LEAVING RELIGION
Finding God

Rediscovering a Faith Worth Believing
and a God Worth Following

D1523970

DR. T. S. WISE

Leaving Religion: Finding God
Rediscovering a Faith Worth Believing and a God Worth Following

ISBN: 978-0-9860613-4-9

Published by
Dr. Terry S. Wise
With kind assistance from Servant Communications, Inc.
Ottumwa, Iowa 52501

Cover picture combines two photos:
File ID 179903260 | © Dmitry Potashkin | Dreamstime.com
File ID 73775381 | © Ali Osman Pekoglu | Dreamstime.com
Used with permission.

Cover and Interior Design: Terry S. Wise and Lissa Auciello-Brogan
Cover and Interior Setup: Lissa Auciello-Brogan

Printed in the United States of America.

14 13 12 11 10 / 10 9 8 7 6 5 4 3 2 1

DECDICATION

· · · · · · · ·

Dedicated to the Fringe

To those outside the mainstream who see God with fresh eyes.

To those who are weary and instead of giving up have offered us a better way.

To those who have left religion to discover a faith worth believing.

To those who live on the fringe and challenge our comfortable paradigms.

Dedicated to the Writers

To those who swim upstream because it is right, not because it is convenient.

To those who study, learn, and communicate new insight to others.

To those who plow the hard soil of ignorance and plant seeds of growth.

To those whose intellect wards off bad theology.

Dedicated to the Supporting Cast

To those who serve so writers can swim and the fringe can see.

To those whose behind-the-scene activities occur without fanfare.

To those whose joy in life is to help others succeed.

To those whose acts of service make life a little bit sweeter.

To those who challenge, encourage, and love me just the way I am.

W. Babcock   July 2021

TABLE OF CONTENTS

· · · · · · · ·

LEAVING RELIGION
The Problem of Behavior

The Problem of Belief
The Credibility of Scripture

The Credibility of Jesus

The Credibility of God

FINDING GOD
A New Beginning

PREFACE

· · · · · · · ·

WHAT IF I CONFIRMED THAT YOU WEREN'T CRAZY or heretical for questioning the traditional teaching of the church? After all, we are asked to believe some pretty unbelievable doctrines regarding Scripture, Jesus, and God, especially in light of modern knowledge that tells us they can't literally be true. Many walk away from the faith, become disengaged, or live in exile as closeted Christians because the traditional Christian message no longer makes sense to them. What if I told you that intellectual integrity and faith can co-exist—that Scripture reveals profound truth that is relevant, life changing, and intellectually defensible? What if I could show you a way forward—a path that aligns with Scripture and the twenty-first century? What if I could reveal a God who is real, deep, and far beyond the limits of denominational dogma—or any religious system for that matter? It is time to return from exile and rediscover a faith worth believing and a God worth following.

When Scripture is approached with integrity, we rediscover a faith worth believing. This book will transform your religious perspective. Profound freedom will overwhelm you upon realizing that Christianity is about living, loving, and being in the sacred presence of God, not fulfilling religious requirements to appease a deity who is always keeping score. It is about time that we articulate our faith in a manner that is intellectually honest and relevant to the times. What a relief to realize that you aren't crazy or heretical after all, and that you don't have to leave your brain at the front door of the church before entering its hallowed halls of faith.

This book is worthy of your time and attention, especially if you are a disillusioned believer who sees the chasm between ecclesiastical teaching and present-day knowledge. If you are thoughtful and serious about your faith, this book will open your eyes to new ways of seeing God. Those raised in fundamentalist and evangelical faith traditions will discover a fresh envisioning of God. If you are a young person struggling to align archaic beliefs with the contemporary world, or if you are in the second half of life and things no longer add up for you, this book may be just what the doctor ordered.

Life is lived forward but is best understood backward. Our present understanding is sharpened when we consider the past, and in a sense, this is exactly what has happened to me. I discovered a huge gap between past and present realities. My own personal paradigm shift occurred while deconstructing traditional Christian beliefs and reconstructing them in light of modern sensibilities. It felt like I was tearing down an old engine, throwing away rusted and worn-out parts, cleaning off those that were still useable, and rebuilding it into something that would last for years to come. It was refreshing!

Rebuilding endeavors can be scary projects for some and never allowed or encouraged by others, but for me, it was a lifesaver. My old engine of faith was so worn out that it was on life support. It had to be rebuilt or it would forever remain in the farmer's back forty where broken cars go to die—no longer worth anything at all. Since traditional understandings of the Christian faith no longer function in our postmodern world, our only options are to keep going through the motions while parking our brain in neutral, jettisoning the whole thing as an irrelevant relic of yesterday, or deconstructing it, casting aside worn out parts, and rebuilding a faith that actually works. I chose to rebuild.

This book helps us rediscover a faith worth believing and a God worth following. Far too many Christians walk away from institutionalized religion in an attempt to escape the regular Sunday morning assault upon their intelligence and their humanity. Who can blame them? They hang on by the skin of their teeth, hoping that a lifeline of credible belief will be thrown to them. They choose to live in exile while holding out for a reasonable faith.

I recognize their dilemma, for I lived it myself. Instead of walking away, however, I began rebuilding. My personal mission wasn't some wild concoction crafted in the padded cell of a madman. No, this rebuilt engine not only makes sense to the postmodern mind but is also a more faithful understanding of Scripture. It was my way of leaving religion to find God. When I speak of leaving religion and finding God, I mean leaving the archaic beliefs of Christianity that no longer make sense in the present age and discovering the God behind such beliefs.

If Christianity doesn't add up for you anymore, you have been wounded and disillusioned by the church, you live in spiritual exile searching for a lifeline of credible belief, or you are simply a thoughtful Christian who is serious about your faith, this book is for you. It will challenge your assumptions, preconceptions, and understandings while at the same time clearing a path for maintaining vibrant faith without sacrificing your mind or your heart. As you rebuild your own faith engine, be mindful that you will unlearn a great many things and cast aside once-cherished beliefs that are no longer convincing. When the slag is brushed aside and the fog has lifted, there is a real opportunity for meeting a God you never knew existed. In short, the journey could be as transformational for you as it was for me.

I hereby give you permission to reason, reflect, question, and process. Engage your mind and emotions as you grapple with what is real and true. Don't worry, I won't alert church officials to your inquisitive spirit or your clandestine reading of this book. You are free to question all you want without setting off another Inquisition. When you finish the book, you may say, "Why didn't I see this before?" That, my friend, is an excellent response, for it means that you are open to learning and growing. We do not see what is until we are ready to see, and that is a process we must all undergo in our own timing.

If you are looking for a religious feel-good book that affirms a superficial approach to God, then this book may not be your cup of tea. This is a thoughtful presentation for sincere people who are both genuine and honest in their spiritual quest. Without a foundation, faith is nothing more than wishful thinking and delusions of grandeur. This book scrutinizes even the dearest of beliefs to test what is genuine and what is counterfeit. Being honest—now *that* is a concept the church could use these days. What better way to know God and live in God's presence than with authenticity.

Religion is one of the most powerful forces in the history of the world. Often, its harsh and rigid beliefs become a litmus test in determining who is a true follower of God. I challenged those beliefs and left religion behind. I couldn't be happier, for I moved on—from religion to God, from shadow to Shadow-maker, from form to substance, and from a set of untenable beliefs to seeing God in fresh and relevant ways. After you read this book, I am hopeful that your faith will be renewed and that you will be drawn closer to God, not farther away. It is a journey worth traveling and a risk worth taking. I hope you stick it out to the end and afford me the time and opportunity to make my case.

There are two major sections to this book: (1) Leaving Religion and (2) Finding God. In the first section (Leaving Religion), I expose the credibility problem within Christianity that causes so many to leave the faith. I unravel traditional Christian teaching surrounding the topics of Scripture, Jesus, and God that have come under fire these days, and for good reason. In essence, because of its behavior and beliefs, Christianity is no longer perceived as relevant in the present age. In the second section (Finding God), I chart a way forward—a new reformation of sorts that helps us rediscover a faith worthy of our time and attention, and a faith that makes sense in the postmodern world.

Breaking things down is the painful part, but it must be done. You can't rebuild unless you first break down—much like remodeling a home. Things get a little messy before the finished beauty finally emerges, for we will be challenged to relinquish treasured beliefs that no longer ring true. It is the rebuilding of our faith that is absolutely thrilling—a way forward that doesn't require us to accept the unacceptable or live out our faith in exile. Instead, we leave religion in order to see God with fresh eyes.

People often ask why I write books, and why I would write a book like this one. This is an easy question to answer, as there are many reasons that motivate me to put pen to paper. Let me list a few of them, in no particular order. Writing allows me to process ideas and concepts. It helps me solidify my own thinking on matters of importance to me. As I write, I am clarifying, refining, and settling upon my own perspective.

Writing helps me reflect upon my own life, what has led me to this point, and where I might travel to in the future. I am on a spiritual journey, and I want to be cognizant of my own personal transformation. I am not a biblical scholar, theologian, historian, or philosopher, nor do I hold myself out to be one. I am simply a fellow sojourner learning and growing like everyone else. If anything, I am trying to be more of a mystic these days—ever mindful of God's presence in the ordinary. I enjoy writing about what I have learned, always hopeful that it might assist others and make a positive difference in their lives. I have no interest in debating, arguing, or cajoling. I just lay the smorgasbord out there so you can eat what appeals to your appetite.

I write because that is how I am wired, and quite frankly, I function best when I am simply being me. I have tried to emulate others, but I am no good at it. In the wee hours of the morning when the creative juices are flowing, I am mindful of my father and wish that he were still living so we could discuss the content of my books. Writing is one way I honor his memory and impact upon my life. I think he would have enjoyed discussing these topics.

Finally, I write for my own children, who are now grown with families of their own. My books will long outlast me, and as my children age, grow wiser, and struggle with their own empty nests, they may feel about me as I feel about my own father, in which case, my writings may provide some comfort for them.

But why do I write a book like this one—one that is prone to misunderstanding, one that challenges our paradigms of faith, and one that is subject to significant controversy? The simple answer is that I care. As a passionate God-follower, I realize that for Christianity to survive in the centuries to come, its message must become credible—capable of sustaining the scrutiny of our day. I want Christianity to succeed, for I am thrilled with its message. This is my contribution to such a worthy cause.

I am grateful to numerous authors who have influenced my understanding of Scripture, Jesus, and God. Many are listed in the bibliography, such as John A. T. Robinson, Raymond Brown, David Friedrich Strauss, Paul Tillich, Philip Gulley, Bart Ehrman, Richard Rohr, and others who have altered the religious landscape for me. I wish I had been introduced to them earlier in my life.

Perhaps the writings of John Shelby Spong, Marcus Borg, and Lloyd Geering have influenced me the most. Many of their concepts can be seen throughout this book, which I reference in the endnotes. Like so many others, I am a benefactor of their research, scholarly thinking, and written works. Books are typically the culmination of the influences of others upon the writer, and this book is no different. They have inspired and challenged my own religious perspectives, and I acknowledge them with thanksgiving.

May this book be a catalyst in your rediscovery of a faith worth believing and a God worth following.

TSW
Ottumwa, Iowa

1

CREDIBILITY: A REAL ISSUE
• • • • • • • •

I<small>T IS THREE O'CLOCK IN THE MORNING, AND AS USUAL,</small> I am wide awake. Lottie, my beautiful brown-haired, amber-eyed rescue dog, is comfortably curled up on the floor beside my bed, nestled in her restful place. I am uncertain whether she is snoring lightly or breathing heavily. The presence of my faithful furry friend is reassuring. As for me, I am propped up on my pillows in bed—half of me exposed to the chilly night air while the other half refuses to come out from under the warm blankets. Piercing the darkness is the glow from my laptop computer screen—just enough light for my fingers to dance about the keyboard, transposing internal thoughts to the printed page.

It is not uncommon for me to be awake at these odd hours. My nighttime stirrings have become a regular habit and feel like an old friend I have known for a very long time. Sometimes I yearn for sleep to take me through the night, and at other times, I am grateful for the time alone. Tonight, and most nights, I experience the latter.

A great deal of uninterrupted tranquility can be enjoyed at this time of the morning. It is during these quiet hours of darkness that I feel most alive, and it is absolutely marvelous. Tonight, I hear the fallen windblown leaves skipping across the lawn. An early snowstorm is headed our way, and I just might catch a glimpse of the season's first snowflakes. Old Man Furnace just kicked on and is puffing his warm air throughout the house. In the distance, I catch the rhythmic rumble of train wheels moving along the rails. These familiar sounds comfort me.

It is during this time of solitude and silence that I seem to be in touch with my inner self, for my heart is calmed, my senses are heightened, and my mind is primed for activity. Instead of trying to anxiously navigate my way through the noisy hustle and bustle of daytime, now, in the wee hours of the morning, there are no distractions competing for my attention. I am keenly aware of my own thoughts. I am conscious of my own breathing. I am mindful of my own existence. I am alive, and the life of God is within me. It is peaceful, and my heart is grateful.

In moments like these, I contemplate who I am, what I am learning, and what lingering questions confound me. Since I have no place to be at this hour of the morning, I reflect upon my journey through life. Like buffalo enjoying summer prairies, my thoughts and feelings are unconstrained—free to roam wherever they choose.

I contemplate God and consider how I experience the divine presence in my life, what I have learned from these experiences, and how they have transformed me. I think about my place in the world, my emotions, and how I *actually* live compared with how I *desire* to live. I think about my father who passed away and my kids who are grown and pursuing their own lives. So many thoughts travel along this mental highway of mine that it can be overwhelming, enlightening, emotional, and highly rewarding all at the same time. It is just me being still in the presence of God, profoundly aware of myself and my surroundings. I hope you experience moments like these in your own life, not necessarily in the wee hours of the morning but at some point during the day when you become deeply aware of yourself, your surroundings, and your Creator.

Sometimes I wonder whether I am far too cerebral for my own good and question whether my penchant for intellectual musings is a lopsided personality quirk that inhibits my attempt to be balanced. To be any other way, however, means that I can't be me—the very way I was hardwired to be. And so it goes night after night. It's the way I function. In these silent, precious hours, my thoughts travel a good distance and take me to places that both excite and replenish my soul.

Divine Mystery

During these quiet moments, I not only grasp my "smallness" in comparison to the grandeur of a vast universe but also sense a profound connection to God's presence whereby the source of life flows in me and through me. As my mind wanders to and fro, I have a thousand questions and "I don't knows." When it comes to spiritual things, relatively few answers abound, as I live in a maze of uncertainty. But certainty is something outside of our grasp, for God is too big, too vast, and too mysterious for us to contain—like a handful of sand that keeps slipping through our fingers. Those who believe they have discovered certainty have probably found nothing but stagnation and a false sense of security. Spiritual maturity is maintaining faith in the midst of uncertainty. Yet, at the same time, despite my lack of understanding, I sense a kinship with God that words cannot fully describe.

In my pursuit of God, I keep bumping up against a mystery so great that no amount of reasoning can harness its splendor. My limited vocabulary and finite cognitive abilities are woefully inadequate to grasp even a sliver of its breadth, and yet, here I am, experiencing something of the great mystery in my own life.

Whenever God is brought down to the level of propositional statements, time-bound creeds, words on a printed page, rituals, and symbols, the divine mystery is diminished, for God cannot be contained in things so fragile, so limiting, and so earth-bound. It is like trying to pour all of the water of Earth's oceans into an eight-ounce glass. In like manner, God can only be experienced—never restricted or controlled. These early-morning hours allow me to bypass my appetite for full understanding so that I can experience a portion of the great mystery of God. That's why these moments are so precious to me—I go swimming in God's great ocean. I don't just float; I go all in and immerse myself. I allow the water of God's radiance to surround me as I splash about. As the writer of Psalm 34:8 (NRSV) says, "O taste and see that the LORD is good."

This book is the result of intellectual wanderings during my nocturnal activities—when I go for a nighttime dip in the ocean of God's great mystery. These pages reflect my own journey and my own experiences as well as my own biases and theological leanings. I speak for no one but myself, for I can only share my thoughts on life as I have lived it and experienced it. Accompanying these swimming excursions is an acute sense of humility, for I realize that I am touching only the tip of the iceberg. My hope, however, is that you will find something of value from my nighttime travels that might benefit your own spiritual journey.

The quest for human meaning is something we all pursue, to various degrees and with varying outcomes. In fact, the heart of religion is ultimately a search for meaning. This quest is a human phenomenon—an aspect of self-consciousness that separates us from the animal world. Cows, lizards, and whales don't ask the kinds of questions that keep me awake at night. We mistakenly understand faith to be something we do that secures our entrance into heaven, but the quest for meaning—this faith journey—is valuable in its own right. It is a powerful, living, creative force that helps us feel alive, and at three o'clock in the morning, I feel very much alive as this quest is taking root in my life.

Future of the Church

Lately, my thoughts have turned toward the church and its future. Having spent a good portion of my life in full-time Christian service, I have a great deal of experience with institutionalized religion—its inner workings, its people, its processes, its structure, its impact, its beliefs, and all things church. It is my love for the church that stirs such deep concern for its longevity.

Excuse me while I pause for a moment. The faint whistle of a distant freight train sounds in the background as it moves a heavy load through town. I must pause, close my eyes, and take it in . . . Thank you for allowing me that brief respite.

Now, about the church . . . I was noting my deep love and concern for its future, which seems to fall short of conveying the gravity and depth of my feelings about the matter. If the church desires relevancy to a contemporary and ever-changing audience, it must overcome significant issues. In short, the church has a serious credibility problem undermining its chance for meaningful survival in the centuries to come.

Inevitably, someone will point a judgmental finger while quoting Matthew 16:18 (NRSV): "I will build my church, and the gates of Hades will not prevail against it." It is not Hades that concerns me but the demise of Christianity in this life and upon this Earth. Meanwhile, in my hometown, churches continue to die. I should know, since I have visited many of them. These beautiful buildings are nearly empty, with no one younger than myself in sight—and I am no spring chicken. In essence, they are under the watchful care of hospice, and their glory days are over.

Some of these churches have already been turned into private homes or purchased by investors for commercial space. One denomination with three declining churches in town realized the problem of sustainability. Rather than disband, they voted to sell all three church buildings and consolidate into a new single congregation. In their mind, this was the only viable option available to them. With pooled money from the sale of these underutilized buildings, they hope to remain open for as long as they can, believing that new wine can be poured into old wineskins. Many pastors are merely overseeing prolonged funerals for older parishioners—the funeral of the grey-hairs. This is not a negative comment about older congregants but a recognition that once they pass away, their church building may well be sold to the highest bidder and become commercial real estate. These folks love the Lord and are an integral part of church life, but it is only a matter of time before things shut down. This scenario plays itself out all across America and is nothing more than a long, drawn-out goodbye.

Times have changed, and no amount of wishing for the good ole days will bring back a dying past. No amount of religious zeal can withstand the proliferation of new knowledge now upon us. To ensure longevity in an ever-changing world, our understanding of God must expand beyond the unenlightened explanations of ancient times; otherwise, we find ourselves on the slippery slope of irrelevance.

The prospect of a dying church is alarming and engenders fighting words from those who believe that the darkened embers of ancient days can light the fires of the future. Unfortunately, the church is becoming an extinct dinosaur and is viewed as a bastion of insignificance. There appears to be little disagreement that the church of yesterday is collapsing. What remains to be seen, however, is whether or not it will even survive.

Talk of altering the church's trajectory stirs up fear, and many will view my musings as a significant threat to the traditional boundaries of faith with which they feel most comfortable. With fresh discoveries about ourselves and our universe knocking at the door, will our faith retreat to less enlightened days, or will Christianity keep pace with the present age? I prefer a faith that intersects with current realities rather than one resting upon the laurels of yesterday.

Whether you agree with the results of my nighttime ponderings, or you dismiss them as nothing more than sleepy and sloppy intellectual endeavors, one thing is for certain—the world is changing, and so must Christianity if it desires a seat at the table. I have read that by 1900, human knowledge doubled every century. By the end of WWII, it doubled every twenty-five years. It progressed to doubling every two years, and now it doubles every thirteen months. When the full potential of the Internet is reached, human knowledge is predicted to double every twelve hours. Whether this is accurate or not, I do not know, but I can confidently attest to the growing cloud of knowledge over the course of my own lifetime. The new knowledge economy is moving at such blazing speed that it feels like yesterday's answers are fast becoming today's questions.

I have witnessed the emergence of technology to the point where I struggle to keep up. The first digital native generation has come of age and cannot fathom life without high-tech gadgets. No doubt, the evolution of change has been in the air since the beginning of time, but with the Renaissance, Protestant Reformation, and Age of Enlightenment came new ways of thinking, seeing, and believing, for it is difficult to continue suppressing what can no longer be denied. Traditional understandings of the past fall farther and farther behind in their struggle to keep pace with the postmodern mind. We have reached a point where there is no turning back. It is akin to selling horse and buggy whips in an age of space travel—something our forefathers could not have imagined. Rather than peddling outdated buggy whips, I yearn for a faith that realistically connects to the modern world.

Entryway to Faith

Our faith journey often feels like two steps forward and one step backward as we question, experience, learn, grow, and change. No journey is a linear climb, but rather a slow winding around the mountain—sometimes up, sometimes down, and often through thickets, ravines, and steep and frightening traverses. This journey of ours affects us in all kinds of ways and often in ways that we don't understand and can't fully articulate. Realizing that we are all heavily influenced by our environment, this may be a good time for me to share a bit about my own journey to God, since my upbringing and experiences have influenced my current thoughts. I entered into faith through the doorway of evangelicalism.

My early memories of church are virtually nonexistent. My parents were married at Ottumwa Baptist Temple on April 6, 1957, a church they attended for a short time. At some point in my early elementary school years, I was invited to attend a summer church program for a few hours one day, but other than that, I don't remember a thing. To my knowledge, I never frequented church, or at least I have no memory of it, until my family began attending the local Christian and Missionary Alliance Church (C&MA) while I was in sixth grade.

Two main factors contributed to my entry into church life. First, my father's coworker was a member of this local C&MA congregation and pestered him on numerous occasions. Apparently, a new pastor had arrived on the scene, which gave rise to the plethora of invitations. Second, my younger sister had been nagging my father to attend church, and this provided the perfect opportunity to appease her repeated requests. And so, my entry into faith began with the Christian and Missionary Alliance denomination through the pleadings of my younger sister and the invitation of a kind coworker.

In the late 1800s, a Presbyterian minister named A. B. Simpson traveled to New York City with a deep concern for evangelizing large metropolitan areas, especially immigrants. He did not intend to form a new denomination; instead, he began two parachurch movements called The Christian Alliance, dedicated to a life of holiness, and The Evangelical Missionary Alliance, concerned with sending out missionaries to evangelize the lost and fulfill the Great Commission of Matthew 28.

Realizing that they were of like mind, these two parachurch groups merged in 1897 to form one group instead of two, calling themselves The Christian and Missionary Alliance. It wasn't until 1974, however, that they officially became a denomination. With evangelical fervor, the C&MA has had a huge impact upon world evangelization efforts. In fact, I once dated a girl whose father was instrumental in opening up the primitive tribes of Irian Jaya to the outreach endeavors of the denomination.

The Christian and Missionary Alliance is squarely situated within evangelicalism. In my view, it is neither too far right to be considered fundamentalist, or too far left to be considered mainline Protestant. Although it has some history, via its founder, of being influenced by Presbyterianism and also by the Holiness and Pentecostal movements, the C&MA aligns itself with evangelicalism, where Scripture is considered the authoritative, inerrant Word of God, and where atonement theology reigns, believing that we are all sinners on our way to hell but for the sacrificial death of Jesus, who died on the cross for our sins. By trusting in Jesus as one's Savior, one experiences the grace and forgiveness of God and secures an entrance ticket into heaven.

Our local sanctuary, as with most C&MA buildings, came with no frills, no icons hanging from the wall as in Orthodox churches, and no pomp-and-circumstance architecture as is often seen in Catholic and Anglican structures. One can typically find a cross hanging on the wall, a Christian flag and an American flag, the C&MA logo, a pulpit at center stage, and a couple of platform chairs. Some maintain a prayer rail where individuals can kneel and seek the Lord. Preachers often extend an "altar call" encouraging those in need to come forward for prayer or to "get saved." C&MA churches are nothing fancy, and mine was quite small—around eighty attendees on any given Sunday.

The typical Sunday service consists of several hymns and choruses, a moment to highlight missionary efforts around the globe, a soloist singing a special song, and a pastor's sermon that usually lasts about twenty minutes. I enjoyed the Sunday services and could envision myself one day becoming a pastor. In those days, evangelical churches also offered an additional Sunday evening service that was less formal, with frequent opportunities for testifying to the Lord's goodness. On numerous occasions as a teenager, I would stand up on Sunday evening and extol God's work in my life. That took a bit of courage, but I did it.

As a young elementary schoolboy, I was oblivious to how the C&MA fit into the larger scheme of Christendom. I certainly didn't question or ponder its practices or its theology. At that time in my life, I had little understanding of theology or the differences between Presbyterianism, Lutheranism, Methodism, Pentecostalism, and Catholicism. Those thoughts rarely crossed my youthful mind. I only knew that this congregation welcomed me—a place where I met friends my age and heard about God for the first time in my life.

While staying overnight with my friend, I told a joke about a man getting kicked out of hell for selling ice cubes. Since hell was supposedly a very hot place brimming with eternal fire, I thought my joke was comical. As the evening progressed, however, guilt fell upon me. If hell was real and I was going there, then there was nothing comical about my jesting. My friend scurried upstairs, woke his father, who happened to be my pastor, and escorted him downstairs to share Scripture with me. If I repented of my sins and believed that Jesus died on the cross to save me from those sins, I not only would be forgiven but would spend eternity with God in heaven when I died. With that good news, I kneeled beside the hide-a-way bed and earnestly repeated the "Sinner's Prayer" after the pastor. I went to bed quite pleased that I no longer had to worry about hell. I was "saved."

My heart was warmed by all of this, and it wasn't long before I was involved in all sorts of activities, from singing groups, to church plays, to Bible quiz teams, to youth group, and the like. My involvement in the church came at just the right time. For many, the junior and senior high school years in the public school system can be awkward and tumultuous, but for me, I had the church. It was a gift that kept me out of trouble, instilled values in me, and helped me realize that I was being called to serve a greater good. It was transformative in that it set the trajectory of my life for years to come.

These days I look back and marvel at how far I have come since those embryonic years. Back then, I didn't think much about church structure, scriptural interpretation, or theological positions. I didn't ask the deep and necessary questions that growing Christians inevitably encounter in the advancement of their faith. All I knew was that I loved Jesus with all my heart and was grateful for his costly sacrifice on my behalf. I yearned to give my life away in service to the one who had so generously served me. It was all so simplistic and pure during this phase of my journey—a time when I lacked the life experiences, failures and successes, hurts and joys, and trials and victories that cause us to engage in serious and critical reflection. My faith was rarely tested, and if it was, I could always find some slick Christian slogan to fall back on.

Over time, my beliefs evolved, and my understanding of faith grew. Though I have moved far beyond the convictions of those early years, I am forever grateful for that stage of my life. It was a good and sacred place—a foundation upon which to further build my faith. It was during this chapter of my life that I sensed a compelling desire to serve in full-time pastoral ministry, and so I set my heart in that direction.

After one year at our denominational Bible college near Minneapolis, Minnesota, I transferred to a Quaker college near my hometown in Iowa. This allowed me to live at home and work while attending college, saving money, and paying off tuition. With a Bachelor of Arts degree in history under my belt, I entered an evangelical seminary to prepare for ministry. After two years, I graduated with a Master of Arts degree in theological studies, began serving as the pastor of a Midwestern C&MA church, and became ordained. I would go on to earn several doctorates and pastor other churches, but my point is that those early formative years instilled in me a desire to know and serve God. My heart was ablaze for the kingdom and serving in ministry. To that end, I began gathering experiences and education that would assist me in that endeavor.

Pastoral ministry isn't for the faint of heart. I barely made enough money to survive and care for my family. My young son was hospitalized for a short time, and I remember the tension I felt between adequately caring for him and wondering how in the world I was going to pay the bill. Some days I shake my head in amazement at how we managed on so little. But we did. Like other pastors, my ministerial experience was filled with good and bad, positive and negative, joys and sorrows. I had little understanding, appreciation, or practical experience with church structure, church dynamics, or people problems. I was a solid preacher, but my soul was simply unprepared for the harsher realities of church life.

Unlike some of the mainline denominations where greater structure and protections abound for the pastoral office, the local C&MA church holds great authority for hiring and firing pastors, setting salary, establishing expectations, etc., while the denomination takes a back-seat role. In essence, there are few structural or denominational protections for ministers and scant checks and balances for congregations with ill intent. This is unfortunate, and many exhausted pastors have left the church to join the secular city all because of how they were treated by the local congregation. Sadly, this is commonplace these days.

I remember a time in ministry when I was sitting in my La-Z-Boy recliner in the middle of the night, scouring the local newspaper for jobs while my heart was palpitating erratically. The only opening I could find was driving a local school bus. In that moment, when I could hardly breathe, I thought to myself, "Surely I would be better off driving a big, yellow school bus than enduring the current pain I am experiencing." Many pastors, I suspect, have found themselves in similar circumstances.

I am grateful for the churches I served, the people I encountered, and the lessons I learned. They helped me grow and become the man I am today. Often, we are unable to fully appreciate our experiences until looking back upon them years later when the sting of disappointment has subsided, the soul has undergone healing, and we are well on our way to advanced levels of spiritual maturity.

My district superintendent once said to me, "We have no pathway for people like you. You are smart enough to become an attorney. We just don't know what to do with people like you." After ten years of pastoral ministry within the C&MA, I transitioned into Christian higher education. This was a setting where "people like me" could thrive—encouraged to utilize both critical thinking and business skills without constraint. This was a wonderful move that allowed me to function from more of a "heart and head" perspective.

I appreciated my district superintendent's honesty and affirmation, but it saddened me that so many churches and denominations find little value in thinking deeply about things. Rather than appreciating probing questions about the faith, suspicion arises with the accumulation of too much education and the asking of too many questions. After all, if the faith has been decided once and for all and Scripture is the inerrant Word of God, then any attempts at inquiry, no matter how miniscule, become borderline heretical.

Why is it that churches claiming to have all the answers don't allow you to ask any questions? In claiming to have a corner on the truth, they provide congregants with a false sense of security. Out of all the world's cultures and religions that ever existed, they are the only ones who know and understand the truth. To associate with them is to be one of the exclusive few—the chosen ones. Unfortunately, congregants are discouraged from asking questions that might undermine the well-rehearsed dogma being spewed forth. In many churches, it seems to me, the pastor is merely paid to recite the traditions of the past, not to challenge us in the present.

Clergy with formal seminary training know a lot more about issues of concern than they let on, and I suspect this is due to self-preservation. To critically reflect upon substantive issues of faith can lead to loss of employment and financial hardship. Pastors often tow the party line for economic reasons while maintaining their own doubts as a private matter. I barely survived when I was a good little soldier; I can't imagine the tribulations awaiting me had I wondered off the beaten path to explore some fascinating terrain.

In today's world, we are faced with a terrible dilemma—do we jettison reason in order to maintain our faith, or do we discard our faith in order to maintain intellectual honesty? I want to be associated with a twenty-first-century church where I don't have to leave my intellect at the door when I enter. I will not be forced to bury my head in the sand while ignoring the advancements of the last five hundred years. I will not abdicate my claim to be called "Christian" simply because a cultural orthodoxy is unable and unwilling to be real and honest. I simply cannot fall back upon primitive viewpoints so unrelated to the present age as to be unrecognizable.

Will Christianity survive in the future given our more sophisticated understanding of the universe and our advances in critical scholarship, technology, and science, or, like the *Titanic*, will it continue its steady descent to the ocean floor while Christians insist on polishing the deck rails? I sure hope Christianity survives, but if it does, it will not be in its current form, for it is already losing ground. The story of faith must be untethered from its primal moorings and reframed with relevance for a postmodern world so we are not forced to choose between intellectual integrity and a vibrant faith.

A Growing Faith

As I moved from the evangelical entryway into the larger arena of religious life, I garnered valuable life experiences that caused my faith to morph into something far deeper than the faith of a young lad. Show me an individual whose youthful beliefs about God haven't changed over time, and I will show you someone whose faith is shallow—someone who hasn't wrestled deeply with the things that matter and who forever remains in the entryway of the house of God, never venturing out to explore the wonders of God's great mansion of faith. We begin the journey one way and end the journey another way, for the journey itself changes us.

What we once believed as children changes over time and into adulthood. This is normal and as it should be. It is called growth and maturity. Not many of us still believe in Santa Claus or the Easter Bunny—a false understanding of reality. As adults, we now hold a different view of these two celebrities—still valuing the myth without literalizing the figures. It is the same with our faith, which is ever evolving and expanding from our entry into the kingdom to the exit door at death. Faith is never meant to be static, but active and alive, constantly growing and developing into something more—something deeper.

For some, faith is to be caught, contained, and hidden in a lockbox under the bed in an effort to protect it from harm. But faith was never meant to be hidden away in a lockbox; rather, it was intended to come out from under the bed, meet the world head-on, and be challenged, questioned, and tried. Only then does it grow and function as it was intended. The mustard seed of faith is designed to produce something greater than the little kernel that initially housed it. When that tiny seed is placed into the ground, a transformation occurs whereby new life emerges.

The mustard seed of faith I discovered in sixth grade put a spark in me that eventually lit a bonfire. It grew and developed into a more mature understanding of what it means to follow the way of Christ. Not only was my heart turned toward loving God, others, and myself; the eyes of my soul began to see life from a fresh perspective. I sensed a responsibility to live for a new cause and move to the beat of an agenda higher than my own.

We are tempted to cast aside the faith of our younger days as though it were meaningless and wasteful, and in looking back, we wonder how in the world we could have believed such things! But it is all part of the spiritual journey. Each phase is precious and meaningful, and it is often because of those younger stages of belief that we have arrived at a more seasoned faith. Rather than discard our earlier journey, we should value and acknowledge it as one stage in our search for spiritual meaning.

In my teenage years, I loved God so deeply that I didn't want to be contaminated with sinful worldly influences, so a friend and I burned all of our contemptable rock albums. I even took celebratory pictures of the event. We were taking a stand for God and against the evils of rock-and-roll—or so we thought. In retrospect, I find that to be a foolish way of thinking, and I chuckle out loud. Those rock-and-roll albums would be worth some money these days, and I really did enjoy the music. Did destroying my rock-and-roll collection make me righteous? Was God impressed with such a display of unbridled zeal? I look back with a bit more maturity these days, but I would never cast aside the joy and fire I had in the belly of my youth.

One Christmas, my wife and I decided that instead of giving one another gifts, we would each spend an agreed-upon amount of money to purchase used books or music. We were anxious to see what value our money could buy in used goods. Guess what I purchased? I bought up all of those rock albums I burned as a teenager when I was going through my "holier than thou" phase of life. Now, of course, instead of vinyl records, they were in digital format. Nonetheless, I was able to listen to the classic music I grew up on—once again. It was a marvelous Christmas, and I still listen to the music from days gone by—and just between you and me, I also play a little air guitar when the music is loud and no one is looking. I cherish the zeal and commitment I possessed in those early years and wouldn't throw it out the window for anything. It was a treasured part of my journey and helped mold me into the God-follower I am today.

Thinking Deeply

While flipping through the various television channels with the high hope of finding something interesting to watch, I happened upon a showboating televangelist prancing about on cable television. Of course, we all know that popularity, a national television show, a feel-good religious message, and a large group of wide-eyed followers equate to speaking with trusted authority on every subject touched upon. If you believe that, I have some oceanfront property in Kansas I would like to sell you! Looking straight into the camera, this slick televangelist informed his transfixed and beguiled audience that God dictated every word of the Bible—word for word.

Think of it, the God of the universe dictating every single word of Scripture to various human beings over a period of fifteen hundred years in both Hebrew and Greek. A God who is said to be all-powerful, the grand creator of heaven and Earth, was forced into word-for-word dictation just to get a message to humans. It seems rather anticlimactic that such a powerful entity could create the universe at which we marvel, only to be stuck with dictation. And, after all of that time and hard work, God lost all of those precious writings, for no one can find the original set of dictated manuscripts. I, too, once believed that Scripture was the very words of God to humankind, but even as a young believer, I realized the deficiency of the dictation theory. As for the slick televangelist, I suspect he realized that he could better control his audience and solicit greater funds by portraying Scripture as the dictated words of God, which he alone could rightly interpret and proclaim.

You see, we were lovers of the Bible, but we didn't engage in a great deal of critical thinking *about* the Bible. We simply believed everything the Bible said as though it were straight from the mouth of God. We swallowed it whole—hook, line, and sinker—without giving much thought to cultural context, biases, the Jewish way of writing, critical scholarship, and the like. When God decreed that total villages be slaughtered—every man, woman, child, and animal—we found some sort of justification for that behavior. After all, since God was holy and we were nothing but lowly sinners, we saw no inherent contradiction between a God who loves and a God who kills, for that was God's divine prerogative. Now, Scripture is interpreted with greater scrutiny, and the view that a capricious deity can kill whomever, whenever, for whatever reason doesn't carry much weight.

It is far easier to believe in the God we make up in our minds, or the God a famous televangelist promotes while looking intently into the camera lens, than to actually think deeply through issues ourselves. The path of ease readily gobbles up what others tell us to believe rather than wrestling with God on our own. Even with this book, I encourage you to do your homework, process and ponder, and arrive at your own thoughtful conclusions

As life marches forward, so should our faith. New knowledge sheds light on old perspectives. Forward movement involves deep thinking and pondering—something we are not good at or used to in the contemporary religious milieu. While I am asking you to give serious thought to your beliefs, many will say that I am forsaking the faith or becoming far too cognitive for my britches—like the overeducated professor who lacks the common sense to tie his shoelaces or button his shirt correctly. But this is a smokescreen.

While asking questions and challenging unexamined assumptions can be uncomfortable, is it wise to believe the unbelievable and call it faith? Many choose to ignore the explosion of knowledge around them in an effort to hold on to the comfort of the past. How long can we deny the growth of new knowledge and its effect upon our religious beliefs? We no longer live in the past—in the cultural context and assumptions of an antiquated age. We live in the present—a modern world with unparalleled scientific discovery, space travel, medical breakthroughs, and the constant blooming of new knowledge. The past can be treasured and valued, but it is not something we should cling to, for we can never go back. We can't. It is dying, sinking, and fading away. The world moves on, and so must we.

Telling a New Story

The problem many encounter is this—how can we be honest Christians in a postmodern world when the church still holds fast to the archaic teachings of the past? The church wants to answer questions that no one is asking these days. Telling the Christ story for a postmodern world entails having to unlearn old understandings—like one of those noisy cicada bugs on a hot summer night molting its skin on the bark of a huge oak tree. It is time we grow up and realize that Santa Claus and the Easter Bunny are myths. Past paradigms will die a painful death if the story of faith cannot be told with both relevancy and intellectual integrity.

Some say that all we have to do is change the packaging for each generation. The assumptions of the past remain, but the color of the wrapping paper changes according to the taste of each generation. If the Bible is the fixed Word of God, absolute and authoritative, as many believe, then about all we can do is change the wrapping paper. To alter the message is to deny the faith; at least, that is how the argument goes. With this perspective, the message never changes, only the delivery methodology. The Christ story is simply rewrapped in glittery new Christmas paper and placed under the tree of each generation.

Is that really all that needs to occur for Christianity to survive in the centuries to come? Is merely rewrapping traditional understandings of an unenlightened past going to fool anyone? Have we not reached a point where the very contents of the gift itself must be reexamined in light of new insight? The writers of Scripture wrote from their contextual understanding of life based on the knowledge they possessed at the time of the writing. We certainly can't blame them for that, for we do the very same thing. We don't write from the past, because we have progressed farther down the road. We don't write from the future, because we are not there yet. We can only write from the context and understanding of our own day, which I am attempting to do through this book.

Think about it for a moment—the writers of Scripture had no understanding of the vastness of space and would be shocked to learn that humans landed on the moon, an exploratory spacecraft is sitting on Mars, and a gigantic Hubble telescope is cruising through space, snapping pictures of distant galaxies. Their limited understanding consisted of Earth below and sky above and just beyond that, heaven, the place where God sits upon a massive throne.

They had no awareness of germs, viruses, vaccines, amino acids, cancer, DNA, atoms, chemical reactions, and the like. Because of their limited understanding, many of the illnesses they experienced were attributed to evil spirits.

Their world was vastly different from ours, and they wrote from the experiences, understandings, and perspectives of their day. We live in a totally different era with a more sophisticated understanding of our planet, our universe, and ourselves. Rewrapping such limited and obsolete outlooks in glittery paper and colorful bows won't breathe life into a corpse. Instead of becoming a museum of ancient beliefs, the church must fundamentally rethink voices of the past if there is to be any chance of survival in the world of tomorrow.

By noting that we must progress forward in a faith fit for the twenty-first century, I am not suggesting that we erase our past as if it never existed. We move beyond those obsolete assumptions and beliefs, but we don't bury them or rewrite history so that it becomes more palatable in the present. It is what it is, and it was what it was. Instead of looking backward with disdain and berating ourselves for being so naïve, seeing the past as a valuable part of our faith adventure helps us honor each stage of the journey. Those prior unexamined assumptions helped us climb to higher altitudes on the mountain where extra baggage from the lower levels is no longer useful.

As human knowledge continues to expand, so will our faith. In fact, I believe the Christ story will continue to be reframed as our knowledge increases. Five hundred years from now, will our amended faith story also be viewed as antiquated? Possibly. With new enlightenment comes new ways of understanding and sharing Christianity, and the pursuit of God will always require intellectual honesty.

In the end, no matter what age we live in, the survival of Christianity rests upon freeing it from its unenlightened past. It may be time for a New Reformation that can stand up to the scrutiny of present times. We will have to unlearn many things and unshackle ourselves from ancient worldviews that are no longer viable in today's world. I suspect the story will continue to be told in new ways as our understanding of ourselves, our world, and our universe continues to evolve. This is good, and as it should be, for God's presence always intersects with current realities, whether we realize it or not.

At this juncture, alarm bells may be clanging in your mind with all my talk of sharing the Christian message in a new way. I understand your reticence, since I haven't yet explained what that new message is and why it must be reframed. That, of course, will come in future chapters. Until then, graciously allow me the necessary space and time to fully develop my thoughts. I assure you, we will eventually get to where you want to go.

A Loving & Learning Attitude

Seeing things in a new light is the result of time, experience, reflection, and a fair amount of reading, not to mention a willingness to listen and learn. What is contained in these pages isn't some new concoction that I brewed up on my own—far from it. For me, appreciating new perspectives took time, and it has only been in recent years, during the second half of my life, that I have made significant headway. It wasn't without struggle, for I recall reading one particular author and having to put the book down. At the time, I viewed him as undermining just about everything I believed. He appeared caustic and jaded, and a bit too joyful about it, if you ask me. I read other authors who moved me along at a slower pace until finally, I was able to pick the book up again and finish it. Since that time, I have read it many times over. Like wine lovers who move from sweets, to whites, to reds, I was being carried downriver by powerful currents whisking me away to new places. Though I was venturing from the safety and comfort of old ways of thinking, all I really had to do was float on the inner tube of intellectual integrity and enjoy the ride.

If this book becomes too much for you, put it down and take a break. Come back to it when you are able, but allow my thoughts to percolate in the back of your mind until you are hungry for a hearty spiritual meal. Who knows, this book may force you from the safety of the river bank and into the currents of your own thrilling river ride to new horizons. This could be the adventure of a lifetime—the very thing your heart has longed for and a way to maintain your faith without losing your mind. It is the reality of God you are after, right? If so, then cast off the blinders that prevent you from seeing a bigger picture.

The *experience* of God is different and distinct from the *explanation* we attach to that experience. Rather than blind adherence to a specific denominational explanation, I want to soak up the experience without the label of an "approved" theological viewpoint; otherwise, I wind up restricting God to a specific period in human history—like a snapshot, a moment in time rather than a continuing, living reality. The ancients wrote of their experience in the language they knew and with the knowledge they possessed at that specific time and place. But God is different and distinct from the explanations used to capture and express our experiences. When fixed ancient explanations are no longer relevant and credible, we must find new language to communicate our God experience. Explanations and descriptions change over time as we obtain new knowledge. The limits of human language cannot fully capture and express the unlimited mysteries of God.

Many have journeyed where I am, pondered the same thoughts, and have written on the subject far more eloquently than I am able. In my case, I stumbled into this new paradigm. In fact, that's pretty much how I have grown over the years—not by some mapped-out strategic plan, but by stumbling into things at the right time. "When the student is ready," they say, "the teacher appears." I am grateful for all who have engaged in their own kind of stumbling and written about it so that I could fall into a deeper faith.

Whenever we stumble upon a new paradigm, we are always tempted to judge those who are not quite there yet. This is unfortunate and often creates a spiritual arrogance that is nothing short of nauseating. We see this all the time in the political realm as liberals demonize conservatives, and vice versa. It is typical tribal behavior that equates God with a particular political party in order to justify our own perspective and advance our own agenda. In my own life, I have come to a place of faith where I feel quite comfortable. I suspect many will be forced to stand with me as new knowledge expands and the alternatives become less and less attractive. Yet I don't demonize those who see things differently.

Those who support a new way of sharing the Christ story often look upon fundamentalists, evangelicals, conservative Catholics, and anyone unwilling to squarely deal with the impact that new knowledge has upon antiquated religious worldviews as "less than" individuals—unworthy of love. Fundamentalists, evangelicals, and conservative Catholics, on the other hand, often look upon liberals and progressive Christians as heretics and destroyers who chip away at their beloved old-time religion that has so faithfully stood the test of time. We demonize one another and justify it with select Bible passages ripped from their context. Progressives speak of tolerance, acceptance, and love but can't seem to find it within themselves to extend that love to those who disagree with them. Fundamentalists speak of the love of Christ ruling in their hearts but close themselves off to those who don't see things their way—the right and only way, in their minds. In essence, it is the same demeaning behavior coming from opposite sides of the fence.

This tit-for-tat childish behavior undermines the love that both sides elevate as a core ingredient of their faith. What good is love if it only extends as far as those who agree with us? God's love is expansive and big enough for all. No matter what view you hold—whether you are a fundamentalist, an evangelical, a liberal, or a progressive—there seems to be a knee-jerk reaction toward keeping our neighborhoods small, even though our talk of love is so big. This may be the real test of following the way of Jesus—how we actually love one another.

Both sides are filled with well-intentioned individuals, all pursuing a personal quest for meaning—each on their own journey with God. I will present my journey and my views, but you are free to accept them, reject them, or accept and reject parts of them. But know this: I am a lover of God and a lover of people. No matter your response to my nighttime musings, I share my journey in love. I love you for who you are, no matter where you are on life's journey. I hope that you will extend that same love to me, even if we see things differently.

Chapter Summary

In this chapter, I shared that my entry into faith came through the doorway of evangelicalism. The contents of this book, I noted, reflect my own experience and my own journey, along with my own biases and theological leanings. I speak for no one but myself.

With the burgeoning of new knowledge now upon us, I questioned Christianity's ability to survive into the future. Contemporary Christians are faced with a critical dilemma—do we jettison reason in order to maintain our faith, or do we discard our faith in order to maintain intellectual honesty? Our world is vastly different than the world of ancient times, and yet I believe the Christian story can be told in a manner that allows us to reclaim both our faith and our intellectual integrity. The church is faced with a serious credibility problem that negatively affects its chance of survival in the centuries to come. In the next chapter, I discuss how the personal and historical behavior of the church affects its credibility.

2

BAD BEHAVIOR: PERSONAL & HISTORICAL
• • • • • • • •

M ODERN ENLIGHTENMENT HAS CAST ITS LONG SHADOW upon us, so much so that Christianity isn't taken seriously anymore by our postmodern, or should I say "post-postmodern," society. Many wonder whether Scripture has anything meaningful left to say. For them, making sense of the Bible is like putting together a strange puzzle where the pieces no longer fit together. Western Europe is a prime example of the cataclysmic fall of religious interest. Unable to close the credibility gap, European Christianity has declined so rapidly as to be on life support. Without twenty-first-century relevancy, American Christianity may follow suit, right in line with the many religious one-hit wonders of the past that were unable to withstand the scrutiny of their generation. Imprisoned by an ancient worldview that is no longer credible in the present age, the demise of Christianity seems inevitable without some sort of corrective measure.

This chapter may turn out to be the articulation of your own private concerns, but you just didn't know how to say them, or whether they should be said at all. Credibility issues become the backdrop for assessing unexamined assumptions of previous ages. Think of it as a patient history—useful information for the doctor in making a correct diagnosis and prescribing an appropriate remedy.

Personal and Historical

In this chapter, I consider the behavioral problem from both a personal and historical perspective. In future chapters, I will demonstrate how we arrived at our present dilemma and examine the credibility of belief. Although the church has many endearing qualities for which it can be praised, my purpose here is to examine the problem of credibility. So, buckle your seatbelts—the ride down history lane is about to get a little bumpy.

We are not surprised to learn that the church has a serious credibility problem surrounding its behavior. In fact, it is easily seen in the history of Christianity as well as our own personal experience with the church. If the behavioral problem were simply an issue of personal perception, personal taste, or cynical individuals clutching a jaundiced outlook on life, we might think twice about such sweeping conclusions and chalk it up to an isolated event every now and then rather than the larger systemic problem that it is. Unfortunately, even a meager examination of Christianity through the ages reveals prejudices, justifications, exclusions, tribal mentalities, and quests for power and authority that extend well beyond a few isolated incidents. No, this unsavory pattern of behavior seems to be widespread and tightly woven into the tapestry of the church. Its storied record of abuse and hurtful behavior undermines its very foundation. Bad behavior happened then, and it happens now. The credibility problem is both personal and historical.

A Crisis of Belief

In addition to detrimental behavior, the church also faces a crisis of belief. In light of the expanding knowledge occurring in various fields of study, especially within the scientific and theological community, the core teachings of the church are coming under fire. These ancient beliefs make little sense to the contemporary mind. These are weighty words, I know, and quite disturbing to biblical literalists, but how does the Bible stack up to our advanced understanding of so many things? It's not that we now know all things but that we now know so much more about our world than we did when the Bible was written. The gap between then and now is one of knowledge—of credibility.

Please understand, I am not implying that God is not real, for I vehemently believe that God is just as real today as in the past. I am not suggesting that Christianity has no story to tell, only that its story must be told in a fresh, relevant, and authentic manner that preserves both its true message and our intellectual integrity. If this can't be accomplished, we may as well flush our beliefs down the drain like so many other past religions that saw their day, declined, died, and now live only in history textbooks that nobody reads or remembers.

Whether a religious teaching is true or false is not dependent upon the behavior of its adherents. A particular teaching must stand or fall on its own merit. I get that. Yet we cannot deny the corrosive effect bad behavior has upon message credibility. Its damaging effect cannot be overstated. Though every religion has to deal with the chasm between belief and behavior, people today filter Christian teaching through modern knowledge and the behavior of its adherents. All too often, they shake their heads and turn away in disgust. The incongruity is alarming.

One might think that such dreadful behavior can be overcome with greater commitment or increased education, but, given our past history, I highly doubt that more time on the hamster wheel of religious performance will tip the scale. Even if our blemished behavior were miraculously turned into shining examples, Christianity would still face difficulties, for the message itself is entwined in ancient worldviews that are no longer believable. While the thunderous waves of bad behavior crash against the foundation, the problem of belief is an entirely different matter, for it is a terminal issue—absolutely devastating and without a future. Bad behavior has a way of turning us off to faith, but the problem of belief strikes at the very heart of Christian teaching, and, absent intellectual integrity, we may as well throw it into the trash bin of history—a religious relic of the past whose beliefs stand in contradiction to twenty-first-century knowledge. Will Christianity overcome these obstacles? I believe it can, but to do so, its faith story must become credible to the postmodern world.

You may feel that I am unfairly picking on the church and that my motivation is imbued with ill intention. Nothing could be further from the truth. More than anything, I yearn for Christianity to flourish long into the future. I seek to help it live, advance its cause, and breathe new life into its slumping body so that the faith story aligns with modern sensibilities. "Christianity doesn't need any help," you say. By that response, I presume that you believe the ancient stories that others find unbelievable. Do you believe, for instance, that Earth is the center of the universe, as the church once taught? Science has proven that it just isn't so. Our universe is so vast as to be nearly incomprehensible, and Earth is but a speck of dust in this massive, unexplored frontier of space. If you want to believe that Earth is flat, or that it lies at the center of the universe, you certainly have that right, but it doesn't play well in the theater of common sense.

Do you believe, for instance, that God held up the sun from its rotation around Earth to give Joshua more time to slaughter his enemies, as noted in Joshua 10:13 (NRSV), "The sun stopped in midheaven, and did not hurry to set for about a whole day"? The ancients believed that the sun revolved around Earth. After all, they saw it rise in the east and set in the west. Despite what Scripture says, however, we know that Earth actually revolves around the sun, not the other way around.

How do we intelligently make sense of this text in light of our knowledge of gravitational forces and planetary movements? You can believe that God actually held up the sun, but to do so puts you at odds with demonstrable twenty-first-century data. I yearn for Christianity to survive, but it cannot live outside of intellectual integrity. The Christian story has much to offer, and I, for one, have tasted of its nourishing and wholesome bounty. Nothing would please me more than to see others enjoying its sweet nectar; after all, according to John 10:10 (NRSV), Jesus "came that they may have life, and have it abundantly."

Bashing Christians isn't my cup of tea, either, for in all truthfulness, their behavior indicts them well enough. They certainly don't need my assistance. I will, however, point out what everyone else seems to notice and experience. Sweeping ugly behavior under the rug merely shifts the dirt around, and the temporary cover-up does no good. Eventually, someone has to clean it up. No one expects the church to be perfect, but it sure would be nice to see a bit more consistency between what is proclaimed and what is practiced. Just so you know, I include myself in that admonition, too!

The Behavior Problem

Nearly everyone has a personal story of church disappointment. On a flight from Florida to California, I happened to sit next to a complete stranger who shared her disappointing story with me. Her beautiful daughter, a senior in high school, was killed in an automobile accident. The lingering pain could still be seen in her soft eyes as she opened up. Her church refused to conduct the funeral service, noting her nonattendance and lack of financial contribution. Apparently, she had not done enough to earn herself a child's funeral and was turned away in her hour of deepest need. What kind of church responds like this, whether Catholic or Protestant? Had you been in her shoes, would your view of the church be bolstered or destroyed by such behavior? The answer is obvious. In that moment, the church lost all credibility, for in her eyes, the chasm between proclamation and practice became impassable. She has since turned away from Christianity and now practices Native American spirituality while experiencing the wonder of God in nature. What is your story? Nearly everyone has one.

Personal Behavior

The gap between proclamation and practice—belief and behavior—is often too great to be bridged. We are not talking about hopping over small mud puddles—the kind we used to play in as children. Those paltry potholes are easily dealt with, knowing that no one is perfect, not even those attending church. When we trip over such crannies, we dust ourselves off and move on. It is nearly impossible, however, to leap over the deep chasms that destroy faith in the church and drive people away in droves. Like trying to jump across the Royal Gorge in Colorado—it can't be done and no one is dumb enough to try it. The steep decline to the bottom of the gorge is nearly a thousand feet. A bridge, 18 feet wide and 1,260 feet long, connects both sides, while the Arkansas River swirls below. Though a bit unsettling, I have walked across this bridge. The chasm is too wide, too steep, and too rugged to cross without assistance. The woman on the plane, and many like her, can easily skip across the mud holes in life, but she was facing Royal Gorge circumstances that caused her to lose hope in the church and turn from its message. That is how behavior undermines credibility.

When Christians proclaim forgiveness but harbor resentment and bitterness, a credibility problem exists. When televangelists preach living by faith yet tirelessly and shamelessly plead for money to globetrot around the planet in a shiny new jet, a credibility problem exists. When churches proclaim love, tolerance, and acceptance but treat the poor, downtrodden, females, minorities, the LGBTQ+ community, and all other "cultural misfits" as though they have the bubonic plague, a credibility problem exists. The myriad of ways the church has been a disappointment is the number of ways it undermines its own existence.

Tell me, if we proclaim the transforming power of Christ in our life, and yet there is no visible evidence of that transformation, what incentive is there for anyone to follow our lead? It is an utterly hollow promise that leads down an empty, dead-end street. People readily pick up on such glaring discrepancies, and even Paul addressed this theme in his letter to the Roman church: "You, then, that teach others, will you not teach yourself? While you preach against stealing, do you steal? You that forbid adultery, do you commit adultery? You that abhor idols, do you rob temples? You that boast in the law, do you dishonor God by breaking the law?" (Rom. 2:21–23, NRSV).

Obviously, not everyone in the church behaves this way, but, sadly, in my experience, a great number of them do—enough to earn Christians the derisive moniker "hypocrite." Some may scoff, "That isn't us. Other churches might be that way, but ours certainly isn't," and that in itself might be a tell-tale sign that they have never really engaged in deep introspection or conversation about their behavior and how others perceive them. In my experience, most churches are woefully unaware of their own dismal history of being a disappointment, let alone how their actions and attitudes reflect disparity and mistrust. In those congregations that pride themselves on having all the answers, these types of questions aren't even allowed, for they are viewed as disruptive attempts by Satan to contaminate their version of the truth and undermine their "sound" biblical interpretation. This is similar to lifetime smokers living in denial of lung cancer—thinking all along that the probable outcome surely doesn't apply to them. Despite living in a different reality, they are unable to escape what they so fervently deny.

We Deserve Better

Are we asking too much of the church? Should we just live with the increasing number of impassible chasms and get over it? It isn't perfection we are after but rather greater consistency and alignment. We all get bent out of shape every now and then when we care deeply about an issue, but it isn't our normal way of behaving on a consistent basis. When the church sets itself up as the conscience of society, the harbinger of morality, and the arbiter of all that is good and right, we are devastated when it refuses to conduct the funeral of a beautiful teenager because the family's financial contributions didn't warrant that level of care. I guess $500 bought you a few sermons, $1,000 landed you some pastoral visits, and who knows, maybe $2,000 would have secured a funeral for your teenage daughter. Is that how it works? It is reminiscent of the Catholic Church selling indulgences during the Middle Ages, whereby you give the church some money, purchase your penance, and voilà, your sins are forgiven! This was one of the reasons Martin Luther, acting in protest, nailed his Ninety-Five Theses to the Wittenberg Castle Church door in 1517 CE. It changed everything.

Lest you feel I am picking on the Catholic Church, it should be pointed out that the credibility factor crosses all denominational boundaries. During a worship service I was leading for graduate ministry students, a pastor from the Christian and Missionary Alliance denomination shared his personal struggle with forgiveness. His son was molested by one of the trusted elders of his congregation. That kind of disappointment isn't easy to overcome—another Royal Gorge circumstance. Countless personal stories of hurt and devastation abound from all denominations. The issue isn't a denominational problem but a behavioral problem within all denominations. The unfortunate end result is a loss of credibility. We aren't asking for perfection, but surely we deserve better!

"You are lifting up the minority of infractions as commonplace," you protest. May I ask, "What planet are you living on? What protective bubble suit and rosy spectacles shield you from the reality that so many others readily acknowledge?"

To deny the pain and disappointment created by church behavior is to engage in self-deception when everyone else notices. Without a doubt, there are many good and positive aspects of the church, but my focus is upon those that undermine its foundation—those pesky termites that keep eating away at the timbers. Whenever proclamations are made from a long-standing institution like the church, a local business, an individual, or a product, credibility is damaged when incongruity exists between proclamation and practice.

Far too many people have been burned by religion and its adherents. In my own experience, those who have treated me the worst have proclaimed Christ the loudest. I have been cheated out of money by professing Christians on numerous occasions, lied to, gossiped about, hated, despised, rumored about, and judged by those who proudly strut their spiritual arrogance. We might expect that kind of behavior from nonreligious folks, but it always stings a bit more when it comes from fellow sojourners in the faith. It is a betrayal of the heart that wounds the soul and deepens mistrust.

I readily understand that Christians are often held to impossible standards. As with most things, people hold others to a higher standard than they hold themselves. As a pastor, I was expected to please every person—all the time. The pedestal was so high that disappointment was bound to occur. If the church was only an instigator of disappointment on rare occasions, we could accept that. In reality, however, the church is a disappointment on a consistent basis, and that suggests a gulf between belief and behavior.

Wouldn't it be nice, for instance, if Christians actually honored their word? That is a pretty simple concept, and a biblical one at that, and yet, it is such a rarity these days. I was once asked to pastor a Quaker church near my hometown. Having been scorched so many times before, I sought clarity regarding the specifics of their pastoral invitation. One of their leaders sensed my hesitancy and remarked, "We are Quakers, and Quakers always honor their word." I am sure there are Quakers who fail to honor their word, but this was said with honesty and sincerity. It touched my heart to find a group of believers taking seriously their obligation to align faith and conduct.

This is an issue for all religions, not just Christianity. The hallmark of the Christian faith, however, is love, as Scripture reminds us in 1 John 4:7–8 (NRSV): "Beloved, let us love one another, because love is from God; everyone who loves is born of God and knows God. Whoever does not love does not know God, for God is love." This significant trait also seems to be the very essence of God's nature.

Instead of love, the church is often the progenitor of judgment and hypocrisy, the traits most often experienced by those outside of its walls. Virtually every church functioning today is an offshoot—a split from another group. Someone got upset over something and went off to start "the correct church." Differences couldn't be worked out, personalities refused to work together, and in the end, it was far easier to separate and begin a new denomination with like-minded individuals than to actually love one another. Maybe that is why there are more than thirty thousand denominations around the globe, each one claiming to possess the "right" theology. After all, love is hard work and demands intentionality. Why in the world do we need so many denominations? Does this obnoxious number reflect our inability to get along? What does it say to the world about unity and our love for one another? Certainly the bonds of love extend beyond mere assent to theological dogma. Why can't we just love God, love others, and follow the teachings of Jesus as best we can?

On one occasion, I was called "Satan" by a prominent member within my church. Satan? Really? Those are the words of one frustrated individual who viewed me as an enemy. The aspersion was cast upon me for not supporting a specific theological viewpoint. On another occasion, I addressed the difference between church symbols and the reality to which they pointed. Baptism, for instance, is a symbolic act that points to a truth much larger than publicly getting wet. Communion is another symbolic act that points to a truth far greater than the plastic cups of juice and aluminum trays filled with bread.

This was the straw that broke the camel's back for one couple, and it solidified in their mind what a terrible pastor I was for wandering so far off the beaten path. They weren't going to sit under *that* kind of teaching and left the church in a huff. I guess loving me wasn't an option. In reality, they cherished the symbol more than they loved the reality to which it pointed. My sin was pointing out the difference between the two. This was far too threatening for them, so they slapped a disparaging label upon me and picked up their toys to go play in the sandbox of another church.

Stories upon stories could be told. Some would cause us to laugh hysterically, because that's about all you can do with them. Others would perplex us as we shake our heads, trying to figure them out. Most of them, I imagine, would drive us to sorrow and tears as we realize how harmful the absence of love can be.

Though we have been personally disappointed by the church's behavior, is this enough to question its future survival? Maybe this is nothing more than people learning to take their faith seriously rather than jumping to the conclusion that Christianity may be failing. We do, however, take note of its prevalence and its devastating effect upon credibility. Combine personal disappointment with the information contained in this chapter and those to come, and we see a disturbing pattern of religious views that are no longer viable. Our attention is now turned toward historical examples of shameful behavior.

Historical Behavior

When we see a tree with apples on it, we recognize it is an apple tree. A tree with plums is easily identified as a plum tree. As Matthew 7:15–20 (NRSV) notes, clues to tree identity are found in its fruit. Good trees produce good fruit, and bad trees produce bad fruit. "Thus you will know them by their fruits," Jesus affirms. Similarly, the historical fruit of the church reveals a great deal about its nature and value.

The church has become its own obstacle to faith, and, all too often, the fruit it produces undermines its integrity. Every once in a while, I pass by a church sign that says, "All are welcome." It makes me wonder whether they really mean "all" in the sense that every human being will be received with open arms no matter who they are or where they are on life's journey, or whether it is merely a common catch-phrase—a euphemism for "all who are like us." Would all races be welcomed? Would members of the LGBTQ+ community be accepted with outstretched arms? Would flaming liberals and crusty conservatives be taken in? Would unemployed street persons be received? Would visitors, regardless of skin color, creed, gender, sexual orientation, or marital status, be loved in their own right, or would they be viewed as special projects in need of correction and adjustment so they become more lovable? I wish I could report that throughout its history the church has set forth a sterling example of opening its arms to all, but that would not be entirely truthful. At times, the church even devours its own.

Allow me to demonstrate the tainted fruit growing on the church vine. By citing various examples of bad behavior, we catch a glimpse of its checkered past. These examples are not exhaustive and are listed in no particular order.

The Killing Fields

Only naiveté would lead one to believe that after the death and resurrection of Jesus, out popped a Baptist church on the corner of Jerusalem Street and Temple Boulevard—that Christianity in its present form has always been around. That is certainly not what occurred. The modern church as we know it took centuries to develop. Jesus wasn't a Christian, a Baptist, a Catholic, or any other denomination. He was a Jew, raised in the Jewish tradition. For all practical purposes, he was a traveling sage who taught deep truths through everyday stories people could relate to.

For various reasons, this diminutive branch within Judaism—this Jesus Movement—would be abandoned by the Jews within 150 years of Jesus' death, leaving behind a constituency of mostly Gentiles. As time progressed, the movement would gain structure, adopt a theology, write creeds, establish sacraments, and create various practices associated with institutionalized religion. Jesus's band of followers became a small faction, which turned into a movement, which eventually turned into a structured religion in the form of the Catholic Church. In fact, that's the only church we knew until 1054 CE, when the Great Schism occurred between the Eastern and Western regions of Catholicism. Rome, with its pope, became the center of Catholicism in the West, whereas Constantinople, with its archbishop, became the center of the Eastern Orthodox Church. Instead of one Catholic Church, they broke communion with one another over political and theological differences.

In 1517 CE, Martin Luther posted his Ninety-Five Theses on the Wittenberg Castle Church door, protesting corruption within the Catholic Church, particularly the selling of indulgences to absolve sin, and with that act, the Protestant Reformation began. This unrest spread throughout Europe and became the seedling from which all Protestant churches emerged. Every Protestant church today can trace its roots back to the Reformation. What began as a faction within Judaism eventually turned into a highly structured Catholic Church, which split into the Western Catholic Church and the Eastern Orthodox Church. The Reformation of the 1500s became the incubator for Protestant churches as further offshoots materialized.

Toward the end of the Protestant Reformation, the Thirty Years' War broke out in Central Europe between the Protestants and the Catholics from 1618 to 1648. From military operations, famine, plague, and violence, an estimated eight million people perished as each group tried to impose their view of God on the other. So much for Christians getting along! Instead, they opted to kill one another, with each camp claiming God was on their side.

Unfortunately, this wouldn't be the only time killing would become a part of the Christian story. The Vatican sponsored the Crusades (1096–1291 CE) several hundred years before the Thirty Years' War. The first major crusade began when Pope Urban II called for the invasion of the Holy Land, which was under Muslim control. Two hundred years and nine campaigns later, an estimated 1.7 million people lost their lives in this bloody, violent conflict. Marching under the Christian flag, the church invaded the Holy Land and waged war against Jews and Muslims. The Crusades were initiated in the name of God while carrying the symbol of God—the Cross.

The Hebrew Scriptures tell of God killing the firstborn Egyptian males during the exodus story. It's as if God couldn't wait for the dramatic ending to this suspenseful storyline, even hardening the pharaoh's heart multiple times until the final act of killing ensued. Even during their spectacular escape through the Red Sea, God saw to it that the pursuing Egyptian army suffered death in their attempt to cross. After wandering in the desert for forty years, the Israelites, in the name of God and at the direction of God, began conquering the Promised Land by confronting, capturing, or killing all those who stood in their way.

When Adoni-zedek, Amorite king of Jerusalem, heard that Joshua had utterly destroyed Jericho and Ai, he feared that his own city would be next and established a military coalition with neighboring kings. He moved against the Gibeonites, who had made peace with the Israelites, and this unwise military maneuver prompted Joshua's army to respond. Realizing that he needed more daylight to slaughter his fleeing enemies, Joshua commanded the sun and moon to stand still. According to Joshua 10:13 (NRSV), "And the sun stood still, and the moon stopped, until the nation took vengeance on their enemies." Does this kind of behavior bode well for the biblical story—to command the heavenly bodies in the name of God for the sole purpose of slaughtering more Amorites?

The prophet Samuel informed King Saul that God desired to punish Amalek for its past actions against Israel during their flight from Egypt (1 Sam. 15, NRSV). The Lord commanded, "Thus says the LORD of hosts, 'I will punish the Amalekites for what they did in opposing the Israelites when they came up out of Egypt. Now go and attack Amalek, and utterly destroy all that they have; do not spare them, but kill both man and woman, child and infant, ox and sheep, camel and donkey'" (vs. 2–3). Saul, however, disobeyed: "Saul and the people spared Agag, and the best of the sheep and of the cattle and of the fatlings, and the lambs, and all that was valuable, and would not utterly destroy them; all that was despised and worthless they utterly destroyed" (vs. 9). This infuriated the prophet, who rebuked Saul and took it upon himself to finish the job: "And Samuel hewed Agag in pieces before the LORD in Gilgal" (vs. 33).

In the name of God, war was waged in conquest of the Promised Land. In the name of God, Joshua asked that the sun and moon be stilled so there would be more time for killing. Now, we discover that God commands genocide—the utter destruction of every Amalekite man, woman, child, infant, ox, sheep, camel, and donkey. When the job wasn't fully completed, the prophet Samuel, in the name of God and on behalf of God, finished the job by hacking the Amalekite king into pieces. This story takes your breath away. It comes right out of Scripture and reads more like a mafia hit job than the Christian history that it is. What kind of God takes pleasure in hacking someone into pieces and killing an entire band of people?

So vindictive is God, we are told, that Uzzah was struck down for preventing the Ark of the Covenant from crashing to the ground (2 Sam. 6). Uzzah and his brother Ahio were transporting the sacred item on an incline when the oxen drawing the cart stumbled. This caused the Ark to become unstable and in grave danger of sliding off, which Uzzah prevented by reaching out his hand to steady it. God's response is recorded in 2 Samuel 6:7 (NRSV): "The anger of the LORD was kindled against Uzzah; and God struck him there because he reached out his hand to the ark; and he died there beside the ark of God." I wonder how Ahio, Uzzah's brother, felt about this? Uzzah was merely preventing the Ark from tumbling to the ground, and yet, this angered God so much that Uzzah's life was immediately taken from him. Old Testament history is filled with numerous killing sprees, both by God and in the name of God. What does this do for Christian credibility?

God decrees, in Genesis 7:4 (NRSV), "For in seven days I will send rain on the earth for forty days and forty nights; and every living thing that I have made I will blot out from the face of the ground." Apparently, God does just that, for we read further in Genesis 7:23 (NRSV), "He blotted out every living thing that was on the face of the ground, human beings and animals and creeping things and birds of the air; they were blotted out from the earth. Only Noah was left, and those that were with him in the ark." In Genesis 1, God declares all of creation "good," and yet, six chapters later, God is so fed up with this "good" creation that a cataclysmic flood is sent to blot out humankind from the face of Earth. How does the modern mind process a God like that? These are but samples of blood-spilling in the name of God—repulsive behavior within Christian history.

Power and Corruption

Whenever power is abused, corruption soon follows. During the Middle Ages, for example, the church faced serious accusations of abuse. Highly coveted church offices often became politically charged and, more often than not, went to the highest bidder. These desired positions projected power and held out promise of personal gain. Some individuals even held multiple offices, which helped to consolidate personal influence and control. Political power and financial wealth became the motivation for many bishops and popes. Exploiting one's position for personal privilege was not uncommon, even to the point of ignoring one's vows of celibacy. This was the backdrop to the Protestant Reformation.

It was during this period that the Catholic Church sold indulgences to raise money. For a price, parishioners could actually purchase their forgiveness. In its early years of existence, the Christian church struggled mightily, often being persecuted for its beliefs and practices—like Emperor Nero accusing Christians of burning Rome in 64 CE. It wasn't until the era of Constantine the Great, a Roman Emperor from 306–337 CE, that Christianity began to flourish—much like a state-sponsored religion. Instead of being persecuted as a social pariah, Constantine declared Christianity to be an official, favored religion. With that kind of connection and backing from the state, Christianity achieved a new status with greater influence. Yet with power comes corruption, and this is what the Protestant Reformers rejected about a thousand years later.

Though the Protestant Reformation opposed corruption within the Catholic Church, it also rejected the consolidated authority of the church to be the sole determiner of right and wrong, the sole interpreter of Scripture, and the sole compass of morality. The pendulum swung from a church once persecuted, to a church dripping with power, and now it swings again, this time challenging the church's authority and loosening its grip on power. Why must the church claim for itself the sole right to interpret Scripture, if not for power? Why must the church be in the business of selling indulgences, if not for money? Religious authority was now being questioned like never before, and rampant corruption was destroying its foundational pillars.

Ecclesiastical authority taught that the sun revolved around Earth and that Earth was the center of the universe. When Galileo, an Italian physicist and astronomer, confirmed Copernicus's earlier theory that Earth revolved around the sun and was not the center of the universe, he was locked up, put on trial, and convicted of heresy. Books on the topic were banned, and teaching on the subject was prohibited. In 1633 CE, Galileo was formally convicted of contradicting official church doctrine and branded a heretic. To stand in the path of such a powerful institution, even under evidence of reason and scientific inquiry, was to risk your life. The church had moved from being the persecuted one to the persecutor of its own people. History reveals that an entity designed to serve others had, in many ways, turned out to be an institution seeking to serve itself.

For those choosing to defy church authority, Inquisitions were initiated in the Middle Ages as an internal cleansing mechanism for rooting out dissent and combating heresy. If you didn't believe the teachings of the church, taught a different doctrine, or practiced witchcraft, you were sniffed out by religious bloodhounds, branded a heretic, and imprisoned or banished. It reminds me of the Salem witchcraft trials in Colonial Massachusetts in 1692–1693, where two hundred individuals were accused of witchcraft. Of the nineteen who were executed, fourteen were women and five were men, and this doesn't take into account the five who died in jail or the one crushed to death for failing to plead.

Breaking news of clergy child sex abuse has captured the headlines in recent years. To this day, new tragedies are emerging. In typical fashion, a church bent on protecting its power and maintaining its polished image works hard to shield itself from criticism. Instead of employing corrective action, the church often turns on its victims and initiates cover-up tactics. These are the deeds of an institution motivated by the trappings of power.

Abuse comes in all shapes and sizes and permeates every denomination. Vulnerable women and children become easy targets in a system where those in power prey upon the weak. Churches have been torn asunder by such exploitation. In addition to physical violence, spiritual abuse is also rampant, where religion is used to intimidate, demean, and humiliate others—thus, diminishing their dignity. Tired and worn out from such demeaning behavior, people are leaving the church in droves and opting for better alternatives. Spiritual abuse takes away any credibility the church has remaining.

Challenging the church can be dangerous, and for many, it isn't worth the effort. Instead, they leave. Speaking truth to power, like Galileo did in 1633 CE, often gets you labeled a heretic. Martin Luther was branded a traitor, as were so many others who challenged church authority. The church has lost its way so often that a sad history of abuse may be its keepsake. The exploitation of power didn't die with the Protestant Reformation; it has merely been removed from the limelight. Its harmful consequences remain.

Women as Second-Class Citizens

Some denominations are well on their way to overcoming their treatment of women as second-class citizens. Others, however, continue the tradition without missing a beat. To the chagrin of many, patriarchy still thrives in the world of religion. Can women be considered for the position of pope? How about a priest? Can they become ordained members of the clergy? Are they allowed to administer the sacraments? Hold positions of leadership? Are they viewed as equals or subservient kingdom members? In both the church and society, women have carried the burden of being viewed as the lesser species for far too long.

In the Old Testament, a woman's role was that of domestication. Their wombs were the incubators of babies, and their work was to cook and care for the lordly males. They were not individuals with ambitions of their own but rather chattel—goods in a contract for which damages could be collected should the woman be in breach. They were things to be owned, not equal beings in an equal relationship. Males, on the other hand, were always the injured party seeking a return on their contractual rights. In their daily prayers, faithful Jewish males thanked God for three blessings—that they were not born a Gentile, a slave, or a woman. That tells you what they thought of women!

From the very beginning, and in virtually every religion, the view of women and their corresponding treatment have been demeaning. Paul, in the New Testament, puts women in their place, for they are to keep quiet in church (1 Cor. 14:34) and are forbidden from teaching or having authority over a man (1 Tim. 2:12). According to 1 Corinthians 11:3 (NRSV), "Christ is the head of every man, and the husband is the head of his wife." Women are to wear head coverings as a symbol of respect for male authority, for "man was not made from woman, but woman from man. Neither was man created for the sake of woman, but woman for the sake of man. For this reason a woman ought to have a symbol of authority on her head" (1 Cor. 11:8–10, NRSV). Paul goes on to say that it is better *not* to marry, unless, of course, men are unable to control their unbridled passion (1 Cor. 7:9). The evangelical church I grew up in took such verses seriously and implemented them with loyal obedience since Scripture was considered the very words of God.

As a teenager, I remember our pastor had to be away from the pulpit one Sunday. His wife spoke during the morning service in his stead, and, as expected, this created quite a stir, for how could she violate the clear teaching of Scripture, which expressly forbids a woman to teach a man? Here she was, a female, standing behind the pulpit, preaching before males. Was she exercising authority over men? Women were to be quiet in church and refrain from straying from their God-ordained boundaries. Church leaders didn't seem to mind when none of the denominational women wore head coverings. Why the discrepancy? Head covering, I suppose, was interpreted as an insignificant, localized cultural phenomenon in contrast to the universal command preventing women from instructing or exercising authority over men. I guess the church can be selective in its interpretation and application when it wants to be!

I was taught that God had an established order to things, of which the man was the head of the woman and the home. Jesus reports to God, the Father; men report to Jesus, the head of the church; women report to men, the head of women; and so forth. To obey this established order is to submit to the authority of God's Word. Women who became too vocal in their marriage or ministry were gently reminded of God's divine order. Good Christian ladies were expected to recognize and accept what God had decreed. Male authority was not seen in my denomination as a bad thing, for men were charged with treating their wives well, as Christ loved the church. Most tried to do just that, but the underlying system of subjugation, which was created by men in support of male dominance, was never questioned.

The Christian and Missionary Alliance, a fervent missionary-sending denomination, commissions missionaries to other lands, often as a husband-and-wife team, though only the husband is ordained. In reality, however, female missionaries engage in teaching, discipleship, leading, and a host of other roles that place them over males. While this may not play well in the States, it is over-come by the missionary label, and from what I can surmise, this is somehow acceptable. Missionary women engage in the same work as males but have to do it in another country and under the guise of a missionary title. How absurd is that?

This sense of God's divine order stayed with me for many years. It is difficult to shed theological concepts that have been ingrained in you over time. Throughout the years, many marriage ceremonies I performed included lan-guage of this nature. In my mind, I was merely citing Scripture and following God's established order clearly set forth in the Bible. It is much easier to follow the divine order of things when you are top dog. We discover the fingerprints of male authors all over this concept—men who wrote from a male perspective in a culture of male dominance.

Prior to the start of formal seminary education, I enrolled in an intensive summer Greek course offered right before the fall semester began. A male instructor was flown in from California to teach the course. Though I thor-oughly enjoyed Greek, this kind of language immersion was overwhelming—like drinking water from a fire hose. The teacher returned to California with two weeks remaining in the course, and I realized that the teaching assistant, who happened to be female, would be taking over the class. A convenient excuse for my nonattendance over the final two weeks was that my grades were good enough for me to coast and still pass the class, but in reality, I was wondering how a Bible-based seminary could allow a female to teach males. Was I to sit under her teaching while Scripture was being violated right before my very eyes? I was in a bit of a conundrum.

I passed the course and never did attend the final two weeks of class. What in the world was I thinking? Not only did I pass up two weeks of education that I paid for, but the teaching assistant was an intelligent, gifted, and kind woman who was ready and willing to help us learn. Like any good Pharisee worth his salt, I sat on the sideline and judged. She was good enough to be an assistant, grade papers, and help out as long as she didn't hold the title of "teacher." The inroads of patriarchal thinking had traveled far in my own life, though I would never have labeled it as such, let alone recognize it for what it was. Thankfully, I have moved on from such foolish views, which goes to show that there is hope for recovering evangelicals like me. I thought I was obeying God when I was actually undermining Christian credibility.

I read an article about a fundamentalist Christian man who demanded that his wife call him "lord" just as Sarah called Abraham by that title. His trump card was 1 Peter 3:5–6 (NRSV), which he wielded with great precision in coercing his wife into submission: "It was in this way long ago that the holy women who hoped in God used to adorn themselves by accepting the authority of their husbands. Thus Sarah obeyed Abraham and called him lord. You have become her daughters as long as you do what is good and never let fears alarm you."

The law school I attended was of the fundamentalist sort, far right of where I was comfortable, but tuition was reasonable, the program design worked for a busy working adult like me, and, most importantly, its bar passage rates were very high. As I attended various course seminars, I noticed that the female servers always wore long dresses or skirts. The only skin showing was their face, neck, and half of their arms. Hair was usually pulled up into a bun, and many adorned their crown with a head covering. Their role, I suspect, was to rise early in the morning and prepare and serve meals to law-school students. I didn't complain—my body needed nourishment to keep my mind powered for difficult legal concepts. These women engaged in their duties with joy, and the school's understanding of God's revealed order was on full display.

Another area where women get shafted at the expense of religion is divorce. In the Old Testament, women were not allowed to initiate divorce—a right exclusively reserved for males. A certificate of divorce would later be granted to them as a form of protection from continued exploitation, but wives were excluded from the male privilege. Many denominations have such strict rules regarding divorce as to be senseless. The Catholic Church, for instance, will annul marriages as if they never occurred even after a couple has been married for many years with a house full of children. This fools no one—not even God. Absent adultery, fundamentalists view divorce as a particularly heinous breach of covenantal vows. Yet, the husband can be a pornography-addicted, physically and verbally abusive man who will be considered the innocent party should the abused wife file for divorce. She is excommunicated while he is allowed to remarry with the church's blessing. Go figure! What causes men to hold such low views of the opposite sex? Although many factors are involved, this mindset may have started right out of the gate with the Genesis story of creation.

Created Unequally?

The creation stories occur in Genesis 1 and 2. Fundamentalists believe these chapters were written sequentially; that is, Chapter 2 was written right after Chapter 1, and so forth. But these are actually two creation stories written at different times and under very different circumstances. Many scholars believe they were written five hundred years apart, with Chapter 2 written long before Chapter 1. We readily assume that both Adam and Eve were created in God's image, but a closer look may reveal a male bias even in the creation accounts. According to Genesis 2, Adam was given dominion over all of creation and instructed to name the animals as God brought them to him. It seems that the pristine garden, the ease of work, and the beautiful animals didn't satisfy Adam's need for a helpmate. Was this an "oops" moment for God—an afterthought? Why didn't God simply create Adam and Eve at the same time and in the same way?

God put Adam to sleep, took out one of his ribs, and used it to craft a female. Adam liked what he saw and named her "woman," just like he named all the other animals that God brought before him. Although she was connected to Adam via the rib, she was not formed like Adam—independently created in the image of God. Adam was created in God's image, but the writer of Genesis 2 leads us to question Eve's image status. Instead of being created in her own right as Adam was, she was taken from his rib and is presented as one who is above the animals but not quite of Adam's stature. Like all the other animals, Eve was subject to Adam because she was seen as lower than him. This subjection put her in a lower class—not quite attaining the glory of divine image.

Her chief aim was to please, serve, and support the God-imaged male. Higher than the animals and lower than Adam, she was seen as inferior. Even Genesis 1:27 is a bit awkward in most translations where God is credited with creating both humans, but only the male is expressly said to be created in God's image. That doesn't sound like a ringing endorsement for women's equality.

Do you catch a glimpse of patriarchy and sexism in these creation accounts? Women have been taught to accept this subservient role as the divine order of creation. Yet the implication is that they are less than human—second-class citizens. These days, only the naïve take the Genesis creation story literally, but its impact has been felt throughout the centuries, and the damage has already been done.

Only in recent history have women found their voice of freedom from the constraints of the past. In Christian America, it wasn't until the constitutional amendment of 1920 that women gained the right to vote in national elections. It took men a long time to share their power and believe that women could vote responsibly. The first woman to ever serve on a president's cabinet was Frances Perkins in 1933, the Secretary of Labor under Franklin D. Roosevelt. In 1981, two years after I graduated from high school, President Ronald Reagan appointed Sandra Day O'Conner to the Supreme Court—a first for America. She served faithfully until her retirement in 2006. Hillary Clinton became the first presidential candidate to be nominated by a major party in 2016, while three other woman became major party nominees for the vice presidential role: Geraldine Ferraro (1984), Sarah Palin (2008), and Kamala Harris (2020).

Why did it take so long for women to be seen as powerful and complementary counterparts in the human equation—equals in their own right? There is still plenty of room for continued expansion of women's rights, but it is wonderful to see female CEOs, Fortune 500 board members, lawyers, doctors, business owners, politicians, journalists, scientists, and the like, when not too long ago, they were restricted from such opportunities solely based on gender. Yet today, in many denominations, women are still held back in the name of God and looked upon as subservient creatures whose chief aim in life is to serve the lordly male.

It's All Her Fault

It has long been the universal norm, in virtually all religions, to view women as the lesser of the sexes—weaker in every way than their patronizing male counterparts. When it came time to account for evil in the world, it was convenient to blame the weaker sex. Unfortunately, women were thrown under the bus by the male writers of Scripture. Eve became responsible for the tragic consequences of the fall and opened wide the door of sin. It's all her fault!

As the story is told from an evangelical and fundamentalist perspective, Eve was the first to disobey God and eat the forbidden fruit. In her weakness, she

wilted at the serpent's temptation. Not only did she succumb to sinful entice-
ment; she also caused Adam to disobey God's directive. When God inquired of
them, Adam blamed Eve and Eve blamed the crafty snake.

Eating the forbidden fruit unleashed a chain of unpleasant consequences.
Forced from the pristine garden, never to return, Adam's work would now be
earned by the sweat of his brow, while childbirth for Eve would become painful.
Both would experience mortality. Accordingly, if the woman hadn't disobeyed
God, sin would never have entered the world. That is quite a load of guilt and
shame to cast upon female shoulders. Eve's failure spawned an entire theological
system built around her sin—atonement theology, which will be discussed later
in the book.

Do the creation stories portray women as less than fully human—subservient
members of God's creation, brought to Adam and named like all the other animals? Are women the instigators of all sin and evil in the world? There is yet
another cloud of misgiving surrounding the female gender that must be mentioned—the issue of blood.

The Issue of Blood

Women possess biological functions that men do not, including menstruation
and childbirth. In Old Testament days, it was believed that life and blood were
deeply connected: "For the life of every creature—its blood is its life . . . for the
life of every creature is its blood" (Lev. 17:14, NRSV). They didn't understand
the biological and physiological functions of the human body as we do today. If
life was in the blood, why were women losing blood on a monthly basis and still
able to live? Yet the flow stopped with pregnancy, only to spill out again immediately after birth. Without access to the medical knowledge we currently
possess, these mysterious events must have been confusing to them.

During menstruation and childbirth, women were considered unclean simply because of their special biological issue. The Old Testament goes to great
lengths in describing female impurity, of which Leviticus 15:28–30 (NRSV) is
an example:

> *If she is cleansed of her discharge, she shall count seven days, and after that
> she shall be clean. On the eighth day she shall take two turtledoves or two
> pigeons and bring them to the priest at the entrance of the tent of meeting.
> The priest shall offer one for a sin offering and the other for a burnt offering;
> and the priest shall make atonement on her behalf before the LORD for her
> unclean discharge.*

Was the woman's sin simply that of being female? Was she declared unclean merely because of a biological process intrinsic to her gender that was neither understood nor treatable in that era? She was required each month to present an offering to the priest so that he could atone for her impurity and declare her whole again. The purification process for childbirth was even lengthier and required a lamb for a burnt offering in addition to the regular pigeon or turtle-dove utilized for a sin offering (Lev. 12). How is childbirth sinful?

Today, males not only attend the birthing event with great expectation and joy but understand it as well. I watched the birth of my own two children, although I missed some of my daughter's entry into this world after nearly fainting. There was no ceremonial cleansing that occurred after the baby was born, and no offerings were presented to a priest for atonement. Today, we better understand women's health and grasp the biological differences between men and women. No longer are women thought of as spiritually defiled by their own natural processes.

Women may be treated with greater respect today than at any other time in history, and though we have seen tremendous progress, we haven't eliminated old patriarchal ways of thinking and behaving. Unfortunately, the church's treatment of women, especially in its own Scriptures, has undermined its credibility.

Homosexuals as Despised Minority

Another group Christians have denigrated throughout the years is the LGBTQ+ community, who at any given time make up a small percentage of our population. Just like women were supposedly the cause of evil in the world, these folks get blamed for a host of horrible things as well. And, just like women who were considered impure and in need of atonement by virtue of a gender specific biology, these folks are likewise considered impure, but this time under penalty of death.

Considered an abomination in the Old Testament, homosexuality was punishable by death, according to the Leviticus holiness code (Lev. 18:2; 20:13). This stiff penalty isn't the only capital crime in the Torah; other circumstances deserving of death include children disobeying a parent, being a medium with the dead, having sex with one's mother-in-law (bet you haven't heard that one before), losing one's virginity prior to marriage, committing adultery, blaspheming, breaking the Sabbath, and many others. If we adhered to all of these capital crimes in our day, a sizeable portion of our population would have been dead a long time ago. Biblical literalists, however, cherry-pick the portions that best justify their prejudice and, in doing so, exclusively focus on homosexuality while ignoring other verses, such as killing a disobedient child.

In 2005, the Grand Ayatollah in Iraq, Ali al-Sistani, issued a fatwa for the killing of gays. During that same year in Israel, Yishai Shlisel, a Haredi Jew (those who reject the secularism of modern culture), stabbed three individuals marching in a gay pride parade. After ten years in prison, he was released, and three weeks later, he stabbed another group of gay pride marchers, killing one of them. His violent act was carried out in the name of God.

While America has no homosexual death laws, it can still be a very dangerous time to be gay. In 1998, a gay student at the University of Wyoming, Matthew Shepard, was beaten to a pulp, tied to a log fence, and found nearly eighteen hours later. He died from severe head injuries six days after the beating. During 2007 in Detroit, a 72-year-old disabled gay man, Andrew Anthos, was killed by a man who shouted anti-gay slurs while beating him with a lead pipe.

We could mention the 2016 mass shooting at the Pulse, a gay nightclub in Orlando where twenty-nine-year-old Omar Mateen killed forty-nine people and wounded fifty-three others. Open and affirming churches face acts of vandalism and are commonly referred to as "the gay church" in town. Such hatred abounds worldwide with plenty of examples to draw from, but you get the point.

In an effort to bolster their case against homosexuality, some uninformed Christian pastors engage in scare tactics by linking homosexuality to all kinds of depravity, such as rape, murder, child molestation, and the like. For these ministers, homosexuality isn't just a heinous sin but a perverted sickness that needs to be cured or wiped out.

One Christian pastor advocates locking up homosexuals in a large fenced-in area, dropping in food as needed, and watching them die off over time since they are unable to reproduce. What kind of sick mentality is that? Do differences in belief also require that we hate? Such hatred reflects poorly upon a church proclaiming the love of God for humankind. What does it say about the God they worship? What does it say about them?

Pat Robertson, founder of the Christian Broadcasting Network (CBN) and host of *The 700 Club*, may be the most famous, nationally known Christian preacher to spew forth malicious anti-gay rhetoric. The most cantankerous opponent, however, may have been Fred Phelps, former pastor of the Westboro Baptist Church in Topeka, Kansas, which the Southern Poverty Law Center has classified as a hate group. Though Phelps has since passed away, he was known for his extreme hatred of the LGBTQ+ community. His fundamentalist group could be found picketing the funerals of gays and military veterans while proudly displaying despicable hate signs, believing that their deaths were the direct result of God's judgment. While his charades garnered national attention in the press, it showed America how hateful professing Christians could be. How does this square with the Bible's emphasis on loving your neighbor?

Churches struggle with homosexuality because they view Scripture as the literal Word of God—permanently fixed for all time. The Bible does portray homosexuality in a negative light, but is this how God feels about it, or is this the homophobic perspective of the age in which the words were written? Homosexuality is spoken of in Leviticus 18:22; 20:13; Genesis 19:4–5; 1 Corinthians 6:9; and 1 Timothy 1:10. These passages have been interpreted in various ways by various scholars, and while there may not be universal agreement as to their meaning, they are intensely negative. Interestingly, the Bible doesn't seem to address lesbianism or transgender issues.

While I do not have time in this volume to address these passages with the depth they deserve, my point is that homosexuals have been ill-treated in the name of God, and Scripture is often used to underscore how much God hates them. That's how the Fred Phelpses of the world use the Bible. These passages are typically taken out of context without considering their underlying worldview and then used to clobber the victims of prejudice. When pouncing on others, it is always helpful to have God on your side!

For many, this issue is a dividing line they cannot cross and is viewed as another, if not the final, indicator of how contemporary culture is sliding off the cliff and into the abyss of immorality. Since homosexuality is most often framed by its opponents as a choice rather than an orientation, the solution for America's depravity is to simply turn back to God—choosing holiness rather than unnatural sexual perversions.

I imagine some engage in same-sex behavior out of curiosity or as a response to bad experiences with heterosexual relationships, but for the most part, sexual orientation is hardwired into us. I was born heterosexual. I had no choice in the matter, just like I had no choice in my eye color, my height, and my right-handedness. Being heterosexual isn't something I choose; it is something I am. It would be difficult, awkward, and wrong for me to behave any other way. Demanding that LGBTQ+ individuals change their internal hardwiring is asking them to rewire their very nature. Biblical literalists can be found bellowing, "The Bible says it, I believe it, and that settles it." That's a nice little slogan to carry in your back pocket, but it does little justice to the complexity of issues involved. I guess we just aren't in agreement on what the Bible says and what it actually means, and thus, we "settle it" in different ways. As we shall see in upcoming chapters, how we view the Bible shapes our understanding of God and Scripture.

Denominations struggle in their approach to same-sex issues. To move forward in total acceptance of the LGBTQ+ community is to split the church, while not accepting them violates their conscience and understanding of the love of God. Meanwhile, as the church wrestles with whether or not to fully embrace such diversity, its credibility erodes even further. We know more about same-sex attraction than at any other time in history. Research continues, but, as with all data, if your mind is already made up, any information that contradicts your position is quickly dismissed and viewed as "flawed."

While serving as the head of academic affairs at one university, I attended a training seminar on conflict resolution with several of the faculty members, one of whom was gay. This young fellow was an exemplary professor who cared for his students and demonstrated excellence in the classroom. He knew I held ministerial credentials, and over lunch we had a very good conversation. To answer his question as to why Christians are so judgmental toward gays, I explained to him their views and why they held them. Near the end of lunch he said to me, "I knew you were a pastor when they hired you, and I thought you would be like all the other Christians I have met. I have never been able to have the kind of conversation with a Christian that I have had with you. Thank you. I am sorry that I initially judged you the way I did." That made my heart smile. He sensed the presence of God in me rather than some pious, condescending attitude.

Not too long ago, as I was enjoying the Sunday worship service with an open and affirming congregation, a transgender women walked to the pulpit to read the morning Scripture. Tears welled up in my eyes as I thought to myself, "Where else could a transgender woman be asked to publicly read Scripture in church and still feel loved and valued by the congregation and by God?" I was proud of this church for offering an extravagant welcome to all without judgment or ridicule.

At the heart of every prejudice is fear, which prompts us to devalue others in an effort to elevate ourselves. Taken to the extreme, fear expresses itself in violence. Afraid of Black people, we segregated them and sought to restrict their civil rights. Afraid that women would gain more power than they deserved, we discriminated against them to maintain male dominance. This mentality is often referred to as "tribal religion," where our God hates everything we hate.

By attaching a divine imperative to our fears, we justify our behavior, take a few verses out of context, act in a shameful manner, and call it the will of God.

"Love the sinner, and hate the sin" is a popular and familiar saying, though I have never known anyone who could actually pull it off. Most often, the recipients of this mentality only hear "sinner" and "hate." The love part can't be seen or heard because of the noise level of hate. The Bible was written in a specific culture, under specific circumstances, and with limited knowledge. By promoting the Bible's negative treatment of homosexuality without an honest appraisal of Scripture and its contextual environment, all we do is perpetuate a theology of ignorance. Scripture must not only be read through the lens of past worldviews; it must also be brought into the twenty-first century in a credible manner. Merely advancing antiquated understandings does little to bolster confidence in a God for the twenty-first century.

Every now and then, I meet parents who were steadfast in their opposition to homosexuality until, of course, their own child turned out to be gay. This put them in a theological bind, and many are now proponents of loving those who are constitutionally oriented to the same sex. They chose love and acceptance over hate and division. Members of the LGBTQ+ community are just like you and me, with hopes, fears, talents, weaknesses, etc. They are in all ways like us, except for one thing. And for this, they have experienced intense hatred from those who feel most holy. The very heart of tribalism is aligning God with viewpoints that allow us to discriminate against others in the name of God. We have seen this dog-and-pony show before in church history. This time, a new age, a new issue, and a new expression, but the same old hatred bolstered by the battle cry, "God's Word says . . ."

Jews as Perpetual Prey

There may not be a more despised people on this planet than the Jews. Calling themselves the "chosen" people of God certainly didn't win them any favors, for this insinuates that others are "unchosen"—the rejected ones. Their move to conquer promised lands in the name of God didn't set well with those about to be displaced. Even so, no one deserves the kind of historical hatred the Jews have faced. After all, Christianity was birthed from the womb of Judaism and cradled in her arms. For Christians to despise Jews is to spit upon the religious mother who gave them birth. Jesus was a Jew; should he also be despised and classified as evil?

I grew up in a small, Midwestern river town with blue-collar men and women raising their families as best they could. To my knowledge, I don't remember ever seeing a Jew, let alone being able to recognize one should they be standing right in front of me. I recently became aware that a Jewish synagogue existed in my home town and that our mayor, the owner of a men's clothing store, was Jewish, but then again, I was unaware of a lot of things back then. To me, Jews were a far-away people who lived in Israel. To my dismay, they were beside me all along.

One day, I asked my aging mother whether she remembered Arnie Sigel's Western Store on East Main Street. I recall their television commercials, where Arnie put two minutes' worth of advertising into a thirty-second television slot—"Have I got a deal for you!" Prior to the start of each school year, mom would take us kids to buy school clothes. We were allotted one pair of tennis shoes, jeans, and a few shirts. Anything else was on us. Arnie's store carried cowboy hats, boots, saddles, and cowboy clothing, for which I had no use, but they did stock a large selection of Levi's jeans. Mom informed me that Arnie was Jewish, his brother ran a furniture store, and when she was growing up in the 1950s, that section of town was called "Hymie Town." This was all news to me.

While antisemitism has manifested its ugly presence throughout the centuries, it was the reign of Nazi terror during WWII that made famous their predicament. Between 1941 and 1945, the genocidal plan of the Nazi killing machine put to death some six million Jewish men, women, and children. Referred to these days as "the Holocaust," two-thirds of Europe's Jewish population was exterminated, and German history was marked with a permanent stain long remembered to this day. Unfortunately, both the Catholic and Protestant churches in Germany turned a blind eye to their plight. I own a book titled *The Holocaust Chronicle* that is filled with pictures and information regarding this calamitous event in human history. Every time I look through its pages, I cry. Who could hate so much as to desire the extinction of an entire segment of the human race?

Like many others, Hitler blamed the Jews for the economic woes of the 1930s. While many in Germany struggled to survive this economic downturn, Jews were portrayed as wealthy individuals living beyond the means of the average German. This provided a convenient scapegoat for German nationalism to flourish, which Hitler used to his advantage.

Martin Luther, the great German Reformation leader of the 1500s, wrote disparagingly of Jews. He advocated setting fire to their synagogues, destroying their homes, forbidding their rabbis to teach, denying safe travel passage, and preventing them from securing loans. These were cruel words penned by the very founder of the Protestant Reformation! Debate continues on just how much influence Luther's views and European antisemitism had upon Hitler and his final solution to the "Jewish problem."

The Church Fathers didn't speak well of Jews, either, portraying them as evil, unfit to live, and outside of God. Tertullian (155–240 CE) believed that Christians were to replace the Jews. As a reminder to them that they killed the Messiah, Augustine (354–430 CE) advocated leaving the Jews alone to suffer for their shameful behavior. John Chrysostom (349–407 CE) taught that, since the Jews rejected Jesus and caused his death, they should be killed for their reprehensible action. It was common to think poorly of Jews and blame them for Jesus's death.

In the 1300s, the bubonic plague spread throughout Europe, and within three years, one-third of Europe's population would succumb to the black death. That generation possessed no understanding of the causes or remedy for such devastation. They had no idea that fleas carried a disease that was then transmitted to humans, as rats transported the fleas. In their limited understanding of how the world worked, they believed the plague was punishment sent from God. But for what? They took stock of things and finally figured out the reason for such upheaval—they had allowed infidel Jews to dwell in their midst. Suddenly, the bubonic plague was blamed on the Jews, and persecution broke out against them in the name of God.

We forget that Catholic crusaders of the Middle Ages killed Jews along with Muslims in their attempts to conquer the Holy Land. Scripture itself, in the New Testament, seems to blame the Jews for the death of Jesus, and it was that wretched Jew, Judas Iscariot, who betrayed Jesus in the first place. The history of antisemitism doesn't bode well for Christian credibility. To this day, the Jews are a vilified people.

Slavery as Cultural Stain

Slavery has been a part of the human enterprise for a very long time. As one kingdom dominated another, captured citizens became the slaves of their conquerors. This was a frequent occurrence in the Old Testament, with the very roots of Judaism planted in the soil of Egyptian slavery. Their escape from the clutches of Egyptian bondage became the basis of a famous 1956 Hollywood film, *The Ten Commandments,* starring Charlton Heston as Moses.

In the Old Testament, God seems to condone slavery, especially in Exodus, Deuteronomy, and Leviticus, where guidance is provided on the various types of slavery, the legal standing of slaves, and their economic role. Apparently, the

Israelites were allowed to own slaves but were forbidden to subjugate one of their own. We find no Scripture condemning the practice. This is a prime example of how interpreting Scripture as the literal, infallible, inerrant, unchanging Word of God is fraught with problems, one of which is that it forces us to accept all of these cultural prejudices as God-ordained practices. This, of course, is problematic.

Slavery appears to be a normal aspect of everyday life in the New Testament, for even Jesus references it as a way of teaching his disciples, such as in Matthew 10:24 and 24:45–46. Though Jesus acknowledges the existence of slavery, many are disappointed that he never confronts it directly or speaks negatively of the practice. It is easy to see how Christian slave owners used this to their advantage.

Though the biblical days of slavery are long gone, the slave trade we are most familiar with began in the 1400s as Catholic Portugal and other Christian European countries sailed the high seas, opening up new trade routes. With the availability of well-crafted boats and navigational tools, they were able to reach western Africa, where Africans were encouraged to kidnap their own people in an effort to source the burgeoning slave trade. Both Protestants and Catholics were involved in this endeavor. In reality, one could own, buy, and sell slaves and still maintain a good Christian conscience since, in their mind, the Bible didn't condemn the practice. Would they have felt the same way had the tables been turned and they were the enslaved ones?

All too often, we read Scripture through the lens of what we want to see or what benefits us personally and economically. Slave owners needed some way to justify their actions, and Scripture afforded them this opportunity, even though their interpretations were often strained. Except for the voice of abolitionists, slaves were seen as having their own lot in life while slave owners had theirs. Each was merely fulfilling God's established order.

In America, the issue of slavery would reach its zenith during the Civil War (1861–1865 CE), where 620,000 soldiers gave their lives fighting over this very issue. If the South could no longer own slaves after their surrender, it would at least vigorously pursue its ugly stepchild—segregation. After Reconstruction, state and local legislative bodies in the South, dominated by whites, passed Jim Crow laws designed to safeguard racial segregation in all public facilities. This lasted until 1964, when the federal Civil Rights Act was passed, banning not only segregation in public places but also employment discrimination on the basis of race, color, religion, sex, or national origin. This was followed by the Voting Rights Act of 1965 that ended discriminatory voting practices.

American slaves were denied an education and severely punished if efforts to better themselves were discovered. This, of course, was an attempt to keep them poor and unaware lest they rise in knowledge and break from the heavy yoke upon their shoulders. Religious slaveholders quoted Scripture as their authority but wouldn't allow slaves to read or question the basis of that authority. A segregationist understanding of the Bible was commonplace for those trying to protect their business assets. In Virginia, a Baptist minister named Rev. Thornton Stringfellow gave voice to these views in his published works, *A Brief Examination of Scripture Testimony on the Institution of Slavery* (1850); *Scriptural and Statistical Views in Favor of Slavery* (1856); and *Slavery: Its Origin, Nature, and History* (1861).

The familiar story of Genesis 9 was even twisted into support of slavery. After binge drinking, Noah falls asleep naked, when his son Ham walks in on him. Rather than cover him up, Ham informs his brothers, who walk in backward and place a blanket over their father. When Noah wakes from his drunken stupor, he is furious that Ham left him uncovered. Noah then places a curse on Ham's son (Canaan), declaring him to be the lowest of slaves to his brothers. According to some, this is the beginning of the black race, and Noah's curse becomes scriptural justification for slavery. With a generous imagination, the Bible can support just about anything we want it too. Interestingly, nothing is said about Noah's shame for his drunkenness or his severe reaction toward Ham. What in the world did Ham's son have to do with this incident? Why was he cursed? We see what we want to see and justify the views that best support our cause.

We have certainly come a long way since the robed gatherings of the Ku Klux Klan, celebrated lynchings, church bombings, attack dogs, firehoses, and Jim Crow laws of our past, but racism has not been eradicated. Slavery isn't one of America's ancient stories, for America is too young to have an ancient history. This oppression of fellow human beings occurred in recent times, just down the street from yesterday. It is fresh in our minds, and I haven't even touched upon the ill treatment of Native Americans, children, the poor, the mentally ill, the divorced, and others. Slavery's presence in Scripture and its past relationship with Christianity beg for explanation in the present age.

Have I presented enough evidence to convince you that Christianity has a serious credibility problem? When we rise above the details of daily living and see the larger picture, we realize that Christian history is replete with examples of shameful behavior—behavior that kills, enslaves, justifies, and blames in the name of God. This overwhelming evidence of incongruity between Christian proclamation and Christian practice stares us down until we blink. It is this incongruity that undermines the credibility of the message itself. It is the problem of behavior—both personal and historical.

The Belief Problem

While I have hinted at the problem of belief, my discussion, so far, has been limited to the church's behavioral issues from both a personal and historical perspective. What remains to be addressed is the predicament with the message itself—the problem of belief. While disappointing behavior knocks us off our feet, it isn't a fatal blow to our faith. What the church believes and teaches, however, becomes the dagger thrust deep into the heart of Christianity.

This problem of belief concerns the church's core teaching. If the Christian story, as it is presently told, no longer aligns with the knowledge we currently possess, the message is cast aside as irrelevant and archaic. Because we no longer live in a pre-enlightened era, the beliefs and worldviews of the past no longer correlate to known truth in the present world. This is a knockout blow to traditional understandings of Christianity.

The God of the ancient world needed sacrificial offerings, unquestioned obedience, appeasement, and worship to avert slinging divine retribution from the heavens. Because our knowledge has increased in so many areas, we see things much differently—more clearly than yesterday. Today, we no longer attribute epilepsy to demons. We grasp plate tectonics and how their movement creates earthquakes and tsunamis instead of attributing these effects to a blood-thirsty God in desperate need of appeasement. It is no longer heretical to believe that Earth revolves around the sun.

No longer do we believe that women are passive vessels who merely lend the nurture of their womb to growing babies; instead, we now recognize their contribution to 50 percent of the child's DNA. We speak of germs and viruses and create vaccines to counter their negative effects. We understand the causes of the bubonic plaque instead of attributing it to God's vengeful anger. Doctors have learned to wash their hands before delivering babies, which reduces infant mortality rates. What if the ancients had learned to do that centuries ago? We have a greater understanding of weather patterns, thunderstorms, and tornadoes and no longer believe they come from the hand of an angry deity. How can Christianity be believed when it advances such unbelievable messages?

Scripture was written in a specific age with a specific worldview and with a specific and limited base of knowledge. We don't seem to realize that Jesus was born a Jew, lived under the Torah, and grew up in a particular time in human history within a particular culture and with a particular outlook on life. In studying the biblical texts, we must keep this in mind. We cannot expect ancient documents to possess twenty-first-century knowledge; neither can we shackle twenty-first-century knowledge to the limited worldview of ancient days. This is the heart of the problem—asking twenty-first-century people to believe ancient worldviews so deficient as to be gasping for their last breath. Soon, the oxygen tank sustaining them will run out of air, and then what?

For many, the Bible is antiquated, outdated, and unable to reach our contemporary world. It is incredulous how modern Christians can literalize the Bible and believe the unbelievable. We often call this credibility gap faith, but in reality, it is nothing short of nonsense. Let's say a prized ancient document written two thousand years ago adamantly declared Earth to be flat, and you, living in the twenty-first century, know that Earth is round; do you (1) throw out the ancient text, (2) throw out your knowledge of Earth's spherical shape, (3) explain the gap as a matter of faith, or (4) understand that a flat-Earth belief was the worldview of the ancient writer at the time the ancient text was written? The answer seems obvious to me. Somehow the Christian story must be reinterpreted and retold with modern-day integrity. I hope to address this challenge in the chapters that follow.

As I unravel traditional understandings of faith in light of twenty-first-century knowledge, I am cognizant of my own fallibility. I don't possess all the answers. Never have. Never will. Only a fool would make such an arrogant boast. In the coming pages, I share my own thinking and my own spiritual journey with the high hopes that it might unleash your own curiosity and encourage you to read further, think deeper, and ponder your own faith journey. My critique comes with honorable intentions for sharpening the message of our beloved Christian faith. To survive in the twenty-first century and beyond, the Christian story must become viable, and this entails unlearning, rethinking, and retelling a message that is no longer contradicted by current knowledge. I believe this can be done, and I hope to bridge the gap between an ancient account written in an ancient time and an exciting story that captures the attention of the postmodern mind.

All I am doing, according to some, is playing fast and loose with God's Word, and you just don't go messing around with the Holy Bible or water it down in any way. In the coming pages, I will devote an entire section to whether or not the Bible is actually God's Word. I can relate to this fear, for I once elevated Scripture to be the fixed and immutable words of God, which made it difficult for me to rethink my traditional understandings of faith. You have heard it said, "It is sinful culture that must change, not God's Word. Culture needs to turn back to God; that's the problem." This view merely reflects a present comfort level with traditional teaching. Any other view is uncomfortable and unthinkable. Stepping back and looking at things from a new perspective takes enormous courage, especially when the headwinds are against you.

We keep asking culture to go backward when humanity is ever progressing forward. It is our understanding of the ancient text that must change. Holding on to the world of yesterday locks Scripture into the time frame in which it was written, along with all of its prejudices, misunderstandings, and inaccurate statements. No, I am not playing fast and loose with the Holy Writings; I am trying to bring them to life and discover a universal faith that can speak to all generations.

When "belief" and "change" are mentioned in the same sentence, warning bells begin to clang. In fact, the only person amenable to change may be a baby with a wet diaper, and even then, I have encountered resistance. This kind of talk is frightening—it was for me in the beginning. It took me a long time to come to grips with the reality right before my eyes. You don't see what you don't see, but once you see it, you wonder how you ever missed it. I don't write of altering our understanding of treasured beliefs in some willy-nilly, frivolous fashion, for I have wrestled with the issues myself.

Does it help if I speak in terms of seeing things with a fresh perspective, correcting a misunderstanding, or sharpening our vision with an adjusted prescription? Maybe it is best to say we are not adding to the Christian message but rather stripping away antiquated beliefs—unlearning bad habits. It is like a treasured portrait hidden beneath multiple layers of paint that have been applied over the years. We only see the beauty of the portrait once the layers of paint covering the prized image have been scraped away. We once believed in Santa Claus and the Easter Bunny, and it served us well for a time. But as we grew up and matured in our understanding of life, we "unlearned" those beliefs—we scraped them away. Whatever word picture best opens up this truth to you, one thing is certain: old paradigms must be scraped away so the beauty of new perspectives can emerge.

Chapter Summary

I assert, in this chapter, that the church has a credibility problem that undermines its ability to survive into the future. I divide the credibility problem into two main areas—behavior and belief. When there is a gap between what is proclaimed and what is lived, credibility is undermined. We see this incongruity through our personal experience with the church and throughout the church's history.

It is the credibility of belief, however, that is the more destructive of the problems, for if the teachings of the church are no longer viable, then its very survival is at stake. The problem of belief will be tackled in future chapters, since this one is already too long and I have much to say. In fact, a good portion of this book will be given to the problem of belief as I scrape away layers of paint covering the beautiful Christian message as it was meant to be told. I hope you will take this journey with me, but before we begin exposing the belief problem, we must first discuss how we got into this mess in the first place.

3

HOW WE GOT INTO THIS MESS
· · · · · · · ·

EFORE WE CAN SCRAPE AWAY THE LAYERS OF traditional Christian teaching
and unearth a new, treasured understanding of the faith story, a final intro-
ductory chapter is necessary. Previously, I noted how the church loses credibility
through its own shameful behavior—both personally and historically. Credibility
further erodes over its staunch adherence to ancient beliefs that cannot withstand
the weight of modern scholarship. We will explore the various ways this occurs in
the chapters to come, but for now, I share how we arrived at this point in the first
place. What has caused us to question the traditional understandings of the past?

I happen to be a forest guy rather than a tree man. Some are just the opposite.
Trees are interesting to study, but I find they are much easier to examine once I
survey the overarching forest and get my bearings. In other words, I grasp the
big picture before I swoop down and examine the details. This way, if I get lost
among the trees, I have a good idea in which direction I must travel to exit the
forest. To that end, I share four epoch religious periods in human history as a
way of helping us grasp the lay of the land—the forest. Once we understand what
has transpired in the progression of religious thought, we will then be ready to
swoop down and examine in greater detail the extraordinary age that is most
familiar to us—the Modern Age.

My simple historical overview will be a disappointment to well-studied historians, anthropologists, and theologians who possess far more knowledge in
this area than I do. My goal, however, is a simple one—to unveil how Christianity's
credibility problem has progressed over time to the point where we are questioning the relevancy of the church. My brief historical fly-over will help us do
that. Unfortunately, the gaze of each generation typically looks only to the
skewed reality of its own culture without stepping back and scanning the horizon

of a broader landscape, all the while believing that the values and perspectives they presently hold have been around since the dawn of humanity.

I am convinved that our understanding of God progresses over time. If that is true, which I believe it is, then the ramifications are enormous. If, in the beginning, we believed one way, progressed to another level of understanding in a subsequent age, and now, in our present age, are moving even further into new insights, then our understanding of God is continually evolving— ever-expanding and moving forward. To be shackled to the views of previous ages is to stunt our spiritual growth.

Notice that I did not say that *God* changes, for what changes over time is our *perspective*. As knowledge expands, our understanding of God must also be enlarged. God hasn't moved—we have, and that is a good thing. Too often, we fasten on to antiquated outlooks when new knowledge reveals something different. Embracing a fresh perspective scares us into feeling we have somehow abandoned truth. What is abandoned, however, isn't truth but an antiquated perspective that can no longer be regarded as truthful. Though God is constant, our understanding is in perpetual motion, trying to keep pace with the growth of new information. This is positive—the way it is supposed to be.

Like a bulldog unwilling to let go of its bone, we clench down on antiquated beliefs while a torrent of new knowledge washes over us. The difference between outdated perspectives and modern knowledge is like a cross-country race between a fighter jet and an automobile. One travels from Los Angeles to New York City at 70 miles per hour, while the other travels at 1,500 miles per hour. The car may be comfortable and may have served its purpose, but it will lose the competition simply because it cannot keep pace with the fighter jet. In a race to the International Space Station, neither the fighter jet nor the automobile will suffice. We need a space shuttle to boost us into orbit while traveling at 18,000 miles per hour upon liftoff. Our beliefs must keep pace with reality, for change bombards us at an alarming and unprecedented rate.

The Idea of Progress

What became new knowledge in one era becomes the anchor holding us back in another. The increasing speed of progress simply cannot be stopped. As we ride the tilt-a-whirl of life, we instinctively reach out for stability only to realize that the things we once held on to are themselves crumbling. While life whizzes by at breakneck speed, we remember that it is our *experience* of God that provides assurance, not our *explanation* of that experience. Explanations morph with the shifting cultural landscape and the expansion of new insight. What remains stable is the fact that God *can* be experienced in this life, no matter what age we live in. So, grab on, soak it up, and experience the thrilling ride. Though we may not be able to fully explain our experience in wholly satisfying terms, we hold on to the comforting fact that it is God we are experiencing.

This dizzying pace of change can be difficult to accept, and our longing for stability is understandable. We must fasten on to something far deeper than the crumbling traditions of the past. When I was a young boy growing up in the Midwest, I played sports, explored the ditch behind our house, and participated in bicycle races up and down the street, and life was grand. I didn't have a care in the world. No stress, no politics, no deep thinking, no decisions, no responsibility—just plain ole fun. Times sure have changed. My father has since died, and my mother is struggling to accept that she will someday follow suit. Even the town I grew up in is different. My elementary and junior high schools have been demolished, and the church of my youth cleared out all of its pews in favor of stackable chairs. A sign of the times, I suppose.

As I grew up and began raising my own family, the bicycle races gave way to hard work and heavy responsibility. Stress, lack of sleep, and difficult decisions became the props in my juggling act. I much prefer playing Little League baseball, enjoying Mom's homemade goulash, and allowing Dad to handle the hard things in life. My world is so different now, and I have entered an entirely new phase of the journey. My children are grown, have families of their own, and are walking into the stiff headwinds of responsibility, decision making, and stress, while I am left trying to sustain a meaningful connection with them. Inescapable and relentless, change is at it again.

Despite its many challenges, I have experienced the transformative effect of change upon my life, for I am a much deeper and wiser individual. If constant change is present throughout our life, why would we expect our understanding of God to remain stagnant? If you maintained the understanding and maturity of a four-year-old into your adult years, you would forever struggle to survive. From birth to death, we are in a constant state of transition. If faith is unable to keep pace with the times, it gets left behind as a relic of the past.

The transitions brought about by science and technology have been astounding. Where is the limit to progress and new insight? Maybe there isn't one. Maybe it just goes on and on; after all, we have an entire universe to explore. When change happens, and it does happen, we are forced to make adjustments and reevaluate things. What we thought we knew for certain must now be reinterpreted in light of new knowledge, and that kind of reevaluation is exactly what has transpired over the centuries. At the very heart of Christianity, and life itself, is the notion of change—an evolution of the heart and mind. Rather than something to be feared, change is the inevitable by-product of being human. It is the path to transformation and seeing things with new eyes. Following God in the midst of uncertainty is the essence of faith and maturity. Is there a way to understand God that allows for this continual evolution of progress while rising above it at the same time?

In presenting these historical transitions, I hope to unveil a progression of thought, carried along by certain people and events that bring us to the point where we are today. Without this larger picture of reality, we wind up thinking that the way things are is the way they have always been. But that is dead wrong. Our current understanding is built upon past progress.

To show the progression of religious understanding, history can be divided into four major periods: Pre-Axial Age, Axial Age, Post-Axial Age, and Modern Age.[1] In fact, the term "Axial" simply means "pivotal." An axial age is a pivotal age—an age where great change and major advancement occur in religious and cultural thought, the outcome of which is the altering of our assumptions about life and God. The greatest of these periods is the Axial Age from which the founders of the major religions emerge. We could call these four periods whatever suits our fancy, but in our attempt to unveil the progression from where we were to where we are now, the term "Axial Age" becomes a line in the sand from which we can point to what came before it and what came after it.

Four Epic Religious Periods

Pre-Axial Age	Axial Age	Post-Axial Age	Modern Age
Beginning—800 BCE	800 BCE—200 BCE	200 BCE—1500 CE	1500 CE—Present

Pre-Axial Age (Beginning—800 BCE)

The Pre-Axial Age refers to the period of time before the major upheaval in religion took place. It stems from the beginning of humanity to around 800 BCE, when the founders of the great religions spring forth. So hampered are we by the hustle and bustle of our present age that we fail to realize that a progression of religious thought has taken place. We experience Judaism and Christianity, but what existed prior to their entrance on stage? We don't think much about that. We are aware of Islam and Buddhism, but what came before their rise to prominence? What existed prior to the great world religions is the very period of time we are referring to when we speak of the Pre-Axial Age—a time before the founding of the major religions.

Imagine the moment when self-consciousness became part of the human experience. Though cognizant of their surroundings, there came a day when humans became aware of their own awareness, and that must have been an anxiety-filled moment. In this Pre-Axial Age, humans were establishing their existence. With a functioning self-consciousness, they moved from little communication to language, from hunting and gathering to farming, from nomadic living to civilization, and from survival mentalities to tribal gods.

People lived close to the ground during this age, and their many gods and spirits directly related to life on Earth—gods that assisted with daily survival. Their religion wasn't concerned with abstract questions, deep theological thought, or deities outside of the world in which they lived; instead, their gods were found in and around the natural world. If they were in need of protection, robust harvests, and healthy childbirth, they invented rituals and traditions for such important occasions, like dancing, singing, beating drums, shaking objects, and the like. These rituals were often tied to the cycles of nature and passed down from generation to generation. Religion became part of their social structure. Life, culture, and the gods were intertwined. Things were simple, and there was no need to challenge their own assumptions or invent complex explanations.

The big questions we ask today were not foremost on their minds. Thanks to progress, we have the luxury of theorizing, philosophizing, and pondering a plethora of deep subjects that cut across multiple disciplines. In the Pre-Axial Age, life expectancy was shorter, modern conveniences we take for granted didn't exist, and knowledge about the world was limited.

Growing up, I heard about primitive tribes in faraway places who struggle to grasp the modern world. Their environment is very different from our own, and to me, this may well represent what it was like in the Pre-Axial Age. There is no need to figure out grandiose questions of life, for they pretty much had it all down pat, according to their culture and understanding. In the Pre-Axial Age, religious stories were passed down by word-of-mouth, and the gods were as diverse as the people and geographical boundaries in existence at the time. Their religions were nameless—just various deities closely associated with nature.

Axial Age (800–200 BCE)

The Axial Age was a time of great advancement in religious thought—a pivotal period that altered the axis of thinking and pointed us in a new direction. It was the dawning of major world religions. From the prophets in the Middle East arose Judaism, Christianity, and Islam. Zarathustra of Iran established Zoroastrianism. Confucius and Lao-Tzu arose in China, from which Confucianism and Taoism sprang forth. In India, Hinduism emerged while Siddhartha Gautama initiated Buddhism. The great philosophers like Socrates, Plato, and Aristotle emanated from Greece.

This was an age of religious birth—new thought was rising in the world, and the world was ready to receive it. If the womb of innovation contained multiple new religions, the attending midwife was the expansion of humanity. Cultures were developing, cities were blossoming, new trade routes were undertaken, and new conquests were initiated. Humans began interacting with people from other cultures, which exposed them to differing viewpoints and perspectives. Whenever new ideas are brought to bear, curiosity awakens, and probing questions provide fodder for deeper thought regarding the world in which we live.

Religions of the Axial Age

Founder	Religion	Region
Abraham/Prophets/Jesus/Paul	Judaism (Christianity later)	Middle East
Abraham/Prophets/Mohammed	Islam	Middle East
Zarathustra	Zoroastrianism	Middle East
Confucius	Confucianism	Far East
Lao-Tzu	Taoism	Far East
Siddhartha Gautama	Buddhism	South Asia
No founder	Hinduism	South Asia
Socrates, Plato, Aristotle, et al.	Philosophy	Mediterranean

As self-awareness evolved alongside our longing for discovery, humans began thinking in ways that surpassed geographical boundaries and transcended the everyday world of survival. When discovery creates a thirst for knowledge, the quest for understanding is given flight. Unlike in the previous age, Greek philosophers began asking big questions about our very existence and the nature of reality. Instead of focusing solely on this world, they, along with all of the major religions, began to ponder a world beyond this one. Distinctions were drawn between the body and spirit, the seen and unseen, the temporal and eternal, this world and another world. God was no longer viewed as dwelling within nature—among the trees, wind, and people; instead, there was now a separation between heaven and Earth—nature and deity.

In India, God was perceived as an eternal reality. In Taoism, God was beyond all description, while the Buddha presented a way of living irrespective of God. In the Middle East, God was viewed as a holy and separate being who was beyond nature—the creator of all things, including nature itself and all humanity. As the Axial Age gave birth to the founders of the great religions, our view of God and the world changed. This wasn't a tiny pebble thrown into a small farm pond but a large boulder thundering down the mountain and creating such change as to redirect the human understanding of life itself—thus, the term "Axial Age."

Big questions surrounding who we are, why we exist, and how we understand reality didn't garner the same level of significance in the previous age. Instead, the focus was upon this world and the daily task of survival. In contrast, there emerged from the Axial Age a fascination with life as self-awareness led to a curious sense of contemplation. It's as if an awakening of intellectual sophistication charted the course of human understanding for centuries to come.

The previous age worshiped many gods and spirits who were associated with nature and who helped with everyday concerns, like capturing or growing food. The Axial Age, however, raised its gaze from the here and now, believing that God, or an ultimate reality, existed beyond this world. Belief became personal and individualistic rather than tribal and social. These novel religions created systems and structures for understanding life that had never before existed, and this new reality extended far beyond the geographic regions in which people lived. They formulate new ways of knowing, understanding, and explaining God, all the while believing their way was the true way.

From our current setting on the timeline of world history, the perspectives of the Axial Age may not sound like much, but at the time, these monumental changes altered the paradigm of reality. Think of the shift from local gods tasked with overseeing the harvest to a god connected with ultimate reality—indescribable and other-worldly. Consider the change from a localized religion consisting of traditional rituals and oral stories passed down from generation to generation to a more structured and unified explanation of existence, reality, and life itself—a belief system that, if followed with sincerity, would grant salvation. Finally, think of the change between a reality grounded in the natural world to a God who lives outside of this world. The Axial Age is indeed a pivotal period, for it planted the seedlings of how we would understand God for years to come.

Post-Axial Age (200 BCE–1500 CE)

If the major world religions were birthed during the Axial Age, they grew up to become highly structured and refined in the Post-Axial Age. Judaism, Christianity, Islam, Hinduism, and Buddhism began to blossom—growing and developing to the point of dominance. These were the major religions of the world during the Post-Axial Age.

We see it over and over again in life—a novel idea comes along, takes root, grows, and replaces old perspectives. It happened with transportation: from foot, to animal, to horse-drawn wagons, to boat, to train, to automobile, to bus, to airplane, to space shuttle, to whatever comes next. The seed planted by the founders of these religions now grows into a fully developed system of thought. Their teachings are memorialized in sacred Scriptures that are utilized in worship, declared to be inspired by God, and eventually canonized into a set of officially approved holy writings.

Religions typically create a set of guiding documents that are assigned holy, inspired, and authoritative status. This not only provides cover for declaring their teaching to be from God but also becomes the basis for promoting their beliefs as the right way by which all others must come to know God. In Catholicism, the pope is infallible. In Protestantism, the Bible is inerrant. In Judaism, the prophets are God's mouthpieces, and in Islam, the Qur'an is God's dictated message to the prophet Mohammed. Each religion establishes an authority source from which to operate. This allows them to feel superior to all other religious systems, since they alone possess God's truth.

The definition and description of God acquired greater shape and clarity during this period. Theologies developed, church structure was built, and doctrines, dogma, and creeds were erected like scaffolding around a building. God is no longer seen in nature as one who lives among us; instead, God was now a deity who lives beyond us. Doctrines of salvation were outlined for those who desired entrance into the realm of God, and a three-tiered universe emerged— heaven above and Earth below, with the canopy of sky in between.

The prophets became the cornerstone of Judaism, and out of Judaism arose Christianity. Jesus lived and died in this age. Christianity sprouted up and eventually structured itself into the Catholic Church. Because someone must interpret the holy writings, oversee the rituals and sacraments of the church, and boldly proclaim its message, the role of clergy developed.

In this age, the teachings and practices of the major world religions morphed from their founders' messages to organized, structured, and coherent models of belief. This refinement led to clarity about the nature of God, the creation of inspired holy writings, and the development of religious doctrines and practices overseen by ordained clergy. This age lasted until the dawning of the Renaissance and Protestant Reformation.

Modern Age (1500 CE–Present)

Over time, the structures, doctrines, and practices of the church became corrupt and stifling. In many ways, the church had become a monument unto itself until the Enlightenment ushered in the Modern Age, of which we are a part. Change is brewing, and it still isn't over. Some believe we are living in a second Axial Age—another period of significant advancement in our faith development.

Like a steam train that starts out slowly and picks up speed, change in the Modern Age has gained significant velocity. In the Pre-Axial Age, things moved slowly, since the wheels were laboring to gain forward momentum. In the Axial Age, the train began moving down the tracks as humanity embarked upon a thrilling ride. It reaches cruising speed in the Post-Axial Age. Things kept moving faster and faster, and in the Modern Age, it feels as though the steam engine has given way to a high-speed bullet train traveling so fast that we cannot get off. The last five hundred years have brought about such rapid changes in science, philosophy, religion, medicine, and all sorts of fields as to be once again turning the world on its axis.

Now would be a good time to swoop down and examine in more detail the trees of the Modern Age. This is the period we most readily relate to, and it is also the age where a significant amount of erosion occurs surrounding the credibility of Christian teaching. We must catch what is going on here and how it necessitates a retelling of the faith story.

The Post-Axial Age lasts around sixteen hundred years—enough time for the major religions to become highly refined and structured. The Dark Ages came and went (476–800 CE), and Catholicism fractured in 1054 CE, leading to the formation of the Eastern Orthodox Church. A Papal Schism followed in 1378–1417 CE, where three different individuals all claimed to be pope at the same time—each excommunicating the others. A German by the name of Johannes Gutenberg invented the printing press in 1440 CE, initiating mass printing and distribution of information. Access to Scripture soon became available to all, not just clergy.

Human imagination lay dormant during the Post-Axial Age. Nothing extraordinary occurred in the way of altering our understanding of life and God. The Catholic Church in the West possessed both the lock and key to interpreting

Scripture, life, and God. This was all about to change with the Modern Age. Occurring in rapid succession, the Renaissance, Protestant Reformation, and Age of Enlightenment greased the skids for another pivotal age of history.

The Renaissance

The Renaissance is birthed in 1300 CE, with a renewed interest in art, literature, philosophy, and learning. The human imagination is once again stirred. Franciscan philosopher and theologian William Ockham lays the groundwork for what is now known as the scientific method. Ockham invites us to investigate our world on the basis of its own natural laws, not upon the dictates of the church. Nature can be explored in its own right without intermediary ecclesiastical interpretation that filters our attempts to understand the world. Ockham's predecessor, Franciscan philosopher Roger Bacon, also explores the natural world through empirical study. During the Renaissance, the embers of new thought are once again being fanned.

The Protestant Reformation

In 1517 CE, Martin Luther nails his Ninety-Five Theses to the door of the Castle Church, and the Protestant Reformation begins. Luther is fed up with the corrupt practices within the Catholic Church, and the selling of indulgences becomes the straw that breaks the camel's back. The ecclesiastical hold on interpreting Scripture, life, and God is being pried open by those seeking to reform it. These efforts are resisted, and thus begins the Protestant line of faith. The groundwork laid by Bacon and Ockham helps free Europe from Catholic dominance, while the Protestant Reformation spurs the movement away from a Catholic-centered understanding of Scripture. The firm grip of Catholicism cannot withstand the human quest for knowledge, and the invention of the printing press helps disseminate these new ideas.

The world is no longer confined to Europe, and ships begin sailing the high seas. Christopher Columbus, an Italian explorer, convinces Spain to fund his explorations across the Atlantic Ocean. He intends to chart a new route to China and the Far East; instead, he opens up the Americas. It will be the Portuguese explorer Ferdinand Magellan who first circumnavigates the globe, from 1519–1522 CE. The exploring and conquering of other cultures allow humans to interact with one another. A whole new world is opening up, and fresh ideas are emerging. Meanwhile, the church is losing its grip on interpreting and dictating our understanding of the world.

Heaven and Earth

Astronomer and mathematician Nicolaus Copernicus contributes to the evolution of new ideas with his published research of 1543 CE, just two months before he died. According to the church, Earth is the center of the universe, and the sun revolves around our planet. This is self-evident, and Joshua 10:13 (NRSV) is quoted in biblical support: "And the sun stood still, and the moon stopped, until the nation took vengeance on their enemies. Is this not written in the Book of Jashar? The sun stopped in midheaven, and did not hurry to set for about a whole day." The Bible says it; therefore, it is true. This is all the proof the church needs. Any other perspective is simply not tolerated and labeled heretical.

When Copernicus discovers that the world revolves around the sun, old understandings of how the world works are challenged, and Earth is removed from its pinnacle status as the center of the universe. Copernicus's insights open the door for others to inquire, and it isn't long before the telescope of an Italian named Galileo Galilei (1564–1642 CE) affirms Copernicus's theory. The Catholic Church brands Galileo a heretic and banishes him to house arrest. Finally, in 1992, the pope half-heartedly admits that Galileo was right—better late than never. In the 1600s, German astronomer and mathematician Johannes Kepler confirms the results of both Copernicus and Galileo.

Next in this line of scientific heavy-weights is Isaac Newton of the same generation. He discovers the laws of gravity that we rely on to this day, and his research advances the realm of modern science. We owe a great deal to these brave men who follow the facts rather than the restraint of erroneous church doctrine. Human understanding of the world is changing, and the church will soon have to reevaluate its stance on many issues. Interestingly, as new insights about our world are being discovered during this time period, Catholics and Protestants are killing one another in the Thirty Years' War (1618–1648 CE). The juxtaposition couldn't be more obvious.

Enlightenment: The Age of Reason

The curiosity of the Renaissance and the Protestant Reformation's challenge to the Catholic Church are followed by the Enlightenment—the Age of Reason. The Enlightenment (1685–1815 CE) becomes a line of demarcation in the history of human thought. Once crossed, humanity can never return to the way things were before. The Age of Reason is a time when great thinkers and philosophers challenge the very foundations of society. They question sources of authority and notions of human nature, something that couldn't have occurred without the work of courageous predecessors.

For centuries, the church based its understanding of the world on a perspective anchored to divine revelation, not concrete observation. As Copernicus, Galileo, Kepler, and others begin looking to the natural world for explanation instead of Scripture, divine revelation as the source of knowledge is replaced with reason, critical thinking, and careful observation. The scientific method of systematic observation, measurement, experiment, and modification or confirmation of a hypothesis is being established. The church no longer possesses unquestioned authority. The times are changing.

Philosophers like David Hume, Emmanuel Kant, and G. W. F Hegel live during this time, and their ideas dominate the cultural conversation. They usher in an era of skepticism, where the authority of both the church and the monarchy is being deconstructed. Are we to believe the church on the basis of divine revelation, or are we to embrace the power of reason and empirical evidence? This questioning of church authority and church teaching continues the erosion of credibility. Should we believe because a religious institution tells us what is true, or should we believe empirical evidence even when it is contrary to church teaching? This is quite a dilemma and, as one might suspect, threatening to the church.

The Nineteenth Century
Ludwig Feuerbach

Questioning Christian underpinnings continues during the 1800s, as German philosopher and anthropologist Ludwig Feuerbach critiques Christianity in his 1841 book, *The Essence of Christianity*. For Feuerbach, humans are conscious and self-conscious beings who mold God into a reflection of their own human nature. In other words, God is nothing more than the projection of human needs. Feuerbach's novel views influence the communist Karl Marx, who believes religion is the opiate of the people. Austrian psychoanalyst Sigmund Freud, who theorizes about the id, ego, and super-ego, is also influenced by Feuerbach, as is the German philosopher Friedrich Nietzsche, who proclaims that God is dead. Feuerbach's work generates invigorating conversations that could not have occurred in previous ages. After the Enlightenment, nothing seems to be off limits.

David Friedrich Strauss

Another individual to make a significant impact upon our view of Christ and Scripture is David Strauss (1808–1874), a German theologian who publishes *The*

Life of Jesus, Critically Examined. In this prominent work, Strauss approaches Scripture through careful critical analysis. Biblical scholarship is emerging. Strauss investigates the historical Jesus—the Jesus of history, as opposed to the Jesus portrayed in Scripture by authors with an agenda. This distinction is huge and creates quite a stir.

Strauss recognizes the time lapse between the actual life of Jesus and the date the Gospels were written. Before the writing of the New Testament Gospels, stories about Jesus circulated orally during this gap in time. Strauss sees reflections of the Old Testament in the New Testament stories, such as how the birth of Jesus mirrors that of Moses. Most importantly, he realizes that the world of the ancient writers was significantly different from his own world. For Strauss, the virgin birth, incarnation, and resurrection communicate truth, but not a literal and historical truth. This type of scholarly analysis and critical distinction is entirely new.

Of course, trailblazers are always demonized, and Strauss is no exception. Fired from his university post, he is unable to secure another teaching job. Though he is ostracized by fellow members of the academy, his courage blazes the trail for future theologians, such as Albert Schweitzer and Rudolph Bultmann. Even the *Jesus Seminar*, in its search for the historical Jesus, stems from the work of Strauss. His writings are instrumental in moving theological conversation to a whole new level.

By applying elements of the scientific method to the biblical texts, a new way of seeing the Christian story emerges. Strauss makes a distinction between what is history (death, burial, and crucifixion of Jesus) and what he calls myth (resurrection and ascension)—those non-historical elements designed to augment Jesus's stature in the eyes of the reader. Instead of interpreting the Bible literally, a higher level of scrutiny is applied, for Scripture is now being investigated and analyzed like any other object of scientific inquiry. This is a monumental shift in religious thinking and practice.

Charles Darwin

The most recognizable figure of this period may well be the Englishman Charles Darwin (1809–1892). Darwin originally sets out to become a clergyman within the Anglican Church, but his love for natural history wins the day. In December 1831, Darwin boards the HMS *Beagle* for his infamous voyage to the Galapagos Islands off the coast of Ecuador. The eventual result of this expedition sends shockwaves throughout the world.

An inquisitive fellow, Darwin marvels at the diversity of life. After careful research, he introduces the theory of evolution—that every species of life evolves from a common ancestor. This, of course, becomes the general belief within the natural sciences, although it still garners the ire of biblical literalists. This branching out from one common ancestor occurs through a process called natural selection—the survival of the fittest. In 1859, Darwin publishes *On the Origin of Species*, and our understanding of the world has never been the same.

Darwin's hypothesis eventually leads to the famous 1925 Scopes trial in Dayton, Tennessee, where it was illegal to teach the theory of evolution in public schools. In reality, the literal understanding of the Bible is on trial, and this high publicity courtroom drama brings national attention to the gap between fundamentalism and a modern understanding of life. The Bible and science are at odds with one another.

Science, which promulgates clinical observation and empirical research, is being fast-tracked, while past understandings of the Bible become a boat riddled with holes struggling to stay afloat. Evolution requires time for mutations to occur—lots of time. This means that Earth is much older than the Bible portrays, and the fossil record, geological record, and DNA evidence all seem to favor Darwin's theory. If Darwin is correct, the creation stories in Genesis are sorely in need of reinterpretation. No longer do literal creation accounts seem plausible, for Earth is billions of years old, not thousands.

The advancement of science begins to erode the very foundation of past religious belief. Darwin's theory challenges a literal understanding of Scripture. The biblical account of creation and its ensuing timeline of Earth's age cannot be taken literally. The evidence points elsewhere. More importantly, evolution implies that there was no perfect creation to begin with. According to traditional Christian theology, God created Adam and Eve in complete perfection. Through the sin of disobedience, creation was marred, and humans fell from perfection into a state of depravity.

If evolution is true, however, there was no such thing as a fall from original perfection, for there was no perfection from which to fall. The very nature of evolution implies a process of moving from something imperfect toward something more perfect, the very opposite of Christian teaching. Evolution not only questions the literal interpretation of the Genesis creation account, but also questions the very heart of Christian theology regarding the nature of humankind. We are not fallen, sinful creatures in need of forgiveness but rather imperfect people in need of being made whole. The gaze of science is moving from the divine hand of God toward naturalistic explanations.

The sharpened axe of scientific inquiry and critical thinking keeps chopping away at the root of Christian theology to the point where our faith story, as it is currently told, has little relevance to the world in which we live. Trailblazers are always excoriated by the religious protectors of the past, and, in predictable style, Darwin is labeled a heretic. The church struggles to keep pace with the change happening all around us, and its initial reaction is to resist and label new findings as heresy. That's what the church did to Galileo, and that's what the church did to Darwin.

In my experience, the average congregation is always playing catch-up—slow to embrace new ways of thinking and doing. Like anything else, science can be misused to promote a specific agenda, but the church's go-to response, along with its inherent distrust of anything new, falls back upon resistance and fortification of archaic positions. Scripture need not be at odds with science, yet the contemporary church drags its feet and throws a temper tantrum as it is led into the future.

The Twentieth Century

The Enlightenment opens the door to science, and through it comes Darwin's theory of evolution, the sending of humans to the moon in 1969, and on to exploration of the galaxy. This progression is simply astounding, and I suspect it will continue to expand. In the twentieth century, the social sciences are added to this growing body of knowledge—new fields of study, like sociology and psychology. These disciplines simply didn't exist prior to the Modern Age. The social sciences supplant religious explanations for human behavior with biological and natural explanations.

For sociologists, religion isn't initiated by divine revelation but arises out of society itself. It is a man-made, social creation intended to fulfill human needs and desires. As society is studied as a whole, religion merely becomes one data point of consideration. Do you see what is happening? Our understanding of God and life is being flipped upside down. God and religion become a social invention rather than a product of divine creation or revelation.

Psychology, another rising field in this era, begins studying the observable behavior of individuals and discovers that human beings react to impulses and stimuli in measureable ways. Once again, human curiosity seeks empirical evidence to confirm careful observations.

Sigmund Freud, the father of psychoanalysis, focuses his attention on how the unconscious influences the conscious. Regardless of what one thinks of

Freud's theories, his work opens the door for natural explanations of our inner selves that were once attributed to God. According to Freud, what we attribute to God's work in our lives is nothing more than a manifestation of the unconscious part of our personality. Human investigation into our world is no longer limited to the heavens or to the historical Jesus; now human life itself and the inner depths of humanity is being explored.

Something important is occurring. As humans become curious, the teachings of the church lose credibility. The heavens are investigated with telescopes, the world with microscopes, society with sociology, and the inner workings of humans with psychology. In every area, natural explanations are advanced for things that were once attributed to God.

Several key theologians rise to prominence during this time. No longer is Scripture interpreted literally; instead, higher criticism and biblical scholarship are brought to bear on the biblical text. With a powerful magnifying glass, the Bible is scrutinized in the twentieth century by such theologians as Karl Barth (1886–1965), Rudolph Bultmann (1884–1976), Albert Schweitzer (1875–1965), Reinhold Niebuhr (1892–1971), Paul Tillich (1886–1965), and others.

I remember discussing Wolfhart Pannenberg (1928–2014) in the evangelical seminary I attended. I didn't think much of his work, and neither did my professors. After all, we were Bible-believing evangelicals who despised those lacking a proper understanding and respect for God's Word. Their writings were the shenanigans of liberal theologians off in left field promoting religion, not God. To our detriment, we weren't expected to think too deeply, for we were far too busy being indoctrinated by well-meaning professors.

In Tillich's view, for instance, God is no longer a being up in the sky but the very ground of being. To my young, idyllic, and judgmental mind, this was all gobbledygook. When discussing the quest of the historical Jesus, I simply cast those efforts aside with my holier-than-thou aspersions. Who could believe such foolishness? Adolf von Harnack (1851–1930) was a duped liberal theologian who simply didn't know Jesus as his Savior. He applied a critical approach to biblical interpretation and questioned many of the doctrines I held so dear. How dare he!

In 1963, New Testament scholar and Anglican Bishop John A. T. Robinson (1919–1983) published a highly controversial book titled *Honest to God*. It merely states what had been articulated by prior theologians, but Robinson writes in a manner easily grasped by the average layperson. According to Robinson, believing in God as an actual being in the heavens can no longer be sustained in light of our present knowledge and a critical analysis of Scripture. Like Tillich, Robinson promotes God as the ground of being, or being itself, rather than an actual being—a thing or entity in the sky. The old understandings, myths, and symbols of God are crumbling.

I remember hearing the name Albert Schweitzer (1875–1965), who published *The Quest of the Historical Jesus*. Schweitzer reveals how our understanding of Jesus has changed over time, and yet, there we were, holding fast to the Scriptures telling us that God does not change. I thought Schweitzer's work stemmed from a lost liberal who wouldn't recognize God if God were standing right in front of him. As a young Bible-believing seminarian, I trusted no one except those who promoted my own brand of self-deception. Rather than advancing the faith, Schweitzer's work, and the work of others like him, was actually damaging the faith—or so I thought. How infantile was my thinking back then, not to mention my arrogance and ignorance, so blatantly evident to others more mature than myself.

I am not a theologian by any stretch of the imagination and do not hold myself out as one. I am merely trying to point out, as best I can, that new ways of approaching Scripture are occurring in the theological realm. The Bible is being looked at through a critical and scholarly lens. The type of scrutiny applied elsewhere is now being applied to the study of Scripture. The historicity of the Gospel of John is being questioned. The difference between the historical Jesus and the Christ of faith is being articulated. God is no longer spoken of as a being in the heavens but the very ground of all being. This kind of talk would not have been tolerated in ages past.

Summary of the Ages

Pre-Axial Age	Axial Age	Post-Axial Age	Modern Age
Before World Religions	Major Religions Born	Religions Structured	Religions Questioned
Beginning–800 BCE	800 BCE–200 BCE	200 BCE–1500 CE	1500 CE–Present
Many gods & spirits	God is other-worldly	Refinement of theology	Scientific method
Geographically limited	God is ultimate reality	Greater structure	Church authority waning
Gods of nature/culture	Asking big questions	God is better defined	Scripture challenged
Earth-centered gods	Personal/Individual	Scriptures/Practices	God/Jesus reexamined
Unexamined assumptions	True way to salvation	Dominant religions	Biblical scholarship

Landing at Our Doorstep

The four epoch ages act as a map that guides our understanding of large chunks of time, and though there is overlap from one age to another, the emphasis of each becomes a trail of white stones, similar to the ones laid down by Hansel and Gretel so they can find their way back home. The ages help us connect the dots from time past to our present thinking, and though we could explore the many inspirational sights along the historical trail, it becomes obvious that we didn't just wake up one morning questioning Christian teaching.

The skepticism of our day isn't the work of an inexperienced and unappreciative generation who should know better than to fall out of step with past traditions. The problem extends far deeper than scapegoating others in an attempt to salvage bad theology. This storm has been brewing for quite some time. We know more about our world today than at any other time in history, and unfortunately, the religious answers of the past no longer stand up against this wealth of knowledge. This is the heart of the problem that has been building over time. The protective layer of ecclesiastical hierarchy has finally been peeled back, exposing the vulnerability of flawed thinking. Something has to give, and it won't be the findings of science.

The Danger of Tribalism

The downside of religion is tribalism—that is, a herd mentality or a clan perspective. In other words, the world is divided into us versus them, right versus wrong, and those possessing truth versus those who are lost. Religion and politics, it is said, are the two most divisive topics of conversation on this planet.

Christianity doesn't play well in a pluralistic world. In fact, any religion with exclusive truth claims struggles to relate to, interact with, and tolerate another way of thinking. Taken to the extreme, tribalism leads to fundamentalism, the most radical form of one's religion. Every religion seems to have a fringe element dwelling within its borders. Tribalism prompted Catholics and Protestants to kill one another in The Thirty Years' War. During the Crusades of the Middle Ages, tribalism motivates Christians to kill Jews and Muslims in an attempt to conquer the Holy Land.

The killing of infidels wasn't limited to the Christian Crusades, for Muslims have their own brand of fundamentalism, too. They kill just as well as others, and history reminds us of their own Crusades. The "us versus them" mentality inspired Islamic extremists to fly large passenger jets into New York City's Twin Towers on September 11, 2001, in their attempt to strike terror into the heart of the demon West. Even Judaism contains an element of fundamentalism that prizes strict expression and interpretation of the faith. Fundamentalism doesn't necessarily lead to killing, but it can, and it always distorts the very message one's faith is trying to convey. It is the kind of distortion that leads pro-life advocates to kill abortion doctors. Do you see the inherent contradiction in using premeditated murder as a way to advance the cause of protecting life? The two don't line up. The dangers of tribalism affect every religion, and Christianity is no exception.

By nature, tribalism is divisive and can lead to acts of violence in the name of God. It brings out the worst in people, as their warped perspective justifies the destruction of others. Tribalism can lead to prejudice, prejudice can lead to violence, and violence leads to the downfall of both the victim and the victimizer. Tribalism and prejudice diminish our humanity. By appealing to the self-serving authority of Scripture, moral absolutes are dictated, identities and boundaries are established, and we begin to think in terms of right versus wrong, us versus them, saved versus lost, holy versus profane, enlightened versus unenlightened, and our way versus the highway. This kind of thinking leads to wars, conflicts, destructive prejudices, and justification of bad behavior. It is not only divisive but antithetical to the very message of Jesus.

Many take note of this destructive cycle and discard religion altogether. Their ears hear a faith that proclaims love, but their eyes see a faith that perpetuates hate, so they vomit up its very presence in their lives. Equating the message of Scripture with the many ways people distort Scripture certainly isn't the answer. That's like casting aside all food because you don't like the taste of peas and broccoli. Yet, the unfortunate effect of tribalism is the distancing of faith from reality, which causes many to turn away from the church. Who wants to be a part of such prejudicial behavior?

The Curiosity of Investigation

As humans progress through the ages, so does their curiosity. Pondering allows the powers of reason, research, and observation to shine forth. The rise of curiosity begins slowly and is followed by the establishment of major religions. This quenches the appetite for a season until the floodgates are opened during the Enlightenment. As civilizations grow, the world shrinks. Curiosity piques as people and cultures begin interacting with one another. The end result is new knowledge that transforms our understanding of life.

This inquisitive bent inspires a closer examination of both Earth and the heavens as a distinction between nature and divine revelation comes into focus. Curiosity finds expression through the scientific method. Research findings defy religious explanations that no longer provide satisfying answers. Though people are entitled to their own opinion, they are not entitled to their own facts. The path of curiosity leads away from religious answers that once held sway. Curiosity promotes questioning, which leads to investigating, which leads to informative data, which leads to reevaluating, which leads to replacing old paradigms of understanding with new ways of seeing the world.

God Redefined

The progression of religious thought also leads to redefining our understanding of God. The gods used to dwell among the trees, winds, mountains, and prairies as an integral part of this life, assisting in the needs of daily living. Curiosity spawns dualistic thinking, whereby the gods who were once present in this world transition to a God who lives out there in another world—sitting on a heavenly throne, dispensing wrath, justice, and mercy. Even this view of God begins to change after the Enlightenment.

God as a being who lives in heaven is now under fire as theologians postulate that God may not be an entity or a thing at all but, instead, the very ground of being itself—a difficult concept to grasp. Religion is given a run for its money with the introduction of science. Did God create everything as the Bible indicates, or did humans create the notion of God? One rises from the hand of God and is revealed to us through divine revelation, while the other rises from human need and is revealed to us through scientific investigation. The very concept of God is up for grabs.

Scripture Challenged

Not only is the nature of God being questioned; the authority and interpretation of Scripture is also being challenged. Scrutiny leaves no rock unturned. There was no such thing as Scripture until humans learned to write and communicate. As the major religions emerged, sacred writings were created to offer support, meaning, and value to the founders' message. After all, it is easier to wield authority when your holy writings are declared to be from God. For centuries, people looked to the Bible as the sole source of knowledge, but this changes over time as curiosity introduces other sources of insight.

As the scientific method produces evidence contrary to church teaching, Scripture falls under higher levels of scrutiny and begins to be studied through the lens of critical analysis. Biblical authority is challenged, and literal approaches to Scripture are questioned as a valid method of interpretation. Science undermines orthodoxy, while evolution queries human origins. Biblical scholarship is born as Scripture comes under the magnifying glass of higher criticism. We now live in a world where the Bible is held up to the penetrating light of modern-day knowledge.

Church Authority Waning

In days of old, the church filled an important role in society. When knowledge of our world was limited, the church became the "go-to" source for answers. However, as knowledge increases, church authority decreases. Where understanding is lagging, one can declare, "Thus saith the Lord" and get away with it because there is no data to prove otherwise. This changes as both the heavens and Earth are investigated. In a sense, we have pulled back the curtain in the Land of Oz and discovered that the great and powerful wizard isn't so great and powerful after all.

Contrary to church teaching, humans discover that Earth rotates around the sun, not the other way around. No longer is Earth the center of the universe. The scientific method is born, and Darwin advances the theory of evolution. Reason interprets our world outside of religious explanations. The church's answers are found wanting—insufficient to counteract the onslaught of new knowledge. Couple this with the credibility problem addressed in previous chapters, and it all adds up to the church's diminishing role in the real world. The influence of Christianity is waning, and its message is becoming more irrelevant every day. To put it bluntly, the church is dying—moving toward extinction.

Jesus Revisited

Our very understanding of Jesus is also under current review. No longer can the Gospels be viewed as historical, literal, and biographical accounts of Jesus's life. Instead, they are a rhetorical means of conveying the profound meaning and message of Jesus in ways that are neither historical nor literal.

Scripture is written in a Jewish context, from a Jewish perspective, using Jewish literary methods. Any understanding of the Gospels must take into account this Jewish influence. As enhanced scrutiny is applied to the study of Scripture, a separation occurs between the historical Jesus who lived and died during the first century and the Christ of faith portrayed in Scripture decades after his death. The creeds about Jesus, the doctrine of the Trinity, and the "fully

God–fully human" nature of Christ are doctrines developed centuries after his crucifixion. Jesus, the central figure of the Christian faith, is scrutinized in a way never before seen in history.

The progression of religious thought throughout the ages is easily discernable. Whether or not the Christian story, as it is currently told, can survive into the future is a fair question. I believe it will survive, but not in its current form. The Christian story must be retold in a manner that is both faithful to Scripture and relevant to our world, for its powerful and freeing message is sorely needed in our day.

Chapter Summary

Our understanding of God and life progresses over time. The four epoch ages of religious history reveal how our current state of skepticism wound up on our modern-day doorstep. Today's understanding is built upon the progress of the past, and unfortunately, the advancement of knowledge has not been kind to the church or its teachings. The Enlightenment opens wide the door of critical analysis and biblical scholarship. It paves the road for colossal change by introducing us to the scientific method. Things will never be the same.

Today, the church is being challenged like never before, and unless a relevant message for the postmodern mind is forthcoming, Christianity will continue its rapid descent into oblivion. In the chapters to come, I will expose the credibility issues surrounding the ancient stories, traditions, and doctrines of the Bible. It is the problem of what the church believes and teaches.

LEAVING RELIGION

☑ **The Problem of Behavior**

The Problem of Belief
The Credibility of Scripture

UP NEXT →

The Credibility of Jesus

The Credibility of God

FINDING GOD

A New Beginning

4

HUMAN OR DIVINE WORDS
• • • • • • • •

S CRIPTURE ACTS LIKE A COMPASS—SETTING THE course of our travels. Because of their directional nature, how we approach the sacred writings is paramount to where they take us. Boarding a train on the wrong track or throwing a rail switch at the wrong time leads to a destination different from the intended arrival point. If you seek passage from Chicago to Nashville but inadvertently follow directions from Chicago to San Diego, you wind up in the wrong city, even though your intentions were honorable. Approaching Scripture in the proper manner keeps us on the right track so we arrive at our intended destination. Listening to the cacophony of voices selling train tickets these days can be confusing. With more than thirty thousand different denominations across the globe, each one claiming that its train will get you to the destination of your dreams, which one do you board?

Growing up in the synagogue, the Jews naturally understood their own method of sacred storytelling. After Jesus's death, stories about him were first told in the synagogue—the incubator of early Christianity. Around 88 CE, however, the growing Jesus Movement began separating from the Jewish synagogue. By 150 CE, the split was complete, and the movement birthed in the womb of Judaism would now live within an exclusively Gentile environment that neither knew about nor understood Jewish history, tradition, liturgy, or their method of sacred storytelling. A book written by Jews and arising from Jewish tradition and culture would no longer be interpreted through Jewish eyes.

At one point in Christian history, Scripture was even interpreted allegorically. For example, Origen of Alexandria (184–253 CE), one of the early Church Fathers, understood that a literal interpretation of Scripture eventually leads down a nonsensical path toward the impossible, so he taught that Scripture should be interpreted allegorically on three levels: flesh, soul, and spirit. With allegory, there are layers and layers of meaning that must be sifted through. Yet is this how the biblical authors intended their writings to be understood—allegorically? How to interpret Scripture has been an ongoing debate over the centuries, and the allegorical method was long ago debunked as a legitimate interpretive option. Biblical scholarship as we know it today wouldn't come into existence until some fifteen hundred years after Origen, and with the Jewish nature of storytelling lost upon a Gentile audience, literalism rose to dominance and continues to this day.

Two Tracks

When all the dust settles, approaching Scripture basically boils down to two main train tracks. One track is called literalism, and the people who frequently ride this rail are evangelicals and fundamentalists. The other track is a nonliteral approach where liberal and progressive Christians feel most comfortable. The track of literalism includes such traditional views as atonement theology, where Jesus dies to save us from our sins; being born again; going to heaven in the afterlife; and entreating the lost to "get saved." The nonliteral train runs a scenic route that focuses upon this life rather than the afterlife and makes frequent stops at such places as acceptance, tolerance, and loving others, while fully embracing God's expansive love for every human.

The literal track focuses upon correct doctrine and obedient behavior with tireless efforts toward converting the lost. It leads right back into the past, where ancient understandings struggle to survive. The nonliteral track, with its focus on God's extravagant welcome for all humans, works in this life toward justice, peace, equality, and assisting others in knowing and experiencing God's inclusive love. This rail leads into the future, where deeper levels of understanding God and the Bible exist. These two ways of looking at Scripture bring about such sharp differences that one might think they are two different religions. One Bible, two trains, two tracks, two routes, two destinations, and two options. Which one is correct? Does it really matter, and if so, why? It certainly does matter, and it matters so much that the future of Christianity depends on which track the train travels.

You may be thinking, "Why all this fuss about our approach to the Bible, anyway? Just read the darn thing and interpret it however you want!" That would solve everything, wouldn't it? We need to be a bit more realistic than that. The reason for the fuss is that the Bible needs to be interpreted just like any other writing. We wouldn't allow contracts, wills, or other important documents to mean whatever anyone thinks they should mean at any given time for any given reason. That's a recipe for chaos and confusion that eventually leads to meaninglessness.

We primarily communicate through a spoken and written language. Words become the vehicle for conveying thought. Understanding isn't as easy as it seems, since words can take on various meanings in different contexts. Just because I write words down on paper intending one meaning (like I am trying to do in this book), doesn't mean that you won't understand it in a completely different way. Whether it is the Bible, a legal contract, a poem, a history, or a narrative, words have to be interpreted so we can assign them meaning.

Let's say I write about a trunk. Am I referring to a car trunk, a tree trunk, an elephant trunk, a suitcase trunk, the trunk of a person's body, that part of a fish between its head and its anus, the shaft of a column, the main channel of a river, the main body of an artery, shorts worn by swimmers, or a passage through the bulkhead of a ship utilized for heating and ventilation? Am I speaking literally or figuratively? Is the story itself and the method of writing intended to convey a literal, historical truth, or is it merely a literary device for relating a profound truth, much like a fable, myth, or fairy tale? Combine these factors with language differences, cultural differences, geographical distances, time differences, historical differences, and a whole host of other differences, and things get a little more complicated than "just read the darn thing and interpret it however you want."

If the Bible is a significant sacred text, which most Christians believe it is, and if certain approaches lead to certain destinations, then how we interpret Scripture is essential to our understanding of God and how we align our lives to what we understand to be true. One day I boarded an Amtrak train from small-town Iowa to downtown Chicago. It was my first real train adventure, and I loved every minute of it. The return trip required a bit more vigilance on my part, because the large metropolitan train station was far more complex than the tiny station house in Iowa. There were more trains, more people, more commotion, and I had to pay closer attention to things. Had I boarded the wrong train, I would have arrived at the wrong destination. The moral of the story is to choose your train wisely. If you seek to understand the meaning of Scripture, it matters which train you jump on.

Bibliolatry

In the world of evangelicalism and fundamentalism, the Bible is looked upon as the very words of God. Along with such veneration comes the real danger of Scripture becoming a tangible replacement for an intangible God, just like Israel's golden calf incident when Moses lingered on Mt. Sinai. In light of the fact that God cannot be seen, touched, tasted, smelled, heard, or communicated with like other relationships we experience on Earth, having some golden calf to worship—something tangible to assuage our anxiety—brings a sense of comfort and security, even if it is misplaced. When we elevate the Bible to God-like status, we become idolaters who worship the Word of God instead of God. That is called bibliolatry.

We see this veneration in numerous ways. Prior to the Gospel reading, Episcopal priests proceed from the altar out into the congregation with the Gospel book held high above their head, as if it is something to be worshiped, while Lutherans, on the other hand, stand during the reading of the esteemed Gospels. Many churches, after publicly reading Scripture, declare, "This is God's Word," or "This is the Word of God spoken to us today. Thanks be to God," or "May God add His blessing to the reading of His Word." Like something out of a slick sales convention, I have watched spellbound audiences raise their Bibles high in the air while the pastor leads them in some mantra about the Bible being the inspired, inerrant, and authoritative Word of God. Of course, this recitation strategically occurs right before a "thus saith the Lord" sermon and is designed to bolster the pastor's own words. For televangelists, this part of the show sets the stage for the ritualistic fleecing of the flock from their hard-earned money.

After recommending a book to a study group looking for something to read, one of the threatened participants remarked, "I am open to reading anything as long as we all agree up front that the Bible is the inspired, inerrant, and authoritative Word of God." This, of course, is a safety measure designed to protect treasured views—an escape hatch for when the heat is turned up too high. Unfortunately, it unveils an attitude that God is done talking.

With this perspective, everything we need to know about life and faith is placed in the good book. Anything that falls outside of the book or contradicts the book cannot be from God. Asked if God still speaks to us today, we get the typical "yes—but" answer. Yes, but God cannot contradict what the Bible says. Yes, but God cannot fall short or go beyond what the Bible says. Yes, but anything that goes against my understanding and interpretation of the Bible can't possibly be from God. In reality, God doesn't do a whole lot of talking these days, and when God is allowed to speak, it is merely the regurgitation of what has already been written—interpreted, of course, through the grid of one's preferred theological bent. With so many denominations, each interpreting the Bible differently, it seems that God is not only silenced but also confused and psychotic. The Bible, in essence, replaces a God who is no longer allowed to communicate. This is nothing less than Word worship—bibliolatry.

Historically, progressive elements within the Religious Society of Friends, often known as "Friends" or "Quakers," seem to have a pretty good handle on this. While the Bible is important, it is not of the highest importance—a designation reserved for God alone. Scripture is the written record of individuals who loved, served, and experienced God, and as such, it becomes a useful tool in our own spiritual growth. However, it is not God, and it is not the only means God uses to speak to us. Though our faith may be two thousand years old, our God is still moving and inspiring afresh in the present moment. When Scripture is elevated as "The" Word of God rather than words *about* God written by those who loved, served, and experienced God, we have invented our own golden calf to worship.

Sola Scriptura

The emphasis on Scripture as the sole source of spiritual authority rose to prominence during the Reformation when Martin Luther aired his qualms with the Catholic Church. Were ecclesiastical teaching and the words of the pope also the authoritative Word of God, or was that designation reserved for Scripture alone? Much to the chagrin of the Catholic Church, Luther advocated for sola scriptura as the sole rule of faith and practice—not the pope, the church, or ecclesiastical teaching.

However one views Scripture, the fact remains that it must still be interpreted. The easy part is reading the printed words on the page. The more difficult step is discerning their meaning, and this is influenced by which train you decide to board and which denominational perspective most appeals to your spiritual taste buds. To our benefit, the Enlightenment triggered the beginning of biblical scholarship, which reached its full stride in the 1800s and beyond. Scripture is now studied through the lens of critical and scholarly analysis.

A former employee of mine often pressed this very point. His side hobby was filling pulpits whenever he could and serving in local interim pastoral ministry roles. He yearned to become a full-time minister and be known as the man with all the answers. His know-it-all attitude and quest for spiritual power caught up to him when he was asked to leave an interim pastorate. When you get asked to leave an *interim* position, that ought to tell you something! It was a painful time in his life, so I took him out for dinner to lessen his pain and lend a listening ear.

Studying the Bible

When know-it-alls encounter differing opinions, defense mechanisms kick into high gear, and he would condescendingly respond, "Well, I just believe what the Bible says." As a tall, lanky individual, he took full advantage of his height, pronouncing judgments on others while literally looking down on them. If he couldn't convince them with his superior Bible knowledge and flawless understanding of Scripture, his intimidation tactics might work. He tried it out on me, and from his lofty perch, proudly proclaimed, "Well, I just believe what the Bible says," to which I replied, "We all know what the Bible says. The real question is, what does it mean?" He had no comeback, for he had backed himself into a corner without an escape route. Reading the Bible is good, but studying the Bible is even better, and since the 1800s, when biblical scholarship first began to blossom, new light has been cast upon the sacred text.

Though it is difficult to critique something that is worshiped in God-like fashion, studying the Bible from a critical perspective frees us from the bondage of literalism. Today, scholars analyze the history of literary forms, such as parables and psalms, in order to determine their original form and context, known as form criticism. Scholars seek to establish the various sources used by the biblical writers, known as source criticism. They attempt to recover the original text of a document, known as textual criticism. These faithful men and women work to discover the setting and theology of a writing by studying how subsequent writers altered a text to fit their own intentions, known as redaction criticism. There is also literary criticism, canonical criticism, and other specialized forms of biblical study. And by the way, criticism in this context doesn't mean being critical or having a critical spirit; rather, it means analyzing something through the grid of critical thinking.

The average layperson knows very little about this, but the cat is now out of the bag, and the information is readily available. In my experience, Christians typically crack open the Bible only when they have a personal need or desire a quick answer that helps them through an acute crisis. Scripture is something occasioned upon, not something to be studied, and when it is read, it is read through the lens of twenty-first-century literalism. But asking ancient authors to write according to the knowledge and understanding of the modern world is far too much to ask. What did Scripture mean in the culture and understanding of the author at the time it was written? This, of course, takes meaningful study, critical analysis, and the type of biblical scholarship that has arisen over the past four hundred years. Today's biblical scholars spend their entire lives studying the sacred text, and while we may not agree with all of their conclusions, we can certainly appreciate their diligent efforts in advancing the cause of biblical understanding.

Unfortunately, biblical scholarship isn't given the credit it is due in literalist circles. No doubt, academics can be annoying, as they sometimes write and speak in ways that only other academics understand, and yet their work is invaluable. The very Bible you hold in your hand had to be translated by someone who made intelligent decisions on structure, context, and meaning in order to best translate variant Greek and Hebrew manuscripts into English. This isn't something the average Christian could have accomplished with any semblance of proficiency. This effort took scholarship. We like the benefits scholars bring us, especially when their insights support our preferred beliefs, and yet they are often maligned as disconnected, high-falutin, bow-tied, over-educated individuals who not only lack common sense but have abandoned the faith in pursuit of reason. "Why can't they just accept the literal Bible in faith?" some say. "After all, it is impossible to please God without faith" (Heb. 11:6).

Most Christians I know struggle to even read Scripture, let alone study it. We can't all be scholars with PhDs in our back pocket while being paid to scour over the sacred text. But certainly the Bible can become more than a book we occasionally visit with an eye toward plucking verses out of context that appeal to our emotional needs. Reading the Bible is a good thing, and in no way am I criticizing the practice. It has become a valuable daily habit in my own life. I am merely pointing out that studying the text is a worthwhile endeavor that unearths precious jewels of understanding far beyond what mere reading could produce.

A deeper study of the creation accounts in Genesis, for instance, reveals more to us than occasional reading can provide. We could just read it, and read it literally, but that leads to nonsense. How do we approach the Genesis creation accounts in chapter 1 and 2 when we realize that chapter 1 was written five hundred years after chapter 2? Yes, you read that correctly. Chapter 1 was written some five hundred years *after* chapter 2. How do scholars know this? Just like we can tell the difference between the writings of Shakespeare, Dickens, and Tolkien, so too can Hebrew scholars identify the differences in Hebrew writings. We can interpret the six days of creation literally, like many do, or, after careful study, we may come to the realization that the Genesis creation accounts are not intended to be literal accounts at all.

Studying the Bible with a learning attitude and an open mind is like eating chocolate pie. When we simply read it for devotional purposes, we are merely licking off the whipped cream on top. It is tasty and satisfies to a certain degree, but it is only as we engage in deeper study that our fork reaches into the texture and flavor of the rich chocolate center and the flaky crust below. For those satisfied with eating only whipped cream, talking about the glory of chocolate filling and flaky crust is rather boring. Some people never ask the kind of questions I ask and have no need for answers beyond their present comfort level. They love God with every fiber of their being and savor whipped cream. They have no idea there are deeper levels, and even if they did, they would have no interest or need to go there. Their dedication and love for God are not in question, but one must ask whether this approach can sustain Christianity for the long haul.

Sadly, for many, Christianity is nothing more than the enjoyment of a Sunday morning praise band while raising their hands in adoration, listening to a preacher in faded blue jeans and tattoos share a pump-you-up message that charges up their spiritual batteries until the following Sunday. It reminds me of the lyrics to many of the contemporary Christian songs played on radio stations these days—a kind of "hang-on-by-your-fingernails" theology. Life can indeed be difficult, and people surely need uplifting and moments of inspiration, but if this is the essence and depth of one's Christian faith, then we are in trouble. Why settle for merely licking whipped cream when the whole pie is available?

The point is to put some teeth into your faith. Give it longevity, depth, strength, and stability by learning to study Scripture more objectively. Lay aside your stained-glass lenses and study, learn, question, analyze, and go where the data lead you. Taste the succulent chocolate pie awaiting you and enjoy all of the layers and flavors, not just the topping. Your faith will be strengthened, not destroyed. You will be able to withstand the gale-force winds of life rather than living from spiritual paycheck to spiritual paycheck.

Inspired, Inerrant, Authoritative

The foundational battle cry undergirding the faith of countless Christians around the world is the declaration that Scripture is the inspired, inerrant, and authoritative Word of God for all time. Though this is proclaimed with fervor, most believers remain clueless as to how the Bible came into existence. Somehow, the Bible is thought to have dropped right out of heaven, neatly divided into chapters and verses, with all of the books in correct sequential order and written in the language of God—the King James Version with the words of Christ in red letters. This is pure nonsense, and nothing could be further from the truth.

It is misleading to think of the Bible as one book, when in reality, it is a collection of sixty-six smaller books written by various authors over the centuries that have now been bound together under one cover. Since the printing press wasn't invented until the 1400s, the manuscripts we possess were written on papyrus or parchment scrolls. People didn't have Bibles in their home, and no Christian bookstores existed. Approximately 95 percent of the population was illiterate. The only time they heard Scripture read was in the synagogue.

The thirty-nine books of the Old Testament arose from within the Jewish community and became their sacred scriptures that Jesus knew and lived under. The twenty-seven books of the New Testament were written during the Christian era and arose from within the early Christian community of the first century. The Bible, so readily accessible in our day, is entirely based upon various manuscripts that are either copies or fragments of copies. These manuscripts were disseminated by hand-copying them word for word—a tedious and time-consuming process fraught with all of the human frailties associated with such an endeavor. Unfortunately, not one "original" parchment or papyrus has ever been found for any of the sixty-six books of the Bible. The Bible we possess today isn't the original writings dropped out of heaven in polished form. Instead, there is a fascinating history behind their formation that many have never considered.

From a structural standpoint, the Old Testament's thirty-nine books can be divided into (1) the Law or Torah, consisting of the first five books of the Old Testament; (2) the Prophets, which include the major and minor prophets as well a few historical books; and (3) the Writings, consisting of Psalms, Proverbs, Job, Ecclesiastes, and other such books. The New Testament's twenty-seven books can be divided into (1) Gospels—Matthew, Mark, Luke, John; (2) Letters—twenty-one of them from the likes of Peter, Paul, John, James; (3) History of the early church—Acts; and (4) Apocalyptic writing—Revelation. There is more; Catholic, Eastern Orthodox, and Anglican churches also take note of the Apocrypha, a collection of Jewish writings compiled a few centuries before Jesus that didn't make it into the Jewish Scriptures of the Old Testament or the official listing of canonized Scripture. Ecclesiasticus, Wisdom of Solomon, Judith, and 1 and 2 Maccabees are the most familiar of the bunch.

The books of the Bible are not arranged chronologically but placed in the order preferred by the church. For instance, Mark is the first Gospel written, not

Matthew, even though Matthew is placed before Mark, and the writings of Paul occur chronologically before all other New Testament books. It is also worth noting that we have no writings of Jesus, the central figure of the New Testament. Instead, we possess only hearsay—that is, what others say he said.

The Bible is a treasured book within the Christian tradition and is filled with profound meaning for the community of faith. We read it, memorize it, meditate upon it, preach from it, make decisions based on it, and hold it dear to our heart. Its sacred-cow status, however, may be the reason Christians are only expected to read it and obey it, not critically study it. Asking difficult questions is taboo. When it comes to Scripture, the heart of the issue is how we interpret the Bible. Division occurs over its origin, authority, and meaning (interpretation). The same Bible viewed differently leads to completely different outcomes. Each group believes the other is wrong and prays that the blinders will fall from their eyes. I know a young biblical literalist who is highly motivated to serve God, and yet, as he confronts others for not living up to his standard of holiness, informs them, "I am not judging. I am merely speaking the truth of God."

Inspired

When evangelicals and fundamentalists speak of "inspired" Scripture, they mean that the authors of the Bible, both Old and New Testaments, were under the influence of God in such a way that their writings can now be viewed as the very words of God. Since we have never discovered an original inspired writing, the various manuscript copies are viewed as true representations of the original autographs. It may be said of many people that they were inspired by God to write a song, a poem, engage in acts of service, etc., but this ordinary sort of inspiration isn't what is intended. For biblical literalists, every word in the Bible was placed there by God (verbal inspiration), and this direct-from-God inspiration applies to all parts equally (plenary inspiration). Every word in every part of the Bible, whether history, poetry, wisdom, law, narrative, or apocalyptic writing, is viewed as the inerrant, inspired, and authoritative words of God for all time. God just happened to use human authors as writing instruments.

This is quite a claim, especially for original writings not even in existence, and one has to wonder whether the Bible's promotion of slavery, its insistence on women's silence and subordination in the church, genocide, and the killing of homosexuals, disobedient children, adulterers, and those worshiping false gods are also the inspired words of God. This is a big problem for literalists. To say that Scripture is the very Word of God for all time means that one must also accept the cultural prejudices, biases, and horrible acts in the Bible as the very words of

God, too. This, of course, is just plain nonsense. In 2 Samuel 12, for instance, the prophet Nathan confronts King David about his affair with Bathsheba, who becomes pregnant and bears David's child. Nathan informs David that God will kill the child as punishment for David's affair. Is this the Word of God for all time? Does God kill innocent babies as a way to punish parents? This isn't right or fair. What kind of God would do such a thing? This is the kind of absurdity that occurs when viewing Scripture as the literal Word of God for all time.

Inerrant

By "inerrant," literalists mean that the Bible is without error in all of its statements and teaching. Because it contains no errors of fact, it is viewed as a trustworthy guide. This is an amazing statement, and for many, if one error were ever discovered in the biblical text, their entire belief in God would go up in flames. How could a perfect God create an imperfect Bible? Yet does the sun, in fact, rotate around Earth, as noted in Joshua? Is this not a factual inaccuracy? Why can't we recognize it as a misstatement of fact but a statement of belief uttered in a pre-scientific era? If the tower of Babel story is merely a literary device designed to communicate a profound truth rather than a literal, historical tower that reached all the way into heaven, would that cause faith to come crashing down? Each of the Gospels provides an account of the resurrection, yet they all differ in their details. Which Gospel account is correct? For inerrant die-hards, one statement that is not literally, historically true would cause their faith to collapse like a house of cards. They have a lot riding on the concept of inerrancy, and maybe that is why they defend it so vigorously.

Authoritative

The formula for evangelicals and fundamentalists looks like this:

$$\frac{\text{direct-from-God inspiration} + \text{total inerrancy}}{} = \text{absolute biblical authority}$$

If the Bible is the direct revelation of God communicated to us through divinely influenced human authors, and if the Bible contains no errors and is factually true in all of its dealings, then it is easy to see how one could hold the Bible in such high esteem, believing it to be the authoritative Word of God for all time. Combine this with a literal interpretation of its contents, and you have the ingredients for a lethal concoction of legalism, judgmentalism, and fundamentalism, all huddling together under the umbrella of God's authority.

I understand this perspective, for it is the outlook of the denomination I grew up in and initially became ordained with. It is the perspective of the seminaries I attended, the churches I pastored, and the educational institutions I served. At one time, I wholeheartedly agreed with this outlook and marched as a good little soldier to the beat of an evangelical drum. In my thinking, I was merely safeguarding and honoring the very words of God—something all good Christians should do.

Whenever questions about inerrancy, inspiration, and authority arise, certain Bible verses are raised in defense of the faith as though they are trump cards that quickly extinguish the fires of intellectual inquiry. Revelation 22:18–19 (NRSV) warns against adding to or subtracting from God's Word. In other words, woe to the person who messes with Scripture:

> I warn everyone who hears the words of the prophecy of this book: if anyone adds to them, God will add to that person the plagues described in this book; if anyone takes away from the words of the book of this prophecy, God will take away that person's share in the tree of life and in the holy city, which are described in this book.

This isn't a threat against messing with the Bible; it is merely the author of Revelation telling readers not to alter this particular apocalyptic writing that relies extensively on symbols and imagery to communicate its intended message. The author's protective warning seems appropriate, given the type of writing it is. Messing with the symbols and imagery affects the story he is trying to tell through them. However, it is not a general warning concerning the sixty-six books of the Bible, which didn't even exist at the time.

2 Peter 1:20–21 (NRSV) is another passage often brought up to defend God's Word: "First of all you must understand this, that no prophecy of scripture is a matter of one's own interpretation, because no prophecy ever came by human will, but men and women moved by the Holy Spirit spoke from God." There is much to be studied here against the contextual backdrop of false prophets, but if the point of quoting these verses is to say that those who wrote scriptural prophecy were moved by the Holy Spirit, I would agree with them. It seems to me that those who wrote Scripture did indeed feel that they were inspired to do so. In fact, people are inspired every day to write something, do something, or give something while sensing the Spirit of God moving within them. But to claim the product of their "moving" is the inerrant Word of God goes far beyond what the text actually says.

The ace up their sleeve is 2 Timothy 3:16–17 (NRSV): "All scripture is inspired by God and is useful for teaching, for reproof, for correction, and for training in righteousness, so that everyone who belongs to God may be proficient, equipped for every good work." Since the New Testament canon was not official or complete until some three hundred years after Jesus died, the author of this passage did not have the completed Bible in mind. Paul relates a similar thought in Romans 15:4 (NRSV): "For whatever was written in former days was written for our instruction, so that by steadfastness and by the encouragement of the scriptures we might have hope."

The Old Testament writings were so highly regarded within the Jewish community that they were thought of as coming from men who were moved by God. Again, there is no problem with God inspiring individuals to write down all that is on their heart, but this doesn't equate to being the once-for-all Word of God for all time. There is a difference between being inspired to write something based on one's experience and understanding of God and then claiming that those writings are the very words of God.

Does it seem odd to you that in order to prove that the Bible is directly from God, claimants use the very book they are attempting to prove up? This wouldn't be allowed anywhere else—certainly not in a court of law. Listen to the argument:

The Bible is the direct-inspired and inerrant words of God.
How do we know this?
Because the Bible tells us it is so.
How do we know that what the Bible tells us is true?
Because it is the direct-inspired and inerrant words of God.

This is circular talk based on circular reasoning. Evangelicals and fundamentalists presuppose inerrancy. In other words, their entire understanding of the Bible presupposes that it is the very Word of God for all time. It becomes the foundation upon which all else is built, and great deference is given to this supposed truth. What happens when cracks appear in the foundation and it begins to crumble under the weight of biblical scholarship and modern science? You guessed it—the magnificent edifice raised upon its foundation begins to falter.

For biblical literalists, the Bible's authority is grounded in its divine origin. This belief, however, is a matter of faith, not fact. Of course, people can believe whatever they want for whatever reason appeals to them, but that doesn't mean their beliefs are reasonable, based on data, or accurate. People are entitled to their opinions, but not all opinions carry the same weight. This is where biblical scholarship over the last four hundred years has been extremely valuable. By studying Scripture with an eye toward critical analysis, we begin to see that the good book is not a divine product dropped from heaven in fully written and polished form. Instead, we recognize its human origin, birthed in the ancient community of Israel (Old Testament) and the early Christian community of the first century (New Testament).

The authors of these books weren't writing to us or for us—twenty-first-century people light years from their own thinking and purposes. No, they were writing to those living in the cultural context of their own world. For instance, in writing his letters to specific churches of his day, Paul had no idea that they would be perceived by later generations as the very words of God for all time. He wrote to the believers in Rome, not to the believers throughout the world—throughout all of time. His letters were particularized to specific churches dealing with specific issues, and Paul's specific responses were based on his own specific understandings within the specific cultural context of his day. That's a lot of "specifics," but you get the idea. The Christian community cherished his writings, but they are Paul's words, not the very words of God for all time enshrined in the meanings and prejudices of the first century.

Viewing Scripture as a human product written from the limited understandings of a particular cultural viewpoint with all of its biases and prejudices of the day doesn't negate God's existence or God's inspiring presence in the lives of the various authors. They indeed sensed God's moving in their lives and felt inspired, just as we feel inspired by God's presence in our own lives. Scripture is a record of how ancient followers saw God from their own perspective, not how God actually sees things. We struggle to fully appreciate this distinction. Their stories, proclamations, wisdom, and understanding are reflections of *their* story. Fortunately, God is still speaking, still inspiring, and still moving, and we are still experiencing the sacred presence, just as they did.

Why do religions elevate their holy writings as originating directly from God? Furthermore, why is it important to us that this be true? Christianity isn't the only religion to claim sacred writings from God—every religion has them. I wonder whether it has something to do with security, authority, and orthodoxy.

Security

In this transient journey we call life, people yearn for security. Instead of stumbling around in the maze of meaninglessness, they seek assurances that there is something more to this life than this life. Possessing tangible writings from an intangible God soothes our anxiety and helps us feel connected to an ultimate reality. We feel more secure dragging around a comforting security blanket no matter how dirty it gets. The purpose of religion, some would say, is to provide psychological security, and that is why religions claim direct-from-God holy writings—to provide assurances to insecure people. Unfortunately, no religion can provide the type of security we long for, not even Christianity. Instead of certainty, Christianity imbues us with courage—the courage to be, to live, and to love in a world filled with insecurity. Rather than providing absolute truth, Christianity lends us the courage to embrace life and walk through it even though "for now we see in a mirror, dimly" (1 Cor. 13:12, NRSV).

I wonder whether a significant factor in the growth of evangelical and fundamental churches has to do with their offer of security amid uncertainty, such as the certainty of heaven over hell, right belief over all other beliefs, right conduct over all other conduct, and being God's chosen over all those who are lost. Whenever cultural change outpaces our ability to cope and absorb such change, there is a return to religious interpretations that offer up authoritative security systems. These systems of certainty help to navigate the ever-changing landscape of life. Unfortunately, having the courage to travel by faith in an uncertain land isn't as satisfying as claiming the certainty and security a direct-from-God writing provides. Many prefer false security to the power of courage.

Authority

When our "blankie" is imbued with divine authority, our internal comfort meter goes up. Scripture becomes the "go-to" place we return to over and over again—a tangible document directly from the God of heaven and the lifeboat of absolutes in a sea of relativity. If the Bible says something is wrong, it is absolutely wrong. If it says something happened, it absolutely happened. Any statement it makes is absolutely and literally true. Scripture is looked upon as the divine book of absolutes.

If Einstein's theory of relativity is correct, however, we live in the created world of time and space. If time and space are relative to one another, then our world is a relative world. All events, circumstances, writings, etc., are relative to the time and space in which they occur, and the Scriptures are relative to the age in which they were written. They cannot speak for all time and all circumstances, for they are products of time and space—born out of a particular contextual environment. The words of one generation cannot capture in absolute terms the meanings, events, and circumstances of another.

Recognizing the time-bound, culture-bound nature of the Bible helps us understand how cultural prejudices found their way into Scripture, such as slavery, subordination of women, male hierarchy, genocide, and a God who rewards and punishes. Scripture is not the absolute truth of God for all ages, for all created things are relative things. Unfortunately, that doesn't provide the security and authority we crave. It is much more comforting to proclaim Scripture as the absolute, authoritative Word of God for all time, even if that belief ignores the nature of ancient writing practices, the relative nature of words, and the limitations of ancient authors tied to a specific generation, culture, pre-scientific knowledge, and so forth.

Orthodoxy

Finally, divine origin and absolute authority provide the basis for right belief, or orthodoxy. In other words, we seek to align our lives with truth, something that assures us that we are correct and part of God's chosen people. After all, individuals don't follow something they believe is false. Claiming orthodoxy allows us to justify our prejudices, embrace tribal mentalities, and engage in discriminatory behaviors. Those adhering to the same security, authority, and orthodoxy are embraced as friends—everyone else is our enemy. God hates all those the chosen people hate. It is the familiar "us versus them" mentality, and out of all the people on this planet, we are the only ones possessing the true, inspired, direct-from-God writings. As such, it carries the authority we need for becoming fruit inspectors in the lives of others, always scrutinizing whether their life measures up to our standard of orthodoxy, which, in its extreme form, can even lead to violence in the name of God.

In a world of uncertainty, religion provides the security, authority, and orthodoxy people long for in their search for meaning. Unfortunately, it comes with a dark side known as tribalism, or, in the vernacular of our day, "We are right, and you aren't. God is on our side, not yours." This provides ample ammunition for justifying the rightness of our cause while condemning the wrongness of others.

What If?

What if the Bible isn't the very words of God for all time, as many believe? What if it merely contains words *about* God—a human product written by human authors trying to describe their human experience and understanding of God from the worldview of their day? What if the Bible contains relative truth rather than absolute truth—relative to the time and culture of its day? What if the Bible is meant to provide courage to live this life rather than security for the next life? What if the Bible conveys profound truth through various literary means instead of literal truth with historical, geographical, scientific, and biographical precision? What if we esteem the Bible not because of its divine origin but because of its role in assisting the community of faith throughout the centuries? What if the Bible reminds us that God is still speaking today, just as God has always spoken to the community of faith? Instead of viewing Scripture as the once-for-all literal Word of God, what if we understood it as the faith journey of those who have traveled before us so we could benefit from their experience?

How We Got the Bible

Before we delve into the hazards of literalism and examine Scripture with new eyes, it will be both interesting and helpful to discover just how the sixty-six books of the Bible came to be thought of as sacred Scripture. If the Bible wasn't dropped from heaven directly by God, then how did we wind up with the resulting Scriptures we now currently possess?

For literalists, the authority of the Bible rests entirely upon its divine origin. Every word in every part of the Bible is exactly the word God placed there in this once-for-all communication to humans. What happens to this authoritative underpinning if the Bible didn't originate from God, as literalists believe, but instead is the product of human authors writing from their own God experience within the worldview and cultural setting of their day? Why is it considered sacred at all, and why should we give it any authoritative value?

A Declared Authority

The short answer is that the weight of the Bible is a *declared* weight. The Bible holds esteemed value because our ancestors in the community of faith found wisdom and guidance in its pages and declared it to be sacred. Out of all the writings that could have been selected, these particular sixty-six books were chosen to be included in the biblical canon. The word "canon" simply means "rule" or "standard." When we refer to the canon of Scripture, we mean those books the church views as the genuine, official writings of their faith. It is the church that has bestowed upon them the elevated status of sacred Scripture, not God.

Establishing which writings would be considered official and genuine is the product of a long process, not something dropped from heaven overnight in final form. Any authority Scripture holds, any esteem it garners, is not because it is the direct, once-for-all, inerrant Word of God but rather because the community of faith looked to it for guidance and inspiration and decreed its sacred status. The authority it carries is a declared authority, not an authority derived from divine origin.

The various books of the Bible weren't originally thought of as Scripture. When Paul wrote his letters to first-century communities such as Rome and Corinth, the recipients of these letters didn't perceive them to be the inerrant, authoritative Word of God for all time. Paul's letters were just that, letters from a recognized leader in the church, not letters from the hand of God. It was only centuries later that his writings would be declared sacred Scripture. The same could be said of the Old Testament books. They gained sacred status long after they were written.

Our inquisitive nature seeks to know who actually decided such things and what criteria were used in the decision. If it were possible, we would demand to see official minutes of such important meetings. Though a great many questions arise over this process, we simply don't have the kind of detailed answers we would like because record keeping and tracking events wasn't as easy as it is in our day. They worked with clay tablets, papyrus, parchment, and memory; we work with computer software programs that track changes and easily store them on powerful, tiny hard drives. For the purposes of this book, a broad conceptual overview is about as deep as we need to go to show that biblical texts morphed from mere writings to esteemed sacred status.

From Writing to Scripture

The first section of the Bible to become sacred Scripture was the Law, also known as the Pentateuch—the first five books of the Old Testament.[2] Beginning with Genesis, we start off with the creation of all things and end in Deuteronomy with the Israelites finally arriving at the front door of the Promised Land—ready to enter and conquer. While the exploits of these first five books are thought to occur in the 1200s BCE, the best estimate of biblical scholars is that they were declared sacred Scripture around 400 BCE.

Next in line for sacred Scripture status were the Prophets, which include the major and minor prophets as well as historical books, like Joshua, Judges, Samuel, and Kings. Though the narrative action in these books takes place between 1200 and 400 BCE, it wasn't until 200 BCE that they would be thought of as part of the Old Testament canon.

The Writings become the last section of the Old Testament to be considered sacred Scripture and include such books as Psalms, Proverbs, Job, Ecclesiastes, and Esther. Scholars estimate that these books were canonized around 100 CE, partly because the New Testament, largely written in the first century, only mentions the Law and the Prophets, not the Writings. Thus, the canonization of the Writings must have occurred after this, since only two sections are mentioned, not three.

We begin to see time gaps between the writing itself and its declaration as sacred Scripture. The New Testament isn't any different. Additionally, before the stories were written down on papyrus or parchment, they were circulated orally and often told within the synagogue. The typical process goes something like this: first there is the event itself, followed by oral storytelling about the event, followed by a writing to memorialize the event, followed by that writing becoming treasured by the community of faith and finally being declared sacred Scripture. This is a lengthy process that occurs over time.

The same thing happened with the life of Jesus. In the early first century, there was a historical figure named Jesus who actually lived, traveled, taught, and was crucified. After his death, there was a period of time when Jesus was remembered orally through various stories about him and his teaching. It wasn't until forty to forty-five years after his death (around 70 CE) that the first written story of Jesus appears in the Gospel of Mark, the first Gospel to be written. And yet, it would be another three hundred years before the New Testament canon was finalized.

This evolving process from oral transmission, to writing, to declared Scripture also applies to biblical stories that are not meant to be understood literally or historically. Instead, they are intended to convey a profound truth through the story itself. Jonah being swallowed by a large fish and living inside its stomach for three days before being expelled on dry land is not an actual historical event but a story intended to show that God's love extends far beyond the limits of our own ability to love. Building a Tower in Babel so tall that it threateningly reaches into the heavens is not literal. Was God worried that the tower would actually breach the heavenly throne room? Did God fragment human language in order to hamper the building project and stunt human ingenuity? Of course not. This is not a literal story but a way of describing something else, such as how language can become a barrier to living together harmoniously. Stories are first told orally, then written down, then cherished by the community of faith, and then declared to be sacred Scripture.

By the time the Council of Nicaea met in 325 CE, there was little consensus regarding an official listing of New Testament books. Still up for grabs were James, Jude, 2 Peter, 2 John, 3 John, and Revelation. Even in the 1500s, Martin

Luther lobbied to remove Hebrews, James, Jude, and Revelation from the Bible. In 367 CE, Athanasius (296–373 CE), the Bishop of Alexandria, wrote a letter that contained the first listing of all twenty-seven books of the New Testament. This didn't put a conclusive end to things, however, for even after Athanasius, other lists containing fewer than twenty-seven books existed. The book of Revelation is the last writing to be declared sacred Scripture.

The point I am trying to make is that the canonization of the Bible was a process rather than an instant revelation from the throne of God. The Bible is not the authoritative Word of God for all time because of its divine origin, for it is a human work that evolved from story, to writing, to treasuring, to finally being declared sacred Scripture by ecclesiastical authority. The Scriptures are held in high esteem by the faith community because it is the church itself that declared them to be their genuine, official holy writings. Every religion has its own declared sacred texts, and for Christians, the Bible is an integral part of our life and identity as followers of God.

Redeeming the Word

Many of us have grown up referring to the Bible as the Word of God—myself included. It is a hard habit to break, and many wonder whether that must also be relinquished. Is there a way to redeem the phrase or make sense of it, given the distinction between the Word of God and the words of God? Evangelicals and fundamentalists use the term "Word of God" as a title or overarching phrase to refer to the Bible when they really mean that each and every word found in the Bible actually originates from God. From their perspective, the Word of God and the words of God are the same thing. This, however, blurs the line of distinction between the two terms.

The Bible has been called the Word of God for a very long time, as Christian history reveals, but it is understood metaphorically, not literally. To say that the Bible is the Word of God is to say that it is a vehicle or pathway for experiencing God. It is not God, as bibliolaters imply, nor is it the very words of God, as literalists suggest; rather, it is a means or avenue for communing with God. There is, in essence, a sacramental nature to it, and yet it is but one vehicle assisting in our God experience. Its origin isn't a divine, straight-from-the-hand-of-God writing but a human product, written by individuals communicating their experience and understanding of God in the time in which they lived. In essence, they created a sacred tool that augments our own experience and understanding of God. The Spirit uses this sacramental vehicle as a means of ministering to us, and in that sense, it can be referred to as the Word of God. This is a subtle distinction worth noting.

In John 1:1–5, Jesus is called the Word of God who became enfleshed in human form. He was, as Colossians 1:15 (NRSV) says, "the image of the invisible God." If we want to know what God is like, we look to the example of Jesus. He is not a literal word on a page but the metaphorical Word who served as a tangible vehicle for others to experience and commune with God. Jesus is the Word of God, and the Bible is the Word of God because both reveal God to us, allowing us to taste the character, nature, and passion of the Holy One.

Can there be other "Word of Gods" that reveal the divine to us? After all, we experience God in many ways and through various means. In one sense, every created thing bears the stamp of its creator and reflects God's image back to us. Unfortunately, the canon of Scripture is currently closed, with no new books being added. This gives the impression that God spoke once in the past and has nothing more to say in the present age. This is an unfortunate effect, for God hasn't stopped speaking—we merely muffle the Spirit's voice and restrict it to a vehicle of the past.

Many mainline churches publicly read Scripture in their Sunday morning services—typically an Old Testament lesson, a Psalm, a New Testament lesson, and a Gospel reading. What may be missing is a contemporary lesson. How is God speaking to us today—in the here and now? What if we read something from Martin Luther King Jr. as God's voice to us in the present age? How about Dietrich Bonhoeffer, the German theologian executed by the Nazis in 1945? Could the writings of Julian of Norwich, the great mystic of the 1300s, be a means of God speaking to us in the present moment? What about Richard Rohr, Marcus Borg, and a host of others who, through a contemporary song, poem, or writing, reveal God's continuing presence among us?

The Heart of the Issue

This distinction between the Word of God and the words of God is helpful, for one views Scripture as a powerful sacramental tool for revealing the character, nature, and passion of God, while the other sees each word in every part of Scripture as the inspired, inerrant, and authoritative words of God for all time, entrapped, as it is, in the prejudices and worldviews of its day.

Earlier I noted that we must be careful which train we jump on in our approach to Scripture, and now you get a taste of why I see it as an essential first step to everything else. In my mind, it is a core issue in the raging debate about the

Bible's origin, purpose, and meaning. We have got to get this right. It is that important.

Chapter Summary

Two trains. Two tracks. Two destinations. One train circles back into past understandings of the Bible that struggle to survive in the contemporary world, while the other escorts us toward the world of present-day relevancy with a scenic ride into the modern age. The train we board has a lot to do with our interpretive destination.

For evangelicals and fundamentalists, Scripture is the inspired, inerrant, and authoritative words of God for all time. Basically, God has spoken and is done speaking, and we now look to the final canonized Scripture as the sole source of authority. This, of course, allows literalists to maintain a sense of security in an insecure world, possess a source of authority from which to operate, and feel superior to others who do not hold their beliefs. Unfortunately, it is a false sense of security, for it is unable to withstand the biblical scholarship of the present age as Scripture is placed under the light of reason, knowledge, and scholarship. It is always more comfortable to embrace a degree of certainty, even if it is a false assurance, than it is to live with courage and faith in an insecure world.

The Bible didn't fall from heaven in complete and final form, for its development took centuries to establish. Its declaration as sacred Scripture occurred centuries after the writing itself. Its value and esteem arise not because God wrote it but because the community of faith has declared it to be the official, genuine documents of the Christian faith. Scripture isn't the literal, inerrant, and authoritative words of God for all time as many claim, for it is a relative document—relative to the time and circumstances of the age in which it was written. Scripture is the Word of God only in the sense that it is a vehicle for experiencing and communing with the divine, not that every word originates from God.

This chapter initiates our excursion into Scripture and literalism. How we approach the sacred text determines our eventual interpretive destiny. Will we read the Bible literally or metaphorically? That is the essence of our next chapter on literalism, to which we now turn.

5

THE DANGER OF LITERALISM
· · · · · · · ·

HOW WE APPROACH SCRIPTURE IS FOUNDATIONAL to understanding its message, and in the previous chapter, I likened it to boarding the correct train so a proper outcome could be attained—arriving at our intended destination. Since the Bible is a Jewish book, written by Jewish authors within a Jewish context, it behooves us to examine Scripture through Jewish eyes—a key element in boarding the right train.

To the surprise of many, the Jesus Movement was actually birthed within the Jewish synagogue. Christianity didn't begin as a separate, independent religion. After the crucifixion, the memory of Jesus lived on through the synagogue—the very heart of Jewish life. In Jesus, the God-presence was so powerful that his life was interpreted through the Hebrew Scriptures of the past. In essence, they enfolded the Jewish Scriptures around their experience of Jesus.

Viewing the Jesus experience through Jewish eyes was easy to do in the early years, at least until the year 88 CE, when synagogues began rejecting the Jesus Movement. By the year 150 CE, the break was virtually complete. Migrating from synagogue life and into a Gentile world meant that Jewish context and understanding would be lost. Gentiles knew very little about Jewish ways. None of the early church fathers were Jewish, yet they were the ones writing commentaries, interpreting Scripture, and developing the various Christian creeds. Viewing Scripture through Jewish eyes was replaced with the lens of Gentile understandings. Within sixty years of Jesus's death, the wrong train pulled up to the station house, and by 150 CE, the Scriptures were whisked away on a locomotive conducted by Gentiles and headed toward the land of literalism.

What in the world is literalism? Is there nothing literal in the Bible? How should modern-day believers approach Scripture? Since formal seminary education isn't an option for most people, is it unrealistic to expect laypersons to explore Scripture at a deeper level? Maybe we should just leave all this interpretive stuff to the heady folks with a penchant for big theological words like supralapsarianism and hypostatic union. Just so you know, hypostatic union is a fancy way of saying that Jesus possessed both human and divine natures, while supralapsarianism, another impressive theological term, concerns the doctrine of election—whether God decreed that certain individuals would be saved *before* God permitted the fall to occur. Now, you will be able to sleep better at night knowing what these terms mean. After all, they were the most pressing items on your mind, right?

While it is true that formal theological education is not in the cards for most people, the good news is that a seminary degree isn't required for increasing one's understanding of Scripture or enhancing one's experience of God. Like a power-hungry police officer boldly flashing his badge around, those possessing degrees of higher learning shouldn't thrust their credentials in the faces of others who haven't had the opportunity or inclination to pursue higher education, nor should those with formal training be looked upon as arrogant elites, disconnected from the real world and unable to relate to common folk.

May I let you in on a secret? No matter how much formal or informal learning we acquire, no one knows everything, and if we are being honest, we only know a fraction of what we think we know. Exploring God is not like studying any other subject, for God is not something you can get your arms around. God is not a body of knowledge to master, an object to dissect and place under a microscope, or a complex mathematical formula to be solved. God is a labyrinth of twists and turns so complicated that no one person or group of persons is able to fully grasp the mystery we call God.

Since we are unable to fully comprehend or explain God, we must simply walk into the cloud of mystery and allow it to envelop us. Far be it from mere humans to explain the creator of the universe, for that would be like asking a catfish to describe what it is like to be human. When people tell you that they have God all figured out, that they alone possess correct doctrine, and that their way is the only true way of knowing and experiencing God, rest assured that their boastful claim rests upon a foundation made of straw. About the only thing we can do is experience God for ourselves and study the experiences and writings of others who claim to have experienced God, which is exactly what Scripture is. In Jewish thought, God is a presence that permeates all of life and is experienced in everyday living—not a doctrine to be mastered or a being to be captured and analyzed.

More will be said about God in upcoming chapters, but for now, I invite you to walk into the great cloud of mystery. Maintain a learning attitude, appreciate those who devote time and energy to advanced learning in biblical studies, and realize that no matter how much we think we know about the Holy One, God is simply too big to be harnessed by our feeble minds. That should take the pressure off of feeling like we have to understand it all, and it should encourage us to jump on the bandwagon and join in on the discussion. Ask questions, challenge yourself, and crawl out from under your limited assumptions and presuppositions. Experience God's presence in your life.

Am I asking you to cast aside the pursuit of knowledge in order to focus solely on experiencing God? No, not at all. Just because we are incapable of understanding *everything* about God doesn't mean we can't ponder things deeply, think things through, and learn all we can about the things of God—all part of being inquisitive human beings. It is when we arrive at all the answers, the correct doctrine, the right and only interpretation of the Bible, and develop entire theological systems that demonstrate haughty and arrogant perspectives that we get into trouble. Remember, like catfish, we are merely humans trying to describe what it means to be God.

Learning and growing begins as an internal posture of the heart. If you want to expand your understanding, you can, for knowledge is at your fingertips in a way never before seen in the history of the world—thanks to science and technology. Educating ourselves takes time and effort as well as exercising our mental powers. Instead of making the investment, many would rather leave their understanding of God to others. Life can be overwhelming, as the tyranny of the urgent shoves all other priorities aside, while the path of least resistance creeps into our lives. It is far easier being told what to think than actually reasoning through our own beliefs. Yet moving from a second-hand religion to our own first-hand experience is a worthy endeavor.

Don't make the mistake I made of confusing my spiritual journey with the accumulation of knowledge. In one sense, I was trying to master God instead of experiencing God. Growing, learning, and acquiring knowledge are certainly worthwhile endeavors, and I am grateful for the privilege of pursuing advanced degrees, but it is not an end in itself. Our spiritual journey is never about arriving but only about becoming. We never reach the pinnacle of full comprehension, but we do get to taste the glory of God's presence as we progress up the mountain. Although knowledge is never an end in itself, it is an investment worth pursuing when kept in proper perspective, for it can open doorways of insight into the mystery of God. This is what the journey is all about—experiencing God's abundant presence while being transformed from the inside out.

What Is Literalism?

Is there nothing literal in the Bible? Of course there is! When the Bible refers to Jesus, we believe that an actual, literal person named Jesus lived and died in the first century. When Scripture speaks of the Jewish temple, we know that a literal, physical temple existed. When the Bible speaks of the Egyptians, we know there was a literal land called Egypt. In combating literalism, we aren't denying that the Bible contains literal references or is ever speaking literally; rather, we are decrying literalism as the approach for interpreting things that shouldn't be taken literally. By discussing what literalism is and showing how it misunderstands Scripture, we will gain a better idea of how to approach the holy book.

Biblical literalism is most often associated with the evangelical and fundamentalist wing of Christianity. In its strictest sense, this view interprets every word of Scripture literally, but most of us know that leads to nonsense. For instance, when the Bible speaks of wine growing on the vine, we realize the author isn't implying that a glass of fermented grape juice is patiently waiting to be plucked from the vine. No, we realize the author has in mind the end product the grapes will eventually become. In Isaiah, we are told that God will bellow like a woman in labor. We know that God is not literally a woman in painful labor. When the psalmist notes that God is like a wild dog, we don't believe for one moment that God is literally a special canine breed.

No one that I know of takes every word literally, for even evangelicals and fundamentalists take note of the different genres of Scripture, such as history, narrative, poetry, apocalyptic, and so forth. Obviously, you don't interpret 1 Kings in the same manner as the book of Revelation. But this isn't what I am referring to when I speak of biblical literalism.

An interpretive approach revered among evangelicals and fundamentalists, known as the historical-grammatical method, is what I learned while in seminary. Mainline denominations, on the other hand, pursue a historical-critical methodology that not only provides greater leeway in interpretation but also seeks to understand the world behind Scripture through investigation and scholarly criticism.

The historical-grammatical method made good sense to me at the time since it emphasizes the "plain-sense" meaning of the text. This view recognizes those pesky obstacles in the interpretive path, such as the distance of time, culture, language, and geography, and it also appreciates the historical and cultural background of Scripture. It makes sense to study the sacred writings in their historical context. Additionally, this methodology emphasizes the grammar and syntax of the writing itself by studying the words of Scripture and their relation to one another. There is nothing wrong with studying grammar and syntax, which to me seems like a useful thing to do.

The historical-grammatical approach to biblical interpretation seeks the "plain sense" of meaning while emphasizing the historical and grammatical aspects of Scripture. If the "plain sense" of Scripture, however, is the most faithful way to interpret the Bible, why has it led to so many different opinions among the evangelical and fundamentalist camps who champion this methodology? What is "plain sense" to one is nonsense to another. In essence, the very method promoted as the "correct" approach to understanding Scripture produces inconsistent outcomes among its most ardent supporters. It seems that the "plain sense" of Scripture isn't so "plain" after all.

These approaches miss the mark, for they seek to understand a Jewish book through Western, Gentile eyes rather than through a Jewish lens. While the historical-grammatical method recognizes various genres of writing, it views Scripture as the literal words of God, often without the rigorous application of higher criticism and without an understanding of the Jewish method of sacred storytelling.

For many years, this is the way I approached Scripture. It was the evangelical way, and it caused me to miss a broader and deeper understanding lying beneath the layer of literalism. My ears were listening for literal truth rather than profound truth, and my error didn't dawn on me until I was in my fifties. I was a slow learner.

If the Bible told a story about a tower in Babel that rose high into the heavens, I never suspected that the story could just be a story—the author's way of conveying a profound truth instead of a literal truth. I read Jonah the same way, as a literal story about a literal boat ride, a literal fish that swallowed a human who literally lived in its belly, who was literally spewed forth on dry land, and so forth. So deep was my respect for Scripture that it never occurred to me that what I was reading might be a nonliteral tool of sacred storytelling. Though I see Scripture with new eyes these days, my respect for Scripture has actually increased. Literalists aren't the only ones with a healthy regard for sacred writing—we just disagree on how to interpret the writings we hold so dear.

Biblical literalists view Scripture as the very words of God and interpret those words in a way that seeks to discover a literal truth when the method of Jewish storytelling may actually be trying to convey a profound truth. There is a big difference between the two approaches. The Bible contains hyperbole, similes, metaphors, history, apocalyptic visionary language, and so forth, but when Jewish storytelling, intended to convey a profound truth, is interpreted as a literal truth, we have boarded a train that takes us to a destination never intended by the author.

Once Upon a Time

The difference between a profound truth and a literal truth might be likened to our modern-day fairy tales, or our myths about Santa Claus and the Easter Bunny. When we begin a story with "once upon a time," everyone knows the story is not to be taken literally but designed to convey a profound truth such as a moral to the story. "Once upon a time" is merely a literary device for communicating profound truth, not literal truth.

To literalize fairy tales is to read them incorrectly and is similar to what literalism does to the Bible. It is boarding the wrong train. Humpty-Dumpty isn't a literal person but an egg that fell and cracked into many pieces. It is an ingenious method for getting the truth across that some things in life just can't be put back together again. It is not a literal story, and we shouldn't interpret it literally. This is where biblical literalism goes awry.

Little Red Riding Hood is another story that shouldn't be literalized. The wolf doesn't literally talk to grandma and the young girl, and neither does the wolf literally eat both of them. Grandma isn't literally being digested inside the wolf's stomach, and wolves don't literally talk. To literalize the story is to misconstrue its meaning and damage the literary device utilized by the author. We know better than that, for we recognize its "once upon a time" nature. Little Red Riding Hood illustrates how young girls must be careful on their path to womanhood lest they stumble and succumb to temptation.

In the story of Pinocchio, a wooden puppet comes to life whose wooden nose grows every time he tells a lie. We know better than to literalize the story. We do, however, grasp the profound truth the story is intended to convey—that good little boys shouldn't lie. In the story of Jack and the Beanstalk, Jack sells his cow for three magic beans that grow into a huge beanstalk so tall that it reaches beyond the clouds, where a large ogre lives in the sky. Jack climbs up the beanstalk, has quite the experience, and makes his way back down before finally chopping the whole thing down. There are no such things as magic beans that can grow stalks into the sky. There is no ogre who lives above the clouds and no beanstalk for Jack to cut down. No one takes this story literally. To do so is to miss the point and focus on the wrong thing. It is a fairy tale—a story designed to express powerful truth, not literal truth.

Fairy tales are literary mechanisms for expressing life lessons. Other fairy tales could be addressed, such as Cinderella, Beauty and the Beast, and Tom Thumb, but you get the point. No fairy tale is interpreted literally. These stories don't have to be literally true in order to be profoundly true because the stories themselves are designed to convey something beyond literalism. We must recognize the nonliteral form of the story, but we must also look beyond the form to ascertain the deeper truth the story is attempting to convey.

There comes a time when even six-year-olds no longer accept the myths of Santa Claus and the Easter Bunny as literal figures. Yet despite their nonliteral nature, we still find value in sharing them with our children. We perpetuate the folklore over and over again at Christmas and Easter, knowing full well they are not literally true. Children seem to make the transition from literal truth to profound truth much better than adults do, but when it comes to the spiritual realm, Christians struggle to accept that a story can be profoundly true without being literally true.

We recognize "once upon a time" stories in every other area of life except when it comes to Scripture. Since the Bible is considered by literalists to be the very words of God, believing that it could contain anything other than literal truth is implausible. For them, using literary devices for conveying profound truth runs against the grain of an inspired, authoritative, inerrant Word of God. Our default propensity, it seems, is to literalize all of our stories and myths, and when it comes to the Bible, we erroneously think that if it isn't literally true, it can't be true at all. What a terrible mistake this is, and what a harmful constraint it places upon Scripture. We readily grasp this distinction in all other areas of life but are reluctant to admit its presence in Scripture.

If Grandpa says, "My granddaughter is an angel," we understand that the little girl isn't literally a being from the realms of heaven. If she were, we should interview her and learn all we can about "the other side." If someone says, "My father-in-law is a big-hearted man," we should call the ambulance right away since an enlarged heart could be a life-threatening condition. Back in my high school days attractive girls were referred to as "foxes." Inevitably, someone would remark, "She is a fox." But if that were literally true, we might want to call animal control and have the wild animal removed from the high school campus. This sort of nonliteral understanding makes sense to us, yet many refuse to allow this literary mechanism to exist in holy writings.

The distinction between literal truth and profound truth is threatening to those who long for certainty in an uncertain world and who need some sort of authoritative source upon which to build their sandcastle. This is why the pope is declared to be infallible, the Bible is declared to be inerrant, and holy writings are declared to be the true message from God. These kinds of declarations provide the certainty we long for in an uncertain world. What would we do if we didn't have a "thus saith the Lord" biblical text to bolster our security needs? I guess we would just have to live by faith and move forward as the wind of the Spirit blows upon us. That almost sounds exactly like what we are supposed to do. Imagine that!

This quest for certainty prompts us to clench literalism so strongly that it becomes a death grip. Even though a literal reading of the Bible leads to nonsensical outcomes, it is the easiest and laziest way to approach Scripture. All you have to do is take things literally—no deep thinking, no wrestling with God, no searching for profound truth, and no allowance for anything other than literalism. It is truly the path of ease and most always wrong. Boarding the literalism train takes you to destinations of the past that cannot survive in the modern world.

Middle Eastern Exaggeration

When we hear "once upon a time" at the beginning of a story, we immediately recognize a nonliteral storyline. The Middle Eastern mechanism for expressing a "once upon a time" story is the use of exaggeration—the clue for a nonliteral reading and the conveyance of profound truth. When facts are so out of proportion to reality, Middle Easterners realize the story is not to be construed literally. This, of course, is what biblical literalists are unwilling to admit. Exaggeration is the Middle Eastern way of saying, "Once upon a time." Let's look at some examples of Middle Eastern exaggeration in Scripture.

Creation

Staunch biblical literalists still believe that Earth was created in six literal days of twenty-four hours' duration. Science, however, has thrust upon this unenlightened view a mortal wound, and many literalists have been forced to retreat from their literal six-day creation stance to understanding "days" as ages consisting of millions of years. When confronted with scientific data of the modern era, literalists are pressed to look at things differently, and this is exactly what new information does for Christians—it challenges them to reevaluate traditional beliefs in light of new data.

Literalists believe that the order of creation listed in Genesis is the exact sequence of how everything was made. For instance, God created Adam from the dust of the ground and later formed Eve from Adam's rib. They lived in a literal garden called Eden, along with a literal talking snake that tempted Eve, and God literally descended from heaven in the cool of the day to walk and talk with the newly formed couple. After all, "That's what the Bible says, and that's what it means."

Does the Genesis creation story square with any reality you have ever known or experienced? Has any human ever been formed out of dust? Given the abundance of scientific data available these days, does any thinking person really believe Earth was formed in six literal twenty-four-hour periods? Has any human life ever been created out of a rib? Have you ever known anyone to hold a cogent conversation with a talking snake? Did the creator of the universe literally descend from heaven and walk in a garden, conversing with humans? Taking things so literally encourages a gullibility that cannot stand up to reason, and without common sense, faith becomes nothing more than religious daydreaming.

To interpret this story literally is to damage the author's intent and blunt its literary effect. The Genesis creation account is an exaggerated story designed to elevate God as creator and explain how evil entered the world, but it is not a literal story. No one was around to witness the creation event, not even the authors of Genesis. This is Middle Eastern exaggeration meant to express a profound truth, not a literal truth. Besides, which of the two creation accounts in Genesis is the true literal one?

Cain and Abel

Are Cain and Abel literally two siblings, the offspring of Adam and Eve, or are they merely characters in a storyline fabricated to communicate a deeper truth? According to the biblical story, Cain takes up farming, while Abel becomes a shepherd. When it comes time to present offerings to God, Abel's offering of meat is acceptable to the Lord, while Cain's produce of the land is rejected. This upsets Cain so much that his raging jealousy becomes more than he can bear. In anger, Cain kills his brother Abel and secures his spot in history as the first murderer in the biblical record. It sure didn't take long for the worst of humanity to emerge.

Taking seriously God's command to be fruitful and multiply, the newly formed couple reproduce. One wonders whether Cain, Abel, and their later brother Seth are their only children and whether Cain's wife was actually his sister. Were other humans created by God besides Adam and Eve? This story has huge gaps in it, and to take it literally is to blindly accept its many problems.

Immediately upon exiting the garden, the family takes up farming and shepherding. How does that happen overnight? Cain goes on to build a city. How does that occur with such a small group of people? Humans were first hunter-gathers who then transitioned to nomadic living before moving to an agrarian society, and then on to the urban environment. Did Cain bypass this lengthy cycle and immediately jump from the hunter-gatherer stage to the agricultural and urban stage? This is not a literal story but a communication of truth far beyond literalism. We spend so much time focusing upon the minutia of literalism and its many conundrums that we wander into the wasteland of irrelevance and miss the deeper point altogether.

Noah's Ark

Did a universal flood occur whereby the existence of humankind was blotted from the face of the planet with the exception of Noah and his family, who escaped in a large boat? Does that seem a bit far-fetched to you? "Well," you say, "that's what the Bible says, and if the Bible says it, I believe it." That's a literalist talking as they try to elevate Scripture at the expense of common sense and contemporary knowledge.

Constructing a boat the sheer size of Noah's Ark was a Herculean task when one considers that Noah and his family had no idea what rain was or how to build a boat. Its massive dimensions were 450' x 75' x 45'. For all intents and purposes, it was nothing more than a floating zoo of mammoth proportions built by only a handful of people. This is mind-boggling since nothing like this had ever been seen before, built before, or even conceived of before. There were no shipbuilders around and no shipbuilding tradition to rely upon for such a massive project. No understanding existed of the mathematical calculations necessary for building a cruise ship of this magnitude that could withstand the forces of nature about to be applied to the craft. Ships of this scale wouldn't be built until the 1850s. It was the transition from wood to iron and steel that allowed for construction of this size with the ability to withstand the type of forces larger ships would endure.

According to the Bible, the ark took eighty-one years to build. That's an awfully long time. Wood used in the early years of construction could have easily rotted after eighty-one years. The wooden deck on most houses would be long gone by that time. Covering the inside and outside of the ark with pitch would have required enough for 229,500 square feet. Fortunately, there just happened to be enough easily accessible pitch lying around for the small family to gather and apply.

This floating zoo had to hold all kinds of animals, which was quite a feat. Discerning the difference in sex for all of the animals may have been a problem all its own, not to mention determining their space requirements and grappling with parasites and disease. Finally, are we to believe that God literally shut the door of the ark and sent them on their way? Does this seem like a "once upon a time" storyline?

The tale of Noah's Ark is an exaggeration that can't possibly be literally true. In fact, it mimics other versions of the same Mesopotamian story, like the Sumerian tale of Ziusudra and the Babylonian epics of Atrahasis and Gilgamesh. What would a literal reading of this story say about a God who wipes out the entirety of human life on Earth except for one chosen family and who later laments the devastating action? Are the beautiful rainbows we see in the sky the result of God placing them there as a sign that God will never again kill off humankind, or does this meteorological phenomenon exist because of reflection, refraction, and dispersion of light in water droplets? The exaggeration is overwhelming.

Tower of Babel

Soon after the cataclysmic waters subside, the flood survivors begin building a city with a huge tower. Since God supposedly lived just beyond the clouds, the citizens of Babel sought to construct a tower so tall that it would allow them to walk directly into the abode of God. In trying to literalize the story, some have suggested that they were building a ziggurat—a stepped tower similar to other ziggurats discovered in ancient Mesopotamia.

God looks down from heaven, sees what they are up to, and confuses their language in order to stop the construction project and disperse the city's inhabitants. Are we to believe that in a moment's notice, the inhabitants of Earth suddenly began speaking and understanding different languages? Have you ever known anyone who could immediately understand and speak other languages? Of course not. Is there such a thing as a tower so tall that it could reach into the abode of God? Of course not. This is a myth—a nonliteral story designed to explain how different languages came about and how language can keep us from working together. The story finds parallels in a Sumerian account called Enmerkar and the Lord of Aratta as well as a similar Assyrian myth written before the Genesis account ever existed. Literalizing the story misses the intent of the author and misunderstands the nature of Old Testament storytelling.

The Red Sea

The exodus from Egypt and the long journey into the Promised Land is a central piece of Jewish identity and history. Just how the Hebrews wind up in Egypt in the first place is an interesting story. Joseph, who was sold into slavery by his jealous brothers, is taken to Egypt and, through a variety of circumstances, eventually rises to second-in-command to the pharaoh. Known for his wisdom and administrative abilities, Joseph prepares Egypt for seven years of severe famine. In order to survive this life-threatening event, Joseph's brothers are forced to seek out food in Egypt, where they eventually become aware of Joseph's identity. This comes as a complete surprise to them, given their ill-treatment of him. In the end, Joseph's entire family is reunited, including Jacob, his aging father. They move from Canaan to Egypt, settle in the land of Goshen, and become known for raising sheep. This is how the Hebrews rise up in Egypt.

Over time, the family grows in number to the point where their undeniable presence is perceived as a plausible threat to those in power. To prevent this potential risk from becoming a reality, the Hebrews are forced into servitude, and the cities of Egypt are built upon their backs. This is when Moses, the greatest hero of the Old Testament, steps in to save the day. He confronts pharaoh and calls down ten plagues upon the Egyptians. The last of these plagues, and the one that secures their freedom, is God's angel of death killing all first-born Egyptian sons while the chosen Hebrew children are spared from this devastating mass execution. With the pharaoh finally giving in to Moses's demand for release, the Hebrews initiate their long trek to the Promised Land—a journey with its own dramatic twists and turns.

When their getaway path is blocked by the Red Sea, the possibility of failure reaches a new level of urgency. No worries—Moses and his staff come to the rescue. As their hero-leader lifts his staff into the air, the waters of the Red Sea part, and the fleeing Hebrews cross to the other side on dry ground. All you have to do is watch *The Ten Commandments* starring Charlton Heston each Easter season, and you can see this played out in Hollywood style. The pursuing

Egyptian army, however, isn't so fortunate. Entertaining second thoughts about allowing their worker bees to fly away, they chase the Hebrews down like a band of outlaws in a classic western movie, and the Red Sea becomes a point of drama as to whether freedom or bondage will be their fate. Once the Hebrews have safely crossed to the other side, the waters of the Red Sea come crashing down on the pursuing Egyptian army, killing every last one of them. Apparently, God isn't fond of Egyptians.

Some believe the parting of the Red Sea was accomplished by a strong wind that dried up marshlands, but this is mere speculation. Given the size of the Red Sea, the time frame in which the Bible tells us they crossed, and the great numbers of people fleeing Egypt, others note that a twelve-minute-mile pace would have been necessary. How could such a horde of people consisting of elderly, infirmed, infants, young children, livestock, etc., move at such a pace? It is totally unrealistic. I can't even run a mile in twelve minutes on my own, let alone with a goat by my side, a baby in one arm, and Grandma hanging on to the other. Had I been a part of the exodus, I would have slowed them down or been left behind.

Was there some event in past history prompting the telling of this great story? Probably. Did it happen exactly as the story describes? Probably not. The narrative is embellished and exaggerated for the purpose of elevating the Hebrews as God's chosen people, called and destined for conquering a land they claimed was given to them by God. It is a story about moving from bondage to freedom.

Jonah and the Fish

Another self-evident exaggeration occurs when Jonah is swallowed by a large fish. Instructed by God to warn the Ninevites of the impending wrath to be unleashed upon their city, Jonah decides to take another course of action. Harboring such disdain for these people, the last thing Jonah wants to see is their repentance and the extending of God's grace. He would rather savor their demise than be a catalyst for their salvation.

Jonah boards a ship to Tarshish and flees in the opposite direction of where he is supposed to go. Unfortunately, the ship encounters a raging storm at sea, caused, of course, by the Lord, who is steering Jonah back to his original assignment. Realizing that the seas are thrashing about because of his disobedience, the prophet asks to be thrown overboard. Better to face death than face the Ninevites. At just the right moment, however, a big fish swallows Jonah and spares him from drowning. One wonders whether Jonah even got wet. For three days and three nights, he survives in the belly of the large fish as it swims to its assigned drop-off point, where Jonah is miraculously spewed forth on dry land—alive and well, with no noticeable wear and tear from the journey. In this "once upon a time" story, Jonah is swallowed by a large fish during a raging storm at sea, lives in its belly for three days and three nights, and is miraculously spewed forth on dry land—all by the hand of God.

Jews would have easily grasped the exaggeration of this fanciful event. Was there really a large fish that followed the boat on its voyage in wait for Jonah to be thrown overboard? Did the fish actually swallow a human being who then lived inside its digestive tract without food and water for three days and three nights, or is some sort of symbolism going on? Was Jonah literally coughed up on dry land at just the right time and place? Even the size of Nineveh seems to be exaggerated from what we currently know about the city. This is Jewish story-telling at its finest—a "once upon a time" way of revealing how God's love reaches far beyond the limits of our own love, for God's love extends to our enemies— even those despised Ninevites.

Literalists spend a great deal of time on the minutia of their viewpoint and wind up chasing rabbit trails into Neverland. In an attempt to prove their literal-ism, they hunt for a fish large enough to consume a human being and search for examples of people who were swallowed by a fish or who survived for a period of time inside a fish belly. Focusing on this kind of frivolity is a waste of time, misses the point, and limits the discovery of profound meanings.

Other Examples

The Old Testament is filled with "once upon a time" tales that are not intended to be interpreted literally. Elijah, for instance, faces 450 prophets of Baal on Mt. Carmel in a battle of the gods. An ox is slaughtered, cut into pieces, and laid upon firewood. Whichever god can light a fire when called upon and consume the offering is the true god. To dramatize the situation, when it is Elijah's turn to call upon the God of Israel, he soaks the firewood in water. His God is so powerful that even water-logged wood will be consumed, and that is exactly what happens. God slings fire from heaven and consumes the wet firewood, the slaughtered ox, the overflow water in the trench, and the stones of the alter itself. That is cer-tainly an "in your face" way of saying, "My god is bigger than your god."

Did water-logged wood actually catch fire? Were the stones of the altar liter-ally consumed by fire flung from the sky above? Could it be that this narrative conveys a profound truth rather than a literal one? Once God's power was so evidently demonstrated, did Elijah literally murder 450 prophets of Baal as

Scripture reveals? Is that the kind of God we serve and the kind of people who follow God—killers of those who worship other gods? Do the facts of this tale extend beyond the realty of life? Of course they do. This is an exaggerated, "once upon a time" story.

There are plenty of other Old Testament examples. Did Balaam's donkey speak intelligible human words while complaining of Balaam's treatment? Is this literal or merely a "once upon a time" event designed to convey a nonliteral point? Was Samson's power actually tied to the length of his hair? Have you ever known anyone in this world whose strength was derived from hair—let alone the length of it?

Was Elijah literally escorted directly into heaven by riding a magical chariot of fire in a whirlwind sent from heaven, thus bypassing death that comes to all of us? What in the world is a chariot of fire anyway? Is this literal, or is this a literary method for elevating the status of Elijah?

When Shadrach, Meshach, and Abednego were cast into Nebuchadnezzar's fiery furnace that was heated up seven times hotter than usual, they miraculously survived without smelling like smoke, without a single singed hair, and without becoming crispy critters in a hot, burning oven. Have you ever known anyone who could withstand such an ordeal? Of course not. This isn't a literal story but an exaggeration intended to convey a profound truth, not a literal truth.

These examples defy human logic and common sense. Because these stories exaggerate events to a large degree, we know the author intends to convey a profound truth, not a literal truth. Authors use stories to get their point across, and Jesus, known as a masterful storyteller, did the exact same thing. Literalism reads what is intended to be a "once upon a time" story as a literal story, and in so doing, boards a train headed in the wrong direction.

The Gospels

The New Testament has its own "once upon a time" stories, particularly within the Gospels. We erroneously assume they are historical and biographical accounts that lay out everything Jesus said and did, and in the exact sequential order as presented. If the Gospel says Jesus was on a mountain delivering the Sermon on the Mount, we believe he was on a mountain and that every word placed upon his lips is exactly what Jesus said. We don't take into consideration that the Gospels were written well after Jesus died and that the authors lived within cultural, religious, and political realities that influenced what they wrote and how they wrote it.

The major source of historical information about Jesus comes from the Gospels. Jesus left no writings of his own, and we are uncertain whether he could read and write since he came from the lower class. What we know about his life and teaching comes only from what others said he said—hearsay. And, most Christians believe the Gospels were written by Jesus's disciples, who were eyewitnesses to everything he said and did. That's what I was taught and believed for years. After all, the Gospels are titled after Jesus's disciples Matthew, Mark, Luke, and John, who traveled with him and heard and saw all of these things. This is good evangelical theology, and to say otherwise is to place yourself squarely in the crosshairs of their holy indignation.

But the Gospels weren't written by eyewitnesses, as we are led to believe. They were penned between 70–100 CE, some forty to seventy years after the death of Jesus. Since the average life expectancy in the first century was around thirty-five years of age, two to three generations had passed after the death of Jesus before any story was ever written about him. Any eyewitnesses would have been long gone by that time.

There are many reasons to suspect that the Gospels weren't written by eye-witnesses, but my point is that they are not literal, historical, and biographical accounts of the life of Jesus. Instead, the authors were painting an interpretive portrait of Jesus that Jewish readers would easily understand—a way that acknowledged the God-presence in Jesus of Nazareth while connecting him to their Scriptures and past heroes of the Jewish faith. Although Mark was the first account to be written, around 70 CE, the Gospel of John, written between 90–100 CE, will serve as an example of why we shouldn't take the Gospels liter-ally. Over and over again, this gospel writer warns his readers against interpreting his work literally.[3]

Nicodemus

John 3 contains the story of Nicodemus, an individual identified with the Pharisees and a member of the Jewish ruling council. This makes Nicodemus a religious leader, who was well-versed in the traditional Jewish way of looking at things. In sneaky fashion, he meets with Jesus under the cover of darkness, for he cannot deny the presence of God in Jesus on the one hand, and yet he is blinded by his own religious limitations on the other hand.

Jesus informs Nicodemus that no one can see the kingdom of God unless they are born again or, as some translations have it, "born from above" or "born anew." Jesus isn't referring to the contemporary notion of accepting him into your heart through some emotional religious experience. He would have had no inkling of an altar call during a morning church service or tent revival meeting while the congregation quietly sings "Just as I Am." The concept of accepting Jesus as one's personal Lord and Savior wouldn't arise until centuries later. Jesus is referring to something far deeper and far more transformative than the development of a doctrine created long after his demise.

The "born-again" transformation Jesus refers to isn't some emotional "come to Jesus" experience but a new way of thinking, seeing, and living. It is an entirely new dimension of life and thought—a change in perspective. Nicodemus is being asked to see with new eyes and perceive things differently than the way he currently sees them. He is asked to go beyond the boundaries of his own religious limitations and barriers. In essence, he is asked to embrace a paradigm shift.

Being the good literalist that he is, Nicodemus finds this kind of talk difficult to understand, for his perspective is confined to traditional understandings of God. He has locked God in a box, and this talk of being born again doesn't make much sense to him. How can individuals crawl back up into their mother's womb to be born a second time? He responds to Jesus's nonliteral point by interpreting his words literally and, in so doing, misses the point altogether. This is how literalism works. It destroys the true meaning of the text and damages the intent of the author while exchanging a profound truth for a literal one. Jesus isn't speaking literally, for no one can crawl back into their mother's womb to be reborn. The story is conveying a profound truth, not a literal one. It is a story about transformation—seeing things afresh with new eyes.

Jesus further informs Nicodemus that in order to enter the kingdom of God, one must be born of water and the spirit. Literalists struggle to grasp this talk of water and spirit and seek to read back into Jesus's words doctrines that didn't exist until centuries later—a kind of revisionist theology. Jesus isn't referring to the doctrine of baptism or some doctrine of the Holy Spirit. Instead, he is relating a simple truth that one must be born not only physically (of water) but also spiritually, for flesh gives birth to flesh, and spirit gives birth to spirit. It is another way of conveying his "born again" message.

How much clearer does it have to be? All humans are born literally, that is, of water, but the kingdom of God requires that we be born again, and that isn't a second physical birth, but a spiritual birth—a transformation from within that opens our eyes to seeing things differently. This new birth isn't something we capture, analyze, and explain; rather, it is a mystical experience, much like trying to capture the wind as it blows wherever it pleases. Instead of asking people to accept him as their own personal Lord and Savior, Jesus asks people to begin seeing God in new ways and to move beyond the religious boundaries that blind them.

Nicodemus is a literalist, and literalists always miss the moving and meaning of the blowing wind. They are stuck in the limits of their own religious perspective—a kind of group think or God-in-a-box mentality. "The wind of God must blow this way or that way," they cry out, never allowing it to blow in its own direction. Yet Jesus becomes a doorway for the blowing wind of God. He didn't fit the mold or expectations of the ruling religious elite, and yet the presence of God was strong and evident in his life. Surprise! God is moving outside of Nicodemus's comfort zone.

Nicodemus processes, analyzes, and considers, but he never seems to cross the line into new thinking and a transformed consciousness. Jesus draws the line very clearly. To be a part of God's kingdom and catch the blowing winds of the spirit, an internal transformation must occur whereby one's perspective is forever altered. No longer are they bound by their own prejudices and religious limitations. Instead, they are open to a new dimension of God's presence in their lives. No longer do they seek to direct and control the blowing winds of the Spirit; now they simply recognize it, allow it, and embrace it.

The Samaritan Woman

John's story of the Samaritan woman illustrates the lunacy of literalism. In John 4, Jesus makes his way from Judea to Galilee and stops at Jacob's well for a refreshing drink of water before continuing his journey. The well happens to be located near Sychar in the region of Samaria.

While his disciples enter the city to purchase food, Jesus remains at the well, where a Samaritan woman arrives to draw water. Jesus asks whether she might give him a drink from the water she has drawn. Since Jews and Samaritans loathed one another, she inquires how a Jew could ask her, a Samaritan, for a drink. Jesus responds by offering her living water to drink, from which she will never thirst again. This astounds her, since he has no means of drawing water out of the well. Only she has the bucket, and he had to ask her for water. How can he provide water for her? She wonders whether Jesus is greater than Jacob, the one who gave them the well in the first place. Jesus notes that everyone who drinks from Jacob's well will thirst again, but the living water that he offers will quench one's thirst forever.

The woman understands this statement literally, for such an offer is indeed enticing. After all, drawing water from the well every day is a pain. If there is a way to circumvent this daily chore, she is all ears. Never having to draw water again would certainly make her life easier. But this isn't what Jesus has in mind at all, for he isn't referring to literal water but to the deep satisfaction one enjoys when connected to the God he espouses.

Upon returning from their city errand, the disciples are amazed to find Jesus talking with a female Samaritan. Women held little status in the male-dominated world of the first century, and in addition to her lowly gender, she was also a despised Samaritan—half-breeds who contaminated Jewish blood, worship, and belief by marrying outside pagan foreigners. And here he is, interacting with a loathsome woman and despised enemy, once again breaking the boundaries imposed by religious prejudice.

Now that the disciples have acquired food from their excursion into the city, they urge Jesus to eat. Instead of partaking, he reminds them that he has food to eat that they do not know about. The disciples are literalists and wonder how he has obtained food of which they are not aware. Once again, Jesus isn't referring to physical, literal food but to the feasting and sustenance he receives from being in communion with God. Literalism destroys the meaning of the text and, like the Samaritan woman and the disciples, misses the point.

The Bethesda Healing

In John 5, another story is told of a man who has been sick for thirty-eight years before Jesus heals him. The event occurs in Jerusalem at a place called Bethesda—a pool with five porticoes located near the sheep gate. It is a popular hangout for the infirmed, who gather at the pool with the high hope of being healed. The sick, lame, and paralyzed wait for the angel of the Lord to stir the waters during certain seasons, and the first one to enter is healed. It seems a bit odd, and a bit cold-hearted, to heal only the first person fast enough, or able enough, to move their infirmed body into the water. If you were paralyzed, there wasn't much hope for you. The person who could walk would always be able to enter the water faster than you.

This man lies there day after day, waiting for his opportunity, only to miss out because of his inability to walk for thirty-eight years. The power of Jesus enters the picture, and healing is bestowed upon the man. Thirty-eight years isn't a long time in our world, for the life expectancy of the average American male is nearly eighty years. In first-century Palestine, however, the average life expectancy was fewer than thirty-eight years. It wasn't enough to merely heal someone who was sick; that had been done before. John notes that the presence of God is so great in Jesus that he can even heal a man who has been sick his entire life. Only someone with God's power flowing through them could do something like that.

As the story goes, the religious elite are upset that this momentous event occurs on the Sabbath when carrying one's pallet is not permitted—healing or not. Keeping the Sabbath means resting, not working, and Jewish religious leaders spend a considerable amount of time defining what is considered work on this holy day. They appear to be more interested in rule-keeping than performing good deeds, like healing a man who has been paralyzed his entire life. On one occasion, Jesus reminds them that the Sabbath is made for humans, not the other way around (Mark 2:27).

We interpret this story literally when that is not the author's intention. Thirty-eight years is the exaggerated interpretive clue that sets up the conflict between the limits of traditional ways of seeing, as illustrated by the Pharisees, and the new way of seeing God, as illustrated by Jesus, who opens up windows to the soul where new light rushes in.

Literalists, however, cherish their boundaries, their certainty, their structures, their religious operating manual, their clear lines of demarcation about what is true and what isn't, and their rigid understanding of how things ought to be done. They would enjoy defining what work can't be performed on the Sabbath and then holding everyone else hostage to their definition. However, the wind of the Spirit blows wherever it chooses, oftentimes outside the lines of what is considered acceptable and appropriate. Jesus seeks transformation, a new way of seeing that is less certain, less authoritarian, and often outside the boundaries established by good religious folk. Jesus represents wholeness, which the crippled man experiences. Jesus is about living life abundantly, about becoming whole, and about connecting with God. Religion has limits; God does not.

Feeding Five Thousand

Moving on to John 6, we discover that a large crowd follows Jesus to the other side of the Sea of Galilee, for they are impressed with the signs he is performing on the sick. As he moves up the mountain to spend time with his disciples, he takes notice of the multitude. In typical Jesus fashion, this becomes a useful teaching moment, as he inquires of Philip where they can buy bread so the crowd can eat. Philip, the literalist, responds that even two hundred denarii worth of bread would be insufficient to feed everyone. Andrew offers up that a young lad nearby has five barley loaves and two fish, but even that scant amount isn't enough to feed the multitude.

After giving thanks, Jesus distributes the lad's meager resources, and everyone eats their fill. There are enough leftovers to fill twelve baskets. The crowd interprets this miracle as a sign that Jesus is truly a prophet from God. In fact, they desire to take him by force and declare him king. We can't really blame them. After all, he gives them free food from just five barley loaves and two small fish. Just think what he could do as their king! Who wouldn't want a king like that—one who can feed people for free?

This isn't a literal story, for even Philip realizes the absurdity of feeding so many with such meager resources. Even if they had the money to buy food for five thousand people, the logistics of doing so would be extremely difficult. Jesus is testing Philip's spiritual understanding, which stops at the limits of literalism. Do you see the exaggeration—five thousand people, five barley loaves and two fish, and twelve baskets of leftovers? The author is using the story to reveal a profound truth, not a literal truth. Twelve is an important symbolic number in Jewish history, for it represents the twelve tribes of Israel. As a new prophet announcing a new vision of the kingdom of God, there must also be twelve tribes associated with Jesus as well. It is a messianic sign indicating that the Gospel writer sees Jesus as the promised Messiah. This is a story linking Jesus with the messianic expectations of the Jewish people.

Walking on Water

After feeding five thousand people, Jesus withdraws from the crowd to be by himself. Since darkness is beginning to fall upon the land, the disciples seek to cross the Sea of Galilee in their journey to Capernaum. Apparently, they leave Jesus behind on the mountain and proceed without him. To their dismay, they encounter a threatening storm while rowing their boat, and when they hit the middle of the lake, they see Jesus walking toward them on the water. Jesus hops into the boat, and immediately they find themselves at their destination.

Does this seem like exaggeration to you? Jesus just happens to be left behind, walks on water to the middle of the Sea of Galilee, jumps into the boat with the disciples, and immediately they are at the shoreline of their destination. The fact that Jesus withdraws by himself after feeding the huge crowd sets the stage for his coming to the disciples on the water. The author wants to show that just as Moses feeds hungry people with manna, so too does Jesus have the power to feed a huge crowd. Just as Moses crosses the Red Sea by parting it, so too does

Jesus cross the sea by walking on it. The feeding of the five thousand and walking on water aren't literal stories but "once upon a time" stories carefully crafted to portray Jesus in light of the Jewish Scriptures. They portray Jesus as the anticipated Messiah, for he even has the power of Moses, the greatest of all Jewish heroes.

A Man Born Blind

As Jesus passes by a man born blind in John 9, the disciples ask whether this blindness is the fault of the man's sin or the sin of his parents. Jesus replies that the man's blindness is not the result of sin at all. Sickness, conventional wisdom suggests, is a matter of personal sin or divine punishment upon the afflicted. Of course, this kind of reasoning prevailed in a world that knew nothing of germs, viruses, vaccines, and the like. From their limited worldview, sickness was a punishment from the hand of God or some ailment brought on by a demon.

Jesus wets the ground with his own saliva, and after making a small batch of clay, applies it to the blind man's eyes with instructions to go wash in the pool of Siloam. The man does as he is told and sees for the first time in his life. This creates quite a controversy among the Pharisees, who are frustrated that Jesus has violated the Sabbath. How dare he heal a blind man on a day the Torah set aside as the holy day of rest! He isn't resting as the law requires but working. Surely this is proof that Jesus is not a prophet from God!

Many figures in the Gospel of John may not be literal people at all but representative symbols—literary creations that stand for something other than a literal person. Here, the blind man may be a symbol of the Johannine community being kicked out of the synagogue for their increasing proclamation of Jesus, while the Pharisees may represent the Jewish synagogue leaders. Is the point being made that Jesus literally healed a blind man, or is this a carefully crafted way of saying something much deeper?

This man isn't an ordinary blind man but a man who has been blind since birth. He has never experienced the sight he now enjoys. The text, in fact, states that since the beginning of time, no one has ever opened the eyes of someone born blind. In other words, the God-presence in Jesus is being shown as something new—something that surpasses all that they have ever known and seen before.

Although the Jesus Movement was initially cradled within the Jewish synagogue, tension grew between the synagogue leaders and the followers of Jesus. After his death, Jesus's followers began wrapping their hero in the fabric of Old

Testament Scriptures. They weren't trying to start a new church; they were simply bringing their sacred Scriptures to bear upon their experience of Jesus. How else were they to understand and interpret the life of Jesus other than through the cherished Scriptures that were so integral to Jewish life?

There was a time when only the Torah existed as Jewish Scripture, but then the prophets came along, and they were grafted in, now becoming the Law and the Prophets. Later, the Writings would also be grafted in, expanding Scripture to be the Law, the Prophets, and the Writings. These three scriptural divisions didn't start out that way. Over time and as circumstances changed, the Scriptures grew as new segments were added. And then Jesus came along, a man in whom the presence of God was experienced like no other. Could the Scriptures also be wrapped around him? Would he become the next addition to Jewish life and culture? Would he, in a sense, also be grafted in to the holy writings? Looking to connect the present Jesus with their past Scriptures seemed like a natural thing to do.

There came a point, however, when Jewish leaders sensed the Jesus Movement had gone too far in its claims about Jesus. It was one thing to see him as a prophet with a contemporary message, but to think of him as anything more than that was too much to bear. Yet Jesus's message was one of seeing with new eyes, which only comes about by a change in perspective—being born again.

This healing story contrasts those who live in darkness with those who live in light, reflecting the very tension the Johannine community was experiencing. Jewish synagogue leaders were resolutely committed to their traditional way of seeing things, so much so that the followers of Jesus were no longer welcomed in their midst. The Johannine community had crossed a line and was seen as undermining Judaism. But like the blind man, their eyes had been opened. No longer would the *form* of religion remain the *essence* of their faith. Their eyes could see new truth, new life, new perspectives, and a new way of living and being. A paradigm shift had occurred. That's what happens when you come into the God-power found in Jesus. You feel like a man born blind who has had his eyes opened and can see for the very first time.

The Pharisees are the ones who remain in their blindness. Their closed minds were not a sign of virtue but a clear indication of traditional "group think." This isn't a literal story but a symbolic way of showing that the way of Jesus opens our eyes to new perspectives. The author of John also states that Jesus is the way, the truth, and the life into this new consciousness. His message becomes the doorway to removing blindness, walking a new path, and embracing and experiencing the kingdom. Jesus is the light of the world because his life and his message allow us to transcend the limits of religious form and traditional group-think that locks God into a box. That's what this story is all about. It isn't describing a literal truth but presenting a profound truth about the kingdom of God amid the circumstances of the Johannine community.

Lazarus

In John 11, we read the fascinating story of Lazarus being raised from the dead—a story found only in the Gospel of John. If Lazarus was literally resuscitated back to life after four days of lying dead in a grave, why is this stunning account not mentioned in any other Gospel? Paul knows nothing about it in his writings, either.

For Christians, the story is a familiar one. The brother of Mary and Martha is sick unto death, and Jesus, who is known for his healing power, is asked to come and heal him. Jesus lingers, and by the time he appears on the scene, Lazarus has been dead for four days. Martha is quite upset about this. Had Jesus arrived sooner, her brother may still be alive. Moved by his love for Lazarus and his sensitivity to Mary and Martha's pain, Jesus commands that the stone be removed from the entrance of the burial cave where Lazarus has been laid to rest. Realizing that a foul odor would be present after four days in the grave, Martha warns Jesus of the impending stench. Having previously mentioned that he was the resurrection and the life, Jesus reminds her again to simply believe. After Jesus calls the dead man to come forth from the grave, Lazarus staggers out, wrapped from head to toe in grave clothes. What a miracle!

Do you see the exaggeration that is occurring? Dead people had been raised before by the likes of Elijah and Elisha, but never a person who had been dead for four days. That was unheard of. Do you know what happens to a dead body in four days? Decomposition begins minutes after death. Without life-giving oxygen flowing through our veins to fuel various parts of the body, the onset of decay is immediate. Rigor mortis sets in within 3–4 hours of death, peaks at 12 hours, and declines after 48 hours. Within 24–72 hours, the internal organs break down. Within 3–5 days of death, the body begins to bloat, and blood-containing foam leaks from the nose and mouth. This is not a pretty sight, and the odor Martha refers to is the stench of decomposition. Does this four-day-old dead-man story seem like an exaggeration to you? Is the Gospel telling us a literal story or is the story merely the vehicle for conveying a profound truth?

In reality, Lazarus may not even be a real, literal person but rather a symbol—a sign of something more significant. Jesus is depicted as a light who brings sight to the blind and life to those who die. He is portrayed as the sustaining bread of life and the doorway to new ways of seeing and being. John is trying to convey a message about the Jesus whom the Johannine community loves and proclaims—the Jesus who got them booted from the synagogue.

Jewish synagogue leaders were beginning to view Jesus as a threat to their tradition, to their faith system, and to their understanding of God. We do well to remember that this Gospel was written somewhere between 90 and 100 CE, which means that the Jewish temple, destroyed by the Romans in 70 CE, was nothing but a heap of rubble and had been that way for twenty to thirty years. The old way of doing business as usual was changing, since the Jewish cultural and religious centerpiece now lay in ruins. How does Israel continue when the heart of Judaism has been ripped from the nation?

Change was all around them, and it was not well-received. This talk of Jesus having been resurrected from the dead, being the promised Messiah and even being God, was disturbing to synagogue leaders. It was but one more challenge to their religious tradition, which was already in upheaval. Though the Johannine community was ostracized from the synagogue, they discovered new life in the teachings of Jesus. Lazarus wasn't a literal person who was literally resuscitated from the dead after four days of decomposition; rather, he was a symbol of the new life that one experiences in following Christ. Despite the Johannine community's rejection by local synagogue leaders, the Gospel of John is written from its understanding of Jesus whom they loved and proclaimed.

Other Examples

The Gospel of John is filled with numerous nonliteral images and stories. At the urging of his mother, for instance, Jesus miraculously turns water into wine during a wedding feast in John 2. When the wine has run out, the only available liquid is in six stone pots, each holding twenty to thirty gallons of water used for Jewish purification rites. Jesus ensures that each of the stone pots is filled to the brim with water, miraculously turns that water into wine, and asks that a sample be taken to the headwaiter, who is perplexed as to why this wine, the best of wines, is now being served to the guests instead of being the first wine to be served.

Jesus doesn't simply turn water into wine; he turns 180 gallons of water into wine, and it isn't ordinary wine. The exaggerated quantity of the fermented beverage is complemented by the over-the-top quality of the wine—the best of the best. This larger-than-life story is designed to convey a nonliteral message about Jesus. Could this account have something to do with the difference between the purification rite, as represented by the water, and the refreshing drink that comes from Jesus? Jesus is being depicted as the one who brings refreshing new wine to the old ways of Judaism.

John also calls Jesus the bread of life, but is he literal bread that you bake and eat, or is the phrase trying to convey a nonliteral, profound truth about Jesus? The answer is self-evident. Jesus purportedly says in John 6 that unless we eat his flesh and drink his blood, we have no part in him. Is that literal? If so, Jesus is promoting cannibalism. Written from the cultural and religious realities experienced by the Johannine community of the late first century, the Gospel of John utilizes a plethora of stories, images, and symbolic figures to convey profound truths about Jesus and the kingdom of God. Over and over again, the Gospel writer warns us not to take his writing literally, for literalism misses the point and ignores the deeper truths being communicated.

A Deeper Truth

The art of sacred storytelling allows for the transference of deep truth. A good story—an exaggerated story—is a wonderful literary device for getting a point across, much like Jesus's parables. It is not important that the story be literally true or that the events literally happened, for it is merely a literary tool—the scaffolding surrounding the communication of deeper truth.

All too often, however, Christians interpret these exaggerated stories literally when they were never intended to be understood in that manner. It was Jesus scholar John Dominic Crossan who said, "It is not that ancient people told silly stories which we, because we are so smart, should not take literally or factually but symbolically or fictionally. It is the ancients who knew how to tell a good metaphorical story (a parable if you prefer) and we moderns who are silly enough to take them factually."[4]

Strong differences may arise over what profound truth is actually being communicated, but there is common consensus that the authors never intended them to be taken literally. Unfortunately, in an effort to safeguard the integrity of Scripture, biblical literalists trot down the literalism trail to find nothing but inconsistencies and nonsense. Their effort to protect Scripture, as though it needs to be protected at all, actually accomplishes the very opposite. In an age of unprecedented scientific discoveries about our universe, their unyielding insistence upon a literal interpretation appears more and more foolish. Their idea of living faithfully into the future is to travel back into the past where unenlightened perspectives prevailed. It will never fly as more and more people abandon the church in search of a view that squares with current realities.

Chapter Summary

Literalism is construing literally what was never intended to be taken literally. It is analogous to interpreting literally the stories of Santa Claus, the Easter Bunny, Little Red Riding Hood, Humpty Dumpty, Pinocchio, and so forth when they were never meant to be understood that way. Many of the biblical stories, just like our "once upon a time" stories, are designed to communicate profound truth, not literal truth. This is the problem of literalism and why it forever misses the point. While literalists seek faithfulness to the meaning of Scripture, their good intentions can never mask their incorrect approach to the religious text. If I intend to climb Mt. Everest but mistakenly scale Mt. Kilimanjaro instead, my good intentions cannot erase the fact that I ascended the wrong mountain.

Exaggeration—facts so out of proportion to reality—is the interpretive clue to reading these stories from a "once upon a time" perspective. Literalism fails to recognize the nature of Jewish sacred storytelling, where exaggeration becomes the literary pathway for communicating profound truth. Recognizing this fact is one way we read Scripture through Jewish eyes rather than through a Gentile lens.

We delve deeper into the world of literalism in our next chapter, as we explore the nature of Jewish religious life, analyze Matthew's use of nonliteral stories, and investigate how words convey meaning and why literalism embraces the lowest level of meaning possible.

6

WORDS AND MEANINGS
· · · · · · · ·

THIS CHAPTER CONTINUES OUR SCRUTINY OF LITERALISM by exploring the use of nonliteral stories in the Gospel of Matthew, where Jesus is compared to Moses. It is the author's way of portraying Jesus as someone greater than the greatest hero in all of Judaism. Additionally, we must grasp the liturgical nature of Judaism, something many have never considered. Matthew weaves his stories and parables around the Jewish liturgical seasons, and we do well to reflect upon this aspect of the writer's intent. But first, understanding the nature and limitations of words to convey meaning will help us appreciate just how difficult it is to describe the indescribable. We will learn that, when it comes to meaning, literalism embraces the lowest level of understanding possible.

An Imperfect Medium

Words are funny things. We can say or write something, fully intending one meaning, only to have it interpreted by others in an entirely different way. On the positive side of things, words are vehicles for conveying meaning. On the negative side, the meaning we intend is often distorted by the limitations of the vehicle itself. Language arises within a specific time, a specific circumstance, and a specific culture. Whatever is said or written encompasses the understandings, worldviews, presuppositions, biases, values, and knowledge of those living within that particular culture at that particular time. In essence, words are relative to the time and circumstances in which they are produced.

When someone experiences a powerful God-moment in their life, they seek to understand that experience and share it with others. It is a natural thing to do. After all, it was a genuine encounter that cannot be suppressed. The process goes something like this. First, there is the reality of the experience itself.

Second, we say, "Wow, what just happened?" as we process the experience internally. Third, we attempt to describe that experience and share it with others through the medium of language—spoken or written words. Finally, we often go on to create systems, processes, symbols, liturgies, and ceremonies to memorialize the experience.

My point is this: words are not the reality behind our experience, only the vehicle used to describe that experience. The words used to communicate truth are not the truth itself but merely the means by which truth is conveyed. Words, therefore, are limited by the culture, history, worldview, values, and knowledge of the generation living at the time the words were uttered. This presents significant problems when trying to communicate our personal God experiences, for the precarious vehicle transporting that reality is itself an imperfect medium of expression.

It is the kind of problem taught in basic communication courses whereby what is said by one person is interpreted by another only after that communication has passed through various problematic filters of personal perception. It can be quite upsetting to realize that words are not objective, for they always originate within a specific time and circumstance and are constantly being processed by others through the lens of their own perception.

Think of the way word meanings have morphed over time. What was meant by "God" centuries ago may not be our current understanding of the term. The word "gay" once meant being happy and now refers to being homosexual. When words of one culture are interpreted by people of another culture, the problem is further exacerbated. The medium of language is an imperfect and precarious channel for conveying the reality behind our God experiences.

A Limited Option

Unfortunately, language is one of the few options available to us in describing spiritual realities. The delicate nature of words cautions us in calling Scripture the objective, once-for-all Word of God. Words can never be objective truth, for they are merely the medium of truth—the communication vehicle utilized to convey our experiences and understanding to others. Like a kitchen faucet, the water lines in our house are only the delivery mechanism that allows water to flow. In like manner, words are not the truth or the experience itself but merely the conduit of delivery. How else are we to communicate? Pictures? Music? Language is the best option we possess, and it is a flawed and limited communication tool.

Words are like fingers pointing to something beyond themselves—symbols that help us interpret experiences and assign meaning and value to things. If words are not objective and are not themselves the truth, then Scripture cannot be objective truth, for it is nothing more than words fraught with all of the limitations inherent in language itself. As much as it pains some folks to hear, Scripture is relative—locked into the cultural realities of the world in which it was written.

If Scripture is literally God's words to humankind, then we have to question why God hates homosexuals, Egyptians, Amorites, and Amalekites and promotes their killing; why women are second-class citizens; why slavery is endorsed; and why other cultural biases exist within the sacred texts. Scripture cannot be the inerrant, objective, literal, once-for-all Word of God to humankind. No word can ever be that. To view Scripture as literalists do not only denies the very nature of words but also impairs the underlying truth the words are trying to communicate.

The constraints of language may be one reason why religious systems always claim divine authority for their sacred writings. Absent divine authority, the writings are subject to the limitations of words just like any other writing, and out the window goes all hope of an absolute, objective, literal, once-for-all Word of God. It is difficult to break the cycle of circular reasoning that prevails in the land of literalism. We have built theologies, systems, structures, processes, creeds, liturgies, ceremonies, and religious institutions and imbued them with divine status so they are insulated from challenge and scrutiny. This creates a fortress of orthodoxy that erroneously believes the words themselves are objective truth rather than an imperfect medium for communicating truth. This distinction is significant and often misunderstood. In the end, we wind up worshiping the Bible itself when it is merely the inadequate conduit for transporting the religious experience of those who have gone before us.

Metaphor and Mystery

So, here we are as humans, trying to describe an indescribable God. Does that strike you as awkward? It is the "catfish trying to describe what it means to be human" predicament we encountered in the previous chapter. Two problematic issues emerge for us. First, if God is truly a mystery that can never be fully comprehended, then no words will adequately suffice. Second, in our attempt to describe our experience of God, the only medium available to us is the words of language—an imperfect medium chock-full of problems. In reality, the mystery of God is far beyond us, and the means we employ in our feeble attempts to describe God are imperfect at best. Because of this, the only possible way to speak of God is through the use of metaphor.

Metaphor allows us to talk about God without the self-imposed limitations of literalism. It is the difference between saying "God is" and "God is like." Metaphor, in essence, is the language of religion—a way of talking about our God experiences without the trappings of literal nonsense. Thus, we say that God is like a rock. God is like a loving father. God is like a strong mighty tower. These aren't literal "God is" meanings but metaphors that allow us to discuss our God experiences in "God is like" language.

Because literalism interprets nonliteral biblical stories in a literal manner, the unintended consequence is that literalism embraces the lowest level of meaning possible. With only literal meaning available for understanding the richness of Scripture, all other interpretive options become null and void. Literalism is a narrow, limited approach to the biblical text that has no way of reaching the height or depth that metaphors provide.

Metaphors allow for a richness in our discussion of mystery—a richness that is broad, open, and deep instead of narrow, restrictive, and shallow. Literalism snatches the awe and wonder out of mystery. Jesus seemed to understand this very point, for his teaching methodology embraced the use of parables, a form of "God is like" messages. The metaphorical nature of his teaching allowed him to get his point across—deep truths that enabled hearers to move from the river bank to the deeper waters of mystery.

Somehow we have been brainwashed to believe that metaphors water down the message and that they are an inferior way of addressing religious things. This mentality is part of the problem, for God can never be spoken of with the absolute certainty we long for. It is impossible to speak of mystery this way, for certainty seeks to deny mystery, while the imperfect medium of words guarantees that it will never be found. Metaphors, symbols, images, and parables allow us to rise above the limited view of literalism. Going the metaphorical route isn't perfect either, for there is always the risk of misunderstanding. Yet Jesus used parables as his primary method of sharing spiritual truth. Apparently, the hope that some would get the deeper point is a better risk than speaking in a manner that does not allow profound truths to be expressed or explored.

Symbols as Pointers

Words are basically symbols that point to something beyond themselves—just like a musical score represents the sounds of a beautiful symphony. Communion is a symbolic religious act that reflects a truth beyond the literal eating of bread and drinking of wine. Baptism is a symbolic religious act that speaks of transformation rather than the literal elements of the act itself. Virtually every Christian church displays a cross—a symbol of our faith that conveys a truth beyond the symbol itself.

Symbols and metaphors are a good thing, for they become road signs along life's journey that constantly remind us to look beyond literalism—beyond the symbol itself to the greater truth to which it points. Our symbols, images, and metaphors may change as culture progresses. Over time, the image that works for one generation may not work for another. Since it is the meaning behind the metaphor that is all-important, the image itself can morph from age to age because it is merely the pointer. Our role is to maintain the enduring meaning, not the temporary image that transports it. We are after the substance of mystery—the reality itself, not the form, symbol, or pathway. To go back to our kitchen faucet metaphor, we want to drink the refreshing water, not admire the water lines running throughout the house. In other words, we don't want our view of the beautiful sunset to be obstructed by the fingers pointing to it. Sometimes we confuse the symbol for the substance, the form for the reality, and that is the danger of literalism.

Symbols and metaphors become important avenues for embracing the core teachings of the Christian faith. They have the power to express profound meaning. They become arm floaties that allow us to enter the deep waters of mystery without downing. In one sense, all of life is a metaphor. Beautiful sunsets become more than a photo opportunity; they become powerful reminders of the handiwork of God. When appreciating a Kandinsky masterpiece, we see meaning beyond the canvas itself. We can be moved to tears while listening to a song that raptures our soul far beyond the notes on a sheet of music. The words of a poet can usher us into a magical world of thought.

Metaphors, images, and symbols have the power to move us, shape us, and transform us. Their transformational nature lies not in the symbol itself but in the substance to which they point. Our goal isn't to define God but to experience God. In others words, God is not a noun that we spend our life trying to define; rather, God is a verb—a presence we are privileged to experience. It is the tension between transcendence and immanence. While God is far beyond our ability to adequately define and describe (the noun part), we nonetheless experience God in everyday life (the verb part).

Historical-Metaphorical Approach

The powerful use of metaphor has led some to approach Scripture from a historical and metaphorical perspective that welcomes the deep meanings of Scripture without stumbling over the intellectual road blocks of literalism. Many interpret "historical" to mean "factual." In other words, for something to be historical, it must have really happened, an event that could have easily been recorded had digital cameras existed at the time. For these folks, if it isn't factual, it cannot be historical, and if it isn't historical, it cannot be true.

Given this confusion, "contextual" may be a better understanding of the word "historical." A historical approach simply means that we examine Scripture in light of its historical setting and its cultural context, not that it is factual or literal. The approach recognizes that words and meanings are intricately linked to a specific time, circumstance, and setting—relative to the context in which the words are spoken or written. Understanding this prevents us from reading twenty-first-century meanings back into the ancient text—a kind of revisionist history or theology. Words are relative to time and space and are always linked to a context. Taken out of their historical context, they become pretexts for advancing prejudiced and revisionist agendas.

The prophets, for instance, are thought of as predictors of the future who utter prophecies about Jesus centuries before he appeared on the scene. But this is a revisionist perspective. The prophets weren't fortune tellers who predicted the future; rather, the Gospel writers were trying to link their powerful experience of Jesus with the Scriptures of their faith. The prophets weren't looking forward; rather, the New Testament writers were looking backward. They interpreted Jesus while scouring the Jewish Scriptures for ways to connect him with their religious heritage. They discovered verses and sections that they could apply to Jesus, and they wrapped him in those Scriptures.

The prophets largely wrote from the sixth to eighth centuries BCE, when they experienced conquest, captivity, danger, and other dilemmas arising within their own historical context. They weren't writing for first-century or twenty-first-century Christians but for the people of their own time and in the historical context of their own day. The language of Scripture isn't absolute but relative—always related to a specific time and place in history.

The other side of this interpretive coin is the metaphorical aspect, which moves readers beyond the stories themselves to the meaning behind them. In other words, it is the meaning that we are after, the substance to which the metaphors are pointing and not the factuality of the story. We don't interpret the creation story literally, for that leads to foolishness. Instead, we recognize a meaning beyond the details of the story itself. Israel's flight from Egypt may not be a literal, factual account but a story about freedom and how one moves from bondage to the Promised Land. The tower of Babel, the Genesis flood, and Jonah being swallowed by a large fish are other nonliteral examples. Profound meanings lie beneath the surface of literalism.

Moving from the confines of literalism to the freedom of metaphor can be frightening, for we are required to let go of the security literalism provides. That security, however, is a false certainty that keeps us near the safety of the shore. Metaphors, on the other hand, nudge us into deeper waters where we more fully experience the mystery of God. It is a move from symbol to substance, from form to reality, from factuality to meaning, and from shadow to Shadow-maker.

Religious Boxes

Literalism promotes rigid dogma, and for all the certainty it claims to possess, it produces nothing but division within the religious arena. Muslims, Jews, Mormons, Christians, Buddhists, and other religious groups believe their understanding of God is the correct one. In fact, they are so sure of it that many follow in blind obedience, for no one dedicates themselves to chasing after what they believe to be false. We are so certain that our way of seeing things is correct that we become dogmatic about it, oftentimes hateful and mean-spirited. With so many diverse religious perspectives, maybe we should be more gracious and less dogmatic. Otherwise, we may wind up limiting God and restricting the winds of the Spirit.

I find it interesting that an all-knowing, all-powerful God can't seem to create one set of guidelines that can be universally agreed upon as the divine instruction manual. Everyone has their own set of sacred teachings. Trying to discern which one is God's actual guidebook is much harder than it should be. But as long as you live within the preferred religious box you call home, all is well. Christians have their own jargon, beliefs, and practices, and within the confines of the Christian box, all is well. The same could be said about every other religious box. Jesus, however, spoke of the kingdom of God—that transcendent kingdom that rises above all boxes. How do we relate to something that cannot be confined to one's preferred religious box?

It is easy to look at other religious boxes as inferior to our own. Various religions teach contradictory things, and the law of noncontradiction assures us that they can't all be true. The Christian box is my preference, largely because I grew up in that tradition and feel very comfortable with it, and it best expresses my approach to God. I am fully aware, however, that all religious boxes, whether Christian or otherwise, are human creations—systems designed to connect us with a divine reality beyond ourselves. Religious boxes attempt to point us toward the great mystery of God, for God cannot be confined to, or defined by, one particular system. God is transcendent—beyond all boxes and religious systems. We may prefer certain pointers over others, largely influenced by what region of the world we grew up in, but the mystery of God is not confined within the walls of any one religious box. God is not a Christian, a Jew, a Muslim, Buddhist, Hindu, or any other religion. Rather, God is that which the great religions are pointing to.

Loose Change

The principle of loose change helps me navigate the mystery of God amid the many symbols pointing to God. If I hold a handful of coins in the palm of my hand, I can make a fist so tight that the coins are pressed on all sides with no room to wiggle and jingle. It is when I relax my grip that I can feel the coins moving about. Loose change, held loosely, creates the freedom for wiggling and jingling. In like manner, when the grip of our preferred religious box is held tightly, our understanding and experience of God are unable to move about freely. When God is thought of as mystery and spoken of in metaphors, we begin to see that the kingdom is no longer limited to any one religious box but instead transcends all boxes. Without the language of metaphor, our God is too small.

Mysticism seems to be the uniting language that rises above the vocabularies of individual religious boxes. You can read the Buddhist, Jewish, Muslim, and Christian mystics, and they all read just like one another. They have reached the point of metaphor and mystery—a point where words seem to fall apart, and a unifying theme among all religions is discovered. The loose change principle allows the wind of God to blow wherever and whenever it desires.

Though we live in the box labeled "Christian," we understand that the kingdom of God is not restricted to one box, for God is in the box, outside the box, through the box, under the box, on top of the box, beside the box, around the box, and beyond the box. We give God room to wiggle and jingle. I call that maturity. I am not implying that all religions are the same, for they often teach contradictory ideas. I am saying that the more loosely we hold the coins in our hands, the more room God has to surprise us. The loose change principle helps us focus on the substance behind the symbol, whereas literalism is the clenched fist preventing the jingling of God.

The Moses Connection

Our attention now turns from words and meanings to the Gospel of Matthew, where we see how stories are utilized in nonliteral ways for the specific purpose of portraying Jesus as one who is greater than Moses. They are not the recounting of historical, factual incidents but Jesus stories told through the lens of Moses, Israel's greatest hero. We begin with the birth of Jesus.[5]

The Birth of Jesus

The Gospel birth narratives are found only in Luke and Matthew. During the Christmas season, churches blend both of these narratives into one. Luke has no wise men traveling from afar as in Matthew, and instead, shepherds come to see the baby lying in a manger after an angel pronounces the Savior's birth and a heavenly host sings praises to God.

Matthew's account contains none of this and instead relays Joseph's dream about staying with Mary even though she is pregnant, describes the bright star leading Magi to the Christ-child and a run-in with King Herod, and depicts Joseph's flight to Egypt in avoidance of Herod's slaughter of innocent Bethlehem babies. Nothing is said of a manger, no great pronouncement by angels, and no heavenly host sings praises to God. When we see the Magi coming to the manger during church Christmas pageants with children all decked out in Middle Eastern attire, we are witnessing how the church takes two separate birth accounts and blends them into one preferred version.

Matthew's rendition mimics a familiar story already seen in the birth of Moses. Matthew is not writing a historical, literal account but using a well-known story from the past as the parallel foundation for relaying a story in the present—one that every Jew would readily recognize and understand. It was his way of communicating that Jesus is greater than Moses.

If we don't recognize the birth narrative as a Moses story, we are left wandering in the land of literalism without ever grasping its meaning. There is no star that parks itself directly over a specific house. That is impossible. Apparently this shining star takes a wrong turn and brings the Magi to the king's palace instead of Joseph and Mary's house. This malfunction allows the author to introduce a conversation with King Herod about who the baby is and where he might be found. Herod wants the Magi to report back to him as spies for the sole purpose of slaughtering the newborn Jewish king. Of course, Jesus miraculously escapes the king's wicked intentions. The details of this story just don't add up, but then again, making literal sense isn't Matthew's goal. He is conveying a Moses story—his way of portraying Jesus as one who is greater than Moses.

In the book of Exodus, every male baby born to Hebrew slaves was to be killed, according to the pharaoh's command. The Hebrews were multiplying far too quickly for the comfort of those around them and were perceived as a burgeoning threat to the Egyptians. To "thin the herd," every newborn male baby would be killed, while female babies could live.

In the case of Moses, his mother was able to hide him for three months, but there came a time when the risk was too great and concealing him was no longer an option. She placed Moses in a wicker basket covered with pitch and floated him along the bank of the Nile River, where the pharaoh's daughter miraculously rescued him, welcomed him into the royal household, and raised him with the finest of all things Egyptian. Like Jesus, Moses was spared from the evil intentions of a wicked king trying to circumvent God's chosen deliverer. The early chapters of Matthew (1–2) introduce Moses into the Jesus narrative. Gentiles, of course, would not have recognized this, since they were unfamiliar with Jewish Scripture, tradition, practices, and liturgy. Instead, they literalized the account rather than seeing it as a nonliteral comparison to the greatest of Israel's leaders.

The Baptism of Jesus

The comparison to Moses continues in Matthew chapter 3 with the baptism of Jesus in the Jordan River. Water is an important symbolic element in Scripture. Moses parts the waters of the Red Sea and also brings forth water from a desert rock. Joshua splits the waters of the Jordan River, as does Elijah and Elisha, and even Jesus turns water into wine. Power over water becomes the literary means of revealing God's power and presence, and even in Jesus's baptism, we see a comparison to Moses. Realizing the symbolic nature of water, Matthew places Jesus at the Jordan River, for it advances his literary cause.

Matthew's Jewish audience would have easily recognized the presence of God so evident in the life of Moses. That same presence was also upon Joshua, who became the chosen leader after Moses's death. As the Israelite army readies itself to invade Canaan and attack Jericho, Joshua commands that the priests carry the Ark of the Covenant into the Jordan River, an obstacle that stands between them and their promised bounty. As soon as the priests step into the river, its waters stop flowing, and, just like Moses's Red Sea episode, Joshua's invading army is able to cross on dry ground. The presence of God upon Moses is also present in the life of Joshua.

Once Moses and Joshua pass from the scene, the prophets emerge with new heroes like Elijah and Elisha, the twin towers of prophetic wisdom in the Old Testament. Near the end of his life, Elijah desires to spend time alone with God, and Elisha, his protégé, pleads to accompany him. As they journey to their destination, the Jordan River stands in their way. How are they to cross? That's easy—Elijah simply takes off his mantle, folds it together, and strikes the Jordan River with it. Voilà, the waters part so he and Elisha can cross on dry ground.

As Elijah is whisked into the heavens courtesy of a fiery chariot and a blustery whirlwind, his mantle falls to the ground. Elisha quickly drapes the mantle over his shoulders and begins to head back home as the new prophet of God. The mantle was a sign that he had inherited a double portion of Elijah's spirit. He still has to cross the Jordan River on his return, but he would simply do what Elijah had done earlier. As he strikes the water with his inherited mantle, the waters part so he can cross on dry land.

Do you see what is going on here? This is Jewish storytelling—their way of saying that the same God seen in Moses is also seen in Joshua, and the same God seen in Moses and Joshua is the same God seen in Elijah and Elisha. All of them have power over water. Matthew now portrays Jesus as having the same power of God upon him—a power and presence greater than Moses. This was astounding for Jews, for how could anyone be greater than Moses, the greatest of all their heroes?

Jesus isn't simply another prophet who comes and goes with the ability to part bodies of water like others before him. Jesus displays God's power and presence in dramatic fashion by parting the heavens. The creation stories of the Torah maintain that God created a firmament to separate the heavens above from the waters below, and at Jesus's baptism, the heavens split open, the Spirit of God descends like a dove, and a voice from heaven declares, "This is my Son, the Beloved, with whom I am well pleased" (Matt. 3:17, NRSV). Moses could open up Earthly waters, but Jesus can open up the heavenly waters.

Jesus and the Wilderness

Matthew connects Jesus to Moses through birth and baptism, but the parallels don't stop there, for in Matthew chapter 4, Jesus also spends time in the wilderness, just like Moses. Moses spent forty years in the desert wilderness, while

Jesus only spends forty days. In other words, Jesus can do in forty days what it took Moses forty years to accomplish. If this is true, then Jesus must be greater than Moses.

Even the temptations Jesus experienced are intricately linked to specific episodes in Moses's wilderness journey. Though Mark, the earliest Gospel to be written, speaks of Jesus being tempted in the wilderness, it does not go into detail about the nature of those temptations. We learn of these temptations for the first time in Matthew, written some fifty to sixty years after Jesus had died.

The first temptation deals with food. Experiencing hunger from the wilderness fast, Jesus is asked to turn stones into bread. Why not? If you are hungry and have such power, just do it. Jesus responds by noting that humans do not live by bread alone. Jesus is sustained by his purpose and his communion with God. Moses also encounters a food issue in his wilderness journey. The traveling horde of Hebrews are hungry and think about returning to Egypt. Better to be in bondage with food than free and starving. Through the prayer of Moses, manna is miraculously provided for the famished nation. Both Moses and Jesus encounter a food issue.

The second temptation deals with putting God to the test as Jesus is asked to throw himself off the pinnacle of the temple. Surely God will send angels to protect him. Just jump. Jesus overcomes this temptation by noting that it is not proper to test the Lord God. Moses experiences a similar test of faith at Meribah as the Israelites lack water to drink. He is instructed to speak to the rock and water will come forth. Instead, Moses strikes the rock twice with his staff, and while water begins to flow and the Israelites quench their thirst, Moses is prevented from entering the Promised Land as punishment for his disobedience. He will die atop Mt. Nebo, where he can only gaze at Israel's inheritance, not enter into it. Joshua, Moses's successor, would lead them the rest of the way.

The third wilderness temptation involves the worship of God alone. After taking Jesus to the highest mountain so he could view all the kingdoms of the world, the devil offers these dynasties to Jesus if he will bow down and worship him. Obviously, this isn't literal, for you can't see all the kingdoms of the world from a mountain, and you can't go from the pinnacle of the temple to a mountain top in a fleeting second. Jesus overcomes this temptation by noting that only God is to be worshiped.

Moses is also led up a mountain, Mt. Sinai, where he would secure the Ten Commandments. He is gone so long that the nation begins to panic. Searching for security during Moses's prolonged absence, they craft a golden calf to worship.

Seeing this debacle unfold, Moses smashes the tablets of stone in a fit of rage and eventually hikes back up the mountain to procure another set. Would the Israelites, led by Moses, worship God alone, or would they bow before a golden calf forged by human hands? Both Jesus and Moses spend time in the wilderness, but Jesus conquers his testing in forty days, not forty years. The three temptations of Jesus parallel three key incidents in the life of Moses: lacking food, testing God, and worshiping God alone.

Jesus and the Law

Thus far, the comparison with Moses involves the birth of Jesus, the baptism of Jesus, and the wilderness experience. The final parallel for consideration involves ascending a mountain and dispensing the Law. Both Moses and Jesus have something to say on this subject.

Moses, of course, treks up Mt. Sinai, where he receives the Ten Commandments, whereas Matthew places Jesus on a mountain to deliver the Sermon on the Mount (Matt. 5–7). Jesus's mountain journey is not for the purpose of receiving a new Torah but of dispensing a new interpretation of the Law. We find him saying, "You have heard that it was said . . . but I say unto you . . ." It is his way of driving the Law down into the very heart of human motivation instead of focusing on the external act alone. Murder is the deed itself, but according to Jesus, it arises from an internal heart problem that must first be addressed. Adultery, another external deed, is an outgrowth of inner issues within the heart. In other words, unless one deals with the internal motivation of the act itself, simply refraining from the deed doesn't go far enough. From one mountain, Moses gave us the Law, which focused on prohibited external deeds. From another mountain, Jesus gave us a new interpretation of the Law that moves beyond the deed to the level of internal motivation.

When the Gospel of Matthew was written, Moses had been dead for more than fourteen hundred years, and Elijah had been dead for eight hundred years. Much time had passed before Jesus arrived on the scene as one who possessed both the power and the presence of God in ways that surpassed even the greatest heroes of Israel's past. These aren't literal accounts but carefully crafted sacred stories meant to accomplish the author's purpose. Jesus was the new Moses, different and better, who was connected to their cherished Jewish Scriptures.

Other Images

Nonliteral images and stories abound throughout the Gospels. For instance, Matthew, Mark, and Luke all contain the transfiguration story. Taking Peter,

James, and John up the mountain with him, Jesus is transfigured in front of them. By transfiguration, we mean that Jesus's face shone like the sun, and his garments became white as snow while he was talking with Moses and Elijah. Literalists believe that Jesus actually began to glow just like the Bible says and that he was literally carrying on a conversation with two dead people.

The transfiguration story, however, is meant to convey a profound truth, not a literal one. By the time Matthew wrote his message, the esteemed temple in Jerusalem had been destroyed by the Romans. The temple was the one place upon this Earth where the presence of God was thought to dwell. Jesus is seen as the new temple—the place where the God of heaven is present among the people of Earth. Paul reflects a similar perspective when he states that Jesus "is the image of the invisible God" (Col. 1:15, NRSV). In the transfiguration event, Moses and Elijah represent the Law and the Prophets. Jesus wasn't literally speaking with two dead people; instead, the Gospel writers are portraying Jesus in a certain light. He is viewed as surpassing Israel's greatest figures who represent the Law and the Prophets, the very theme presented to us in the Gospel of Matthew. Jesus is the new temple, the place where the presence of God intersects with the people of Earth.

The miraculous feeding of five thousand people (Matt. 14) with a measly five loaves of bread and two small fish isn't a literal event. Instead, it is a parallel story based upon Moses providing manna to hungry Israelites in the desert. Matthew is retelling a Moses story that Jews would easily recognize, except he enriches it and attributes the provision of food to Jesus. The Jews didn't debate the literalness of the story, for they knew the author was attributing Moses qualities to Jesus.

The ascension of Jesus into the heavens was not a miraculous take-off into outer space but an Elijah story retold with Jesus as the centerpiece. As Elijah ascends into the heavens, he sends a double portion of his spirit upon Elisha, his protégé. When Jesus ascends into the heavens, however, he releases the mighty power of God's Spirit upon the community of faith—a power much greater than what Elijah sent. Instead of literalism, these stories reveal an alternative way of viewing the sacred text.

The crucifixion story in the Gospel of Mark is written with the Passover in mind, as Jesus is likened to the Paschal lamb. Mark is a shorter account than Matthew, and his liturgical writing carries Jewish Christians from Rosh Hashanah (the Jewish New Year) to the Passover. The crucifixion is the culminating event in Mark's story. Matthew expands the Gospel of Mark because he wants to cover the entire liturgical year, not just a portion of it like Mark. Fascinating! We never considered that the Gospels contain parallel Old Testament stories written for liturgical purposes. Their relationship to the Jewish calendar didn't enter our minds, for we were reading Scripture through Gentile eyes.

Seeing Through Jewish Eyes

The final area we must address is the liturgical nature of Judaism and how Matthew weaves his Gospel stories around the Jewish calendar. Our eyes have been programmed to read the Bible from a literal perspective. We assume that everything recorded is a literal account of an actual event. This is our conditioned approach, the effect of not seeing with Jewish eyes. We confuse literal interpretation with Jewish sacred storytelling. We must take into account the context and motivation of the biblical writers instead of perpetuating literal misunderstandings from one generation to the next. Since we are not Jews living in the first century, we fail to realize that Christianity was birthed in the synagogue and that Jesus was being interpreted through their familiar Jewish Scriptures.

Jewish Liturgy

Many are unfamiliar with the liturgical nature of Judaism. For some reason, we think Jesus attended a church just like the one we attend. But that isn't the case at all. Jesus knew nothing of our religious denominations and modern-day forms of worship.

Jesus grew up in Judaism, with all of its history, tradition, and liturgy. He was familiar with synagogue life, heard the Scriptures being read, and participated in the liturgy and festivals of Judaism. If Christianity grew up in the synagogue during its early years, and if the New Testament writings were created while Christianity was still intricately linked to Judaism, then the Bible is most certainly influenced by Jewish liturgical forms. Yet most Christians know very little about this.

Jewish worship is liturgical worship. In the beginning, the public reading of Jewish Scripture occurred in synagogues, and an explanation of the reading was later added. After the temple was destroyed, prayer became a part of the worship itinerary, since sacrifices could no longer be offered. Synagogues helped dispersed Jews maintain a connection to their Jewish identity. Torah readings are scheduled around a religious calendar, as are Jewish festivals and events that remember the past, honor the Torah, and recognize God's presence. Evangelicals and fundamentalists know very little about liturgical forms of worship, for it isn't a part of their religious wheelhouse. Mainline denominations often follow a liturgical calendar, but it is the Catholics and Eastern Orthodox believers who excel in this regard.

The Jewish Calendar

Christianity operates on the Gregorian calendar built around the position of the sun—a solar calendar. Muslims build their religious calendar around the position of the moon—a lunar calendar. The Jewish religious calendar takes into consideration the position of the sun and the moon in its liturgical practices—a lunisolar calendar. The choice of calendar is merely the reference point from which certain festivals and celebrations routinely occur in the practice of a specific religion.

For Jews, the time-honored Sabbath is celebrated weekly as a day of rest. It begins Friday evening and lasts until Saturday evening. As a distinguishing practice within Judaism, it is built upon the creation story, wherein God rested on the seventh day of the week. Jesus was very familiar with this aspect of Jewish life and was often criticized for doing good deeds on the Sabbath when he should have been resting. I once pastored in a state where it was illegal to sell liquor on Sunday. As the state reconsidered its blue law, a devout Christian woman expressed her opinion in the local newspaper that selling liquor on Sunday violated the Sabbath. This, of course, reveals a fundamental misunderstanding many Christians have regarding the Sabbath—thinking it is Sunday.

One of the great religious events in Judaism is the eight-day Passover celebration during which Jews commemorate their freedom from Egyptian bondage. Every aspect of the Passover meal symbolizes some memory of the great escape. For instance, unleavened bread is eaten to remind them of their hasty departure from Egypt, for there was no time for bread to rise. Bitter herbs are also consumed as a reminder of the bitterness of slavery. Jesus celebrated the Passover like other Jews of his day.

Following Passover comes another great festival called Shavuot, also known as the Feast of Weeks in English, or Pentecost in Ancient Greece. Originally a harvest festival celebrated at the end of the barley harvest and the beginning of the wheat season, it comes fifty weeks after Passover and now also celebrates the giving of the Torah to the Jewish people. This was a significant holiday in Jewish religious life and was celebrated with a twenty-four-hour liturgy consisting of eight segments of three hours each. Psalm 119, the longest Psalm in the Bible (176 verses), was written for this celebration. The Psalm exalts the laws of God and is a hymn to the magnificence of the Torah. Did it ever occur to you that Psalm 119 could have been written for use in celebration of the Shavuot liturgy?

Matthew's Sermon on the Mount was also designed for the Shavuot liturgy. In essence, it expands upon the blessedness of Psalm 119 by including eight blessings in the opening section of the sermon, the rest of which consists of a commentary on each of these blessed beatitudes. The author works backward so that the very first commentary discusses the eighth beatitude, the second commentary discusses the seventh beatitude, and so forth. My point is that Matthew's Sermon on the Mount is fashioned after Psalm 119. It is designed to lead worshippers in celebration of the festival of Shavuot. It is Matthew's way of incorporating Jesus into the Jewish liturgical season.

The sermon isn't a literal account of a literal speech given upon a literal mountain. It is a carefully crafted story devised for liturgical purposes. Did Jesus ever speak from a mountain? Probably so. Did Jesus ever touch upon some of the topics addressed in the Sermon on the Mount? Probably so. Did Jesus stand on a mountain and deliver a speech that mimics Psalm 119 for liturgical purposes with eight beatitudes followed by eight commentaries working in backward fashion? Probably not. Gentiles would have no clue of Matthew's liturgical end. Instead, everything is interpreted literally, and the meaning and purpose of the text are undermined.

Another important festival celebrated by Jews is Sukkot, also known as the Feast of Tabernacles or Booths. This eight-day harvest festival gives thanks to God for the fruit of the land. It recalls God's provision when Israel wandered in the desert and during harvest season when they lived in temporary huts among the fruit and vegetables they were gathering. In celebration, booths made of branches are erected in honor of God's past provision and present blessing upon the harvest.

Yom Kippur, otherwise known as the Day of Atonement, comes at the end of ten days of repentance that begin with the Jewish New Year—Rosh Hashanah. Yom Kippur is a significant time in the Jewish religious year, as Jews make amends for their sins and seek reconciliation with God.

The stories in Matthew are designed to address the many liturgical needs of the Jewish calendar. The crucifixion is told with the Passover in mind, as Jesus is likened to the Paschal lamb. The story of John the Baptist is told against the backdrop of Rosh Hashanah, the Jewish New Year. Stories of cleansing are told in light of Yom Kippur, while the parables of the sower, the wheat and tares, and the mustard seed are told in relation to the eight-day harvest celebration of Sukkot. The transfiguration story is told against the backdrop of a destroyed Jewish temple. Unless we view Scripture with Jewish eyes, we miss the liturgical nature of Judaism.

Strains of Judaism

When Jesus walked this Earth during the first century, various expressions of Judaism existed, some of which are even mentioned in the Bible. One perspective was that of the Pharisees, who began the rabbinic tradition we recognize today. We don't read of rabbis in the Old Testament—only priests and prophets. Paul self-identified as a Pharisee, and Rabbi Hillel was an early rabbi within the Pharisaical wing of Judaism. Pharisees emphasized the purity code of the Old Testament. They maligned Jesus for eating grain on the Sabbath, healing on the Sabbath, and eating with sinners deemed to be unclean. They were professional interpreters of the Torah, and the New Testament portrays them as focused upon external issues rather than internal motivations of the heart.

The Sadducees were also contemporaries of Jesus. While we don't know as much about them as we do the Pharisees, they appear to be upper-class Jews—elites who were more accepting of Roman life and culture. As Hellenized Jews, they displayed greater acceptance of Greek influence and less concern with issues of purity. They were smaller in number than the Pharisees and did not believe in the afterlife.

The Essenes represent another voice within New Testament Judaism. Though they are never mentioned in the Bible, we learn of them through the Dead Sea Scrolls, discovered in 1947 at Qumran on the northwest shore of the Dead Sea. The Essenes were separatists who protested a religious environment they believed had become contaminated. In their eyes, the elected high priest obtained his position under false pretenses, which invalidated the entire temple practice. So, they began their own movement in protest of the corruption they saw within Judaism. They created their own religious calendar and their own way of observing the Torah. They were a disciplined people with strict religious values who expectantly looked for God's intervention in human history.

Zealots would become the final group within Judaism. Their cause is to free the Holy Land from Roman occupation. Simon, one of Jesus's disciples, was a Zealot. To many Jews, the Zealots were freedom fighters. To the Romans, they were nothing but terrorists. They engaged in guerilla warfare and raided Roman patrols when the numbers were in their favor. Eventually, the Romans became fed up with these annoying and costly disruptions and put an end to them by destroying the Jewish temple in 70 CE.

Even today, we see various strains within Judaism, such as Orthodox, Conservative, and Reformed perspectives. Despite these differing viewpoints, the Jews of Jesus's day held similar core beliefs. They believed in one God, the covenant God made with the people of Israel, and the Torah. They differed in their approach to the Torah's holiness code, as some were stricter than others. The temple was held in high esteem as the center of Jewish religious life—the place where God's presence was most prescient upon Earth.

Synagogues became a place where neighborhood Jews gathered together for the public reading of the Torah. It was the local gathering spot for teaching, reading the Scriptures, and engaging in the liturgies of the Jewish religious calendar. It was the place where the first followers of Jesus began to share their understanding of Jesus and connect him to their Scriptures. In a sense, the early Jesus Movement becomes an additional element within first-century Judaism, while the synagogue serves as an incubator for Christianity. Around 88 CE, the Jesus Movement would separate from the synagogue and follow its own path, completing the separation around 150 CE. This break from the synagogue is an important element in the background of John's Gospel, written at a time when the Johannine community was being ostracized for their understanding and teaching of Jesus.

I grew up in a nonliturgical church where Christmas and Easter were the only two events marking our religious calendar. Though our Sunday services had a routine ebb and flow to them, we didn't adhere to a lectionary like mainline denominations, and we lacked any sense of formality and large-picture perspective of a yearly cycle of worship. A religious calendar to follow? What in the world was that, and how restrictive that would have been to our minds, for we proudly followed the Spirit's leading, not some dry, boring religious ritual. It never occurred to us that the worship of our birthmother, Judaism, was highly liturgical, or that Jesus himself followed a religious calendar. Besides, we were living under the new covenant, not the old Jewish ways of doing business!

But the liturgical nature of Judaism and the fact that it functioned from a yearly religious calendar with various seasons, celebrations, and festivities are actually helpful to us. Every Jew participated in these religious activities, and the Gospel of Matthew, thought to be the most Jewish of the Gospels, is constructed with this liturgical calendar in mind.

Understanding how the early Jesus Movement processed their encounter with Jesus helps us view Scripture through Jewish eyes. Their interpretation of him occurred within the cultural mindset of the day. In Jesus, they saw and experienced a God-presence like no other, and it transformed their thinking and their behavior. They were once blind but now saw the kingdom with a new set of eyes. They processed their experience through the synagogue, the Scriptures, and the liturgical practices so familiar to them. Jesus wasn't just another religious fanatic spouting off pious platitudes. To the contrary; they saw the presence of God in him, and his teaching forever changed them from the inside out. How did they make sense of their God encounter as experienced in Jesus? They processed it from within Judaism—what they knew and what was familiar to them.

They knew of Moses, the greatest hero in Jewish history, so Matthew interprets the greatness of Jesus through the shadow of Moses. You think Moses was great, wait till you hear about Jesus! You think Elijah was glorious, wait till you hear about Jesus! They portrayed Jesus in light of their own history and liturgy. To them, Jesus wasn't initiating a new religion called Christianity; rather, he was a new prophet within Judaism, more excellent than Moses and Elijah.

Chapter Summary

Expanding upon the dangers of literalism, this chapter examined the role of words and meaning, explored Matthew's use of sacred storytelling to convey a message beyond literalism, and described the liturgical nature of Judaism as a backdrop to the Gospel stories.

Human language is made up of words that help us communicate with one another—an imperfect vehicle for transporting meaning and value. Words are never the truth but only the medium through which truth flows. No word can be an objective, once-for-all-time word of God, for all words are relative—that is, related to the specific context and time in which they are uttered. The only way we dare attempt to describe an indescribable God is through the use of metaphors, which provide a depth and richness that literalism cannot touch. In fact, literalism embraces the lowest level of meaning because it splashes about in the shallows of religious expression without entering deep waters.

The Gospel of Matthew, we discovered, uses sacred storytelling to compare Jesus with Moses. By interpreting the words literally, we miss this point altogether. Comparing Jesus's birth, baptism, wilderness journey, and interpretation of the Law to Moses, we realize that Matthew doesn't intend the stories to be taken literally.

To show how Matthew carefully crafted his writing to meet the needs of the various celebrations and festivals, the liturgical nature of Judaism was touched upon. Just as Psalm 119 was written with Shavuot in mind, so Matthew writes the Sermon on the Mount in similar fashion. His stories weave in and out of the various liturgical seasons. Parables of the sower and the mustard seed, for instance, are told in relation to the eight-day harvest celebration of Sukkot. The crucifixion is told with Passover in mind as Jesus symbolizes the Paschal lamb.

There is more to the sacred text than meets the eye, and the nature of words, Matthew's nonliteral comparison stories, and his liturgical purpose help us understand just how shallow a literal approach to Scripture can be. We swim in deeper waters when we speak of God in metaphors and view Scripture through Jewish eyes. One of the ways Christianity loses credibility in the modern world is its insistence that Scripture is the literal, inerrant, authoritative, once-for-all Word of God. As we have seen, that belief no longer holds sway. What then is the value of Scripture? That is the subject of our next chapter.

7

WHAT VALUE IS SCRIPTURE?
· · · · · · · ·

THE PREVIOUS CHAPTERS MAY DISTURB THOSE WHO view Scripture as the literal, inerrant, once-for-all words of God to humankind. From their vantage point, everything in the Bible is absolutely true and absolutely factual, and if you were a really good Christian, you would view the Bible as they do. To question such a perspective is to reveal oneself as a heretic—an enemy of God who undermines the faith. We are quickly wrapped up, packaged, and labeled as part of the problem with modern society and its erosion into godless decay. There is little civil conversation—only judgment and derision. This is merely a "my way or the highway" mentality all dressed up in religious attire.

There are others, however, who will read the previous chapters and say, "It's about time someone addressed the elephant in the room." Their hearts will be lifted and their faith will be strengthened when they realize one can believe in God, follow God, love God, and live for God without being asked to believe the unbelievable. They are tired of disengaging their brain and casting aside good old-fashioned common sense. For them, the contents of this book will ring true, and for every individual who is offended, ten others will be inspired to leave religion and discover a faith worth believing. As it turns out, for one group I am the devil, and for the other, a godsend.

I understand how hard it can be to watch cherished beliefs fall by the wayside. I struggled with it myself, as most thinking Christians do at some point in their lives. As I took stock of what literalism offered, I realized I had to be honest with myself, for the problems of literalism far outweigh its benefits. Literalism offered a forever finalized communication from a God who had once spoken in the past instead of a God that was still communicating in the present.

Literalism gave me a God who was prejudiced in all sorts of unacceptable ways and who enjoyed the killing and punishment of others. A God like that deserves neither respect nor worship. Literalism offered an interpretive approach to Scripture that leads to nonsense and steers us outside the bounds of modern knowledge. Literalism asked me to believe the unbelievable and call it faith. I am not very good at math, but there came a time in my life when even I realized things just didn't add up. Though I loved God with all my heart, I sensed there had to be a better way—an honest way forward filled with integrity.

How does one progress in their faith without a divine source from which to operate? If God didn't write the Bible, then what value does it hold for Christians? Where do you turn when the very foundation upon which you stand is crumbling beneath your feet? When confronted with such challenges, many simply surrender their faith altogether, embarrassed for having been so gullible. Others despair, "If the Bible isn't literally true, then it can't be true at all," and they question God's very existence. But whether or not God is real isn't dependent upon one's approach to the Bible. Though I am sensitive to their predicament, these folks have painted themselves into a corner, resulting in unfortunate, unjustified, and unnecessary conclusions. While no one likes to be duped, there is a better way of looking at things, and that is the focus of this book.

An Essential Decision

We attach value to things on a daily basis—everyday items, like what food to purchase at the grocery store, to big things, like which religion to follow, if any. These values guide our conduct and our understanding of life and God. We readily cast aside that which is deemed worthless and hold dear to that which we value. Is Scripture worth treasuring? Does it hold value for modern humans? If so, how and why, and if not, should we simply discard it?

Our approach to Scripture is like boarding a train—an illustration I have previously used because it captures the idea that decisions lead to consequences. Board the wrong train, and you arrive at the wrong destination. Our choice of train determines our interpretive destination. How we choose to view Scripture is absolutely foundational—an essential, all-important decision that must be considered carefully and wisely. For all of the reasons mentioned in the previous chapters, I can no longer ride the rails of literalism with integrity, for it lacks value for me and conflicts with common sense, scientific data, Jewish sacred storytelling, and reality as we know it. There is a difference between the value of Scripture itself and the value of a specific approach to Scripture. These are two very different things, and this may well be the heart of the problem. Though I highly prize Scripture, I discard literalism as a meritless approach to its contents.

The Heart of the Problem

Many see literalists themselves as the heart of the problem, but this is merely an attempt at demonization. I lived in the land of literalism for most of my life and found my colleagues to be devout individuals with a heart for God. Personally attacking literal train riders has no place in the Christian faith, for it defies the biblical mandate to love others. By disparaging those who disagree with us, we have vacated the principle of love in exchange for a tribal mentality—like two neighbors who can't get along, each acting in the same hateful ways but approaching things from their own side of the fence. Distinguishing between the value of people and the value of their argument is difficult for people to grasp, let alone do, for demonizing others is one way we attempt to justify the rightness of our cause.

We are to love people, even those who march to the beat of their own drum, see the world through multicolored spectacles, and think and live in ways that we wouldn't dare. And by people, I mean all people, regardless of gender, race, ethnicity, sexual orientation, age, religious belief, political persuasion, etc. When I speak of literalists, I am not disparaging them personally as individuals, for I know many of them and have great respect for their sincere devotion to God. Rather, I argue against the literalism they hold so dear. In the court of life, their perspective is no longer compelling.

With that distinction being made, the very heart of our Christian differences lies in our assorted understandings of what the Bible says and means. Both literalists and nonliteralists seek to follow God in the best way they know how, but each rides different trains, whisking them away to different destinations. So you see, our train-boarding decision takes on great significance, since it sets the course for our behavior, worldview, and understanding of God. How we approach the Bible is the heart of the problem. The church faces a credibility of belief that begins with its understanding of Scripture. Simply put, literalism lacks credibility, and for good cause. This book promotes the value of a nonliteral train ride as the best choice, for it not only passes the scrutiny of present-day knowledge but is also a more faithful understanding of Scripture.

The Value of Scripture

You don't have to pitch your tent in the camp of literalism to hold Scripture in high regard. The Bible is filled with wisdom and profound truth that extends far beyond the limits of literalism. I take Scripture far too seriously to take it literally. For biblical literalists, the value of Scripture arises from its divine origin. The previous chapters have already debunked this viewpoint, but the approach sure sounds good, for it provides the security we long for. Often, you will hear literalists say, "The Bible says...," as though they were quoting some international and universally agreed-upon sent-from-heaven rule book for the game of life. Quoting the Bible with such manipulative and self-righteous intent merely advances one's personal agenda through the use of divine authority. The problem with believing that the Bible is the inerrant, once-for-all, literal words of God to humankind is that it simply isn't true. To believe this myth, one has to disengage from reality itself, believe the unbelievable, and travel in the opposite direction of modern knowledge and common sense. You can call it faith if you like, but I call it nonsense. The value of Scripture cannot rest on such tenuous pillars.

What value does Scripture hold if it isn't the inerrant, literal, once-for-all words of God to humankind? Scripture is valuable because (1) it reveals God to us, and (2) it teaches us.

Scripture Reveals God

In previous chapters, I noted that the Bible is not God, even though some well-meaning believers elevate it to a God-like status. This is bibliolatry—worship of the Bible. I have also noted that the Bible is a relative document—directly related to the time, culture, and circumstances of its authors, and as such, it encompasses the biases, prejudices, knowledge, and worldview of its day. The Bible is a human product whose stories, values, history, and teaching arise from within the community of faith itself. It is a collection of writings about human understandings and experiences of God. The Bible was written by humans, for other humans, about how those humans understood God, experienced God, and lived for God in the specific circumstances of their day. The Bible is not God, and it is not the direct words of God memorialized for all time; instead, it is human words about God.

If the Bible is a human product, then its value is tied to its contents and function, not to some divine origin. Scripture is valuable to us not because it is God's words but because it is words about God from within the community of faith. It is considered a sacred book by Christians because the church has declared it so. Our ancestors in the faith found such value in these texts that they declared them to be sacred writings that could enhance our own understanding and experience of God.

Word of God

Scripture can be thought of as the Word of God in the sense that it acts as a doorway into greater communion with God. This distinction between the Word of God and the words of God is significant. One is used in a metaphorical sense to indicate its sacramental nature, while the other emphasizes that every word, every teaching, every viewpoint, etc., is the direct revelation and will of God. One is to be embraced and celebrated, while the other can never be.

Because of its sacramental nature, the Bible plays a pivotal role in the life of Christians. Jesus was called the Word of God because his life and teaching revealed God. If we want to know what God is like, we look to the life of Jesus as someone who embodied the values, compassion, and character of God. The Bible can also be thought of as the Word of God in a similar way. The church treasures Scripture as a means of revealing and experiencing God.

God Is Still Speaking

To view Scripture as the forever finalized words of God to humankind means that God has spoken in the past and is no longer speaking in the present. What more is there to say if God's forever message has already been set in final, unchangeable form? Of course, this places God in quite a jam, for nothing new can ever be revealed, and God is forever associated with the prejudices, tribal mentalities, and reprehensible behavior seen in Scripture.

Many perceive the Bible as a thick book of rules and regulations we must obey in order to appease a heavenly deity, while the role of the Spirit is to help us understand the rules and empower us to obey them. In fact, it seems that the kingdom of God is all about rule-keeping in order to placate a demanding deity. If you are like me, however, you probably fail in this regard a great deal more than you succeed, even when you try to be a good foot soldier in God's army. This view of Scripture is damning, difficult, and disturbing.

Did God speak once and that was it? Is our relationship to God merely one of learning and obeying the many rules and regulations found in the good book? That sort of relationship doesn't inspire me at all. Quite frankly, if the Bible is God's forever finalized form of communicating to humans, then I have to question God's ability to communicate. We send people to seminary just to understand the darn thing, and even then, they come out disagreeing on what the Bible says and means. Is that the best God can do while we are left in the lurch, trying to figure things out and still being held accountable under the threat of eternal damnation?

Why can't we get it through our thick skulls that Scripture is merely human words *about* God, not divine words *from* God? Scripture contains the experiences and understanding of individuals who felt inspired to write things down. They wrote from their own perspectives in their own time and in light of their own circumstances. We are privileged to read their perspectives, and it helps us connect with God in our own spiritual journey. In this regard it becomes a doorway for our own God experience, and our own God experiences are nothing more than God speaking to us in the present.

Have individuals experienced God in the past? Of course, for God was speaking then. Do individuals experience God in the present age? Of course, for God continues to speak. God has always spoken and is always speaking. This notion of a one-time, forever finalized communication doesn't make sense, and it never will, for God is a continuing presence—a present voice to all who are listening.

Certainty vs. Uncertainty

As I have pointed out in earlier chapters, life is filled with uncertainty. With great bravado, we declare what is and what isn't and trick ourselves into believing we have things all figured out, perfectly labeled, and neatly stacked. Even though we possess more knowledge than at any other time in the history of the world, in the big scheme of things, we know very little. When it comes to God, for instance, we literalize, systematize, and analyze so much as to make bold claims when the mystery is far beyond our ability to comprehend, let alone describe. With regard to our age, our health, our finances, our children, our jobs, and our world, the certainty we seek cannot be found. That's just the way it is for finite creatures living in a vast universe.

It can be scary to live in a world of uncertainty. Who wants to live that way? We yearn for security and understanding, and yet it evades us. Since we are unable to define and describe God with the certitude we desire, we must walk forward into the great cloud of mystery that surrounds us. I rise early each workday for a sixty-mile one-way commute on a two-lane highway filled with the danger of hills, curves, ravines, oncoming traffic, drunk and texting drivers, wild animals, and snow in the winter time. When the weather conditions are just right, fog envelops my route, making the trek both fascinating and treacherous at the same time. Each time I encounter these conditions, I think about the presence of God and how it must surround us like a fog so thick that forward movement is more by faith than by sight. Enveloped by this cloud on the ground, I experience both the thrill of being alive and the vulnerability of not seeing as clearly as I would like.

The church's holy book offers hope in the midst of uncertainty, unless you are a literalist and have everything figured out! Certainty and mystery are opposites, and as I go to the Bible on a daily basis to connect with the mystery of God, I do not search for certainty, because I know it is not there. Instead, I seek to be enveloped by the fog—the presence of mystery itself. I am incapable of explaining it; I can only experience its reality in my life, so I merely close my eyes and breathe it in. The Bible is about meaning and experience. It offers hope and courage in the face of insecurity and uncertainty, and, as such, its value is priceless.

Scripture Teaches Us

Scripture is not only a spiritual doorway for communing with God; it also acts as a valuable teacher in our journey through life. Through its pages, we learn a great deal about living in the presence of divine mystery. How do we walk with courage in an insecure and uncertain world? We learn from the experiences of those who have walked before us. How did they deal with things? What did they learn? What pearls of wisdom might we accumulate to assist us in our journey?

When we read the Bible literally, we limit what it can teach us, for literalism embraces the lowest level of meaning possible. When our eyes are open to profound truth rather than literal truth, the doorway into mystery swings wide open, and deeper levels of learning emerge. If the only truth we find in Scripture is literal truth, then we are missing the depth, layers, and texture of profound meaning that sweep us away into deeper waters. It is like visiting the zoo and only seeing the chimpanzees when a vast array of other animals awaits you. Did you see the giraffe, the hippopotamus, the rhinoceros, and the camel? Did you stop and listen to the staff and volunteers explaining how the zoo works, how they care for the animals, and their peculiarities? You were in the zoo surrounded by the wonder of God's creation, and you missed most of it because all you saw were chimpanzees. The truths presented in the Bible go beyond literalism—beyond the chimpanzee exhibit. They are deep, profound truths that assist us in our journey through life.

Values

We pursue life according to our values. Wasting time and effort on the insignificant is unappealing and meaningless. How do we determine what we should value? Our upbringing, our parents, our experiences, and a host of other things help define our values. Christians, however, seek to live life in accordance with the still-speaking God of creation, but how do they do this? What values should be important to God-followers? The Bible offers wisdom, guidance, insight, and values, as seen in the lives of those who have walked before us. We discover, for instance, that love is the heartbeat of Christian conduct and a value that serves us well. The courage to walk in an uncertain world involves loving God and others. The prophet Micah encouraged the people of his day to do justice, love kindness, and walk humbly upon this Earth. The value of those words is immeasurable for our own spiritual journey. We learn from the example and teaching of Jesus. The many stories of the Bible present profound truths that teach us what is important. Scripture offers valuable wisdom and guidance.

Since the Bible is a relative document—that is, related to the specific time, culture, and circumstance of its authors—we learn from the problems they encountered and how they faced them. Their world informs our world. Their encounters inform our encounters. Their lives serve as powerful examples to us. Their sacred storytelling enhances our own God experiences.

Life, Love, and Being

I love reading and studying the Bible. It is a fascinating book that enlightens my own spiritual journey. I don't interpret it as the very words of God to humankind but rather as human experience, understanding, and response to the great mystery of God, written, of course, within the time, culture, and circumstances of its day. These writers' experiences help me assess and embrace the values I seek to live by within my own time, culture, and circumstance.

For instance, if God is the source of life, as Scripture portrays, then I best express my devotion to God by living life to its fullest. If God is the source of love, then I best express my devotion to God by loving expansively and wholeheartedly. If God is the source of being itself, then I best express my devotion to God by being the best me I can be. I live, I love, and I become as a way of living in the presence of God in a world that is bigger than I am. Scripture is a valuable teacher, and by embracing its teachings and values, I am transformed from the inside out into being the best me I can be.

Many literalists are willing to give up on God if the Bible they believe in isn't the literal, inerrant, forever finalized words of God to humans. They can't imagine a God outside of their own preconditions to God's existence. Either the Bible is the historical, factual, literal words of God, or there is no God at all. A bit extreme, wouldn't you say? Yet others abandon the faith for the very opposite reason. If literalism is the only way to understand the Bible, they are compelled to choose between faith and reason. What a predicament to be in as many walk away from the church.

The good news is that God is real and present no matter what approach we take, for God's existence is independent of our opinion about the matter. The good news continues when we realize that one can believe in God, love God, live for God, and experience God without having to forsake our intellect or our faith. It is possible to leave religion and find God—to rediscover a faith worth believing. Scripture holds immense value for people of faith without asking them to pitch their tent in the land of literalism.

Chapter Summary

This chapter answered the question, "What is the value of Scripture?" If it is not the literal, inerrant, once-for-all words of God to humankind, then why bother with it at all? I offered two key reasons why Scripture holds value. First, it reveals God to us by opening a doorway into divine mystery. It is not God, and it is not the very words of God; instead, it is a book the church has recognized as a sacred tool for helping us commune with God. In essence, it has a sacramental nature about it that has long been recognized by the faith community.

Second, the Bible acts as a teacher. As we read its stories and interact with its message, we learn from the experiences of those who have gone before us. The Bible was written by humans, for humans, and reveals how humans experienced God through the circumstances of their own age. This, of course, inspires and informs our own spiritual journey.

Christianity struggles to survive because of what it advances as truth. I call it the credibility of belief. What the church believes about Scripture is no longer credible in light of modern knowledge. Credibility is lost because the church promotes a literalistic view that forces thinking Christians to choose between their faith and their intellect. To believe in literalism is to park your brain at the church door and throw our current reservoir of knowledge out the window. We either embrace modern knowledge and reject faith, or we embrace faith and reject what we know to be true.

This either/or crisis need not exist, for it is entirely possible to be both a thinking and passionate Christian without accepting the tenets of literalism. There is a better way to approach Scripture that is filled with integrity and far more faithful to the sacred text. That is the good news these chapters on Scripture have been trying to convey.

Next, we turn our attention to another key section—beliefs surrounding Jesus that have also lost credibility in today's world. If you think tackling Scripture was a hardy sacred cow to address, the section on Jesus will be even more difficult. I will be entering the forbidden zone where Christians dare not tread. Yet how can we ignore the large elephant in the room?

LEAVING RELIGION

☑ ## The Problem of Behavior

☑ ## The Problem of Belief

The Credibility of Scripture

The Credibility of Jesus

UP NEXT →

The Credibility of God

FINDING GOD

A New Beginning

8

THE CHRIST OF FAITH
· · · · · · · ·

W̶E HAVE BEEN EXAMINING THE CREDIBILITY OF belief that faces the contemporary church—the problem of what the church teaches and believes
about Scripture, Jesus, and God. In our last section, we tackled the traditional
understanding of Scripture as the literal, inerrant, once-for-all words of God to
humankind. Instead of believing the unbelievable, we revealed its numerous
inadequacies and presented an approach to Scripture that honors its immense
value while also maintaining intellectual honesty.

We left traditional understandings of Scripture behind because its integrity
was compromised as biblical scholarship and modern-day knowledge exposed
its many flaws. Because we now possess far more insight than when the Bible
was written, contemporary Christians are faced with either giving up their faith
in order to maintain cerebral sanity or waving goodbye to intellectual integrity
in order to maintain their faith. I presented a way forward that allows us to
believe in God, love God, live for God, and experience God through Scripture
without giving up either our faith or our intellect. A fresh understanding of the
sacred text is one way we leave religion in order to find God and rediscover a
faith worth believing.

The start of a new section now begins in which we examine the traditional
understanding of Jesus. As with the subject of Scripture, I deconstruct another
one of the church's sacred cows and, in so doing, walk among religious land
mines at my own peril. If you thought Scripture was a challenging subject to
address, an even greater sacred cow is about to be scrutinized. As difficult as it
may be, we must approach this subject with intellectual integrity if Christianity
is to survive into the future with any semblance of meaning. The church asks us
to believe what is no longer believable, but how can we maintain such a belief

when contemporary data contradict those traditional understandings? We can't. And that is why we must—we absolutely must—address the elephants in the room.

The Central Figure

No one has changed the world like Jesus. He is the central figure within Christianity who is worshiped, prayed to, and revered as God incarnate—a member of the Trinity. According to church doctrine, Jesus was born of a virgin, was resurrected from the dead, and ascended into heaven. His death by crucifixion is proclaimed to be a sacrificial offering whereby Jesus died in our stead so we could be saved from sin and reconciled to a holy God. These are huge claims attached to a person who walked this Earth in ancient sandals two thousand years ago.

Perhaps the greatest difference between the Jesus of Christianity and the central figures of other religions is one of revelation. Jews see the revelation of God in the sacred Torah, whereas Muslims see God's revelation in the Qur'an. Moses and Muhammed are merely the revealers of the revelation given to them, whereas in Christianity, Jesus himself is the revelation of God. In other words, God revealed Godself in a person, not just a book, and this is a unique aspect of traditional Christian teaching.

While Christians love and worship Jesus, mentioning his name is not always popular. He is often identified with brands of Christianity built around shame, fear, eternal damnation, strict rule-keeping, and his appeasing death. For those living in other countries around the globe, Jesus may be perceived as the central figure from which our nation's politics and policies are built—policies they feel are unjust. Still others wrestle with the various Christian teachings about Jesus. How can he be both human and divine at the same time? How can he be born of a virgin? Did he really die for our sins? How could a loving God require his crucifixion? How can a person literally rise from the dead? How does someone ascend from Earth into heaven? This section of the book touches upon these very issues.

The Historical Jesus and the Christ of Faith

It is helpful to distinguish between the actual person called Jesus who walked this Earth in the first century and the Jesus portrayed in later writings after his death. The two are not the same. One is how he actually was, while the other is how writers intentionally portray him. The story of Santa Claus may help us understand the kind of distinction I have in mind. Santa is based on the fourth-century historical figure of St. Nicholas, who was a bishop in the ancient city of Myra during the days of the Roman Empire. He was known for his kindness and generosity. Legend grew around him after his death, so much so that St. Nicholas was portrayed as giving the gift of money to many in need, healing the sick, and raising dead people back to life.

Our present-day notion of Santa Claus arises from this historical figure of old. Although St. Nicholas may have walked upon this Earth in Myra, his story has been altered, embellished, and broadened so that Santa is now viewed as traveling through the sky on a sled pulled by flying reindeer to homes across the globe in a single night while dispensing Christmas gifts to good little boys and girls. If there really was a St. Nicholas who was generous and kind, and if Santa Claus is based on that historical person, we can easily recognize the distinction between the historical St. Nicholas and the current portrayal of Santa Claus.

We get a further taste of this distinction as we speak of those who have passed on. We knew and experienced them one way while they were alive, and after their death, we remember them in a different manner. One is real, the other is embellished, and we often get the impression that they were superhuman. We have, in essence, elevated them to some saintly status in our memory. These examples help us grasp the distinction between the actual, first-century Jesus whose feet touched Earth's soil and his portrayal in Scripture written years after his death.

This distinction makes sense. Those who wrote of Jesus portray him in ways that further their literary agenda. This distinction may not have been all that obvious to generations before the seventeenth century, for they accepted the portrayal and the historical as one and the same. The Renaissance, Reformation, and Enlightenment unleashed a spirit of inquiry so powerful that biblical scholarship and critical approaches to the study of Scripture were born, and a distinction between the historical Jesus and the Christ of faith came to light.

Pre-Easter and Post-Easter Jesus

One author has labeled this distinction as the pre-Easter Jesus and the post-Easter Jesus.[6] One refers to what Jesus was like before his death, and the other refers to what Jesus became after his resurrection. One is the actual, historical Jesus, and the other is the Christ of faith—the way Christian tradition has portrayed him to be.

That there was a real, actual person named Jesus who walked upon Earth in the first century is not seriously questioned. No writer of antiquity disputed the historical existence of Jesus, and most historians today agree. Several historians of old, such as Josephus and Tacitus, also refer to Jesus as a person who actually lived in history. Though some challenge the veracity of such a historical figure, it seems pretty clear that Jesus was an actual person.

Jesus was born around the beginning of the first century and died by cruci-fixion around 30 CE. He was Jewish; lived in the region of Galilee; engaged in typical human behaviors, such as sleeping and waking, eating and drinking, speaking and being quiet; and was in all respects flesh and blood just like we are. He was born of a woman and had a beginning like we did, while his death ensured that his life also had an ending. That is the historical Jesus. He spent time traveling and teaching and developed a following. That person is no longer living, for he died a painful death centuries ago. The actual, historical Jesus is no longer actual. Instead, he is historical, just like we will be when we die—someone who once lived upon this Earth.

The post-Easter Jesus, on the other hand, isn't a flesh-and-blood figure with bones, muscles, blood, skin, and digestive system; instead, the post-Easter Jesus refers to what Jesus became to the Christian tradition after his death. He is no longer another human being to rub shoulders with but someone we experience in an entirely different way. Although the historical Jesus is dead and gone, the spirit, meaning, and message of Christ are present realities in our daily lives.

Paul had such a powerful vision of Jesus during his Damascus Road journey that it transformed his entire life and ministry. Many disciples also experienced transforming visions of a resurrected Jesus. Eventually, these visions gave rise to the continuing presence of Christ as found in the Gospels. Traditions about him developed after his death, and it is these stories, memories, and portrayals that encompass the post-Easter Jesus. Mark was the earliest account written, penned about forty years after Jesus's death, while John was the last to be written, nearly seventy years after his demise. That is enough time for the memories of Jesus to be told and retold, altered, and embellished until they morphed into the post-Easter representation.

It is helpful to think of Jesus in terms of the man who actually walked upon this Earth and the Christ he became as time went on. Evangelicals and funda-mentalists reject this distinction, for it doesn't fit well into their religious paradigm. When this concept was raised during my seminary training, it wasn't given much airplay because we minimized it as another liberal assault upon our cherished traditional beliefs. After all, if such critics truly knew God, they would surely see things from our perspective—the right way, of course.

When you are too holy for your halo, you aren't open to seeing new things, or you readily dismiss them as anti-Christian—unworthy of further contemplation. As I matured and grew stronger in my faith, I was able to be more objective. Quite frankly, realizing that there is a difference between the real human being named

Jesus who lived and died in the first century and the portrayals of him written long after his death makes a great deal of sense to me. One is the flesh-and-blood Jesus, and the other is the portrayed Christ. One is the actual Jesus, and one is the memory of Jesus. One is the pre-Easter Jesus, and the other is the post-Easter Jesus. One is the historical Jesus, and one has become the Christ of faith.

Titles of Jesus

Stories about Jesus circulated orally after his death as a way of continuing his ministry and memory. Scholars doubt whether these post-Easter titles were claimed by the actual, historical Jesus because he didn't speak of himself in this manner, and an advanced Christology hadn't yet been developed. For example, the New Testament, written after his death, refers to Jesus as the Son of Man, Messiah, Savior, Word of God, Great High Priest, Light of the World, Bread of Life, Son of God, Lamb of God, Son of David, etc. Outside what these writers tell us about Jesus years after his death, there are no writings from Jesus himself for us to consider.

Tension between Judaism and Roman occupation filled the cultural context of the early church. These post-Easter titles assigned to Jesus flow from the dynamics of these two realities. One title allotted to Jesus is the Son of God, a phrase arising from the Old Testament. At the time of Jesus, the term referred to individuals possessing a unique, special, and close relationship with God that was recognizable to others. That is, others recognized his intimate relationship with God and bestowed upon him the title "Son of God." Jesus was the Son of God not in a literal sense but in a figurative sense.

The Roman use of the phrase was quite different. First-century Jews lived in an occupied land as part of the Roman Empire, where the emperor was considered the Son of God, either by conception or by declaration. The title can be found on Roman coins and various inscriptions throughout the empire. By saying that Jesus was the Son of God, the Jews were not only recognizing the special relationship he had with God but also denying the Son-of-God status of the emperor. This post-Easter title assigned to Jesus was a way of challenging Rome while at the same time linking Jesus to the one true God of Israel.

Jesus was also called "Lord," another title the Romans used in reference to the emperor. In Jewish circles, "Lord" conveyed the idea of loyalty, allegiance, and faithfulness. To say that Jesus is Lord is to give one's allegiance to him. He had such a special relationship with God that his teachings were powerfully winsome. Following Jesus entailed loyalty, allegiance, and faithfulness. It was Jesus, not the despised Roman occupier, who was worthy of that kind of devotion.

In a similar vein, Jesus is designated as "Savior," another label with reference to the emperor of Rome. In Jewish terms, "savior" is related to the Exodus story, whereby God liberates the Hebrews from Egyptian bondage, and as such, God is their rescuer. Jesus is also portrayed as a rescuer and linked to the liberation story of the Old Testament. Caesar Augustus was likewise hailed as a savior for bringing peace upon the land and putting an end to the civil war that had raged within the empire. The Roman emperor pursued peace through war and coercion, whereas Jesus pursued peace through love and nonviolence.

"Messiah" is a distinctively Jewish term that finds no parallel within the Roman world. In English, the word is translated as "Christ." The last name of Jesus isn't Christ, and his parents weren't Joseph and Mary Christ. Rather, "Christ" is a title that means "anointed one," a concept that began in the Old Testament with Israel's first king—Saul. The prophet Samuel poured oil on Saul's head and "anointed" him as God's elect. The Jews hoped that someone anointed of God would free them from the yoke of Roman occupation in much the same way that Moses delivered the Hebrews from Egyptian bondage. The authors of Scripture intentionally portray Jesus as the fulfillment of Jewish messianic expectations—an elected deliverer anointed of God.

The historical Jesus didn't carry these titles, didn't promote such titles, and didn't refer to himself with these titles. It was only after the resurrection appearances that these post-Easter titles came to be fully associated with Jesus.

The Jesus Effect

Separating the actual, historical Jesus from the post-Easter Christ is challenging for traditionalists because they view the post-Easter portrayals as describing the pre-Easter Jesus. The historical figure was a man who didn't travel much outside his region, held no political power, had no military might, no wealth, no formal education, came from the lower class, and attracted a ragtag group of wide-eyed disciples, and yet his impact upon the world is astonishing. In all honesty, the fledgling movement should have fizzled out shortly after the fuse had been lit. But that is not what happened.

We watch his disciples scatter after his arrest, disbelieve initial resurrection reports, fear being arrested themselves because of their association with him, and return to their previous way of living. Yet it is these very disciples who eventually turn the world upside down. It isn't long before this small band of brothers expands in number, especially around Jerusalem. After Paul's dramatic Damascus Road vision, he stops persecuting the early followers of Jesus and becomes one of their chief proponents in spreading the good news. Peter seems to have focused his efforts upon the Jews, while Paul turns to the Gentiles. Through three missionary journeys, Paul expands the Jesus Movement by establishing new churches throughout the region. During his fourth trip, he is imprisoned in Rome for his beliefs and activities.

According to tradition, the disciples were so dedicated to The Way that many were martyred for their faith. By all accounts, they faced death knowing that they were following in the footsteps of Jesus, and they counted it a privilege!

Since the church in Rome was situated within the large metropolitan center of the empire, it naturally held more influence than the outlying areas. For many years, Christians were maligned and persecuted for their beliefs—until the early 300s, when the Roman emperor Constantine the Great legalized the Christian religion. This launched the church toward further expansion and grew into what became known as the Catholic Church. That's how Christianity structured itself for centuries, until the East-West Schism of 1054 CE, when political and theological differences caused the Catholic Church in the east to break from the Catholic Church in the west. This was the start of the Eastern Orthodox Church. In 1517 CE, Martin Luther initiated the Reformation, when groups broke from Catholicism to birth the Protestant line of churches.

My point is that the tremendous growth of Christianity began with the teaching of one man who lived two thousand years ago, attracted a hodgepodge of followers who took up the torch after he died, and set the world ablaze. When we scrutinize Christian beliefs, we are referring not to a handful of persecuted believers but to a religion that has spread throughout the entire world. To honestly question the church's teaching about Jesus is a big deal, for the church's impact has been felt globally.

Competing Viewpoints

Since its humble beginnings in the first century, Christianity has blossomed into common beliefs about Jesus, but it wasn't always so. After his death, multiple understandings of Jesus emerged, which led to competing views about who he was and what he stood for. These various perspectives became the backdrop for the great church councils that brought us the creeds of Christendom—creeds designed to clarify these competing views of Jesus centuries after his demise. These church councils were as much a political battle as they were a theological statement. The creeds ultimately reflected the views of those with the most political power and theological clout. Christianity as we know it today would be much different had other viewpoints carried the day.

Today, we pick up our nice-smelling, leather-bound Bibles, thinking that Christianity as we currently know it has always been that way. We embrace the faulty notion that immediately after the resurrection, systematic theologies were developed, church doctrine was established, denominations immediately sprang up, and everything was instantly set. Nothing could be further from the truth. It took centuries for all of this to come about, and early Christians were quite diverse in their understanding of Jesus.

Some followers thought Jesus was merely an anointed human being, while others believed he was divine. Some thought he was exalted to divine status at his resurrection, others said it was at his baptism, and still others said he was exalted to divine status at his birth. Another group believed that Jesus was with God before creation—from eternity past. The Gnostics believed one way. The Marcionites believed another way. The Docetics believed still another way. There wasn't just one way of seeing Jesus but multiple, diverse understandings of who he was. They were all sincere followers, but they simply saw things differently, and each perspective considered itself the correct viewpoint. The church councils changed all of that.

Creeds

Evangelical and fundamental churches aren't much for tradition, and while they accept the Apostles' Creed and the Nicene Creed as truth, they are rarely mentioned backburner issues. In my many years of service to the evangelical world, I don't recall a time when the creeds were ever uttered during a church service. For mainline denominations, the creeds are very much a part of both the religious culture and the Sunday morning services. Many progressive churches do away with them altogether. In essence, evangelicals and fundamentalists suppress the creeds, mainline denominations embrace them, and progressives often ignore them.

For Christians, the creeds act as a common set of affirmations and core beliefs. They are "I believe" statements that the faithful recite without question. But taking the creeds literally is a challenge for thinking Christians, for it is yet another intersection where reason and faith collide. There is nothing wrong with expressing our understanding and experience of God, and the creeds try to do just that. The problem is that their portrayal stems from an ancient worldview that no longer exists. We live in a very different world—one with increased knowledge far more advanced than in the days of old. The dilemma with accepting the creeds literally is that we must either reject intellectual honesty in order to maintain our faith or throw away our faith in order to maintain intellectual integrity. The fork in the road is upon us, and the crossroad is real.

The Apostles' Creed begins with, "I believe in God, the Father almighty, creator of heaven and earth." Is God really an almighty Father? Is God really a male or defined by maleness? What does that say to the value of women? Many have used their belief in a masculine God to support male domination and demeaning views of women. "Almighty" brings into question God's ability or willingness to use that almighty power for good. With personal pain, evil, and natural disasters all around us, we wonder why a God with unlimited power isn't responding. Would an all-powerful, all-knowing, omnipresent God actually advance as literal truth some of the "truths" found in the Bible and discussed in previous chapters? For instance, does an almighty God attribute sickness to sin in our lives? Is God unaware of germs, viruses, bacteria, and the like? Shouldn't an all-knowing God understand that Earth revolves around the sun and not the other way around?

The creed goes on to say that God created heaven and Earth. If heaven is a place believers go to when they die, where is it, and what is it? Are we to believe in a utopian society somewhere "out there"? These ancient authors had no concept of the vastness of our universe or the age of Earth. From their limited understanding, the universe consisted of three tiers: the earth below, the sky above, and just beyond that, the place where God lives—heaven. With just this first statement of the creed, the faith we are to affirm runs smack-dab into the brick wall of reason.

Creeds are often structured around a Trinitarian formula. First, there is a statement about God, followed by a lengthier statement about Jesus, and finalized by a quick statement about the Holy Spirit. The lengthier middle section reflects the contentious issues of the day in which the nature of Jesus was in flux. There were competing views about who Jesus was, and the church councils tried to clarify these issues. Listen to the statements of belief about Jesus.

The creed states, "I believe in Jesus Christ, his only Son, our Lord." If Jesus is the only son of God, then what is our status? Are we not sons of God? Can there be daughters of God? It is then affirmed that Jesus was conceived by the Holy Spirit and born of the Virgin Mary. To understand this literally defies all logic. Is God able to have sex with a human female? Does the Holy Spirit have seed to share? How can a woman give birth without male seed? To literally affirm this belief defies everything we know about human reproduction.

The creed goes on to affirm Jesus's resurrection and ascension into heaven, where he is seated at the right hand of the Father. What is a resurrection? Is it a resuscitation back to life or something entirely different? How does Jesus ascend up to heaven, wherever that is? Does God literally have a right hand? Every Sunday, millions of devoted Christians throughout the world stand and recite their belief in the Apostles' Creed. Do they realize what they are affirming and how a literal understanding of the creed makes little sense in our world? The Nicene Creed isn't any better.

The creeds were not created by Jesus, recited by Jesus, or a part of the Jewish religion of Jesus. Instead, they are post-Easter explanations about Jesus, developed long after his death. The Nicene Creed was fashioned in 325 CE, nearly three hundred years after Jesus died. It was the Roman emperor Constantine the Great who invited bishops to the town of Nicaea, located in modern-day Turkey, to settle their disputes about the nature of Jesus. Though Constantine was the emperor who legalized the Christian religion and became a Christian himself, his motives for hosting such a council may have been less about Jesus and more about bringing peace to the empire. Having lived with his fill of division and discord, Constantine sought to bring the Christian religion into agreement, hoping that Christians could serve as an example of peace and unity within the empire. The last thing Constantine desired was more conflict in his kingdom.

There were competing views of Jesus in early Christianity, from the importance of his death to whether he died at all. Although the various letters of the New Testament were in existence around the close of the first century, they were not yet combined into one book recognized as the official New Testament. In fact, there were numerous other gospels and epistles in existence that didn't make it into the New Testament canon. Christians looked to these various writings in support of their disparate views.

The Docetists, for instance, believed that Jesus was fully divine and, as such, couldn't be fully human. He merely *appeared* to be human. If this is true, then Jesus only appeared to die because God cannot die. Docetists believed that Jesus was fully divine but not a human being. Marcion lived in the second century and believed that there were two gods—the god of the Old Testament who promoted Law and the god of Jesus who promoted grace and came to save us.

The Gnostics of the first century held yet another view of Jesus. Their name comes from the Greek word "gnosis," which means "to know." In other words, this group emphasized the importance of gaining spiritual insight and knowledge as opposed to believing a set of propositional statements. Jesus wasn't one who died to bring us salvation. Instead, he was the conveyor of spiritual insight and knowledge about oneself—a kind of enlightenment figure.

Some Christians believed that Jesus was both divine and human but that he was two beings, not one. Others insisted that Jesus was divine and human but was only one being. How can the Father be God and Jesus also be God and there still be one God? Other Christians believed that there were many gods, not just one. The point is that in the early years of Christianity, there was no consensus about the nature of Jesus. It would take both time and church councils to bring about some form of common affirmation.

Orthodoxy and Heresy

With so many views living together under one roof, which one was correct? Which perspective would win out over all others? As it turns out, certain views did win out, thanks to the ecclesiastical councils, but not because they were the truth; rather, they received more votes than the other views. It raises the question of what is orthodox and what is heretical.

"Orthodoxy" refers to right belief. To be orthodox means that you believe the right things. "Heresy" refers to choice and means that you choose to believe something different. The views that came to be known as orthodox beliefs are the ones that won out at the council meetings. This meant that all other views were heretical. Orthodoxy doesn't refer to what is true, only to what has been declared the winner of the various views. We all think our views are right, so in one sense, we are all orthodox in our own way of thinking. The point is that the church councils occurred within the worldviews and dynamic realities of their day, amid the theological and political powerbase of the various bishops, and among the controversies surrounding Jesus. In the end, one group wielded more power than the others, and the outcome was that the group's views were declared to be orthodox views—the right way to believe. All other views were deemed heretical because people were choosing to embrace another way of believing.

We think that creedal affirmations represent the one true belief about Jesus, when in reality, the very opposite is true.[7] In other words, the affirmations arising from the church councils and considered to be orthodox weren't the original and majority view of early Christians. Instead, orthodox views were developed centuries later. In essence, early on, there were various *original* views of Jesus, but as each group tried to convince others of their perspective, one group won out over all others. The winning views weren't the original orthodox views but merely one of many. They just happened to be the views that won out when all was said and done.

Jesus didn't teach these orthodox views, and neither did his early disciples. They were later developments put into written form in the fourth century. It took time for Christians to think it all through, argue among themselves, and sort out their understanding of God, Jesus, Scripture, etc. The view that finally carried the day is called the orthodox view because it garnered more votes than the other perspectives. Since that time, the other viewpoints have diminished to the point of nonexistence.

Jesus and God

The most notable issue faced at the Council of Nicaea was the relationship of Jesus to God. Was Jesus one with God in substance and nature, or was he a created being who lacked equality with God? Arius believed that Jesus was not equal with God because he was a created being. Athanasius, on the other hand, believed that Jesus was one in substance and nature with God. His view prevailed and has been labeled "orthodox" ever since.

Think about what this decision meant in the context of the Roman Empire. By stating that Jesus was equal to God and that no others were above him meant that Constantine the Great, the Roman emperor who initiated the council to begin with, was below Jesus. In other words, the Nicene Creed affirmed that Jesus was God and Constantine was not. It didn't take long for Constantine to pick up on this, and, as we might suspect, he embraced the view of Arius over Athanasius.

Responding to Creeds

If creeds are to be taken seriously but not literally, how should we approach them, especially when a literal understanding doesn't square with the reality we know? Many Christians simply remain quiet during these recitations or utter them with a nonliteral understanding. The historical-metaphorical approach once again comes to our rescue.

It is helpful to understand the historical context of why the creeds were developed in the first place. What were they trying to accomplish? What were they responding to? With multiple and competing views of Jesus, the creeds tried to bring about one view, a dominant view that would rise above all others. Those views with the most political power and theological punch prevailed and have been advanced as the official teaching of the church since the fourth century on.

We know from previous chapters that no words can be absolute, once-for-all words but are instead relative to the context in which they are uttered. As the church advanced in structure and sophistication, so did its understanding and explanation of Jesus. The post-Easter Jesus was being developed, crystalized, and formed into an orthodoxy of belief, while all other views, even if they were at one time considered original and orthodox, were now designated as heresy. Understanding the history and context of the creeds helps us grasp how their affirmations reflect the issues of their day. If words are relative, I wonder whether we could make up our own creed to respond to the issues of our own day.

Creeds become a method of group identity. Little League baseball teams wear certain colors that identify individual teams. Green and gold were the colors of one baseball team my son played on. When I was growing up, schoolchildren placed their hands over their hearts and began each school day with a recitation of the Pledge of Allegiance, a group-identifying act proclaiming American status and loyalty. For Christians, the creeds become a method of identifying with other believers from around the globe as well as those who followed The Way long before we did.

Though a literal understanding of the creeds makes little sense these days, we can approach them from a metaphorical, nonliteral perspective. Instead of taking every line literally, we recognize that in the fourth century, this was their way of affirming the reality of God, Jesus, and the Spirit. At the very least, the creeds are one way of articulating the reality of God within the time, worldview, and cultural circumstances of their day. Even though they depict God as an almighty male father who possessed a right arm and right hand, it doesn't mean we must accept that as literal truth. Instead, we view it as an articulation of their view of God as understood from the world in which they lived. It can be seen as their way of affirming the reality of God's existence without accepting the literalness of the statements themselves.

The same could be said of the affirmations about Jesus, his virgin birth, resurrection, ascension, etc. Are we asked to affirm that a human being came into existence through a virgin birth when everything we know about human reproduction defies this belief? From their perspective, however, women were merely incubators without further contribution. They didn't grasp the biological complexities of conception and birth as we do, and a virgin birth story was their way of uplifting the divinity of Christ. It was their way of saying that Jesus came from heaven, and the ascension was their way of getting him back into heaven. The relative nature of these affirmations is tied to their limited understanding of the world. From a metaphorical viewpoint, however, we can affirm the centrality and importance of Jesus to Christianity. They saw in him the very image of God, and the creeds were one way of expressing this.

Believing or Beloving

The problem with creeds, however, is that they become tests of faith. You either believe the absolute, literal truth of their propositional statements, or you are labeled an infidel. Instead of relative expressions of the reality of God, they are used to determine who is in and who is out of the kingdom—check marks regarding the validity of one's faith. Is it possible to believe in the reality of God, the centrality of Jesus to Christianity, and the presence of the Spirit without having to embrace the absolute literalness of the creedal statements? I sure hope so; otherwise, the progression of human understanding is forever restrained by antiquated worldviews of the past.

In our way of thinking, to believe means we must affirm propositional statements as literal truth. But is that the correct understanding of what it means to believe? Belief in propositional statements as absolute, literal truth is "believe that" affirmations.[8] In other words, to "believe that . . ." is a mental assent to the literal truthfulness of a propositional statement. James 2:19 (NRSV) notes, "You believe that God is one; you do well. Even the demons believe—and shudder." Notice the "believe that" terminology. But is that the kind of affirmation we are making when we recite a creed? Even demons give mental assent to such propositional statements. There has to be more that unites us than mental assent to "believe that" statements.

Prior to the 1600s, to "believe" meant something different than our current definition. Instead of believing that a particular statement was absolutely and literally true, the word was used in reference to a person as the direct object, not the statement itself. In other words, the subtle distinction is between *believing in someone* and *believing someone*. One refers to the trust and confidence we put in the individual as opposed to merely believing what the individual says. In one, we hold the individual close to our heart with uplifting love; in the other, we merely give mental assent without the delicate endearing of the heart. In one we belove, and in the other we believe.

This distinction between beloving and believing was seen long before the creeds were written. The demons *believe that* God is one, but they do not *belove* God. Jesus never taught us to believe certain creeds as a test of faith. The issue of following God isn't a matter of correct theological doctrine but rather a matter of the heart. The Pharisees of his day were more concerned with correct belief, but Jesus said that following God was a matter of loving with our heart, soul, mind, and strength and loving our neighbor as ourselves. When following

Jesus is based on affirming specific doctrinal statements, our faith becomes as sterile and inviting as a hospital intensive care unit. Emphasis on doctrinal purity as a test of faith leads to rigidity and cold-heartedness. Instead, faith is alive, joyous, radiant, abundant, full of grace, and based on love and relationship emanating from the heart.

What if we looked at the creeds as beloving statements rather than believing statements? That changes things for us. Instead of lines drawn in the sand of orthodoxy, they become affirmations of our love for God that elevate the things we hold dear and give our heart to. In doing so, we unite with millions of Christians around the globe and the faithful who walked before us in beloving God with confidence, trust, and devotion. In this way, the creeds become sacramental instead of doctrinal. They help us experience God instead of determining whether or not we are of God.

Post-Easter Portrayal

A sufficient amount of time passes after Jesus's death for stories and memories about him to develop, become embellished, and morph into higher levels of theological structure. This becomes the post-Easter Jesus—the portrayal created after his death. These after-death depictions are then projected back onto the historical individual who walked upon this Earth. They paint a picture of the Jesus he has become rather than the historical Jesus that he was.

We now see Jesus as God when Jesus never saw himself this way. We now see him as a Savior when Jesus never saw himself this way. We now view him as the Son of God, born of a virgin, and ascending into heaven when Jesus never claimed any of these for himself. You see, the post-Easter Jesus is not the same as the historical Jesus. The embellished Christ of faith developed over the years as a way of uplifting the man and his message into something more than a man with a message. This distinction is essential, for it affects how we view Jesus.

I grew up accepting the portrayed Jesus as the actual, historical Jesus. For me, Scripture was God's literal, inerrant, once-for-all words to humankind. I took it all literally, and I took it all in faith because the Bible says that without faith, it is impossible to please God, and I certainly didn't want to displease God. Like others who were at one time inspired to charge the gates of hell with a water pistol and a bucket of water, my views have morphed over the years. As I grew and matured, so did my understanding of God. My unbridled zeal turned into steadiness, and steadiness turned into knowledge, and knowledge turned into wisdom, and wisdom turned into rethinking, and rethinking turned into intellectual honesty, and intellectual honesty turned into a new understanding of Scripture, Jesus, and God, which turned into leaving religion, which turned into finding God, which turned into having a deeper and more genuine faith.

Many evangelicals and fundamentalists are so blinded by their religious fervor that in their race to live a life worthy of their calling, intellectual integrity is left behind at the starting gate. It is as if the racehorse stormed out of the gate without its rider. This, in my mind, is unfortunate, because without intellectual integrity, the faith we hold so dear matters very little, for it merely becomes another baseless personal opinion. When faith is grounded in intellectual honesty, we are able to move forward with both passion and compassion. It often takes a crisis of faith, a book, a friend, a specific event, suffering, or something outside ourselves to alter our thinking and embrace a personal paradigm shift. When we place upon the historical Jesus all the baggage of the post-Easter Jesus, we create a hybrid Jesus that never existed—a superhuman who is not real. The faith of countless Christians today is placed in the façade of a post-Easter portrayal of Jesus without recognizing the actual, historical one.

The Image of God

The post-Easter titles for Jesus all point to a divine being who descended from heaven, took on human flesh, and fully functioned with both a human and a divine nature. He is God in human form, or what we came to know in seminary as the God-Man. If Jesus is literally an amalgamation of both God and man and functions from this dual nature, then he becomes a standard we are unable to attain. In essence, he cheated, for how can we live like him, be like him, and do what he does without also being both God and man just like he was? This is a post-Easter image created after his death that doesn't represent the Jesus who walked upon this planet.

In our quest to see through the layers of post-Easter portrayals and discover the historical Jesus, we have little to go on other than the Gospels, which are our main source of information about him—even though they are themselves post-Easter portrayals. Moving beyond these post-Easter accounts has inspired numerous scholars over the years to sift for clues of the historical Jesus. It is not an easy task, and one that is rarely appreciated.

It is safe to say that the historical Jesus had quite an impact upon the lives of his followers—so much so that they readily acknowledge the work of God in his life. This is quite different than Jesus actually claiming that he was God—a portrayal written of him after his death. In essence, the post-Easter titles attributed to him merely point to the remarkable power and presence of God upon his life that touched so many. To house all of God in a human body simply cannot be done. We can't comprehend God, let alone describe God's divine qualities with any sense of true justice. What makes us think that an infinite God could be contained in a frail, finite, human body? We might be able to reflect, "Here is a human life lived so wondrously that surely this must be how God is," but we are incapable of saying, "That human being is God." A human life simply cannot contain all the qualities of God, for to be one means that you are not the other.

For instance, God is traditionally thought of as all-powerful, all-knowing, and everywhere present. These qualities are beyond human limitation, for no human is all powerful, all knowing, and everywhere present. To be human means that we are not God and that we lack these characteristics. The historical Jesus possessed none of these qualities, and if he did, he would not be human. When we say that Jesus "is the image of the invisible God" (Col 1:15, NRSV), we mean that Jesus lived his life in such a way that it reflects back to us what God must be like. He demonstrated some of God's qualities, but because he was a finite human, he could not house all the qualities and nature of an infinite God. In the life of Jesus, we sense what God must be like (character) and what God must care about (passion). Pointing out the difference between the actual Jesus and the Jesus we have turned him into is a distinction worth noting.

This kind of talk amounts to gibberish for strong-headed traditionalists steeped in the post-Easter understanding of Jesus. Trying to separate the historical Jesus from his after-death portrayal sends traditionalists into orbit, and we are viewed as heretics of the worst kind. If Jesus isn't the post-Easter portrayal they exalt and worship, then their faith begins to crumble. But pointing out this distinction is something that thoughtful Christians cannot deny. It need not destroy one's faith in God, but it does help clarify who Jesus was and what he stood for. This distinction merely challenges us to be intellectually honest about our faith. We know that the historical Jesus influenced the lives of others who saw in him the very character and passion of God. Jesus is loved not because he was actually God but because he was actually human and displayed within his life and message the very image of what God must be like. That is why we say that Jesus is the revelation of God.

The Message of Jesus

If the world was set ablaze by the early disciples whose lives were transformed by their experience of Jesus, what was his message all about? What did he teach, and why was it transforming? While many have experienced this transformation in their own lives, there appears to be no consensus as to his message. Various aspects of his message minister to different people differently, but just like the question of Jesus's nature and relationship to God, there are still many voices competing for our attention.

Some perceive Jesus as an apocalyptic prophet. In other words, he believed that the kingdom of God was imminent and that judgment was forthcoming. In this view, his message concerned how to best live and prepare oneself for the fast-approaching new kingdom. Others see Jesus's message as one of wholeness and healing. After all, his ministry consisted of numerous healings, of which there are abundant examples in the New Testament.

Some see him as the promised Messiah—the one anointed to overthrow the shackles of Rome. Others view him as the sage on the stage, a traveling rabbi who taught pertinent life lessons through stories and parables. Was Jesus also a prophet of social and political change, as some suggest? Must we choose only one element of his teaching? What is the heart of his message, as revealed in the New Testament? A plethora of books have been written on the subject, but for our purposes, I will simply share my own perspective.

Jesus was primarily concerned about what matters most—the heart. In fact, that seems to be the thrust of his life and ministry. In the Gospel of Matthew, Jesus discusses the Law in his Sermon on the Mount discourse. You would think that any good rabbi worth his salt would embrace the Law of Moses by reminding listeners of its importance and meaning. Repetition is always good, but Jesus doesn't just spout off the traditional understanding of the Law. Instead, he offers a new interpretation of the Law when he states, "You have heard that it was said . . . but I say to you . . ." He recognizes what the Law says, demands, and means, but he expands upon it and moves it forward from the conventional understanding of his day. Instead of focusing primarily on the external act itself, whether it be murder, adultery, divorce, false vows, etc., Jesus drives the Law down into the heart—into the realm of internal motivation. Instead of the external act of murder, he speaks of the internal issue of anger from which murder arises. Instead of the outward act of adultery, he addresses the internal issue of lust. This is a new interpretation of the Law and is consistent with Jesus's emphasis on the heart.

As with any ministry, whether it be the work of Jesus or anyone else, criticism is always present, and it was no different for Jesus. Pretty much everything he said and did was scrutinized, especially by those looking to find fault. He was criticized for healing on the Sabbath, plucking and eating grain on the Sabbath, and for failing to give the Sabbath its rightful due. He was criticized for what he said, how he said it, where he went, with whom he ate, and a host of other things. Those who studied the Torah asked him questions in an effort to trick him, even though they didn't have much luck in that regard. On one occasion, he was asked a question about the greatest commandment, and his answer seemed to boil the Law, the Prophets, and his own teaching down to what matters most—the heart. Jesus purportedly said to the inquirer, "'You shall love the Lord your God with all your heart, and with all your soul, and with all your mind.' This is the greatest and first commandment. And a second is like it: 'You shall love your neighbor as yourself.' On these two commandments hang all the law and the prophets" (Matt. 22:37–40, NRSV). If you want to know what following God looks like, this pretty much says it all. You see, it is a heart thing and not some test of faith that requires mental assent to a creed or set of propositional statements.

Jesus not only emphasized the heart; he actually lived life from the heart. He moved, breathed, and ministered through a heart of compassion. It seems that when we commune with the living God, we always find love flowing from one human heart to another. Jesus was moved by the people to whom he was ministering. Love flowed from his heart to theirs. In looking upon Jerusalem, his words were, "Jerusalem, Jerusalem, the city that kills the prophets and stones those who are sent to it! How often have I desired to gather your children together as a hen gathers her brood under her wings, and you were not willing!"(Matt. 23:37, NRSV). In Matthew 9:36 (NRSV), we read, "When he saw the crowds, he had compassion for them, because they were harassed and helpless, like sheep without a shepherd." In the language in which the New Testament was written, our English word "compassion" arises from the Greek word "splanchna," which refers to the stirring of the bowels. In other words, Jesus felt so much compassion for those he was ministering to that it provoked a visceral response in him. He was so emotionally moved that it literally upset his stomach.

It was this kind of love and compassion that caused many to see the very life of God in him. To look upon Jesus was to see the character and passion of God— the image of the invisible God. What a testimony to the life and ministry of the historical Jesus! Did Jesus sense that the kingdom was upon them and that the judgment of God would soon arrive? Possibly. Was he concerned with healing and wholeness for those in need? Of course. Did his words have implications for social change? Sure. These elements were present in his life and ministry to some degree, but the thrust of his message was one of love. He didn't promote revolution or overthrowing Roman occupation. He didn't heal every single person who came his way. He wasn't a fanatical prophet with nothing to discuss outside the end time. He didn't reverse the political and social structures of his day. Jesus didn't stop slavery, eradicate poverty, change the social view of women, or cure every disease. Instead, he sums up his message as one of love, and that's how he sees the totality of the Law and the Prophets. It is this ethic of love that transformed so many and became the hallmark of Christianity.

Chapter Summary

This chapter introduced another realm of doctrinal teaching advanced by the church that has lost all credibility in the modern world—the beliefs about Jesus. Challenging these long-held beliefs should not be construed as casting aside the central figure of Christianity. Instead, I question the church's portrayal of him that we are asked to blindly believe by faith. This is why the distinction between the actual, historical Jesus must be separated from the myth, legend, and portrayal of him after his death. It is difficult work trying to figure out what is embellished and what isn't because all we have to work from is the post-Easter texts written long after his crucifixion. And yet this is the kind of critical thinking that many scholars wrestle with in moving our understanding of Jesus forward.

The various post-Easter titles assigned to Jesus all point to someone worthy of devotion, allegiance, and loyalty, especially in a world that promoted loyalty to the emperor alone. Though there were competing views of Jesus after his death, the various titles assigned to him reveal how much he was revered. They reflect what Jesus had become to them, not what Jesus thought of himself.

As Christianity grew, these competing views became problematic for those who longed for a single understanding. Was Jesus human or divine? Was he made divine at his death, resurrection, baptism, and birth, or did he exist before all creation? Was he a created being who was subservient to God, or was he equal with God? Did he possess two natures or one? What one believed depended upon which teacher you followed, which community you lived in, and which gospels and epistles you looked to for support.

The creeds changed all of this. Bishops gathered together to hash out a definitive statement about the nature of Jesus. The view with the most votes became the prevailing, dominant, orthodox view—a view that true believers were expected to affirm for the literal truthfulness of their propositions. All other viewpoints were labeled heretical.

Many today are unwilling to recite and affirm the literalness of the creeds; instead, they approach them from a historical-metaphorical perspective. They recognize the historical context in which the creeds were formed, the issues of competing viewpoints regarding Jesus, and the creeds being crafted within a worldview that no longer exists.

With this in mind, they approach the creeds metaphorically instead of literally. The creeds are a reflection of how people in a certain age expressed the reality of God, Jesus, and Spirit in the language and understanding of their day, but we are not bound to affirm the absolute literalness of the statements themselves. In this way, the creeds become sacramental rather than literal. We look upon them as beloving statements rather than believing statements. In other words, they reflect the reality of Jesus in whom we trust, love, and follow rather than propositional statements about him. It is the difference between *believing in* someone and *believing* someone—*beloving* someone and *believing* something.

While there are various opinions as to the message Jesus proclaimed during his life on Earth, I presented the ethic of love as the thrust of his message since it summed up the Law and the Prophets and reflected the very heart and character of God. That is why we are told to love God with all our heart, soul, strength, and mind and to love our neighbor as ourselves. Love becomes the hallmark of Christianity precisely because it is the hallmark of God.

Now that we have introduced Jesus, the central figure of this entire section, it is time to dig into the specific doctrinal teachings about him to discover just how credible they really are. We begin with the virgin birth and ascension of Jesus, the subject of our next chapter.

9

THE VIRGIN BIRTH

· · · · · · · ·

WHILE WORKING ON A PROJECT WITH A FRIEND, I asked whether he believed in the virgin birth of Jesus. He responded affirmatively, so I asked him why he believed the way he did. "You know the answer to that," he replied.

"Because the Bible says so?" I inquired.

"Yes," was his short reply, fearing he was about to get pulled into an uncomfortable conversation.

The reason many believe what they believe about Jesus is because "the Bible says so." Because Scripture is revered as the absolute, literal, inerrant, once-for-all, authoritative words of God to humankind, challenging such a notion gets one into trouble, and no one wants to be labeled a troublemaker. Yet much of what the church asks Christians to believe is based entirely upon a literal understanding of Scripture. Literalism is so foundational to the church's credibility problem that I addressed this very issue first and foremost in previous chapters.

What happens to literal beliefs and their supporting arguments when the very lynchpin of those beliefs is seen in a new light? It changes everything and allows us to inject reason, common sense, logic, scientific data, and modern-day knowledge into our understanding of God and Scripture. Hiding behind the grand illusion of "the Bible says so" no longer works for thoughtful Christians. We live in a very different world than when the Bible was written.

Advancing "the Bible says so" mantra means that literal reasoning must be applied to all parts of the Bible, not just those glorious passages we favor over all others. We also have to say, "I believe the sun revolves around Earth because the Bible says so. I believe God hates Egyptians, Amorites, and Amalekites because the Bible says so. I believe children should be stoned to death for misbehaving because the Bible says so. I believe God supports slavery because the Bible says so. I believe women should be subservient, second-class citizens because the Bible says so. I believe God hates homosexuals and demands their death because the Bible says so." These statements are absurd, and yet this is the outcome of a literal "the Bible says so" approach to Scripture.

Besides, with more than thirty thousand denominations throughout the world, each with its own "the Bible says so" mantra, which viewpoint is the correct biblical stance? In today's world, a doctrine like the virgin birth of Jesus comes under greater scrutiny than a flippant "the Bible says so" response.

The virgin birth story has become a mainstay in the Christian tradition. In fact, I am writing this chapter shortly after attending a traditional Christmas Eve service where Luke's birth narrative was read and the Nicene Creed was recited, each addressing the supernatural birth of Jesus. We are familiar with Luke's birth narrative, in which the angel Gabriel visits Mary in Nazareth and announces that she will conceive a child. Surprised by this, Mary asks Gabriel how such a thing could happen since she has never known a man. Gabriel explains that the Holy Spirit will come upon her, and the child within will be called the Son of God.

That sure explains everything, doesn't it? From a literalist point of view, the miracles Jesus performs, the powerful teaching he delivers, and his ability to become a substitutionary sacrifice for our sins are the result of God being encapsulated in human flesh. In essence, Jesus was no ordinary baby, for he was a God-Man conceived in a virgin woman by the very Spirit of God. Have you ever met anyone who was born of a virgin without male sperm? Of course you haven't. This was simply a miracle of God, the argument goes.

That Mary was a virgin made pregnant by the Holy Spirit is certainly what Matthew and Luke portray and what Christians believe truly occurred. But are we to understand this literally when we know that is not how human reproduction works? That's not the story of the birds and the bees as I learned it. With our current knowledge of human reproduction, we are asked to embrace a virgin becoming pregnant by God. This violates everything we know about biology. "It is a miracle," you exclaim. That is certainly one explanation, and one the church has advanced throughout the centuries, but let's see whether it stands up to the scrutiny of our generation.

The virgin birth narratives are only found in two places within the New Testament: Matthew and Luke. While both accounts entail a virgin becoming pregnant by the Holy Spirit and then giving birth, the stories differ in their details so drastically that they cannot be reconciled. For instance, Matthew tells of a bright star that leads the Magi to the Christ-child, where gifts of gold, frankincense, and myrrh are presented. On their way to Jesus, the wise men make a stop at Herod's palace to ask for directions. This leads to Herod's murderous attempt to wipe out any potential threat to his kingship by sending troops into Bethlehem to slaughter innocent babies. Jesus is spared, as an angel warns the family to flee to Egypt. Additionally, an angel of the Lord appears to Joseph early on and warns him not to divorce Mary, for she is carrying a child conceived by the Holy Spirit. That's the Matthew story.

Luke, on the other hand, sees things a little differently. In his account, it is Mary who receives an angelic visit, not Joseph. The angel Gabriel informs her that she will conceive and bear a son. Because she is a virgin, this confuses her. Upon inquiry, Gabriel relays that the Holy Spirit will come upon her, and for that reason, her child will be called the Son of God. As Mary and Joseph travel from Nazareth to Bethlehem to register for the census, the pangs of birth ensue, and she delivers the child outside the inn, for there was no room for them because of the census travelers. She wraps Jesus in cloths and lays him in a manger, which many believe is nothing more than a feeding trough for animals. King Herod is absent from the story, as are the wise men who travel from afar carrying gold, frankincense, and myrrh. In Luke's story, only shepherds who receive a special angelic announcement are present.

Both accounts acknowledge Mary's virginity, conception by the Holy Spirit, and a birth, but other than that, their details vary considerably and cannot be harmonized. Like so many other stories in the Gospels, the virgin birth episode is not meant to be taken literally. Instead, such stories are meant to convey profound truth, not literal truth. Trying to reconcile events, places, people, content, and timelines within the various narratives is difficult to do. Some want to accept every story, every instance, every event, and every person literally, as though they actually occurred in the exact order in which they are presented. When you lay it all out, however, it becomes painfully obvious that this is no solution at all, for things don't neatly line up, contradictions abound, and Jesus can't be in two places at the same time, doing and saying two different things to different groups of people.

Literalism is an easy approach, for all you have to do is read the words and accept them literally, in the exact order, location, circumstances, and timeline the Bible suggests, even when doing so defies reason. For many, this is called faith, and if the rest of us would simply get on board, we wouldn't be wasting precious time on things like this book. This, however, is nonsense. For the very reasons noted in previous chapters, literalism cannot withstand the scrutiny of common sense, let alone biblical scholarship and the bounty of present-day knowledge.

A Developing Narrative

The virgin birth story developed over time. In fact, it didn't enter the vocabulary of Christian literature until the ninth decade of the Common Era, when it first appears in the Gospel of Matthew, nearly sixty years after the death of Jesus. Mark, the earliest of the Gospels, says nothing of a virgin birth. In fact, Mark begins his account with Jesus's baptism, not his birth. If Jesus were truly conceived by the Holy Spirit and born of a virgin, it seems to me that this would certainly be a relevant and important fact to point out. Apparently Mark isn't aware of it, for he skips over the birth altogether in favor of Jesus's baptism.

The Gospel of John, the last gospel to be written, knows nothing about a virgin birth, either. Instead, the Gospel speaks of John the Baptist bearing testimony to Jesus, who is light. John notes that Jesus, the Word, came into the world, but it says absolutely nothing about a virgin birth or supernatural conception. It is amazing to me that such a story, if it were literally true, isn't referred to by other Gospel writers and in other places within Scripture; and yet there is nothing but robust silence on the matter.

Matthew writes his birth story with the Gospel of Mark in front of him, which he finds deficient and far too short for his own purposes. Considering the issues of his own day, he alters Mark's account by adding a birth tradition and augmenting and deleting various stories to fit his audience and agenda. Luke seems to do the very same thing. Because the four Gospels were written between forty and seventy years after the death of Jesus, one wonders whether the earlier Christian writings of Paul mention anything of the virgin birth. After all, Paul was one of the early proponents of Christianity, spent his life defending the faith, and wrote a good portion of the New Testament. If anyone would advance the virgin birth, surely it would be Paul himself. Unfortunately, that isn't the case. Paul's writings say nothing about a virgin birth. The earliest writings of the New Testament are Paul's letters, with the first being 1 Thessalonians, and yet this epistle is completely silent on the matter.

In his next letter, written to the Galatians around 50 CE, Paul has this to say about the birth of Jesus: "But when the fullness of time had come, God sent his Son, born of a woman, born under the law" (Gal. 4:4, NRSV). There is no miraculous conception by the Holy Spirit, no pregnant virgin, and no angelic announcement. No shepherds. No wise men. No King Herod. No manger. No census. No escape to Egypt. None of it. Instead, we read that Jesus arrived on the scene in God's timing, was born of a woman, and was born under the Law. No new revelation here. Jesus was born just like everyone else.

Additionally, Paul notes in Galatians 1:19 that upon visiting Jerusalem, he actually met with James, the Lord's brother. As noted in Mark 6:3 (NRSV), Jesus had brothers and sisters, according to locals who heard Jesus speaking in his hometown synagogue: "'Is not this the carpenter, the son of Mary and brother of James and Joses and Judas and Simon, and are not his sisters here with us?' And they took offense at him." From Paul's perspective, Jesus entered this world under no special circumstances. He had a common birth and a common family. Mark even tells us that Jesus had a common occupation as a carpenter. Paul's point is that Jesus was actually, historically born and shared in a common humanity like the rest of us.

The only other mention of Jesus's birth in Paul's writing occurs in Romans 1:3–4 (NRSV) where Jesus "descended from David according to the flesh and was declared to be Son of God with power according to the spirit of holiness by resurrection from the dead." No virgin birth is found here, only a resurrection. Although Paul develops a robust Christology in his writings, he does so without knowing anything about a virgin birth—a story that wasn't yet developed and written. The virgin birth is not necessary or foundational for Paul. In fact, it appears that he, too, knows nothing about it. This makes sense when we realize that the virgin birth story was a later addition to the portrayal of the post-Easter Jesus.

Many Supernatural Births

Christians have the idea that there was only one person in all of history who entered this planet through a supernatural birth—Jesus himself. For many, the reason a virgin birth story finds its way into the Bible is because God placed it there. When Scripture is viewed as the inerrant, authoritative, once-for-all words of God to humankind, stories take on a literal, factual reality straight from the hand of God. That is what the evangelical church taught me as I was growing up. The Jesus I worshiped and adored was conceived by the Holy Spirit, was born of a virgin, and saved me from sin. Had I been aware of other virgin birth stories, they would not have been taken seriously, for zeal without knowledge has a way of closing our mind to the reality of new insight.

Yet the existence of other supernatural birth stories before Jesus is exactly what we find. The concept didn't fall directly from heaven into the laps of Matthew and Luke. Instead, miraculous births had been around for a long time, and Christians may have utilized the concept to their own ends. The virgin birth story may be a Jewish adaptation of a concept already in existence before Jesus arrived on the scene. Here is a partial listing of other virgin birth stories that existed before Jesus.[9]

Sample Virgin Births

Name	Date	Birth	Note
Gautama Buddha	600 BCE	Born of virgin Maya	Holy Spirit came upon Maya
Horus	1550 BCE	Egyptian god born of virgin Isis	He received gifts as a baby from three kings
Attis	<200 BCE	Born of virgin Nama	
Quirinus	500s BCE	Roman savior born of a virgin	Universal darkness accompanied his death
Indra	700s BCE	Born of a virgin in Tibet	He ascended into heaven
Adonis	>1200 BCE	Babylonian god born of virgin Ishtar	
Mithra	600 BCE	Persian god born of a virgin	
Zoroaster	1000s-1500s BCE	Iranian leader born of a virgin	
Krishna	1200 BCE	Hindu god born of virgin Devaki	

Many Greek and Roman mythological figures were said to be born of gods. Hephaestus, the god of fire and metalworking, was said to have been conceived by the gods in a sexless, virgin birth. Perseus and Romulus were conceived by gods. Great and powerful leaders like the Roman emperors and the Egyptian pharaohs were thought to have divine origin. Virgin birth examples come from other religions, Egyptian and Classical history, Greek and Roman mythology, and even philosophy, as Plato and Apollonius of Tyana were thought to have divine origins. Matthew and Luke weren't the first to advance miraculous birth stories as a way of describing the origins of heroes.

The point is not whether these stories are literally, factually true, for we now know that human births do not occur apart from a female egg and a male sperm. Virgin or not, that's how the biological process works. The point is that divine birth stories existed long before Matthew and Luke attributed a supernatural birth to Jesus. It was not a novel concept in the ancient world. Whether or not

Matthew and Luke were aware of other miraculous birth stories is debatable. The bottom line, however, is that stories of supernatural births have been around since the days of old as an ancient method of elevating others to prominence.

Elevating Jesus

The idea of a virgin birth didn't enter into the literature of Christianity until the ninth decade of the first century. Jesus doesn't seem to know anything about his alleged virgin birth. Jesus's own family thinks he is out of his mind—not the kind of reaction one would expect from a virgin mother who experienced a supernatural conception. The disciples don't know anything about it. The first-generation Christians never heard of it. Paul in the earliest Christian writings knows nothing of it. The story is only mentioned in Matthew and Luke, writings that would occur much later in the first century.

The virgin birth narrative developed over time as a way to comment on the life and meaning of Jesus. Matthew and Luke were trying to capture his wonder and magnificence—a way of portraying their hero. They were elevating the Jesus who had so profoundly influenced the lives of so many. One method of doing this was to say that he was conceived by the Holy Spirit and born of a virgin. That would certainly have set him apart from the masses. With all the information we know about human reproduction these days, we would probably find another way of elevating our profound experience of Jesus, but in those days, describing someone as being born of a god was not an uncommon method of elevating prominence.

The virgin birth story is one way Jesus morphs from a historical Jesus into the Christ of faith—from the pre-Easter Jesus to the post-Easter Jesus. He moves from a normal birth, normal parents, and normal siblings to being conceived by God and born of a virgin. The legend grows as a way of portraying him as larger than life. In a later chapter, I share how Jesus moves from a mere man to a God in the Christian tradition, but for now, we take notice that the virgin birth story was a later development that arrived on the scene in the ninth decade—nearly sixty years after Jesus was crucified.

Jesus's miraculous birth is a post-Easter myth. Evangelicals and fundamentalists react negatively to the word "myth"—a demeaning term in their mind. I readily dismissed the concept in seminary because my evangelical filter didn't allow me to fully grasp how scholars were using the term. Like many others, I took "myth" to mean that something was untrue and shouldn't be taken seriously. We get our hackles up, and our defense mechanisms kick into high gear in an effort to protect the esteemed Bible from being denigrated to something untrue and unimportant. This, however, is an incorrect understanding of the term.

In the world of religious studies, "myth" has an entirely different meaning than what we commonly attach to it. Myths are stories designed to connect us to the sacred world. In other words, they serve as a bridge for connecting the sacred dimension to our common, everyday life. In this sense, the virgin birth story is a myth because it is a story that connects God with humans—the sacred with everyday life. As such, myths or sacred stories can be powerful ways to convey truth without being literally true. They are often symbolic methods for helping us better relate to God without the story itself being literally or factually true.

It is when we literalize religious myths that we lose all credibility in the modern world. We can literalize God impregnating a virgin if we want, but people living in the present age realize this simply cannot be, for it flies in the face of what we scientifically know. People begin moving away from such unbelievable doctrines. Christianity loses credibility in their eyes, becomes intellectually indefensible, and is quickly dismissed as an outdated relic of an unenlightened past. Something more is being communicated through the virgin birth story than a literal understanding of the details.

The virgin birth narrative is a response to the ministry and impact of Jesus. It is a way of showing that God is present in human history through the person of Jesus. He was someone who moved them beyond their own humanity, and whether it is the story of his birth, resurrection, or ascension, they are all human declarations that Jesus was greater than what his ministry had been. In him, they saw the very presence of God. There was no other way to describe it, for in their mind, no possible human explanation could adequately describe the presence of God experienced in Jesus.

That Jesus was literally, actually born of a virgin through the seed of God is not an historical reality, for we know that to be factually impossible. We also know that the purpose of virgin birth stories is to elevate individuals in the minds of the readers, not provide details of a literal, actual event. Virgin birth stories are a commentary on the meaning and impact of a hero. We don't attribute divine origin to infants; instead, we attribute divine origin as a way of addressing their adult life—a reflection of what they did or how they lived their life as an adult. The virgin birth stories about Jesus were, in essence, a backward reflection upon the meaning and importance of his life written long after he was dead and gone. Matthew and Luke are declaring that the birth of Jesus was a significant event in the history of the world, for from that birth came a man in whom the very image of God could be seen.

Isaiah's Prophesy

To die-hard virgin birthers of the evangelical and fundamentalist persuasion, I am not reading my Bible correctly, for Jesus's virgin birth was predicted centuries ago by Isaiah the prophet. Isaiah 7:14 indicates that a virgin will be with child and bear a son and that his name will be Immanuel. Does it get any clearer than that? There it is, right in front of our noses and stated as plainly as plain can be. Isaiah predicted it, and his prophesy came true. It is so simple—just believe what the Bible says!

If we dig a little below the surface, however, we discover that things aren't as simple as they appear, for the context of the statement and the word translated as "virgin" are not what they seem at first glance. This is where *studying* the Bible instead of merely *reading* the Bible reveals its value and allows us to maintain intellectual integrity in our faith. Does Isaiah really say that a virgin will be with child? Let's look at the facts.

Let me state it forthrightly: the word "virgin" is nowhere to be found in Isaiah 7:14. It simply isn't there. The Hebrew text literally reads: "a woman is with child." Not "a virgin will conceive" or "a virgin will be with child." Saying that a woman is with child is quite different than saying that a virgin will conceive a child. The nature of the person with child has changed from a woman to a virgin, and the timing of the conception has changed from a woman already pregnant to a virgin who would become pregnant centuries later. Why does Matthew's quote of Isaiah 7:14 not line up with the actual Hebrew text?

Maybe the difference can be explained by Matthew quoting the Septuagint, a Greek translation of the Hebrew text. But this can't be, because Matthew's quotation even deviates from the Septuagint version. Matthew seems to be relying on some other Greek translation of Isaiah that we are unaware of and do not currently possess. Matthew's quotation of Isaiah 7:14 actually differs from both the Hebrew text and the Greek Septuagint translation in two places. First, Matthew says that the virgin will be with child, whereas the Septuagint states that the virgin will conceive. Secondly, Matthew uses the third-person plural in saying "they" will call him Immanuel, while the Septuagint uses a second-person singular "you" will call him Immanuel. Both Matthew's version of the Old Testament quote and the Septuagint's translation into Greek do not accurately reflect the actual Hebrew text of Isaiah 7:14 (NRSV), which uses a third-person singular. The New Revised Standard Version of the Bible gets it right: "Therefore the Lord himself will give you a sign. Look, the young woman is with child and shall bear a son, and shall name him Immanuel."

My point is that the Old Testament Hebrew text has been mistranslated so that its meaning changes. This isn't something I just pulled out of a hat. Scholars have known about this for quite some time. The average layperson may not be aware of how the Hebrew text has been altered in support of a virgin birth narrative, but even Justin Martyr, in his dialogue with Trypho in the second century, was fully cognizant of this issue.

A writing exists titled *Dialogue with Trypho*, written between 155–170 CE, in which Justin Martyr argues that Jesus was the Messiah. We are uncertain if the dialogue was a real one or whether Trypho was a fictional character created by Justin Martyr in a mock argument. Nonetheless, Justin, who is a new convert to Christianity, invites Trypho to also convert to the faith. This spawns an interesting dialogue between the two of them. Trypho notes that "virgin" is a mistranslation of the Hebrew text, the very point I have raised. Unfortunately, Justin doesn't listen, for his mind is already made up on the matter. Justin won the second-century battle, but given our modern-day knowledge, it seems that Trypho has won the war.

The Hebrew word "almah" is used in Isaiah 7:14 and refers to a young woman of childbearing age, not a virgin. If Isaiah wanted to refer to a virgin, he would have used "betulah," the only Hebrew word for virgin. In fact, "betulah" is used more than fifty times in the Old Testament. People knew what a virgin was, but Isaiah doesn't use the word. Instead, he chose "almah," which refers to a young woman. Even our English Bibles can't escape the pressure to conform, for they merely reference "young woman" in a tiny footnote. The Septuagint, however, mistranslates the Hebrew "almah" into the Greek word "parthenos," which can mean virgin or maiden. Trypho realizes that there is absolutely no connotation of "virgin" in the Isaiah text. It is only in the translation from Hebrew to Greek that "almah" is mistranslated as "parthenos" and the connotation of virginity arises.

Isaiah's Context

As Matthew seeks to connect Jesus to the Jewish Scriptures, it is helpful to understand the actual context of Isaiah 7:14. Was Matthew stretching things in order to make his point, or did he accurately reflect the context surrounding the verse? Is Isaiah 7:14 a prophecy about the virgin birth of Jesus uttered eight hundred years beforehand, or is the verse commenting on the immediate situation occurring in Isaiah's time?

In previous chapters, I noted how Scripture is relative—that is, related to a specific time, place, and circumstance. When we yank verses from their historical context, they become nothing more than out-of-context justifications for however we desire to use the passage. All one has to do is examine the context of the chapter to realize that Isaiah 7:14 is not referring to a virgin birth occurring centuries after the fact. It isn't rocket science. Here is the condensed version of what was happening in Isaiah's day that prompted the infamous verse about a young woman with child.

Assyria was a powerful and threatening kingdom with a thirst for conquering. It had both the drive and resources to be successful. Three neighboring kings were very concerned about their ability to withstand an assault by the Assyrian army. These three kings were Ahaz, the king of Judah in the south; Pekah, the king of Israel in the north; and Rezin, the king of Syria to the northeast. If the three kings could combine forces, they might have a chance against the Assyrian invaders.

King Ahaz declines the invitation to join the three-king alliance, which angers Pekah and Rezin. Rebuffed, they bring their forces upon Jerusalem with the hope of deposing King Ahaz and replacing him with someone who will agree to their alliance. The people are frightened when the armies of King Pekah and King Rezin surround the city of Jerusalem. This is when Isaiah speaks to King Ahaz and encourages him to take heart, for the Lord will give King Ahaz a sign if he will only ask for one. Though Ahaz refuses to ask for a sign, Isaiah gives him one anyway. The sign given to King Ahaz is that of a young woman who is pregnant with child. She will give birth to a son whose name will be Immanuel.

People immediately think that Isaiah is speaking of Jesus, when he isn't. The Isaiah context goes on to say that the boy will eat curds and honey, and before he reaches the age of being able to discern good from evil, the kings camped outside Jerusalem will be gone. In other words, in a short time, King Pekah and King Rezin would no longer be a worry, and beyond that, the Assyrians would eventually be destroyed. As things turned out, Pekah and Rezin were wiped out by the Assyrians within two to three years, and though the Assyrians overtook Jerusalem, at least the people survived, even if under the thumb of Assyrian rule. Their trouble was only for a season, but they lived through it rather than being obliterated like Pekah and Rezin.

The sign Isaiah provided to Ahaz was that of a pregnant woman who would give birth. In other words, it was a symbol of life and continuance. It was a living sign that God had not forsaken them. Despite the siege, life would continue on for the people of Jerusalem—just look at the pregnant woman who will give birth. As the child grows, he will be a constant reminder of God's presence. The crisis will pass, and life will go on. Many scholars believe that the child may have actually been Hezekiah, who would later become king of Judah.

Neither the Isaiah text nor its historical context suggests anything about a virgin birth. The reference to a young pregnant woman has nothing to do with Jesus, who would arrive on the scene some eight hundred years later. What good would a sign about Jesus have done for King Ahaz in his present crisis? He needed immediate encouragement, for his city was surrounded by Pekah and Rezin and would soon be overcome by the Assyrians. How would a reference to Jesus relate to them, and how would they even understand it to be referring to Jesus? They would have no clue to who Jesus was. The sign of the pregnant woman who gives birth to a son was to show King Ahaz, in that moment of time, that Judah would live on, life would continue, the crisis would pass, and God would remain in their midst. The boy's very presence signifies God's presence during this difficult time.

Matthew's message is written primarily with Jews in mind, as Jesus is presented as the Messiah. In his zeal to connect Jesus to the Jewish Scriptures, Matthew actually misquotes the Hebrew text of Isaiah 7:14 to support a developing tradition surrounding the birth of Jesus. Other than Matthew and Luke, no other Scripture addresses the supernatural birth of Jesus—a new addition to his growing legend. Matthew tries to link this developing tradition to supporting material from the Old Testament. The rest of Scripture, however, is dead silent on the matter.

Overcoming Original Sin

The virgin birth story made perfect sense in the ancient world as a means of elevating Jesus. In fact, theologians believed that his virgin birth overcame the issue of original sin passed down from Adam. Our present-day understanding of the woman's role in human reproduction, however, completely obliterates this belief.

The doctrine of original sin teaches that the first human beings, Adam and Eve, disobeyed God by eating the forbidden fruit. The perfection they once enjoyed was now lost as the taint of their sin entered the stream of human existence to be passed down to all subsequent human beings. When a male impregnated a female, the stain from Adam and Eve's original sin was passed down to the offspring.

Jesus, however, couldn't be a sinner like the rest of us. He had to be viewed differently, for you couldn't elevate him only to have him brought down by the taint of sin. There had to be a way of separating him from this generation-to-generation sin problem. The virgin birth narrative solves this dilemma and allows Jesus to escape the corruption infecting all of humanity. The solution is simple—Jesus was conceived by the Holy Spirit, not male seed, thus breaking the cycle of sin. This allows him to bypass a stain the rest of us are said to possess. Adam wasn't his father; the Holy Spirit was. Because of this, original sin couldn't have possibly been passed down to Jesus.

This was an ingenious explanation at a time when the woman's role in the reproductive cycle was understood to be one of passivity. In other words, women merely lent the nurture of their wombs to the life planted inside by the male. Women were not considered co-creators because there was no understanding of their contribution to the reproductive process. Sin was passed on by male seed, and because Jesus's father was the Holy Spirit, he was immune from the transfer of original sin.

This outlook changed a few centuries ago with the discovery of female eggs and male sperm. With this relatively new milestone in human understanding, it became clear that women could no longer be considered passive participants in the reproductive process. Instead, we now realize that they are an integral part of creating life and contribute 50 percent of the genetic makeup of the child. Oops! This sure changes the meaning and impact of a virgin birth protecting Jesus from the taint of sin, for if Eve is now a contributor instead of a passive incubator, the protection once relied on no longer exists.

Prior to the knowledge that women contribute to human conception, the virgin birth story was an accepted explanation of how Jesus escaped original sin. Because sin was passed on by male seed, the woman's role was irrelevant, and Jesus had nothing to worry about. Now that the woman is seen as a contributor to human creation, the transfer of sin becomes problematic. With the advent of science, the discovery of a woman's egg cell, and her genetic contribution of DNA material, the virgin birth story is no longer credible in the modern world.

Realizing this sinking dilemma, Catholics invented a new doctrine known as the Immaculate Conception of Mary. In 1854, Pope Pius IX declared it so. It was their way of dealing with the new knowledge of a woman's contribution to the creation of human life. Instead of changing their view on the virgin birth of Jesus in light of scientific evidence, they broadened their theology to say that God even spared Mary from the stain of Adam's sin as a way of preserving their commitment to this doctrine.

It reminds me of the joke about a man who thought he was dead. The doctor drew blood from his vein to show that he was alive, but it did no good, as the patient exclaimed, "So, dead men do bleed after all!" Like the man convinced he was dead, it is difficult to alter the perspective of closed minds unreceptive to new information, especially when it affects a long-held belief.

If Jesus was conceived like the rest of us, then he was born into original sin as we were. This simply couldn't be, for it would destroy the very doctrine taught by the church for centuries. As quick thinking preservationists, they invented a new doctrine called the Immaculate Conception of Mary, whereby God miraculously cleansed Mary so she was unable to pass Adam's sin down to Jesus. She, too, was also conceived without sin. This change in theology—this invention of new doctrine—doesn't bode well for intellectual integrity, and it does nothing to dispel the problem of credibility. It goes to show how far the church will go to preserve its dying doctrines. I guess dead men do bleed after all!

The virgin birth story really wasn't a miracle of birth, because Jesus grew in the womb and was delivered like every other child born of a woman. Instead, the miracle was one of conception—of a woman becoming pregnant without male seed. We call it a birth story when it is really a conception story. Impregnating a virgin female with male sperm through artificial insemination is achievable these days, but pregnancy without male sperm is not.

The seed that impregnates Mary wasn't male seed at all, for if it was, the original sin of Adam would have been passed down to Jesus. Instead, it was God's seed. The fact that God has seed to give to Mary or that God would impregnate a human being is an alarming revelation. Not only does it elevate Jesus above the masses as someone special; it also becomes a method for overcoming the transfer of original sin from generation to generation.

The idea that a virgin birth would somehow prevent the transfer of original sin onto Jesus was destroyed when science discovered that women were active participants in the creation of life. No longer could they be viewed as passive incubators, for they actually contributed 50 percent of the baby's genetic makeup. If Mary was tainted by original sin, then Jesus was tainted by original sin. This scientific discovery has created quite a theological challenge for the doctrine of hand-me-down sin.

In light of this new knowledge regarding women, something had to change with the status of Mary to prevent sin from reaching Jesus. The doctrine of the Immaculate Conception of Mary does just that, an innovation that miraculously cleanses her from all sin. This newly invented doctrine cures the problem, for now we have holy seed from God and a holy cleansing of Mary. Rather than altering Christian teaching to align with new knowledge, we simply created a new unbelievable doctrine to explain an outdated and intellectually deficient theology.

Impact on the Incarnation

The transfer of sin, however, is only one issue affected by the scientific discovery of a woman's egg cell and her contribution to the baby's genetic makeup. The doctrine of the incarnation is also affected. Traditional Christian teaching asserts that Jesus was a God in heaven who voluntarily left his high and lofty abode to become a human being. Jesus had to be fully human, I was taught, in order to be our human representative, and he had to be fully God in order for his substitutional, sacrificial death to be applicable to all who believed in him. We will discuss the doctrine of atonement in the next chapter, but for now, Jesus is promoted as being fully God and fully human in one body—a doctrine known as the incarnation.

When asked how this can be, fundamentalists respond as they typically do to such conundrums: "It is a miracle of God. Just believe." The doctrine, however, makes no sense whatsoever. If the seed of God and the egg of a human were united, the outcome would be a baby that was neither fully God nor fully human. To be one is not to be the other. Being human is to possess all the limitations and encumbrances of humanity. Being God is to be free from the limitations and encumbrances of humanity. Uniting a God and a man creates neither a God nor a man. If Jesus was both, then he was an anomaly—a human standard we can never rise to or achieve, for we are not God-Men or God-Women.

I was taught that Jesus was the God-Man and that everything he did was the result of being fully God and fully man—a new strain of being with the merging of humanity and divinity. In human form, the powers associated with deity were restrained, while Jesus's human powers were augmented so that he could heal, read the thoughts of others, and outwit the religious elite who tried to trap him with tricky questions. To be truthful, I couldn't really explain how all this worked, and I didn't think much about it at the time. I simply believed the doctrine because, after all, no one can explain God, and this was just one of those things you had to accept in faith. The Bible taught it, and because the Bible contained the very words of God, it was my solemn obligation to accept its teaching, which I dutifully did.

Does God possess sperm to impregnate a human being? Would the sperm of God and the egg of a woman produce a baby who was fully God and fully man or an offspring who was neither fully human nor fully God? Is this virgin birth narrative a literal story providing us with factual details of what actually occurred, or is this a sacred story designed to convey a profound truth about Jesus rather than a literal truth? Saying that the Holy Spirit came upon Mary was an ancient way of recognizing that Jesus couldn't have been the kind of person he was without the presence of God upon him.

Scandalous Illegitimacy?

If there was no miraculous conception and a virgin teenage girl didn't become pregnant with seed from the Holy Spirit of God, then the implication is clear: Jesus had a human father. But who? Did Joseph and Mary have premarital sex in which Mary became pregnant? Was the father someone other than Joseph? If so, did Mary engage in intercourse willingly, or was it forced upon her without consent? To even suggest such a thing is taboo. How dare we tarnish the reputation of Mary! Yet such questions must be raised if we seek intellectual honesty in our faith. If Jesus wasn't miraculously conceived by God, then he must have had a human father like the rest of us.

Some scholars smell the scent of scandal surrounding the birth of Jesus and pick up hints scattered throughout the Gospels. Even in John 8, where a woman caught in adultery is brought before Jesus for condemnation, he allows her to depart without judgment. Could this be reflective of a sensitivity to his own past? Some scholars think so.

Everything we know about human reproductive biology tells us that Jesus was conceived by a human father as opposed to a supernatural father. This doesn't change the value seen in Jesus or the image of God reflected in his life, but it does make us wonder who his earthly father was. In another sense, does it really matter? God is seen in all people, regardless of race, religion, pedigree, belief, or birth father. However Jesus came into the world diminishes nothing of him in my eyes, for the life of God was upon him in such a way as to be transformative in the life of others, including my own.

The progression of my faith may not be different from the journey others travel. First, I became cognizant of God and entered into spiritual awareness through the doorway of evangelicalism. Second, I read the Bible literally and learned the stories contained within. Third, I sought higher education in the realm of theology and learned how to interpret the Bible from an evangelical perspective. Fourth, I entered full-time ministry and spread the evangelical dogma. Fifth, I garnered valuable real-life experience, where I realized that church teaching didn't square with reality. Sixth, I began to read, study, and broaden my perspective until I arrived at an understanding of faith that I could embrace wholeheartedly without casting aside intellectual integrity.

My understanding of God has changed so much that Jesus doesn't have to be impregnated by the Holy Spirit for me to see the image of God in him. In fact, Jesus becomes a much greater example to me by not having a supernatural birth. In this way, it gives me hope that by following his ways and living a life of selfless love, I might also be able to reflect a positive image of God's life flowing through me. As I bring up the scandalous notions surrounding the birth of Jesus, I do so realizing that it is necessary to identify all the elephants in the room. I doubt we will ever have all the answers we desire, but at least we are talking about things head-on and up-front. Questioning, probing, and seeking are not threatening; doing so is merely a part of the spiritual journey that I embrace. It is allowed and encouraged. How else do we arrive at authentic faith?

Mary

It must be remembered that the accounts of Jesus's birth were written long after he died. They are post-Easter stories crafted with a particular agenda and audience in mind. Some scholars believe that Mary and Joseph were not historical figures at all but rather composite fictional characters necessary for the storyline. The first mention of Mary as the mother of Jesus occurs around the eighth decade when Jesus speaks in his hometown synagogue. One of the listeners inquires, "Is not this the carpenter, the son of Mary and brother of James and Joses and Judas and Simon, and are not his sisters here with us?" (Mark. 6:3, NRSV). In Matthew, we get our second reference to Mary, around the ninth decade. Luke brings her up as well, but in the Gospel of John, she is not called by name but merely referred to as "the mother of Jesus."

While Mary has become a focal point in Catholic theology, she isn't often spoken of in the New Testament, and when she is, it isn't always in a positive light. For instance, John merely refers to her as the mother of Jesus without mentioning her name. When she notifies Jesus that the wine has run out while they are attending a wedding in Cana, Jesus responds in John 2:4 (NRSV), "Woman, what concern is that to you and to me?" That isn't a flattering or respectful way to address one's mother. In the Gospel of Mark, the townspeople struggle to understand how Jesus could speak so powerfully, having been "the son of Mary," possibly a derisive comment regarding a charge of illegitimacy. She is said to come from a lowly estate in Luke, and Matthew notes Joseph's surprise when Mary is expecting a baby that is not his. Additionally, Jesus is implicitly accused of being the son of illegitimacy in John 8:41. Mary even believes Jesus is out of his mind in Mark 3.

Recognizing this uncomplimentary view of Mary, both Matthew and Luke delete Mark's reference to Mary believing that Jesus was out of his mind, and they delete Jesus's uncomplimentary comment toward his relatives who refused to honor him as a prophet in Mark 6.

A charge of illegitimacy was leveled at Jesus that Matthew and Luke seek to clear up, for they are trying to spread the good news about him in the midst of these spurious accusations. While Scripture doesn't come right out and openly declare illegitimacy, many scholars believe the hints are too significant to ignore. After speaking in his hometown synagogue, Jesus is called "the son of Mary." Given the hierarchical nature of the male-dominated society and the emphasis on male offspring and lineage, male inheritance, male rights, and males as producers of life, referring to Jesus as the son of a woman instead of the son of a man was an insult suggesting that his father was unknown.

Matthew may have also hinted at this illegitimate charge by noting that Joseph was surprised when his betrothed became pregnant by someone other than himself. In Luke, Mary is portrayed as someone from a lowly estate. What could be lowlier than pregnancy outside of marriage? The Gospel of John also records someone questioning Jesus's birth: "We are not illegitimate children" (John 8:41, NRSV). The implication is obvious—Jesus was. One way of handling the illegitimacy issue is to write a virgin birth story that proclaims God to be the father of Jesus. Matthew also addresses Jesus's lineage with a genealogy filled with some interesting people.

Genealogy of Jesus

In seeking to elevate Jesus in the minds of his Jewish audience, Matthew links him to the father of the Jews: Abraham. He also traces Jesus to King David, who is intricately associated with Israel's messianic expectations. For Jesus to be considered the Messiah, the very thing Matthew was trying to show, he had to be linked to David. What is even more fascinating is how the genealogy connects four well-known women from Jewish history to the virgin birth story.

Tamar, the first woman mentioned in the genealogy of Jesus, is Judah's daughter-in-law. Judah is one of the twelve sons of Jacob, and he impregnates Tamar, his daughter-in-law. She gives birth to twins: Perez and Zerah. Jesus's line comes through Perez. Rahab is another woman named in the genealogy whose story we are more familiar with. She is a prostitute in Jericho who protects Joshua's soldiers tasked with spying on the land. The next woman of notoriety is Ruth. Ruth is a widow who gathers leftover grain from the field of Boaz, a distant relative. She seduces Boaz by giving him too much wine. In his drowsy state, he falls asleep. Ruth climbs under the covers with him and in the morning pleads with him to marry her. Boaz can't find anyone more closely related to Ruth for her to marry, so he takes it upon himself to be her husband and protector. The final woman of note in Matthew's genealogy is Bathsheba, the wife of Uriah the Hittite. Involved in an adulterous affair with King David, she becomes pregnant and gives birth to their child.

Do you see a pattern here? The line of Jesus flowed through a woman involved in incest, a woman involved in prostitution, a woman involved in seduction, and a woman involved in adultery. How do these women with sordid pasts relate to the virgin birth story?

Matthew may have introduced his virgin birth story with a genealogy that included incest, prostitution, seduction, and adultery in order to address the illegitimacy issue. If the life of God can be seen in all kinds of people, even these disreputable women in Israel's history, then surely the life of God can also be seen in Jesus, who was hanged on a tree like a common criminal and suffered charges of illegitimacy.

What the Virgin Birth Means

I have no idea whether Mary engaged in intimate relations with Joseph prior to the ending of the betrothal period, or with another man, either voluntarily or involuntarily. There is just no way for us to know these things for certain, given the limited information we have about Mary, Joseph, and Jesus. I do know that to interpret the virgin birth story literally violates everything we know about human biology. Myths, the sacred stories of religion, were never meant to be literalized, for their role is to present profound truth, not literal truth, and to serve as bridges between the sacred and the ordinary. For all the reasons mentioned in this chapter, God impregnating a virgin female doesn't pass the sniff test of credibility.

Reading the birth narrative literally cheapens the Jesus story and is entirely unnecessary. The sacred story is loved and valued, but not because it is a literal account. Rather, it reveals how the life of one man can be so meaningful, loving, and impactful. The virgin birth story reflects a belief that no human life could be lived like Jesus lived it without God being involved. The supernatural birth story was a way of connecting the human life of Jesus with the sacredness of God. In Jesus, we see the intersection of the sacred upon the ordinary.

Jesus was a man in whom the image, power, and presence of God could be seen like no other, but that wasn't because he was God and possessed an advantage unlike the rest of us. No, the power of the Jesus story is that he was a human being whose life of selfless service and love for others demonstrated to all what God must be like.

Virgin birth language is ancient language, a way of elevating the status of Jesus more than two thousand years ago. That language no longer resonates with our world of science, technology, and advanced knowledge. We no longer talk that way or see things that way, and we would never use ancient language in light of the wisdom we now possess. Do we continue speaking ancient code in a postmodern world, or do we somehow find relevant and credible ways of addressing the experience and reality behind the virgin birth stories? Continuing to advance literal interpretations is to speak ancient code that no one speaks these days. It is a language of the past that will soon die out. The virgin birth story says a great deal about how Jesus was perceived that is valuable and profound, but it is not a literal story, as many believe.

Ascension to Heaven

Before leaving this chapter, there is one more item that must be addressed. The virgin birth was Jesus's entrance into this world, while his ascension depicts his exit back into heaven to be seated at the right hand of God. We surely don't know all there is to know about the universe, but we certainly know much more than first-century biblical writers. Ascending from Earth up into heaven doesn't pass muster.

Another way of elevating the status of Jesus is to say not only that he came from God but that he also returned to God. Unfortunately, a literal interpretation of the ascension also loses credibility in light of present-day knowledge. The ancient world maintained a three-tier view of the universe: the abode of God beyond the clouds, Earth below, and the sky in between. God lived "up there" just beyond the clouds.

Since the discoveries of Copernicus and Galileo, however, a three-tiered universe has come under fire. Ancients would be astounded to learn that we have sent men to the moon, possess giant telescopes that peer into the night sky, and even sent hurling through space a traveling telescope snapping pictures of far-away galaxies. We even have exploratory probes moving throughout our galaxy. My mind is blown away with all of this, and I live in the time when it is all happening. The difference in knowledge between then and now is astounding, like the gap between a two-year-old and a Harvard graduate with a Ph.D. in biophysics and sixty years of life experience. The knowledge gap is huge.

If Jesus ascended up into heaven, what is meant by the term "up"? Going straight up from Chicago takes me in one direction, while straight up from Seoul takes me in an entirely different direction. Up from one location in the world may actually be down or sideways from another location around the globe. "Up" doesn't make much sense in a vast three-dimensional universe, but it does if you believe the world is flat, sits at the center of the universe, and exists in three tiers—heaven, sky, and earth. Going straight up beyond the clouds to arrive at God's home made perfect sense in their world. We know today, however, that if we went straight up from any location on Earth, we would not arrive at God's doorstep. Instead, we would be stuck in Earth's gravitational pull and find ourselves orbiting the planet. If we were to somehow escape Earth's gravitational pull, we would find ourselves floating in space, not standing in the throne room of God.

Think about the pure physics of an ascension. Even if Jesus ascended at the speed of light, which is 186,282 miles per second, he would still not have escaped our galaxy on his way to a heavenly destination somewhere out there. Unlike first-century Christians, we have actually been beyond the clouds, orbited Earth, and explored space, and we have yet to discover heaven just beyond the clouds. Like the virgin birth narrative, this ascension story simply cannot be taken literally. It is intellectually indefensible in light of the knowledge we currently possess, and yet we ask people to jump on the bandwagon. When they don't, we label them as bad Christians or, worse yet, unbelievers.

The virgin birth is an incredible story about how Jesus enters the world. The ascension is its corresponding tale of how he gets back to where he came from. Neither of these stories can be taken literally, but they can be valued and loved as sacred stories—human attempts to connect the sacred with the ordinary. For first-century people with first-century knowledge and a first-century worldview, what better way to do that than by using first-century language of a virgin birth and an impressive ascension?

Greater Than Elijah

In previous chapters, I noted how the Gospel of Matthew, written primarily for Jews, compared Jesus to Moses. One can easily discern how Matthew used Moses as his comparative inspiration. Comparing Jesus to Moses was his way of elevating Jesus in the eyes of his Jewish audience. If you thought Moses was great, wait until you consider Jesus, for he was greater than our greatest hero.

Luke's account, however, is written for a broader audience in an attempt to attract Gentiles. Unlike Matthew, who compares Jesus with Moses, Luke uses Elijah as his comparative measuring rod. If you thought Elijah was great, wait until you consider Jesus, for he was greater than our great prophet Elijah. Moses and Elijah represent the Law and the Prophets, and Jesus is greater than both of them. Jesus was the new Moses and the new Elijah.

The Gospels of Matthew, Mark, and Luke were all written for use in the life of the synagogue. The stories are framed with the various parts of the liturgical year, seasons, and practices in mind. Writing to Jews in the homeland, Matthew's genealogy of Jesus is traced back to Abraham, the father of the Jewish nation. Luke, on the other hand, is writing to dispersed Jews who were in greater contact with Gentiles and could attract a larger audience. His genealogy extends farther back than Abraham, for Luke extends his lineage all the way back to Adam, the father of humankind, which opens the appeal of Jesus to a greater audience.

The Gospel of Luke reflects a connection to Elijah. For instance, just as Elijah raised from the dead the only son of a widow, Luke has Jesus doing the very same thing by also raising the only son of a widow (Luke. 7). Just as Elijah healed a foreigner (Naaman) of leprosy, Jesus also heals a foreigner (Samaritan) of leprosy (Luke. 17).

The granddaddy comparison of them all is the story of Elijah's ascension. Just as Elijah ascended into heaven, Jesus also ascended into heaven. It took a chariot of fire and a whirlwind to get Elijah off the ground, but Jesus was greater than Elijah and didn't need a chariot or a whirlwind. Instead, he ascended in a cloud on his own accord. As Elijah ascended, he dropped his mantle for Elisha, his star pupil, as a sign that he would inherit a double portion of Elijah's spirit. Jesus's ascension was grander, for he released the Holy Spirit of God at Pentecost upon people from every tribe and nation. Do you see the comparison Luke is making? He is elevating Jesus to one who is greater than Elijah, one of the greatest heroes in the history of Judaism.

Many Christians today believe that Jesus literally lifted off this planet to begin his journey beyond the clouds and up into God's heavenly abode. For them, this was an actual, factual event; had there been streaming video in that day, they could have captured it live and streamed it to the world. I suggest that the ascension wasn't an actual event at all but rather a way of relaying profound truth that is real, valued, and loved, but not literal.

Not only is Luke elevating Jesus as someone greater than Elijah; we are also reminded of the enduring presence of Jesus. The ascension places Jesus back into the presence of God, and if God is said to be everywhere, then Jesus must also be everywhere. Because he is no longer living on Earth as a flesh-and-blood person, his presence is no longer restrained by time and space. Jesus can be experienced anywhere and everywhere. Placing Jesus at the right hand of God portrays him as one who holds authority and honor. In other words, he is Lord, not the Roman emperor. Jesus is the one worthy of our loyalty.

The point is that the ascension is symbolic and metaphorical, not literal. It speaks of a valuable and real truth, but not a literal event. Jesus is greater than Elijah, and he is greater than the Roman emperor. He is worthy of our respect, trust, and loyalty, for his enduring presence is with us always.

Chapter Summary

This chapter dismantled a literal interpretation of the virgin birth story. In an effort to elevate the status of Jesus in the eyes of their readers, Matthew and Luke fashion their birth stories—an ancient way of uplifting someone above all others. The virgin birth stories are not to be taken literally, for humans do not give birth apart from conception with male seed. The discovery of a female egg and a male sperm prove this.

The entire virgin birth story erroneously stems from Isaiah 7:14, which is mistranslated. The Hebrew text only says that a young woman is with child, not that a virgin will become pregnant by the Holy Spirit some eight hundred years later. Isaiah 7:14 is speaking to the immediate context of King Ahaz, not some prophecy about an event centuries later.

In his attempt to elevate the status of Jesus and possibly address a question of illegitimate birth, Matthew quotes a Greek mistranslation of Isaiah 7:14, for it supports his cause and helps advance the developing narrative around the birth of Jesus. No one knew about a virgin birth until the ninth decade, when Matthew brings it up. Neither Jesus, Mary, the disciples, nor Paul had ever heard of such a thing. The story was developed in the late first century.

The bookend to Jesus's miraculous entry onto this planet is his miraculous exit from Earth as he ascends into heaven to secure his seat at the right hand of God. Like the virgin birth narrative, this story is not to be taken literally, for it, too, is a myth—a sacred story designed to convey profound truth about Jesus, not literal truth. His ascension is likened to that of Elijah, one of the great heroes of the Jewish faith. Jesus is even greater than Elijah. The virgin birth and ascension stories are literary methods of saying that the life of God was seen in Jesus like no other.

This chapter briefly mentioned the impact of the virgin birth upon the incarnation, but it is our next chapter that delves into the matter more deeply. According to traditional Christian teaching, the reason Jesus left his heavenly abode and entered human history was to die on the cross and atone for our sins. Is this another doctrine gasping for its last breath in the contemporary age? I answer that question in the next chapter.

10

THE ATONEMENT

· · · · · · · ·

ET'S FACE IT: CHRISTIANS ARE ENAMORED WITH the blood of Jesus. We sing songs about the blood. We symbolically drink the blood during communion. We wash ourselves in the blood according to the lyrics of one of our great hymns: "Are you washed in the blood, in the soul-cleansing blood of the lamb? Are your garments spotless? Are they white as snow? Are you washed in the blood of the lamb?" The blood of Jesus carries theological significance for traditional Christians.

The way to overcome any problem, according to one of my former ministry students, is to simply "plead the blood" of Jesus. His class presentation included a large chart with Scripture verses to bolster his case. The core of his entire ministry consisted of pleading the blood of Jesus—whatever that means. He didn't much care for my probing and clarifying questions. I guess he had things all figured out, and my role as professor was to simply acknowledge his impressive biblical interpretation skills. It goes to show just how potent the blood of Jesus can be, as the hymn states: "There is power, power, wonder-working power in the blood of the lamb."

My days as a youngster in the church were filled with plenty of hymn-singing that exalted the blood of Jesus with such songs as "There Is Power in the Blood"; "Are You Washed in the Blood"; "Covered by the Blood"; "Nothing but the Blood"; "There Is a Fountain Filled with Blood." Those songs held deep meaning for me, and even though my theology has changed significantly since my early years, I still love me some good ol' hymns. Recognizing that some hymns can become dated and theologically awkward, several denominations have updated their lyrics while keeping the familiar melodies. I recently attended a denominational conference where great hymns of the past had been outfitted with modern lyrics. For me, this was the best of both worlds. The recognizable melody brought back wonderful memories while I stood with a host of modern-day worshippers giving voice to a faith that touched our contemporary reality.

Radio, television, and online religious programming are jam-packed with preachers recounting how Jesus died on the cross for our sins. The cycle is one of sin, guilt, repentance, forgiveness, and restoration—all based on seeing the death of Jesus as the substitutional and sacrificial offering that placated God's wrath. This idea that Jesus's death was a spilling of blood for all humanity is deeply ingrained in us. It is another doctrine of the church we readily embrace without much scrutiny, and it takes a bit of thinking to wrap our arms around its disturbing implications. Will we once again watch another long-held doctrine disintegrate before our very eyes?

Atonement Defined

A fancy theological word like "atonement" needs some defining. In simple terms, atonement refers to the death of Jesus as the satisfaction or reparation for our sins. The story goes like this: When Adam and Eve ate of the forbidden fruit in the Garden of Eden, they disobeyed God's clear instruction. Defiled by sin, their disobedience opened the door for a defect to enter into the stream of human existence as their sinful contagion was passed on to the rest of humanity. According to Christian teaching, we enter this world with a sinful nature that befalls all of us. Not only is our human nature totally depraved; we also choose to sin on a daily basis. Trapped in this ghastly predicament, we find ourselves alienated from a holy God by nature and by choice. We need to be forgiven and brought back into a right relationship with God. In essence, we need a Savior—someone who will rescue us from our helpless plight.

As diseased individuals unable to produce an effective antidote, we are unable to save ourselves, for God's holiness and justice cry out for satisfaction. Like oil and water, sin and holiness do not mix. Something has to give. The cure is an unblemished, perfect sacrifice that appeases an angry deity. That's where Jesus comes into the picture. God the Son left the splendor of heaven, descended to Earth, and took on human form to become a Savior who died for our sins. His death was sacrificial in that he gave his own life as a ransom for many, but it was also substitutional because he died in our stead. An unblemished sacrifice has to be without sin, and his conception by the Holy Spirit assures us that the stain of Adam did not reach him. Born without a sinful nature and having lived a sinless life, Jesus became the perfect, unblemished sacrifice offered in our place.

Because all of humanity is infected with this dreadful disease and we are unable to offer ourselves up as blameless sacrifices, we need help. As a human, Jesus could be a representative for all humanity, and as God, his sacrifice could be applied to all those who respond in faith. This idea of Jesus dying for our sins is the story of atonement.

From pulpits across America, this doctrine is proclaimed Sunday after Sunday. Churches are filled with symbols, rituals, and sermons that constantly keep the death of Jesus before us. We cannot escape it, for the story is tightly woven into the very fabric of Christian teaching and has been for centuries. Crosses adorn our sanctuaries. We wear them as shiny pieces of jewelry around our neck. Hung on the walls of monastic sleeping quarters, crosses are the last thing monks see before they go to bed and the first thing they see when they wake up. With atonement theology set in religious concrete, am I really going to question this core belief?

Many enjoy splashing about in the shallow waters of faith, but as they wade into the river of new insight and the water rises to their waist and chest, they panic and high-tail it back to the safety of the shore. No matter what doctrine is being examined, the elephants in the room must always be identified and scrutinized. You might want to tighten your seat belt, because this chapter will severely test whether you want to splash in the shallows or float in the deep waters of transformation. Are you willing to identify elephants in the room and view doctrine with greater objectivity, even when it comes to your most cherished beliefs, or are you too far into the black hole to ever consider an alternative perspective?

If the death and resurrection of Jesus are seen in a new light—if the old, traditional way of understanding the Jesus story is no longer credible—can we even call ourselves Christian anymore? That is a reasonable question. The answer is a resounding "yes," and I will address this very issue later down the road. For now, open your mind and your heart to a new way of seeing. As you think things through and wrestle with your own understanding of faith, don't abandon common sense and the bounty of present-day knowledge. Questioning beloved doctrines is not an easy thing to do. It takes courage and honesty. Rest assured, God is not threatened by inquisitive minds and probing endeavors, and no lightning bolt slung from heaven will strike us down for being intellectually and spiritually curious.

Jesus presented no test of creed or list of approved doctrinal statements that must be affirmed in order to experience, love, and follow God. So, let go of the many theological restraints the church uses to define and control who can be God-followers. Before we jump right in, however, let's get a handle on the last week of Jesus's life to gain a clearer picture of his death.

Jesus's Last Week

The fact that Jesus lived and died is not seriously questioned by historians. When it comes to the Apostles' Creed and the Nicene Creed, however, about the only historically accurate statement is that Jesus was crucified under Pontius Pilate, suffered death, and was buried. On the one hand, there is the actual, historical reason why Jesus was killed, and on the other hand, there is the theological explanation of why he was executed. Historically, Jesus died because he was charged with a political crime, which was treasonous to Rome. Traditional Christians, however, believe that Jesus came to Earth for the express purpose of sacrificing his life to save us from sin. One is a historical reason for his death, while the other offers a theological interpretation of his crucifixion.

Jesus's public ministry began shortly after his baptism in the Jordan River by John the Baptist—a relative of Jesus. John was a fiery preacher who spoke forcefully of repentance and the necessity of being prepared for the coming judgment. Apparently, Jesus was moved by John's message and sought to be baptized, after which he initiated his own public ministry. How long was Jesus's ministry? We are unsure. Some believe that his public ministry lasted one year, because in Matthew, Mark, and Luke, he attends only one Passover in Jerusalem, while in John, he attends three different Passovers—leading some to conclude that his ministry lasted three-and-a-half years.

Near the end of his life, we find Jesus in the city of Jerusalem, a word that means "city of peace." The irony is that, for Jesus, the city was anything but peaceful, for it would be the place of arrest, condemnation, and crucifixion. Matthew notes that after the transfiguration, "Jesus began to show his disciples that he must go to Jerusalem and undergo great suffering at the hands of the elders and chief priests and scribes, and be killed, and on the third day be raised" (Matt. 16:21, NRSV). Peter took exception to this crazy talk, pulled Jesus aside, and rebuked him. Luke also notes this unwavering commitment to enter Jerusalem: "When the days drew near for him to be taken up, he set his face to go to Jerusalem" (Luke. 9:51, NRSV).

Remember, Matthew and Luke are writing decades after Jesus's death in an attempt to elevate his stature in ways that support their cause. They are looking backward as they write—trying to put into their own words what his life meant.

Whether or not Jesus actually stated his intention to go to Jerusalem, we will never know, because the authors of Matthew and Luke were not disciples of Jesus who followed him around. It is quite possible that Jesus yearned to take his message to a larger crowd found in Jerusalem during the Passover celebration, but did he purposely intend to die? Was he on a "suicide-by-crucifixion" mission, purposefully entering Jerusalem with the specific intention of being hung on a cross? His death stunned his disciples and all who followed him, leaving first-generation Christians struggling to interpret his shocking demise. Placing words of intention upon his lips is an after-the-fact, post-Easter, backward-looking way of attaching significance to his death. Once Jesus's death was adequately interpreted, second-generation Christians moved on to explain his birth.

Jesus may have known that a trip to Jerusalem could easily cost him his life—a risk he was willing to take. After all, if you interrupt the temple activities, overturn the tables of the moneychangers, upset key religious leaders, speak of new interpretations of the Torah, proclaim a countercultural message, and enter Jerusalem to a noisy crowd bowing before you and placing garments and palm leaves on the ground, the risk of danger increases dramatically.

Like other devout Jews, Jesus celebrated the Passover in Jerusalem. His message had previously been proclaimed in rural areas of Galilee, but here was an opportunity to declare his kingdom message before a larger crowd in the big city of Jerusalem. Because Jews were expected to celebrate the Passover in Jerusalem, the city swelled two to three times its normal size as visitors arrived for the annual celebration. It was congested and hectic with the possibility of tense and dangerous moments, for which the Romans were prepared. Extra troops were brought in to quickly squash any disturbances that might erupt.

During this last week of his life, Jesus entered the temple and didn't like what he saw. Was he upset that the moneychangers were making a profit off sincere worshippers who had traveled a good distance and were in need of sacrificial offerings? Was he dramatically acting out a parable of God's soon-coming judgment? Whatever his intention, interrupting the operations of the temple during such a busy time was not taken lightly, for it upset the religious leaders, who would seek to stop Jesus from further disruption.

During this week, he celebrated a meal with his disciples, took time to pray in the Garden of Gethsemane, and was betrayed by one of his disciples: Judas Iscariot, who was bribed into providing pertinent information about Jesus to the Jewish authorities. What information did Judas provide that led to the arrest of Jesus? Did he merely share the location of Jesus so he could be quietly apprehended away from the crowds, or did Judas provide something more—information that would somehow serve to justify an arrest?

Jesus not only taught crowds of people who came to hear him speak; he also taught his own disciples privately. Some wonder whether a private teaching of Jesus could have been used against him. For instance, Jesus taught his disciples that in the future kingdom, they would rule over the twelve tribes of Israel. But who would rule over the twelve disciples? Jesus, of course. Could Judas have shared this new kingdom teaching in which Jesus would be a ruler?

If Judas provided this information to Jewish authorities looking for a reason to quiet Jesus, this talk of ruling in a new kingdom could have easily motivated their desire to shut him down. You don't talk about being a ruler, your disciples ruling over the twelve tribes of Israel, and implementing a new kingdom without someone in power taking notice, especially those upset with Jesus. Rome guarded its empire with iron fists, and this kind of talk would not have been well received. The religious leaders saw this as a way to stop Jesus, for they already viewed him as a disruptor of the status quo. They took him into custody and turned him over to the Roman governor, Pontius Pilate. The death of Jesus has often been laid upon the shoulders of the Jewish people, but it was only a small circle of Jews who initiated this action, not "the Jews" as a people or nation. Jews get blamed for many things, even the killing of Jesus. Although both played a role, it was the Romans who condemned Jesus and carried out his execution.

Rome was unconcerned with trivial religious scruples. As long as things didn't get out of hand, and there were no riots and no disruption or threat to Roman authority, the Jews could quibble all they wanted about religious matters. A charge of religious blasphemy meant nothing to the Romans, but a political charge of claiming to be a future king was a potential threat to the authority and longevity of the empire. It was a charge that perked their ears and garnered their attention.

Pilate asked Jesus directly whether he was the King of the Jews, and by all accounts, Jesus responded affirmatively. Those words provided Pilate with the necessary grounds for condemning Jesus. After his flogging, he was made to carry his own cross, hoisted upon a wooden beam, and crucified along with two other criminals. Crucifixion was a dreadful way to go. It brought excruciating pain to its victims, sent a message to others of Rome's power, and brought despair unto Jesus's disciples.

The Gospels agree that Jesus was arrested, condemned to die, and crucified under Pontius Pilate. That is the underlying plot. Discrepancies in other details exist and are difficult to harmonize, such as what day did Jesus die? Was it after the Passover meal, as noted in Matthew, Mark, and Luke, or before the Passover meal on the Day of Preparation, as noted in John? Historians cannot firmly rely on the Gospels as factual accounts of what actually occurred because of the inconsistencies in the stories, the biased purpose of the authors, and the nature of Jewish storytelling, meant to convey profound truth rather than literal truth. The Gospels are not historical, factual, literal accounts of the life of Jesus but interpretive portraits of what his life meant.

Cause or Effect

For those who traveled around the countryside listening to him, believing his words, loving him, and anticipating the new kingdom, his death was a total shock. The man they loved, followed, believed in, sat under, and assisted for a season of powerful ministry was now dead. This must have rocked their world and brought on despair, frustration, disillusionment, and enormous pain. With their hopes crushed, the first generation of followers struggled to explain this unexpected outcome. How could it have happened, and what did it mean? The man sent from God had been killed in a most inglorious manner. He was supposed to be the Messiah, an anointed messenger of God, sent to usher in a new kingdom, and here he was, dead. How does one deal with that?

Is the issue one of cause or effect? In other words, was Jesus's death the consequence of his message and actions, or was it his very intention to begin with? Did God predetermine Jesus's death so that he purposefully sought crucifixion by Roman authorities, or was Jesus's death the unfortunate outcome of the message he was proclaiming? Was Jesus going to be killed no matter what, for any reason, just as long as he died, or was his execution the possible end result of a message that others didn't like?

First-generation Christians were stunned by Jesus's death and struggled to find some rationale, some explanation, for why it happened. In trying to account for his death, they searched their Scriptures for an answer—a justification. They came to the conclusion that God had ordained his death and that Jesus had been sent to die for our sins. In their minds, the Jewish religious leaders refused to recognize Jesus as the Son of God and were ultimately responsible for his death, even if they did hand him over to Roman authorities. But this is a backward reflection—an attempt to explain an event they didn't understand at the time. It was a post-Easter explanation of a pre-Easter event.

Though a small circle of Jewish leaders conspired against Jesus and the Romans found reason to execute him, his death was the end result of the message he spoke and the actions he took. It was not a preordained incident but a matter of risk while proclaiming a message that powerful people didn't like. Jesus may have sought to enter Jerusalem in an effort to spread his teaching to a larger audience, and he may have realized the risk in doing so, even the risk of losing his life, but he believed so strongly in his cause that he willingly assumed the danger.

From both a religious and political standpoint, his message and his actions infuriated protectors of the status quo. Danger always arises when the dominant powerbrokers are challenged. It happened to Martin Luther King Jr., Abraham Lincoln, Gandhi, and a host of others whose message got them killed. History is replete with examples of such people. Their deaths were not preordained, nor did they intentionally choose to die. Instead, they assumed the peril engendered by their cause. Their deaths were the unfortunate outcome of standing up to the powers that be with a message that challenged the status quo. Jesus's purpose wasn't to die but to transform the world with a life-changing message. For that, he was killed—the unfortunate consequence of promoting a cause from which he would not back down.

Paul

Because Paul's epistles are the earliest-known Christian writings, we get a sense of how he worked out the death of Jesus in his own mind. He was a learned man, a Pharisee who studied the law, knew the Scriptures, and was a pupil of Gamaliel, an early-first-century rabbi of high stature. For Paul, and many others, the death of Jesus simply didn't make sense—it didn't fit the mold of Jewish messianic expectations. He put his mind to work in searching for an answer.

Although messianic expectations of the first century varied, not one of them anticipated a Messiah like Jesus—convicted and crucified on a cross. That kind of death was reserved for criminals, and no one believed that the Messiah would be a convicted criminal. In their minds, and according to Deuteronomy 21:22–23 (NRSV), hanging on the timbers of a tree was to be accursed by God:

> *"When someone is convicted of a crime punishable by death and is executed, and you hang him on a tree, his corpse must not remain all night upon the tree; you shall bury him that same day, for anyone hung on a tree is under God's curse. You must not defile the land that the LORD your God is giving you for possession."*

Jesus was indeed hung on a tree—crucified upon a wooden beam with outstretched arms. This was not a noble act because it was akin to being accursed of

God—the very opposite of existing messianic expectations. Additionally, Jesus came from Nazareth, where the conventional wisdom of the day was expressed by Nathanael: "Can anything good come out of Nazareth?" (John 1:46, NRSV).

Nothing about Jesus fit messianic expectations. He was a carpenter, not a king. His own family and hometown certainly didn't view him as the Messiah. His disciples didn't always understand his teaching, and one of them betrayed him to the Jewish authorities, which led to his eventual death. He had no power, no prestige, no money, no formal education, and no place to call home. He didn't teach revolution or overthrowing Rome, and he didn't ride a stallion, own armor, or oversee a militant resistance. Instead, he spoke of peace, forgiving, serving, and becoming like little children. No one even considered a Messiah like that. Any hope that he might be the expected one was extinguished as he was hung on a tree, had a spear thrust in his side, and was buried in a tomb that was not his own. That isn't the image of a kingly Messiah, strong and mighty, able to cast off the yoke of Roman occupation. The hopes aligned with Jesus were quickly dashed against the rocks when he died.

Paul, once a persecutor of Christians, would have been pleased with the death of Jesus, except for his famous vision on the road to Damascus. That life-changing event altered his religious perspective and forced him to reconcile his personal encounter with the risen Christ and the dissonance within his own mind. How does one explain such an extraordinary incident when all roads lead to Jesus being accursed of God and defying all messianic expectations?

After his powerful encounter, Paul didn't sit under the disciples' teaching. Instead, he spent three years alone in Arabia, somewhere near Damascus, sorting things out in his own mind. Only after this time of personal reflection did he make his way to Jerusalem to meet with Peter and James. At the end of this season of pondering, he found a way to bring coherence between his personal experience and his messianic understanding—a view that has stuck with the church ever since.

Because the death of Jesus destroyed all messianic expectations, his death had to be explained in a new way. First-generation Christians linked Jesus's death with sin and salvation. By the time Paul wrote in the 50s CE, the idea was pretty well set. He declares in 1 Corinthians 15:3 (NRSV), "Christ died for our sins in accordance with the scriptures." His time of personal reflection and scouring Scripture helped him arrive at this conclusion. He deduced that our sins required a sacrifice and that Jesus was that sacrifice. For Paul, Jesus died so that sinners could be justified by the blood of Christ and saved from the wrath of God (Rom. 5).

Taking their lead from Paul, the Gospel writers add to this sacrificial language by noting that Jesus's death was a ransom for many (Mark 10:45). Paul's writings also prompted Mark to place Jesus's death in the context of the Passover so that he could be identified with the Paschal lamb of the Passover meal. As you recall from the Exodus story, it was the blood of the slain Paschal lamb that allowed the firstborn Hebrew children to escape death when God's angel of death flew over the land, killing children. Early Christians read this story in light of Jesus, whose death would now be connected to the blood of the Paschal lamb—now applied on the doorposts of human hearts to save them from death.

As time progressed and other Christian writings emerged, the story became more defined. In Hebrews, written in the 80s CE, Jesus is portrayed as a perfect sacrifice, much like the Yom Kippur lamb in the ritual of atonement. Because Jesus was an absolutely perfect human sacrifice, there was no need for additional sacrifices to be offered. His was a once-for-all sacrifice. As the church became more structured and refined in its theology, the idea of Jesus as the sacrificial Lamb of God became more pronounced. The creation stories were interpreted literally, and the doctrines of Christ become clearer. The traditional Christian story of redemption took flight.

Implications of Atonement

Paul's articulation of Jesus's death would become a central pillar in Christian teaching. This understanding arose in less enlightened times and within a worldview that included sacrificial offerings to the gods, an angry deity in need of appeasement, and a negative view of humanity. Will this explanation survive in a world of scientific inquiry, advanced worldviews, and a greater reservoir of knowledge?

It is now time to examine the many problems associated with atonement theology—issues that Christians either ignore or are unaware of. I will surface these issues so that ignorance can no longer be an excuse. I am, in a sense, pulling our collective heads out of the sand so that we can confront our doctrines with intellectual integrity.[10]

Denial of History

To say that Jesus died because of our sins is to soft-pedal the actual historical reason for his death. Pontius Pilate didn't execute Jesus to play a role in God's salvation story or to facilitate a death that would cover the sins of humanity. That thought wouldn't have entered his mind, and it didn't enter anyone's mind until years later as a post-Easter explanation. Pontius Pilate executed Jesus because he admitted to being the King of the Jews after Pilate asked him whether it were true. Pilate was certainly aware of the Jewish leaders' dislike for Jesus, but even they didn't arrest Jesus as a means of helping him fulfill a death wish that was ordered from above. Their actions were motivated by hate and disdain for the man who stood as a threat to their power and profit.

If Jesus merely had to die to save humankind, he could have enjoyed a full life of teaching and writing, gathered more followers, and simply awaited his natural and eventual human demise. Historically, however, he didn't just die; he was killed. Murdered. Publically executed. Neither the Jewish religious leaders nor the Romans liked what they saw and heard in Jesus. He had a following; was causing quite a stir with powerful religious leaders; was upsetting the status quo from a social, political, and religious perspective; and claimed to be a king.

His execution was public and demeaning—the type of death reserved for the worst of the worst. For Romans, crucifixion was a way of saying to the world, "This is what happens when you challenge our authority." His death also pleased the Jewish leaders, for they were the ones who arrested Jesus in the first place. Jesus's death served their purposes, too, as they gloated with a similar line of thinking: "This is what happens when you challenge our authority." To say that Jesus was crucified in order to rescue humanity from sin obscures the historical reality behind his death. Atonement theology arose after his crucifixion and attempts to find significance in the cross while soft-pedaling the historical reason for his demise.

Distorted View of Humanity

Have you ever thought about what this understanding of the cross says about us? We call Jesus the rescuer of humanity, which implies that humans need to be rescued. We call Jesus the Savior, which implies that humanity needs to be saved. We call Jesus the Redeemer, which implies that there is so little intrinsic worth in us that we must be purchased by his blood like a used, broken-down violin in a two-bit junk store. Traditional Christianity sees the very core of our human identity as one of guilt, sin, and shame. Human life is corrupt at its core, and everything about the church operates off this main assumption. Institutional religion would be lost without this theology, for it provides the necessary power and control to corner the market on forgiveness and dictate human behavior. The main problem with humanity, traditionalists believe, is that we are fallen sinners and our guilt is universal. So depraved are we that we are born into sin, and our very nature is corrupt. Is this an accurate diagnosis of our problem, or is this a distorted view of human nature? We have got to get the diagnosis right if we seek to offer an appropriate remedy.

According to the Genesis story, God's creation was originally perfect and good, and it would have remained that way had the forbidden fruit episode not occurred. With Adam and Eve's disobedience came the opening of the doorway to sin, and God's punishment quickly ensued. Kicked out of the Garden of Eden, the snake would now slither on the ground, life would become difficult, the ground would produce only with the sweat of our brow, women would experience painful childbirth, and death would be our destiny. When we look at the world today and see slithering snakes, life's difficulties, hard work, painful childbirth, and death, it is nothing more than the result of our own doing—the punishment of God and proof of our unworthiness.

Adam and Eve's sinful actions triggered God's redemptive process, and we watch it slowly unfold in the Scriptures until it culminates in the sacrificial, substitutionary death of Jesus on that fateful day when he was nailed to a cross. Now that his death has been accomplished, our job is to go into all the world and convert others to believe this story. Why God didn't rectify such a devastating situation immediately, no one knows. Instead, it took centuries upon centuries of pain, suffering, guilt, and shame before the final rescue operation took place in the first century. In reality, the full benefits of his death and resurrection have yet to be realized, as millions of Christians expectantly await Christ's return to Earth in power and glory.

The cure brought about through the death of Jesus seems to be a partial cure, one that must await its final effect in our lives. Meanwhile, those who aren't aware of this story or who happen to live in parts of the world where Christianity is not the dominant religion are simply out of luck, for the benefits of the cross apply only to those who believe. The rest await a destiny in hell, the place a jilted, loving God created for those who don't love God back. That is a pretty harsh way for God to implement a remedy for humankind, don't you think? I guess the antidote really isn't for all humans but only for those lucky enough to hear and believe such a message. The rest are doomed to become crispy critters in the eternal fires of hell—at least, that's the traditional way of seeing things.

We are slow learners. First, the Law arrived to aid us, but all it did was open our eyes to our many shortcomings and made us feel even more guilty. It had no ability to correct the problem; it merely pointed it out by throwing it in our face. A system of sacrificial offerings was implemented to temporarily appease an angry God and momentarily relieve our burden of sin until the next offering was due, but that system became corrupt and meaningless and merely masked the problem for the short term. It wasn't a cure but a Band-Aid. Next, the prophets arrived on the scene as a contemporary voice in leading God's people, but instead of listening and learning, the people killed the prophets for their message. Not even the Law and the Prophets could alleviate our sin problem. Finally, God sent Jesus, God's very own son, as a perfect, once-for-all, substitutional sacrifice for human sin. The sin problem was now cured on a permanent basis for all who would believe. That's the story we have learned over the years. But what does that story say about humanity? What is the underlying view behind such a narrative?

The underlying concept behind Jesus as the divine rescuer, Redeemer, and Savior of humanity is that we are intrinsically sinful, dirty, corrupted, evil, depraved, unworthy, and guilty. Can you imagine raising a child with this type of underlying assumption? If every morning, every night, and every day, we reminded the child of her unworthiness, depravity, sinfulness, and evil nature, would she grow up to be a healthy, balanced, functional adult? Of course not. But that is exactly what we find in Scripture. For instance, we are told in Isaiah 64:6 (NRSV), "We have all become like one who is unclean, and all our righteous deeds are like a filthy cloth." Referencing the Psalms, Paul asserts in Romans 3:10–18 (NRSV) that "there is no one who is righteous, not even one . . . there is no one who seeks God." Paul further declares that "all have sinned and fall short of the glory of God" (Rom. 3:23, NRSV).

There are plenty of other verses to remind us how wretched we are. In fact, one of our most beloved hymns, "Amazing Grace," informs us that the most amazing thing about God's grace is that it saved a wretch like me. We are wretched people deserving of God's wrath—a worm theology. We got ourselves into this predicament, and it's all our fault. I remember singing a Christian song that was popular in my earlier years that said, "And I'm the one to blame. I caused all the pain. He gave himself, the day he wore my crown." That's the view of human nature from the perch of traditional Christianity. We are evil people in need of rescue. Thank goodness for God's divine rescue plan, where the substitutional and sacrificial death of Jesus saves us from sin.

I possess a tiny booklet with a stitched binding and pages of different colored felt. This visual aid is often used in children's work to explain how their evil nature can be cleansed. The first page in the booklet is a piece of black felt that represents sin, that dark spot on our heart that makes us unclean and evil in the sight of God. It is followed by red felt representing the blood of Jesus that was shed on the cross in order to save us from the blackness of our soul. Next up is blue, the color representing baptism and the washing away of our sins. After blue comes the white felt page that reflects our cleansed hearts becoming whiter than snow because of what Jesus has done for us. Now that we are forgiven and cleansed, the next page is green and speaks of our responsibility to live for Jesus and grow in our faith. The last page of the book is yellow, a color representing heaven, the place where forgiven sinners are privileged to go when they die.

When I knelt beside the hideaway bed at my friend's house many years ago, a similar story was told to me as his father led me down this path of faith. This was the faith formula—the only way evangelicals and fundamentalists know how to understand the cross. That night, the night I followed the evangelical formula, I sensed that I had made a momentous decision for my life. I am grateful for entering into faith through the doorway of evangelicalism, for it brought to me a personal and literal way of understanding God—something I needed in my life at the time. The formulaic story shared with me in my early years is the same story that I learned in seminary and the same story I told others. Whether we used a little felt booklet, pointed to select verses of Scripture, or walked forward during an altar call to say the sinner's prayer, it was an encounter with God.

For me, it was the first time I experienced God in a meaningful and momentous way. Now that I have matured, garnered valuable life experience, studied Scripture to greater depths, and taken time to reflect and process, I find the story of the little felt book to be deficient and disturbing in many ways.

I make a distinction between my experience of God and my explanation of that experience. This is an important difference worth pointing out. As I knelt beside the hideaway bed, I experienced God's presence in my life, but I now have a different way of explaining that experience, and it doesn't entail the traditional theology of the cross. For many, these are difficult words to hear, but bear in mind that I am in no way denying the reality of God or the personal nature of our God encounters. People experience God in different ways and at different times that are personal to them. Liberals, progressives, evangelicals, fundamentalists, and even atheists can, and have, experienced God. It is not the reality of the experience that I question but the explanation itself, for the story we embrace either lends itself to credibility or fantasy.

From an evangelical and fundamentalist viewpoint, the entire story of the Bible is one in which God is working to restore a right relationship with a fallen, distorted, and sinful humanity. That is the backdrop upon which all else is built—the unfolding story of a fundamentally flawed humanity in desperate need of forgiveness and restoration. Does this explanation ring true in our world—a world where the light of knowledge shines more brightly than at any other time in history?

Darwin and Evolution

The cross is a universally recognized symbol of Christianity, along with its story of a once-perfect creation that fell into sin. The cross of Christ is the Christian remedy for our sin problem. But then came along science, the scientific method, Darwin, and the theory of evolution, which would shake Christianity to its core. How does the traditional Christian story stand up to this new source of knowledge? Not very well, I am afraid.

Darwin lived with competing passions—God and science. At one time, he sought to become a member of the Anglican clergy, but his love for natural science won out. Darwin's famous voyage to the Galapagos Islands would forever change the way we look at human origins. The published findings of his research knocked the church off its feet. As science grew and expanded in knowledge, the church found itself retreating into defensive positions that still exist today.

Darwin introduced evolution to the world, the theory that all species of life evolve from a common ancestor. This branching out of species occurs through a process of natural selection—the survival of the fittest. Evolution takes time for mutations to occur, which means that Earth is older than the biblical record suggests. Scientists exploring the fossil record, geological record, and DNA evidence agree that Earth is billions of years old, not thousands.

Darwin's findings challenge traditional Christian teaching in two primary ways. First, they challenge a literal understanding of the Bible. In light of the current scientific knowledge we now possess, a literal six-day creation is not supported by the evidence. Faced with contrary data, many traditionalists are forced to expand their understanding of a literal six-day creation. Begrudgingly, they may adjust the time it took God to form the world, but they are unwilling to accept the full implication of science upon their faith. What else in the Bible doesn't match up with the knowledge we now possess? Is the talking snake of the creation story literal? Is the Garden of Eden literal? Is the story of Adam and Eve literal?

The creation stories were written in a different time with a different worldview, under different circumstances, and with a different base of available knowledge. The story of creation, as told in the Bible, may have been the only way people could conceive of creation at the time, for the knowledge we currently possess was not available to them. The story of the Bible is now placed under the microscope of modern knowledge, modern circumstances, and modern worldviews.

In the past, I felt uneasy with the relationship of Scripture to science. Science is always moving forward, always growing and expanding in its knowledge, and sometimes it gets things wrong. Theories are merely theories that are continually in motion and in need of adjustment. How and why would I put my trust in science when it is ever evolving? I wanted to place my faith in something solid and unchanging, like Scripture. But science was eroding my trust in Scripture as the literal, unchanging Word of God. No longer could I square core biblical teaching with scientific data, and my literal views were crumbling. Either science was a heap of rubbish and the biblical stories were literally true, or science was providing new evidence and my understanding of Scripture had to change to fit a new reality.

As you can tell from the writing of this book, I have traveled beyond the base-camp of biblical literalism. No matter what we believe, whether it is a religious belief or not, we must always be willing to alter our perspective as new evidence becomes available. We must go where the evidence leads us, even if we struggle with the new direction. It is the right thing to do. My faith is not in science, for science isn't something in which faith is placed. Science is merely one tool out of many that gathers data for understanding the universe. It is a useful and good tool, but it's certainly not the only tool in the shed.

Science is uncovering new knowledge all the time. Our understanding of the world is evolving. Centuries from now, we will know more than we do at this time, and our views may have to adjust even further. Although I am grounded in the existence of God, my understanding of God will grow and expand as new knowledge comes to light. I understand the internal wrestling match that ensues when evangelicals and fundamentalist clash with science. The answer isn't a rejection of science or a rejection of the Bible but rather an appreciation for science and a new understanding of Scripture.

What do Christians do with evolution, knowing that even this theory may be adjusted over time? For many, if evolution is true, they can no longer believe in God, and their faith is destroyed. The issue isn't whether God exists or not but whether their understanding and explanation of God can coexist with the information that science is revealing. Evolution doesn't deny a creator, only the means by which creation occurred. Science may alter how I view and interpret Scripture, but it does nothing to destroy my belief in God. Darwin's theory of evolution, which is supported by a plethora of evidence, challenges a literal understanding of the Bible, a view that collapses under its own weight.

The second impact of Darwin's research is even more significant than the first, for it undermines the very foundation upon which the Bible stories are told. In other words, it challenges the notion that human beings were originally created perfect and fell from that perfection through sinful disobedience. Evolution undercuts the very foundation of atonement.

Evolution moves in the opposite direction of the biblical story and contradicts the fall of humankind. According to the Bible, human movement goes from perfection to imperfection. Evolution, on the other hand, moves from imperfection to something more perfect. Life began with one cell that learned to divide into two cells, and then thousands of cells, and on to various structured forms of life over billions of years. Humans, with their self-conscious abilities, are a relatively new form of life in the grand scheme of Earth's history. That kind of story is a very different story than what is presented in the biblical creation accounts.

If humans evolved over time as evolution suggests, then there were no first parents handcrafted by God out of the ground and placed in the Garden of Eden; rather, life evolved from a single cell. Do you see the enormous impact this theory has upon the biblical story? Darwin implies that life is still evolving and in the process of adapting and becoming. Perfection has yet to be achieved. At this very moment, galaxies are still being formed as the creative process continues. If there is no such thing as original perfection, then there can be no such thing as an original fall. You can't fall from something that doesn't exist.

This destroys the concept of original sin, the corruption of human nature, and the need to be saved from sin by the death of Jesus. If evolution is true, it is absolutely devastating to the traditional way the Christian story is told. Does this mean that God is not real and doesn't exist? No, it means that our understanding and explanation of the biblical story has to change, for the old story, as it is currently told, is no longer credible in light of present-day knowledge.

When we strip away the traditional storyline, what else is there? We are at a loss for what to replace it with (the last section of the book will address this). Viewing humanity as totally depraved and in need of forgiveness through the shed blood of Jesus is a distortion of the real message of the Bible. If there is no original perfection, no original sin, and no original fall from perfection, then the problem is not one of forgiveness but rather a problem of not yet evolving into what it means to be fully human, something I will address in future chapters. For now, my point is that Darwin's theory of evolution challenges not only the literalness of the Bible but the very foundation of the redemption story as a fall from perfection.

Distorted View of God

In addition to the damaging nature of Darwin's theory of human origins, have you ever considered what the theology of atonement actually says about God? Not only does the traditional story imply that humans are sinful, corrupt, evil, depraved, and in need of redemption; it also holds disturbing implications for God as well.

When you step back and consider the redemption story, it is rather appalling. We focus so much on our unworthiness and how good God is to rescue us, we forget how repulsive the story can be. What kind of God requires a blood sacrifice in order to forgive? Is God's justice so unwieldy that the only way to overcome the offensiveness of sin is to require that Jesus die? What kind of satisfaction is that? What kind of God requires that kind of payment?

Jesus instructs his own disciples to forgive those who offend them, and they should do it seventy times seven times, a number that indicates forgiveness without limits (Matt. 18:21–22). If we—as sinful, unworthy, evil people—are expected to forgive without end, without condition, and without a blood sacrifice, why doesn't God do the same? In order for God to forgive, however, someone must die and pay the ultimate price. God's forgiveness is conditioned upon a human blood sacrifice. Can you imagine if we required that kind of sacrifice before we extended forgiveness?

You say, "Well, you are not God!" That is exactly my point! It seems that our own sense of justice is far greater than God's, for God asks of us what God will not do Godself. Is God's sense of justice so warped that a bloody sacrifice must be offered in appeasement? That is disgusting and repulsive. Certainly an all-powerful, all-loving God could have found it within Godself to forgive, just like we are asked to forgive, without the spilling of human blood. How is it just to require the death of an innocent man to satisfy the justice of God? It seems like the *ultimate injustice* to me.

If God requires that the Son of God pay the ultimate price for sin with his own life, does that make God the ultimate child abuser? Which one of us, as parents, would demand that our child be flogged and crucified to appease our sense of justice? In any other walk of life, this kind of behavior would be unacceptable, if not criminal. Yet Jesus becomes God's victim, the one who is beaten and condemned to die in order to appease the Heavenly Father's holy anger. In essence, God the Father demands the death of God the Son as a payment for sin. Who of us would treat our own child like that? Does this sound like justice to you?

To further our human guilt, we are told over and over again that we are the ones responsible for Jesus's death—that he died in our place. God's wrath is so severe that God would have easily killed us, for we are worthy of death. In fact, if we don't get our act together and believe in Jesus as our Savior, we are bound for eternal damnation in the fires of hell. Think of it—a loving and benevolent God doling out eternal punishments for temporal sins. That hardly seems like justice. It would be similar to punishing a child with eternity behind prison bars for stealing a piece of candy at the grocery store. The punishment doesn't match the crime. Eternal hell for a temporal sin? Does it bother you that God even requires a death at all—the sacrifice of a human life? It ought to. It is repulsive.

The story of the cross, as told by traditional Christians, reminds us of ancient worldviews where fickle gods demand sacrifices of appeasement to stay their hand of punishment. While the intent was to create a story to explain the death of Jesus, the outcome produced a God who wasn't worthy of our affection. The story makes God out to be a punitive God who can't seem to forgive without a blood sacrifice. The story makes Jesus out to be a victim, as God's punishment is taken out on him in exchange for forgiveness. The story perpetuates the familiar guilt-laden view of humanity and elevates the church as the place that speaks for God, houses forgiveness, and controls the behavior of others. Do we really think that kind of story can withstand the test of time? Who are we kidding?

Is that the story of the cross or a distorted understanding of the Christian message? Atonement theology is an ancient story—one that is no longer credible in our sophisticated age. The world of Old Testament sacrifices and competing gods who hurl thunder and lightning from above no longer exists. We do not live in the first century, with its limited base of knowledge. We have progressed from the fourth century and from medieval times. We are now a twenty-first-century space-age generation with medical, scientific, and technological breakthroughs occurring regularly. The message of a bloodthirsty God whose justice demands a bloody human sacrifice finds no traction in our day. The Christian message has to be bigger, grander, and deeper than this ancient perspective.

Unworthy or Incomplete

Is this guilt-laden message of the cross the correct diagnosis of the human condition, and is the shedding of Jesus's blood the correct remedy? Is escaping the wrath of God really what Christianity is all about? Is punching our heavenly entrance ticket in the afterlife the meaning of this life? What if the framework we have been operating from for so long is incorrect? What if the problem with humanity is not that we have fallen from perfection, are infected with sin, and are in dire need of forgiveness?

Instead, what if humanity is incomplete and evolving—in need of being made whole, more complete, and more fully human? How could we have fallen from a perfection that never existed in the first place? Our problem is not that we are sinners but that we are incomplete people on a journey toward wholeness where we become more fully human. The theology of atonement keeps us shackled to the Christianity of yesterday, but the power of God, as seen in Jesus, moves us beyond our incomplete selves and toward a greater humanity where the life of God flows in and through us.

A Gentile Distortion

This distortion of the cross can be attributed, in part, to the move from Jewish beginnings in the synagogue to Gentile understandings away from synagogue life. When Christians speak of Jesus as the Passover lamb, they are often unaware that they are identifying Jesus with the Paschal lamb of the Old Testament, whose blood was spread on doorposts to prevent the Hebrew firstborn children from being slaughtered by God's angel of death. Additionally, on the Day of Atonement during Yom Kippur, a lamb was killed and its blood placed on the Mercy Seat.

Coming from a non-Jewish world, Gentiles took these symbols and animal sacrifices to mean that an angry God needed to be appeased by sacrifices that paid for sin. This idea of animal sacrifices seems so archaic in our age. In Jewish terms, the lamb was sacrificed not to appease an angry God but to recognize that humans have not achieved the fullness of their humanity. We long to be whole, complete, and all that God intends us to be, and an unblemished lamb represented the wholeness we long for. God is whole, complete, and perfect, while we are still on that journey. The lamb is a symbol that represents our journey of becoming.

Misrepresents Christianity

We have leaned on atonement theology for so long that we rarely ever question it. It is simply accepted as true. All this talk of Jesus paying for our sin, being forgiven, and securing an entrance ticket to heaven when we die isn't the thrust of the Christian message. This perspective may have prevailed in a flat-Earth, three-tiered understanding back in the day, but it actually obscures the real meaning of Christianity—the meaning of transformation. If Christianity is about changing, growing, becoming, and transforming ourselves and our world, then making forgiveness the sole issue of Christian meaning misses the greater point.

When we literalize the creation story, the fall, the eating of the forbidden fruit, etc., we misrepresent the Christian story and create doctrines covering humanity, heaven, hell, salvation, forgiveness, original sin, and atonement that turn God into a vindictive curmudgeon.

Challenging central doctrines of the Christian faith wins me no favors among biblical literalists. How can we not place them under the light of modern scrutiny when our database of available knowledge has progressed so far? All belief, even religious belief, must continually be updated in light of new knowledge. The death of Christ is indeed filled with meaning, but it's not the literal meaning that we assign to it.

Chapter Summary

This chapter challenges the traditional understanding of Jesus's death—that he died as a substitutional sacrifice in our stead to satisfy God's sense of justice and save us from the consequences of sin. This story arose as a post-Easter explanation of a pre-Easter event that was neither understood nor expected. Caught off guard by his shocking death and the manner in which he died, first-generation Christians linked Jesus's death to Old Testament stories of the Paschal lamb and the lamb of Yom Kippur.

The implications of such a story are incredulous and rarely thought about by Christians. Atonement theology obscures the real, historical reason Jesus died—that he was charged with a political crime that was treasonous to Rome. His death was the unfortunate result of proclaiming a message that offended those in power. The story of atonement presents a distorted view of humanity—once perfect but corrupted through the fall of disobedience. Darwin's research, on the other hand, indicates that humans weren't created perfect but evolved from lower life-forms to more complex forms of life, from imperfection toward greater evolution. If there was no perfection to begin with, then there is no fall, no sin, and no need for a Savior.

The story of atonement also presents a distorted view of God—that grand curmudgeon in the sky who possesses such a warped sense of justice that human blood must be spilled before forgiveness can be extended. To require the death of an innocent human being is an act of ultimate injustice by a deity claiming to be just. God now becomes a bloodthirsty father who victimizes Jesus in an act of divine child abuse. What kind of parents would demand the death of their own innocent son in pursuit of justice? To top it all off, the story perpetuates a negative view of humanity as sinful, fallen, corrupt, and unworthy. This plays right into the church's hands as the powerful arbiter of human behavior and the place where forgiveness can be secured. In essence, the story misrepresents the real message of Christianity.

Now that the birth and death of Jesus have been examined, we turn our attention to his resurrection, another core doctrine of the church. What do we mean when we say that Jesus was resurrected? Is his resurrection to be taken literally, physically, spiritually, or is the story simply a metaphor for something else? The next chapter helps us answer these questions.

11

THE RESURRECTION

· · · · · · · ·

EASTER HAS LONG BEEN ONE OF MY FAVORITE TIMES of the year. I love its message of hope and its bright and cheery colors. As the defining moment of Christianity, it is the glue that holds our faith together. The resurrection, not the death of Jesus, gave rise to our faith. Without a risen Christ, the movement would have fizzled out long ago. Easter is the most celebrated Christian holiday around the globe. In fact, Christians gather for worship on Sundays because it is thought to be the day in which Jesus was raised. Easter lilies, new spring dresses, and early-morning worship services are a part of the American Easter tradition.

The great resurrection hymns that I grew up singing still resound in my mind with such memorable lines as "Christ the Lord is ris'n today, Alleluia"; "Because He lives, I can face tomorrow"; "Up from the grave he arose, with a mighty triumph o'er his foes." Their glorious stanzas hold a special place in my heart as Christians from around the world unite in celebratory voice on Easter morning.

I was told by a reliable source that the pastor of the church I grew up in nearly visited the local funeral home in order to raise a dead man back to life. Apparently, he felt called by God to do so. After all, Jesus was raised from the dead. So was Lazarus and several folks in the Old Testament. For my pastor, it was simply a matter of faith because God certainly has the power, even in our age, to bring life back into a corpse. But alas, raising a dead man lying in his coffin took more faith than he could muster, and he abandoned the idea.

Televangelists in the business of healing boast of God's wonder-working power, but they always seem to be dealing with the lesser illnesses. We don't find them raising dead people back to life, growing limbs that have been amputated, removing metastasized cancer from the body, unclogging blood vessels of the heart, curing diabetes, and healing other seismic health issues. Raising someone from the dead is not something you see every day, and that brings up the issue of meaning.

An Issue of Meaning

What exactly do we mean when we speak of a resurrection? If the meaning is central to our faith, it behooves us to seek clarity on the matter.[11] Our understanding either advances the cause of credibility or hinders it. For my former pastor, resurrection meant altering the nature of a corpse so that life once again flowed through the veins of a dead person. One day, you are dead as a doornail, and the next, you are brought back to life again. What was breathless, cold, decaying, and lifeless now becomes a breathing, living, warm, heart-pumping, blood-circulating, thinking individual. Is that what is meant by resurrection—that Jesus was dead as a doornail and brought back to life again?

Unfortunately, the New Testament doesn't describe for us the rising of Jesus. We are simply told that Jesus is raised and that he appears to others, but the actual event itself is never fully explained in Scripture. Because this matter is left undone, we must look elsewhere for interpretive clues, and this has led to varying perspectives. The precarious nature of language and meaning is another obstacle. We think meaning is easily grasped—that is, the meaning we assign to the resurrection. Yet others may see things differently because they assign a different meaning—the meaning that is easily grasped by them. Realizing that the New Testament leaves out crucial details about the rising of Jesus and that human language is fraught with its own weaknesses, what we assume about the resurrection may not actually be correct. The issue comes down to meaning. What does the Bible mean when it says that Jesus was raised?

A Familiar Story

Early on in my spiritual journey, I learned about the resurrection of Jesus, a core Christian belief. Years ago, I preached at my daughter's church and demonstrated the importance of the resurrection by bringing her up front to illustrate its foundational nature to the Christian faith. Echoing Paul's words in 1 Corinthians 15:17, I believed that if Jesus wasn't resurrected from the dead, then our faith was worthless. I still believe that the resurrection is essential to Christianity, but I now understand its meaning in a whole new way.

The story I was taught to believe went like this: Jesus was crucified, died, and was buried in a tomb. After three days, life was restored to his body, and he walked out of the tomb, showed himself to various people over a period of forty days, ate with them, talked with them, and appeared at will before ascending into heaven to be seated at the right hand of God. Because Jesus could appear, disappear, and pass through walls, his resurrected body was a new kind of glorified entity. Just how that could be, I did not know. I simply took it on faith. Jesus was raised in the manner in which we will be raised from the dead at our own resurrection. Immediately after the rising and prior to his ascension, Jesus's body was in a transition state until he was seated at the right hand of God. Of course, it didn't occur to me at the time that a whole lot of gap-filling was going on with this view. It made for good preaching, but was it actually true?

My ordination with the Christian and Missionary Alliance denomination demanded that I believe in a bodily resurrection of the dead. This included Jesus's resurrection as well as my own at his second coming. Had I questioned the doctrine or articulated an alternative view, I would have been soundly rejected as defective and unfit for Christian service—cast off the evangelical assembly line. So you see, what is meant by resurrection is a matter of meaning. How will we understand the rising of Jesus? What meaning will we assign to it?

Reviving a Corpse

Does resurrection mean bringing something dead back to life—back to its previous existence? Was this a revivification or resuscitation of a corpse, much like the raising of Lazarus, who had been dead for three days? Is that the meaning of resurrection?

If "rising" implies that Jesus was brought back to a previous state of physical existence, then he would at some point have to die again because he was human. It doesn't explain how he could pass through walls, appear, and disappear. What good does it do to be raised only to die another death? What hope and benefit does that offer us?

Some maintain that Jesus was raised in a semi-physical state of existence that allowed him to eat fish, invite Thomas to touch him, talk with people, have bodily form, and yet appear, disappear, pass through walls, and become difficult to identify. Jesus rose, it is argued, with a new, semi-physical body—whatever that is. I have never met a semi-physical body.

Because Scripture doesn't provide the exact details of his rising, we end up with various interpretations based on speculation and conjecture. In fact, we are simply told that God raised Jesus and that he was seen by others. Most of the Christians I have met believe that Jesus was brought back to life in a physical or semi-physical form during a literal, historical event that could have been recorded had cameras been rolling inside the tomb. Just think, if God had waited until video recorders were available for such a historic occasion, we could have had overwhelming evidence of the moment life reentered into the dead body of Jesus. We could have watched him walk right out of the tomb. It would have been insurmountable proof of the revivification of a dead body. Unfortunately, there is no video recording and no eyewitness—merely a statement that Jesus was raised.

No Body—No Decay

Many declare that proof of a resurrection is seen in the fact that a body could not be produced. In other words, if the religious authorities wanted to disprove a resurrection, all they had to do was open the tomb and produce the dead body of Jesus. Because no one would have dared to steal the body and risk Rome's fury, the only conclusion, we are told, is that Jesus was bodily resurrected from the dead.

But why must an empty tomb lead to the conclusion of a resurrection? That seems a bit far-fetched to me—an extreme conclusion given the lack of verifiable facts. If we went to visit a grave in a cemetery and found it empty, would we assume a resurrection for Uncle Johnny—that he had been brought back to life and climbed out of the grave? You might advance a resurrection story if you were writing decades later from a post-Easter perspective and wanted to portray Jesus in a certain light, but it is not a normal assumption one would naturally come to.

We assume that everyone knew where Jesus had been buried and that Christians were proclaiming his resurrection shortly after the crucifixion. In reality, there was a gap between the resurrection and its proclamation. According to Acts, there was at least a period of seven weeks from the resurrection to Pentecost, when the first public announcement occurs. We are uncertain whether Luke's chronology is accurate, but it does suggest a duration of time between the resurrection event and its public proclamation. It could easily have been much longer.

Had Jesus been dead for three days, wouldn't his body have begun the process of decomposition? That's what happens when you die—your body begins to decay. Blood coagulates, the organs break down, and rigor mortis sets in. After lying in a tomb for that amount of time without being embalmed, the body would have been in a severe state of deadness. Realizing this issue of decay, Luke references Psalm 16:10 in his account of Peter's Pentecost sermon: "For you will not abandon my soul to Hades, or let your Holy One experience corruption" (Acts 2:27, NRSV). Some versions use the word "decay" instead of "corruption." The reference is again made in Acts 13:35–37.

Luke uses the psalm to bolster his resurrection claim. But is the psalmist actually referring to Jesus? We certainly wouldn't pick that up from reading the psalm itself. Prior to the resurrection claim, no one had an inkling that Psalm 16:10 (NRSV) was referring to Jesus. Why? Because the psalm is referring not to Jesus but to David, its alleged author. We know this from the context of the psalm. David says, "I will bless the Lord; my heart instructs me; I keep the Lord always before me; I shall not be moved; my heart is glad; my soul rejoices; my body also rests secure." Clearly, David is referring to himself. He goes on to say, in reference to himself, that God will not abandon his soul or allow him to undergo decay. God will make known the path of life, and God's presence brings him joy. That is all about David, not Jesus.

So why is this verse used in reference to Jesus? Because New Testament authors looked backward in an attempt to connect Jesus with their Scriptures as a way of explaining his powerful ministry. King David isn't uttering a prophetic prediction about a future person he knows nothing about, nor is he saying that he won't die and experience decay like the rest of us. Instead, he is saying that through thick and thin, ups and downs, and all of his struggles through life, it is God who preserves him and keeps him from being destroyed. That's it. Nothing more and nothing less. It is his way of declaring that God preserves him throughout all of his troubles and against his enemies. Luke looks back, realizes that he can apply cherry-picked verses to Jesus, and does so. This allows him to connect Jesus with Jewish Scripture and lends credence to his story.

Does an empty tomb prove that a resurrection is the reason for its emptiness? Certainly, there are other reasons why a body might not be produced. Maybe the tomb simply could not be identified. Maybe Jesus was never buried in a tomb to begin with, as some scholars suggest. It could be that those affirming the resurrection now lived away from Jerusalem and could boldly make such a distant claim without threat of Rome. It could be that Jesus was hurriedly laid in a tomb before the start of the Sabbath, and the tomb was not known to the authorities. Someone could have tampered with the body as a final insult to Jesus, and by desecrating his body, they intended to produce fear in the disciples rather than faith. Some even argue that the post-resurrection appearances of Jesus were mere hallucinations, that Mary went to the wrong tomb in the early-morning darkness, or that Jesus didn't even die. There could be any number of reasons why a body wasn't produced, some more probable than others, but to conclude that a resurrection occurred is not the normal and only conclusion possible.

Many scholars today question whether Jesus was actually buried. The biblical story says so, but that doesn't mean the narrative is historically accurate. Some believe that Jesus was left on the cross, as was Roman custom, or possibly taken down and thrown into a mass grave and left to rot along with Rome's many victims. According to the Christian story, Jesus is taken down from the cross and buried in a tomb, which is entirely possible, as the Romans did, on occasion, make exceptions in this regard.

If the burial tomb of Jesus was actually identifiable, it seems reasonable to expect that the early church would have taken some interest in the location where such a momentous event occurred. Yet we find nothing of the sort in early church history or in Scripture. The earliest search for Jesus's tomb didn't occur until the fourth century. Could the Easter story be referring to a deeper truth rather than a literal truth about a dead body coming to life again?

Differing Details

The resurrection narrative differs according to who is telling the story. None of the Gospels are written by eyewitnesses. No one actually witnessed the rising of Jesus, for the Gospels were penned decades after his death. Obviously, there is agreement that Jesus rose, but contradictions abound on just about every other detail. Paul, the only New Testament writer with a personal resurrection experience, states that Jesus was raised but doesn't say that the tomb was empty. The Gospels all declare that certain individuals visited the tomb on the first day of the week, but there is no agreement on who these people were, and how many. Did the women see the risen Lord? Mark and Luke say no, whereas Matthew and John say yes. Which one is it?

Where were the disciples when Jesus appeared to them for the first time? Was it in Galilee, as Mark and Matthew suggest, or in Jerusalem as Luke describes? Maybe it was first in Jerusalem and then later in Galilee, as John notes. Did the resurrection occur on the third day or three days after? Who first saw the risen Christ? According to Paul, it was Peter, but Matthew says it was the women gathered at the tomb. For Luke, it was Cleopas in Emmaus, and for John, it was Mary Magdalene. These are contradictory statements that cannot all be true at the same time. The details of the event do not align.

Christians tend to combine the accounts into one preferred narrative, but that won't do, for there are several resurrection accounts, each with irreconcilable differences from one another. Ignoring those differences is no longer an option. Some attempt to turn the tables by suggesting that the contradictions themselves strengthen the case for reliability. If four different people witnessed the same motorcycle accident, we would expect there to be discrepancies in each of their accounts. That would be normal. By turning the tables, contradictions and irreconcilable differences are now seen as pillars of support.

This reminds me of an old interview trick used by prospective job candidates. When asked to identify their weaknesses, they turn the tables. Rather than admit that they have them, they name an attribute that can be turned into a strength. For instance, they might acknowledge a lack of self-care, all the while using it to prop up just how loyal, dedicated, and hardworking they would be for the company. They identified a weakness, made it into an asset, and turned the tables. It fools no one and tells me that they may be unwilling to admit areas for improvement.

In a similar vein, asking why a loving God would kill people in the Old Testament, commit genocide, and seek the destruction of others is not the real question, according to one famous evangelical preacher and author whose voice crackles over the radio waves. Instead, the real question to be asked, says the acclaimed luminary, is why a holy God would allow any of us to live. In other words, he dodges the negative and turns the question around. It is the same tactic employed by job candidates unwilling to admit weaknesses, except the well-known clergyman won't even entertain a discussion about God's alleged killing spree in the Old Testament.

It must be kept in mind that the Gospel writers were not eyewitnesses to the resurrection. Instead, they were relying on oral tradition, previous writings, and what others had told them. In fact, they were not four independent witnesses to the same motorcycle accident but four writers dependent upon one another. Both Matthew and Luke had the Gospel of Mark before them as they wrote their resurrection narrative, and they copied Mark in some places, changed his work in others, and omitted other parts. To argue that the Gospel writers were four independent eyewitnesses is inaccurate and misleading. They were neither eyewitnesses nor independent.

Some conclude that if Jesus wasn't bodily raised from the dead, then the Gospel writers were liars and should be ashamed of themselves for creating a false narrative. In other words, if Scripture doesn't mean what I think it should mean (a bodily resurrection), then the authors cannot be trusted about anything at all. This is nothing more than a "my way or the highway" mentality—a literal understanding of the resurrection that dismisses other points of data and throws the baby out with the bathwater.

A gap exists between Jesus's death and the story of his resurrection, which was written decades after the crucifixion. Initially, stories about his resurrection began to be told orally—possibly in various versions. Over time, those stories were remolded, retold, and reframed. The Gospel writers, aware of these oral traditions, chose the details that best fit their literary needs and memorialized their versions in written form. They were not liars; they were simply using the means available in their time to communicate a powerful truth about Jesus. They were not relaying factual and literal information for the history books; rather, they were painting interpretive portraits of Jesus to convey profound truth, not literal truth.

No one was inside the tomb to describe for us exactly how a resurrection happened. The Bible leaves out this crucial information, contradictions abound between the Gospel narratives, and the very language used to speak of a resurrection is itself precarious. With such obstacles before us, one wonders whether the meaning can ever be ascertained. To that end, our quest begins with Paul, the earliest of the Christian writers.

Paul

Written twenty to thirty years after the crucifixion, Paul's letters were penned prior to all the Gospels and are, in fact, important works that help us understand the earliest conception of the resurrection. In a sense, they are the clearest, purest, and most authentic rendition of the story that existed prior to the later additions offered by the Gospel writers.

Surprisingly, for Paul, the Easter story has nothing to do with an empty tomb or a body rising from the dead. In other words, Paul didn't believe that Jesus was physically and literally raised into the former existence he enjoyed before his death. No, Paul saw the resurrection as a spiritual act, not a physical one.

In Paul's mind, it was God who raised Jesus from the dead and placed him in the seat of power and honor (Rom. 8:34). "That is true," you say, "because Jesus ascended up into heaven to be seated at God's right hand." But you are forgetting a very important fact. The ascension story was written twenty-five to thirty years after Paul died. Paul knew nothing of an ascension, for the story hadn't yet been invented. For Paul, being raised meant being exalted to the right hand of

God, not that Jesus physically and literally came back to life again. It was not a physical resuscitation but a spiritual exaltation.

Paul writes in Romans 6:9 (NRSV), "We know that Christ, being raised from the dead, will never die again; death no longer has dominion over him." If Jesus has merely been revived back to human life, he would have to die a second time. This cannot be, according to Paul, for the resurrection isn't physical but a new dimension of life with God. Even in Philippians 2:5–11, Paul informs us that Jesus was highly exalted with God. In other words, he wasn't raised to life on this Earth but had entered into the divine realm. In Paul's authentic writings, there is no indication of an empty tomb or a resuscitated human being who is literally and physically brought back to life. When Paul speaks of Christ being raised, he has in mind the immediate exaltation of Jesus to God, with God, and becoming one with God, which has nothing to do with an empty tomb or a physical, bodily resurrection. This comes as a surprise to many, but it is the earliest written conception of the resurrection.

Ephesians and Colossians were not written by Paul, but even these writings were penned before the Gospels. In keeping with Paul's mindset, Ephesians also notes that Jesus was raised to the right hand of God (Eph. 1:20), and Colossians concurs that Christ was raised in this manner (Col. 3:1).

My point is that the earliest, most authentic writing about the resurrection is not the story of an empty tomb or a dead man coming back to life. Instead, it is an exaltation story of Jesus being raised by God into an exalted status with God—a new dimension of life. This certainly changes the Easter story from what we commonly hear and believe. In reality, we take Paul and the various Gospel accounts and meld them into one story that becomes our preferred understanding. The amalgamation of narratives, however, doesn't take into account the delineation of Paul's early writing as a foundational view of the resurrection, and it doesn't take into account the many discrepancies within each of the Gospel stories themselves. It is a shock to most Christians that Paul understands the rising of Jesus as an immediate exaltation into God, not the rising of a dead man back to life.

The Appearances

In support of a bodily resurrection, Christians often point to the many witnesses who actually saw the risen Christ. Paul notes in 1 Corinthians 15:3–8 that Jesus appeared to Cephas, then to the Twelve, then to five hundred brethren at one time, then to James, then to all the apostles, and finally, to Paul himself. His letter to the Corinthians was written around 54–56 CE, approximately twenty-five to thirty years after Jesus's death. What exactly does Paul mean when he says that Christ "appeared" to the people on his list? Is he referring to a physical, bodily appearing? That seems highly unlikely because he already stated that Jesus was raised spiritually to an exalted position at the right hand of God. Even with his own Damascus Road encounter, he saw no one. We are talking not about a physical seeing but about a spiritual seeing.

The word "appeared" (*ophthe* in Greek) is the very same word used in the Septuagint to speak of God appearing to Moses in the burning bush (Exod. 3:2). We rush to judgment that the appearance of God in a burning bush was a physical, literal seeing. In other words, had we been there with our modern tech equipment, we could have actually filmed God hanging out in a bush that was on fire. But is that the kind of seeing Paul is referring to? Did more than five hundred people in Paul's list of witnesses actually see a visible, literal, physical, tangible Jesus? Is that the kind of "seeing" Paul has in mind?

No, Paul is speaking of another kind of seeing—an insight that extends beyond sight and beyond the literal, physical senses. Could he be referring to a new revelation, a paradigm shift, a breakthrough in thinking, and a new understanding? This seeing is a lightbulb that turns on when individuals realize for the first time how the various pieces of the puzzle fit together. It is a spiritual aha moment, like finally understanding a math formula that allows you to solve all sorts of other mathematical problems. Paul found a way to interpret the untimely death of Jesus that opened the door to new understanding. Something good came from something bad.

Good from Bad

Joseph is a prime example of something good arising from something bad. Paul knew the story well. Joseph was sold into slavery by his jealous brothers but wound up rising to second-in-command of Egypt, where he was able to provide sustenance for his brothers and father during a severe famine. What was once a tragic event was now turned into triumph, and powerful life lessons are drawn from the narrative. Did a similar reflection occur with the story of Jesus, where something good came from something bad?

The suffering servant of Isaiah 53 was also a reminder of Jesus. Scholars believe that Isaiah's suffering servant is a symbol of the people of Israel. Isaiah returned home from exile with high hopes for the chosen people of God. But reality hit him hard, and hope dimmed as he surveyed the destruction caused by the Babylonians. The temple lay in ruins, the city was laid bare, and his heart sank into his stomach. The sheer work it would take to restore Israel was overwhelming. Over time, however, Isaiah began to see things from a different perspective.

Maybe the glory of Israel would no longer be tied to such constructs as power, victory, and might. Maybe Israel was being called to a new role—an example to others of how to endure hostility. Maybe Israel's glory was found in suffering—enduring the hostile blows of others without retaliation. Maybe the glory of God could be better seen with responses of love and kindness, and in that way, God would bless the Jewish nation. Similarly, Jesus endured the scorn of Jewish leaders and the hostile blows of the Romans, and yet he did not retaliate or resist. Instead, he loved. He was like the suffering servant of Isaiah. In his suffering, we see the blessing of God. Something good came from something bad.

Although Paul lists those to whom Christ appeared, the various appearances in the Bible do not line up with one another. According to Paul, Peter was the first to see Jesus. Does this mean that out of all the disciples, Peter was the first one to grasp this new insight about Jesus? Was Peter the first to see Jesus as a living example of the ancient stories where something good comes from something bad—that love wins the day despite such cruelty and rejection? Jesus didn't cling to this life with a survive-at-all-cost mentality. Instead, he responded in love to the rejection he experienced. That sounds like Isaiah's suffering servant and Joseph's ordeal in Egypt. It was love that enabled Jesus to freely accept his demise, for love is the universal, all-powerful method of affecting others in transformational ways. Jesus not only taught love as the highest ideal—he also embodied it in his own response. Was this eureka moment a new understanding for Peter? Was he the first disciple to see this, and did he then share this new insight with the others?

Too many Christians focus on right belief when Jesus focused on loving God and others. The most difficult thing for humans to do, Christian or otherwise, is to respond in love during difficult and challenging times. Love is the highest ideal because of its transformative power for both the lover and the beloved. Love has the ability to penetrate the hardest of hearts and open windows of new understanding, especially during difficult circumstances.

An Epiphany

For Paul, the appearance of Jesus was not a matter of life being restored to a dead body. Instead, it was a moment when new insight and understanding gave rise to transformation. Paul didn't see a physical Jesus on the Damascus Road. In fact, he didn't see anyone at all. He saw a light and heard a sound. It was a vision of new understanding that transformed him from a religious legalist and vicious persecutor of Christians to a grace-filled man and ardent supporter of The Way. The resurrection isn't a one-time event but a way of living—an ongoing process of transformation and new insight. It is the continual evolution of our humanity from primal, survival instincts to always responding in love. By choosing love, we change and evolve, become more fully human, and grow into the likeness of Jesus.

Paul's Damascus Road experience was an epiphany. Luke, the author of Acts, mentions Paul's divine encounter on three separate occasions, and in each account, the details differ according to the contextual audience. The gist of the story is that Paul saw a light, heard a sound, went blind, and later regained his sight when Ananias laid hands on him. Much debate occurs over the differences in the various accounts, but one thing seems to stand out: Paul was blind but now sees. Is that not the story of resurrection—moving from blindness to sight? Is that not the paradigm shift that Jesus continually spoke of during his ministry?

Jesus encouraged people to see things differently. Nicodemus needed to be born from above—to experience a paradigm shift—if he ever wanted to know God in this life. Instead, Nicodemus took Jesus literally, wondering how he could climb back into his mother's womb and be born all over again. He missed the point. The woman at the well took Jesus's offer of living water literally instead of realizing the deeper truth. She needed to see things with new eyes. Paul encountered a paradigm shift of the soul on his way to Damascus. It was so revelatory that it shook him to his core and altered the trajectory of his life. It was an epiphany of transformation.

The Gospels

If Paul's understanding of resurrection was spiritual in nature rather than physical, how do the Gospels portray the Easter event? Because they were written after Paul's letters, it will be interesting to see how they frame the narrative. The earliest Gospel is Mark, and many are surprised to learn that it originally contained no account of Jesus appearing to anyone at the tomb. The earliest-known manuscripts of Mark end at 16:8 with Mary Magdalene; Mary, the mother of Jesus; James; and Salome fleeing after learning that Jesus had risen. The remaining verses of chapter 16, verses 9–20, which are contained in our modern Bibles, were added later as editors sought to align Mark's resurrection story with that of Matthew and Luke.

In Mark's account, a young man in a white robe announces that Jesus has risen and gives instructions to inform Peter and the disciples that they will see him in Galilee. This kind of experience would frighten just about anyone, and those who came to anoint the body with spices fled in fear. In Mark, there is no physical resuscitation of a dead body. Instead, the disciples would see Jesus as they returned to their homes and engaged in the normal everyday task of living life. The young man in a white robe is not an angel. He is placed in the story to announce that Jesus is seen in the ordinary course of daily living. That is when their eyes would be opened to seeing him in a new way. The resurrection is not an event but an experience. It is not an objective, historical, literal, resuscitation but an internal, subjective, personal understanding of new insight.

Matthew, written about ten years after Mark, contains approximately 90 percent of the content found in Mark. This tells us that Matthew had access to Mark as he was writing his own resurrection narrative. Matthew, however, makes changes to Mark's version. For instance, the young man dressed in a white robe now becomes an angel whose "appearance was like lightening, and his clothing white as snow" (Matt. 28:3, NRSV). In fact, the angel even descends from heaven and rolls away the entrance stone. Instead of four people at the tomb, as Mark notes, we now have only two women (Mary Magdalene and the other Mary) who come to look at the grave, not anoint Jesus with spices. In Matthew, when the angel announces that Jesus has risen, the women quickly depart with great joy and run to tell the disciples that they will see Jesus in Galilee. Those at the tomb in Mark say nothing as they go away, trembling.

In Matthew's account, the women meet Jesus on their way to the disciples. He greets them, and they take hold of his feet and worship him. Jesus instructs them to tell the brethren to go to Galilee, where they will see him. Matthew records the first mention of anyone seeing Jesus after his resurrection, whereas the earliest manuscripts of Mark say nothing about an appearance. Matthew's resurrection narrative was written in the ninth decade, nearly sixty years after the death of Jesus, and he expands the resurrection story by elevating the supernatural element to meet the needs of his Jewish audience and complete what he feels is left out of Mark's rendition.

Even in Matthew, however, the resurrected Jesus is not a literal, historical corpse revived back to life. The disciples travel to Galilee and see Jesus when they climb the mountain—their designated meeting place. There is no account of Jesus climbing the mountain. Instead, he suddenly appears without the laborious climb. Jesus announces that all authority has been given to him in heaven and Earth. Remember, Paul stated that Jesus was raised to the right hand of God, an exalted position in the heavens. Jesus is not a victim, bloody and bruised from a crucifixion, but is now seen as exalted and imbued with power and authority.

Jesus then announces what has come to be known as the Great Commission, where he directs his followers to make disciples of all the nations, baptizing them in the name of the Father, Son, and the Holy Spirit; teaching them to observe all that he taught them; and reminding them that he is with them even to the end of the age. In evangelical land, this is a charge to storm the gates of hell, share how Jesus died for our sins, and free those held captive by Satan. In essence, it has become the fundamentalists' battle cry and the evangelical fight song for converting lost souls.

But this can't be, for there was no organized, institutional church at the time of this supposed statement by Jesus. The disciples were fresh off a traumatic execution of their leader. Besides, they thought of themselves as Jews, not as adherents of a new religion called Christianity. This Great Commission has nothing to do with converting sinful souls into confessors of orthodox religious statements or becoming members of institutionalized religion. Instead, it has everything to do with going beyond our comfort zones, our boundaries, our fears, our insecurities and sharing with others the way of Jesus—the way of love. A love so boundless and so authentic that it allowed Jesus to face the most difficult of circumstances with the confidence of God. The "seeing" in Matthew is an understanding of what the message and meaning of Jesus really were. The resurrection is about new insight, new understanding, and a paradigm shift that alters the trajectory of our own thinking and behavior.

The next Gospel to be written is Luke, about five to ten years after Matthew. As time progresses, more supernatural and physical elements creep into the story. For instance, Mark has a messenger in white, Matthew has a luminous angel as white as snow, and now Luke informs us that two angels make the announcement of his rising (Luke 24:4). Luke's resurrected Jesus now eats, drinks, interprets Scripture, mysteriously comes and goes at will, and shows his hands and feet. Because Luke's resurrected Jesus is much more physical than that of previous writers, he now has to get Jesus off this planet and into heaven, and that is where Luke's ascension stories come into play (Luke 24 and Acts 1).

For Paul, Jesus was spiritually exalted, as seen in his rising to the right hand of God. Luke, however, places a greater emphasis on the physicality of Jesus and creates an ascension event—a physical liftoff from Earth. Were the physical elements of Luke's resurrection account one way of identifying the Jesus who was crucified with the Jesus who was raised? In other words, did Luke seek to ensure that there was no confusion between the Jesus who lived and died and the Jesus who was resurrected?

The fourth Gospel, John, is the last account to be written. Here, Mary Magdalene is the only one to initially visit the grave. She discovers the stone rolled away from the entrance and runs to tell Peter and another disciple, who desire to see for themselves. The tomb is empty, and though there is no appearance of Jesus to anyone at this time, and even though they do not understand what is happening, we are told that they believe.

Mary Magdalene, after returning to the gravesite, is found weeping outside the tomb when she enters into a conversation with someone she thinks is a gardener. It is only after her name is spoken that she recognizes him as Jesus and embraces him, which he does not allow. The eyes of understanding are opened for her. Jesus later appears to the disciples while Thomas is absent and then reappears eight days later when Thomas is present. The scales fall from his eyes as he recognizes Jesus and exclaims in John 20:28 (NRSV), "My Lord and my God." The issue is one of seeing from a new perspective with opened eyes.

The resurrection of Jesus has nothing to do with a dead person being resuscitated back to life again. It has everything to do with scales falling from our eyes so that we see the love and power of Christ with new eyes. The resurrection isn't a literal, objective, historical event in the first century but an internal, subjective, transformative experience of God. It is firsthand experience of the reality and life of God that prompts us to love with the expansive and inclusive love of Jesus. The resurrection is a reality that comes to us in our generation—to every generation. Rather than being a single moment in past history, it is about seeing Jesus as a continuing presence in this life, over and over again. It gives us hope that we can become more than what we currently are and that our humanity can evolve into all that God wants us to be. It takes a resurrection for that to occur, a new way of seeing Jesus.

Something Happened

While the cross is the most widely recognized symbol of Christianity, it is the resurrection that initiated the religious movement. Had Jesus not been raised, his followers would have become nothing more than a fringe element within Judaism that died out shortly after the death of their beloved leader. Other messiahs had come and gone. Other miracle workers existed before Jesus. There were other religious leaders who had become famous for their teaching, but Jesus was different. Something happened after he died that allowed the scattered disciples to reconstitute themselves and muster up enough courage to change the world. Their lives were so completely transformed that they would set in motion the beginnings of a world-renowned religion with millions of followers.

Once an impetuous loudmouth, Peter was now transformed into a key leader of the The Way. The rest of the disciples experienced similar changes from fear to courage. Even Doubting Thomas had his eyes opened. Once critical of Jesus, James, the brother of Jesus, became a strong follower and an early leader in Jerusalem. A new holy day was inaugurated to commemorate the rising of Jesus and is why Christians worship on Sunday. Something influenced the disciples in such a powerful way that the trajectory of their lives was altered. We call that something the resurrection.

Many believe that the resurrection was a physical or semi-physical resuscitation of a dead body. If Jesus was raised back into human existence, he would be subject to death all over again. For Paul, however, the rising of Jesus had nothing to do with being brought back to life. They could have showed Paul the bones of Jesus, and it wouldn't have changed his perspective one iota. Jesus wasn't physically raised but spiritually raised, and because of that, whether the tomb was empty or not is absolutely irrelevant. Jesus was exalted to the right hand of God. In other words, Jesus rose to an exalted state to become one with God. That is entirely different than saying a dead body came back to life again.

When Jesus "appeared" to people—that is, when they saw him—were they seeing a physical Jesus? If we had snapped a photograph at the time of the appearance, would we have captured a physical Jesus standing next to Peter, Mary, and the other disciples? No, because that is not the "something" that happened. When people saw Jesus, it wasn't a literal, physical sighting but an internal realization of the powerful meaning of his life. What they saw and what they experienced was a paradigm shift, a new revelation, a new understanding in which the life, ministry, and death of Jesus were seen with new eyes.

Jesus suffered greatly at the hands of his captors, and yet he didn't defend himself or lash out to save his life, as 1 Peter 2:23 (NRSV) declares: "When he was abused, he did not return abuse; when he suffered, he did not threaten; but he entrusted himself to the one who judges justly." Instead, he reacted in love and thereby revealed the heart, character, and image of God. How could a man respond like that, given the circumstances? It must be, as 2 Corinthians notes, that God was in Christ. This incomparable Christ "is the image of the invisible God" (Col. 1:15, NRSV). Could this be what they realized and experienced?

The resurrection became the story of exaltation and transformation. From sorrow and pain arise new understandings. In a sense, the resurrection demonstrated the message of Jesus—that we must die to one way of seeing so we can rise up to see another way. It is a concept that permeates his teaching.

For instance, a grain of wheat must fall into the ground and die before it can turn into something else and produce a harvest. We take up our cross daily, a symbol of death, in order to follow Jesus, or, as Paul observes, we crucify the flesh daily. We die to one way of seeing and move to another way of seeing. Nicodemus had to be born from above—that is, change his line of sight if he was ever going to experience the kingdom of God. The blind man couldn't see a thing until he encountered Jesus, who put mud on his eyes and provided the gift of sight. That's what happens when we come into contact with the Christ power, and just like the followers to whom Jesus appeared, we can also encounter Christ, have our eyes opened, and see things afresh. The death and rising of Jesus symbolize the very work of God in our life—the work of transformation, not resuscitation. That is what the resurrection is all about.

Those Who See

Isn't it interesting that after the resurrection, Jesus didn't appear to just anybody? He didn't appear to Pilate, to those who flogged him, or to his executioners. He didn't appear to the Jewish leaders who arrested him or to the crowds who shouted for his demise. He could have easily returned to his itinerant lifestyle, taught in the synagogues, continued his healing ministry, and the like. He could have leisurely strolled down Main Street, flaunting his presence to everyone who looked his way. But that is not what happened. Instead, he appeared only to a select few—to those with faith to believe.

The appearances of Jesus seem to be much more subjective than some highly visible dance down Victory Lane in the face of all the doubters. We discover that the only ones to whom Jesus appears are those with the faith to believe. Jesus appears to those within the household of faith. Even Doubting Thomas was a member of the faith community who finally came to see the risen Lord.

The ones who saw Jesus as resurrected were those who had their eyes opened. Over and over again, we are told how Jesus was not recognized, and then he was. Thomas finally saw the resurrected Christ after verbalizing his doubt. Those on the Emmaus Road finally recognized him after a road-trip conversation. Mary's eyes were opened after she heard her name. The fishermen finally recognized him on the Galilean seashore after he told them where to cast their nets. Even Paul turned from persecutor to believer when the scales fell off his own eyes.

Those to whom Jesus appeared were members of the faith community or had some connection to Jesus. They weren't just people out of the blue. Something happened in their life that enabled them to recognize Jesus as resurrected. Jesus's appearances weren't objective, literal, physical sightings but subjective experiences in those with the capacity and willingness to believe—those whose eyes were opened to seeing Christ in a new way. As best they could, the biblical writers tried to capture this experience with a resurrection story. How can words adequately capture the continuing presence of Jesus experienced after his death? That may be why the Easter moment is proclaimed but never fully described—because it is a personal, subjective experience and not a literal sighting. This powerful experience is what transformed Peter and the rest of the disciples from cowardly, defeated followers into courageous proclaimers of Christ.

Meanings of Easter

What is the underlying meaning of the resurrection? Is there just one value to the story, or can multiple lessons be learned? One significant message is that of transformation, a concept we already discussed. Seeing Jesus afresh speaks of an internal realization about who he was and what he means. The resurrection is a metaphor for dying to one way of seeing and rising to see another way. We shouldn't be afraid of metaphors, for the Bible is chock-full of them in reference to God and Jesus. For instance, Jesus is portrayed as servant, lamb, light, bread, Lord, door, vine, shepherd, Messiah, Savior, priest, Son of God, living water, Word of God, and so forth. Metaphors are vehicles for conveying deep meaning, and it is the meaning of Easter that we are after.

Transformation occurs when we change, grow, and seek to emulate the very life and love of God as evidenced in Jesus. In other words, Easter isn't a one-time event in history but a continuing process of transformation as we die and rise over and over again while change, growth, and transformation occur throughout life's journey. Spiritual evolution is an ongoing process whereby growth plus change equals transformation, and transformation is nothing more than a new way of seeing.

The resurrection also speaks of the continuing presence of Jesus beyond his death. He is more than a past figure of history who lived and died. Instead, Christians encounter Jesus as a spiritual reality. Believers from across the centuries have proclaimed their experience of the risen Christ. They didn't see a physical, literal Jesus but a spiritual Jesus whose abiding presence lives on in the lives of his followers. Evangelicals and fundamentalists do well in this regard, emphasizing the personal nature of Jesus's presence in our lives. As Luke puts it, "Why do you look for the living among the dead? He is not here, but has risen" (Luke 24:5, NRSV). The abiding presence of Jesus in our life is a living, spiritual, ongoing reality, not a physical one.

There is an old hymn titled "I Come to the Garden Alone" whose chorus declares, "And he walks with me and he talks with me, and he tells me I am his own; and the joy we share as we tarry there, none other has ever known." Those lyrics speak of the continuing presence of Jesus. Would we be able to snap a picture of Jesus as he walks beside us and talks with us, as the song states? Of course not. We don't understand the lyrics physically or literally but spiritually. Jesus continues to be experienced long after his death as a spiritual reality.

The resurrection speaks of Jesus's exalted status. Sitting at the right hand of God is one way of saying that Jesus was raised to power and authority. In other words, he is Lord above all others. To be Lord means that Jesus is worthy of our affection, loyalty, and commitment. For Paul, the exaltation became God's mark of approval and vindication of Jesus. That kind of Jesus deserves our loyalty and love, and the exaltation confirms this. Being raised to God's right hand is a metaphor of power, authority, and honor. No longer would Jesus be seen merely as a great teacher and healer who mirrored God; now he became one with God and participated in the authority and power of God. He is Lord.

The resurrection speaks of God's own declaration about Jesus. For Paul, Jesus didn't rise on his own accord, but God raised him and exalted him to the heavens. Paul believes that Jesus became the Son of God when God acted upon him, raised him, and exalted him. In other words, the act of God upon Jesus is not only a declaration of God's power but a declaration of what God thought of Jesus. By exalting him, God was vindicating his life and ministry and putting a stamp of approval upon him. It was a divine affirmation of the work Jesus began.

The resurrection speaks of the birth of Christianity. As previously mentioned, the death of Jesus would have been the end of the Jesus Movement had there not been a resurrection. When the followers of Jesus saw him as the exalted Lord whose continuing presence was still with them, Christianity was given flight. Strength and courage arose as his life and death were interpreted with new meaning. Even though he died, he still lived, and their new understanding changed their perception of everything he ever did and said.

The resurrection speaks of conquering death. Paul states in Romans 6:9 (NRSV), "We know that Christ, being raised from the dead, will never die again; death no longer has dominion over him." For Paul, Jesus was raised to a new dimension of life, one in which he entered into God. Had Jesus merely been raised to his former existence in this world, he would have had to die all over again. What kind of conquering would that have been? Instead, Jesus was spiritually raised from the dead to a place beyond death—a place at the right hand of God. That is a spiritual rising, an exaltation into a new dimension of life.

The resurrection speaks of hope, and humans are always looking for symbols of hope. Conveying meaning through human language is fraught with numerous dangers, especially when it comes to our experiences with the divine. Whether one takes a literal or metaphorical view of Christ's rising, it is the truth behind the resurrection that we are trying to convey through the constraints of human language. Words are never adequate in describing such experiences, and the resurrection is no exception. The story is one way we express our encounter with the Christ power, and when we encounter the Christ, there is always hope.

The resurrection story communicates the hope that we can still experience the presence and meaning of Jesus in our life. We are encouraged that our own life can have meaning. Although death is a reality we must all face as the book on our life closes, we have hope that others may still read it. Our presence can continue in others when life is lived with meaning and purpose. Jesus's life continues to be lived in and through us. He showed us that life is about living, loving, and serving. How should we live? Jesus taught us with his very life. His was a life of service. He gave himself in selfless love and transformed those around him. The book of Christ's life lives on to transform countless others. We have hope that our life will do the same.

Finally, Jesus was raised into God, which gives us hope. Truth be told, we have no idea what exists after death, though many have wagered on a place called heaven. I wonder whether our own death will mimic the cycle of life and death that we see all around us. As a deer lies dead on the side of the road after being struck by a fast-moving vehicle, animals gather to feed on its carcass until it decomposes back into the earth from whence it came. It makes me wonder whether our own death will be similar. In other words, as our body returns to the earth, will our spirit return to its place of origin in God? As Jesus rose to God, will our own spirit also return back to its source?

Though certainty about the afterlife evades us, hope existed in the minds of early Christians that death was not the finality it appeared to be. Exactly what that means is debated in Christian circles. Does our spirit rise and return to its source in completing the cycle of life, or does it simply mean that the impact of our life, when lived in selfless love like Jesus, has the capacity to live on in the hearts of others?

Chapter Summary

The contents of this chapter may have come as a surprise, for the traditional Easter story has been told so often as to be seared into our conscience. To think of the resurrection in any other way feels like we are abandoning the faith—especially with a doctrine so integral to Christianity. While we are not walking away from our rock-solid belief in God or the reality of Jesus's continuing presence in our life, we are moving on from the outdated and illusory manner in which our faith has traditionally been voiced. When ancient beliefs become unbelievable in light of the sophisticated knowledge we now possess, it is time to reexamine those beliefs, get to the heart of what is behind them, and discover new avenues of understanding that make sense to the postmodern mind.

The church has taught a literal, physical resurrection—some sort of resuscitation or revivification of a dead body that came back to life and walked out of the tomb. According to Paul, the earliest of the Christian writers, the rising of Jesus wasn't physical or literal at all but spiritual in nature, as God raised him to a place of power and authority at God's right hand. In other words, the rising was a spiritual exaltation whereby the status of Jesus changed to becoming one with God.

Paul and others experienced an epiphany as Jesus was seen in a new light after his death. Their eyes were opened to new understanding, new insight, and a new way of deciphering Jesus. In the Gospels, Jesus appears only to those who have their eyes opened—those with the willingness and capacity to believe. The resurrection isn't about a corpse coming to life again. Instead, the story is one of transformation and seeing things with new eyes. It isn't a single event of past history but the many eye-openings and ongoing internal realizations that occur during our spiritual journey.

The resurrection speaks of many things, not just transformation. For instance, it speaks of the continuing presence of Jesus in our life today. He is a spiritual and divine reality, not a physical one. The exaltation of Jesus to the right hand of God not only places him in a position as Lord—that is, someone worthy of our commitment, loyalty, and honor—it also serves as God's vindication of his life and ministry. Finally, the resurrection is a symbol of hope. Death cannot suppress the ongoing influence of our life from affecting others, and it is incapable of preventing our spirit from returning to its original source—God.

Today, millions of Christians worship and pray to Jesus, believing that he is God. Did Jesus proclaim divine status for himself, or was divinity attributed to him after his death as part of a post-Easter portrayal? Just how did Jesus come to be thought of as God? That is the subject of our next chapter.

12

WAS JESUS DIVINE?

· · · · · · · ·

THOSE OF US WHO GREW UP IN THE CHURCH DIDN'T think too deeply about
religious things when we were young. We simply attended because our parents dragged us there, it was the traditional Sunday routine, or we looked forward
to seeing our friends. Whether we were bored out of our mind or thrilled to connect with others, one thing is certain: we soaked up the church's teaching like a
sponge. We learned what we were taught without the benefit of critical thinking
or deep questioning. We were young and naive, and even if we had probed
beneath the surface, it wouldn't have been welcomed or appreciated, especially
had we arrived at different conclusions than official church doctrine permits.

For centuries, the Bible was rarely questioned from a critical perspective.
Many couldn't even read, and Scripture was the unquestioned, literal Word of
God to humankind. It held absolute authority that only the clergy could rightly
interpret and understand. That changed with the onset of the Renaissance, the
Reformation, and the Enlightenment, which unleashed a spirit of inquiry like
never before. Probing, questioning, and exploring were seen in a positive light,
the teaching of the church came under scrutiny, and the scientific method was
born. The Bible began to be studied through the lens of critical thinking, and the
birth of biblical scholarship allowed us to see things we never saw before. It
changed our understanding and approach to Scripture.

One insight arising from biblical scholarship was how Jesus came to be
thought of as God. In ages past, this kind of talk would have resulted in excom-
munication, imprisonment, or death, because the Gospels were assumed to be
literal, historical, absolute truth written by eyewitnesses who followed Jesus
around, wrote down all that he said and did, and then provided a factual and

historical timeline of his life. Like the layers of an onion, biblical scholars peeled back previous assumptions and found significant problems with interpretations of the past. Now, Scripture was being studied, analyzed, and scrutinized with a critical eye that noticed discrepancies and contradictions. Scholars realized that the Gospels were not written by eyewitnesses and that their content was not meant to be literal, factual, historical accounts of Jesus's life. Instead, they were a form of Jewish storytelling—interpretive portraits intended to portray Jesus in a favorable light decades after his death.

Biblical scholarship revealed how Jesus moved from being a man to becoming a God in the mind of his followers—how the historical Jesus morphed into the Christ of faith after his resurrection. The perception, understanding, and explanation of Jesus expand over time. This change in status is the difference between the pre-Easter Jesus and the post-Easter Jesus that has been discussed in previous chapters.

How did a first-century itinerant preacher, executed as a criminal by the Romans, wind up becoming an equal member of the esteemed Trinity? This is the kind of question we never considered as young people growing up in the church. No one would have expected us to. But now we are without excuse, for we live in an age when critical thinking is expected and Scripture is being challenged in light of modern knowledge. Just how did Jesus come to be thought of as God?

Ancient Understandings

Throughout this book, I have stated that ancient worldviews were quite different than our own. This is normal and expected, for their reservoir of knowledge was not nearly as extensive as ours. Their worldview was an outgrowth of the knowledge they possessed within the culture of their day. Simply put, the ancients believed that gods could become human and that humans could become gods. We tend to think of God in the singular, whereas the ancients believed the divine realm contained multiple gods at various levels of divinity and power. This is untenable to the contemporary mind but something the ancient world embraced.

We assume that Jesus was the only human to ever be declared divine, but he wasn't the only individual thought to be a god. About fifty years after Jesus, a philosopher named Apollonius of Tyana arrived on the scene. Like Jesus, he had a miraculous birth, performed miracles, cast out demons, healed diseases, raised dead people to life again, and ascended to heaven. In fact, the followers of Apollonius argued with the followers of Jesus over which one was the true Son of God.

To think of someone as divine was not unusual in the Greco-Roman world, for the concept arose out of their polytheistic religious environment, where thousands of gods existed for all kinds of events, functions, rites, places, needs, etc. We imagine a great chasm between God and humans, but in the ancient world, the divide was not so great. In other words, the divine and human realms were viewed more as a continuum. The sliding scale went from humans with little power all the way to gods with great power and majesty. This means that some overlap existed whereby gods could enter the human realm and humans could enter the divine realm. At the lower end of the divinity scale were humans who became divine, followed by spirits, then local divinities, and near the top end of the continuum were the gods of Rome and Greece followed by the highest, most powerful God.[12] This worldview is different from our own and helps us appreciate the context of ancient thinking and its influence upon Christianity.

In the ancient world, humans could become gods in several ways. First, those who showed extraordinary skill or intelligence could possess divinity because they were viewed as more than human. Second, some individuals were thought to have been fathered by the gods. Alexander the Great, for instance, was said to have been fathered by the Greek god Zeus. Finally, individuals could be declared a god. This process of divinization typically occurred after a person's death. Romulus, the founder of Rome, was believed to have been transported to the divine realm upon his death, and Julius Caesar was declared a god after his death. Whether living or dead, emperors could be declared gods. Humans could be considered divine if they possessed special skill or intelligence, were fathered by a god, or were declared divine upon their death, and sometimes even while they were living.

My point is that Jesus wasn't the only individual thought to be divine, for the idea that humans could become divine or that the divine could become human was part of ancient worldviews. This mindset wasn't limited to the Greco-Roman world, for we see elements of it within Jewish Scripture and the noncanonical, apocryphal books.

Scripture speaks of divine entities in the spiritual realm, such as angels, archangels, cherubim, and seraphim. We discover that both God and angels have assumed human form. As three men visit Abraham in Genesis 18, two of them are angels in disguise, while the third is God in human form. Angels are called gods in Psalm 82, and in the apocryphal books of 2 Baruch 51 and 2 Enoch 22, humans can become angels. Some even read from Genesis 6 (expanded upon in 1 Enoch) that the Sons of God (angels) had relations with the daughters of men and produced a giant race of humans. Even the Jewish kings are sometimes referred to as gods (2 Sam. 7:13–16; Ps. 2:7, Isa. 9; 45), although they are never seen as the highest God. There appears to be levels of divine beings, and some humans are considered to be god right alongside God Almighty.

This concept of multiple gods and divine beings seems odd within the monotheistic religion of Judaism. It wasn't always that way for the Jews, for early on they were henotheists, which means they believed in multiple gods but only worshiped one. Of the Ten Commandments, the most well known is the first one in Exodus 20:3 (NRSV): "You shall have no other gods before Me." Out of all the available gods to choose from, the early Jews chose Yahweh as the one worthy of their loyalty, commitment, and dedication. However, as time passed, their understanding progressed from henotheism to monotheism. No longer was Yahweh a god out of many gods; instead, Yahweh became the one and only true God—the rest were merely idols.

My point is to place the divinity of Christ within its proper context. Elevating someone to divine status was not unusual for the ancients, and after Jesus died, divinity was bestowed upon him. This divine declaration speaks not to the truth of the assertion but to the profound value realized in Jesus. His followers found no better way to explain the impact of his life than to say that God was upon him, that he was the image of God, and finally, after his death, that he was divine. He must be divine, they reasoned, for no one could live and love the way Jesus did apart from God's divine presence.

Did Jesus Claim Divinity?

Did Jesus think of himself as God? Did he actually teach and preach that he was an equal member of the Trinity? This has been the teaching of the church, but what if Jesus never claimed that about himself? Then what? In my experience, whenever long-held religious beliefs are questioned, two defenses keep popping up. First, people point to the very words of Jesus to support the truth of what he said, but they never mention the circular reasoning involved in their conclusion. Of course, this assumes that he actually spoke the words attributed to him in Scripture. Second, they note how God values simple, childlike faith. Asking too many questions is a sign of unbelief. No matter how many facts are placed before them, they are merely discarded in pursuit of simple faith. Apparently, we are to park our brain in neutral, believe the unbelievable, and accept the limited worldviews of ancient days. These defenses pop up over and over again in uncomfortable conversations while common sense is viewed as a wolf in sheep's clothing.

Does trusting in God with simple, childlike faith mean abandoning our reasoning abilities? I hardly think so, for the logical end conclusion could lead to gullibility so severe that everyday common sense is thrown out the window. Standing in front of an oncoming freight train traveling at eighty miles per hour while believing you will not be harmed is pure folly, no matter how simple or complex your faith may be. My bet is on the train, not on your faith. As we consider the teaching of Scripture, we must never abandon our ability to reason and think critically, and that is the gift that biblical scholarship has given to us. While I am neither abandoning faith nor implying that reason is the end all and be all, I am saying that simple faith is no defense to sound reasoning and common sense.

When it comes to the words of Jesus in Scripture, we must likewise tread lightly. In reality, we have no recorded words from Jesus himself. He produced no writings or works that we can point to. All we have is what others claim that he said, decades after his death. And the words placed upon his lips by the Gospel writers do not always align with one another. When others point out that Jesus said this or that and use it as proof of the assertion itself, it tells us that they accept those words as the actual words of Jesus rather than as words placed upon his lips by a particular author, writing at a particular time, under particular circumstances, with a particular agenda, decades after Jesus's death. It may be an example of simple faith, but it is not reasonable. Instead of saying, "Jesus said . . .," it is more accurate to say, "The author of the Gospel portrays Jesus as saying . . ." Most Christians I know simply don't think in these terms. But how can we not in light of the knowledge we now possess?

Did Jesus claim that he was God, or did the authors place words of divinity upon his lips in their post-Easter portrayal? Because we have no actual writings of Jesus himself, our main source is what the Gospel writers say he said—hearsay. Biblical scholars pour over Scripture and explore history in an effort to uncover clues to what may have *actually* happened as opposed to what others *say* happened. Do you see the difference?

The only Gospel in which outright claims of divinity are made is John, the last Gospel to be written. The earlier Gospels of Matthew, Mark, and Luke make no such claims. If Jesus was actually God and the Gospel writers knew that, it would seem to be a significant point worth mentioning, but Matthew, Mark, and Luke say nothing about it.

Some point to Mark 2:5–7, where Jesus tells the healed paralytic that his sins are forgiven. After all, who can forgive sins but God alone? But Jesus doesn't say that he forgives sin, only that the paralytic's sins are forgiven. He wasn't claiming to be God in this scenario; rather, he was pronouncing what God has already declared in much the same way that Old Testament priests declared forgiveness of sins on behalf of the nation and individuals offering sacrifices at the temple. The priests only declared what God had already decreed. Jesus does the same thing. Mainline denominational ministers in our day follow suit.

From the earliest Christian writings to the later writings, we see a progression of thought regarding the divinity of Jesus. When well-meaning Christians point to the words of Jesus in the Gospel of John as proof of his divine self-understanding, it should be remembered that the earlier Gospels do not make such claims and that John is the last one to be written. Unveiling this progression of thought in Scripture is fascinating, and it was discovered not by simple, child-like faith but through scholarship and critical examination of Scripture. As a result, it challenges our traditional understanding of Jesus.

A Divine Progression

The perception of who Jesus was progressed from early, less sophisticated views to later, more advanced explanations. There is a difference between the actual, historical Jesus and the Christ of faith portrayed after his death—from the historical pre-Easter Jesus to a post-Easter portrayal. The New Testament was written over time, and the views and understanding of Jesus developed and grew during this period. When I speak of a divine progression or Jesus becoming divine, I am referring to how his status morphed over time from being a historical man who walked this Earth to being thought of as divine. His followers bestowed divinity upon him after his untimely death as a means of explaining the impact and meaning of his life. In their perception, Jesus went from being a human being like the rest of us to becoming the divine Son of God. The Gospels differ in their timing of when they think this happened. These differences reveal how the perception and understanding of Jesus change over time.

The earliest Christian writings of Paul have Jesus becoming divine at his resurrection. Jesus was designated the Son of God, by God, upon his exaltation to the right hand of God. For Paul, divinity was bestowed upon Jesus at his exaltation. In his mind, that was the essence of the resurrection—an exaltation of Jesus whereby he was declared by God to be the Son of God. That was the moment Jesus was made divine. It was a post-death declaration.

Moving from Paul's early perspective, we come to Mark, the first Gospel to be written and the first compilation of the Jesus story. Written about forty years after Jesus's death, Mark accepts Paul's understanding that Jesus was designated the Son of God, as his book opens with "the beginning of the good news of Jesus Christ, the Son of God" (Mark 1:1, NRSV). Mark also accepts Paul's notion that Jesus was declared to be divine by the Spirit of holiness, but he now changes the timing and setting of when this occurred.

For Mark, Jesus was declared to be the Son of God not at his resurrection but at his baptism. The Spirit of holiness mentioned by Paul is now seen in the baptismal event, as the Spirit descends upon Jesus like a dove (Mark 1:10, NRSV). Mark agrees that Jesus was declared to be the Son of God through the Spirit, but he intentionally moves up the declaratory event. This made it easier for Mark to show that God's power and presence was with Jesus throughout his ministry. Mark has Jesus being adopted as the Son of God, by God, at his baptism. The skies open, the Spirit descends upon Jesus like a dove, and the voice of the Father declares, "You are my Son, the Beloved; with you I am well pleased." Mark moves the designation of divinity earlier in the timeline, from resurrection to baptism.

The next Gospels written are Matthew and Luke. Matthew appeared about ten to twenty years after Mark, and Luke was written about five to ten years after Matthew. Both were penned about fifty to sixty years after the death of Jesus. In these books, the moment Jesus is declared the Son of God is moved up even further. It isn't enough to say that Jesus was designated the Son of God at his exaltation or his baptism. Instead, Matthew and Luke become the only Gospels to contain virgin birth narratives. Now, Jesus is declared to be the Son of God at his conception and birth. He didn't become the Son of God at some point during his life or after his death; Jesus was now seen as having been born the Son of God.

For Paul, the resurrection became the moment when Jesus was designated to be divine. For Mark, it was the baptism of Jesus. For Matthew and Luke, Jesus was born the Son of God. Do you see how the portrayal of Jesus progresses from early views to later views? Matthew's and Luke's birth narratives contain the symbols of divinity. An angel sent from God announces the miraculous birth, Old Testament prophesy is said to be fulfilled, and Mary conceives by the work of the Holy Spirit. Paul's notion that Jesus became divine by the Spirit is still present, but the timing moves earlier to his birth.

By the time the Gospel of John appears, sixty to seventy years after the death of Jesus, we read some astounding statements about the divinity of Jesus. Generations had passed since the historical Jesus walked the earth. Life moved on like it always does, circumstances and situations had changed, and the portrayal of Jesus had blossomed. By the tenth decade, Jesus was now so identified with God that John begins his account by saying that Jesus was with God and was God before his conception and birth.

Stating that Jesus became the Son of God at his exaltation didn't go far enough. Saying that Jesus was adopted as the Son of God at his baptism simply wouldn't do. Declaring the conception and birth of Jesus as the moment of divine designation didn't confer justice upon his splendor. Instead, John declares that Jesus was with God from before the creation of the world. He was divine before his birth. Jesus was with God, is God, and existed as God before he was ever born. John opens with the following words: "In the beginning was the Word, and the Word was with God, and the Word was God. He was in the beginning with God. All things came into being through him, and without him not one thing came into being" (John 1:1–3, NRSV). In John's mind, there was never a time when Jesus was not divine.

Contrary to the other Gospels, John goes to great lengths to portray Jesus as God. John 8:58 (NRSV) is a prime example where Jesus purportedly says, "Very truly, I tell you, before Abraham was, I am." Does this not reflect John's view of Jesus as stated in his opening words—that Jesus existed as God before his birth? By saying that he was "I am," Jesus was declaring himself to be God, the great I Am of the Old Testament. In John 14:9 (NRSV), Jesus purportedly tells Philip, "Whoever has seen me has seen the Father." The portrayal of Jesus has really progressed since the early days following his death!

Another instance is found in John 10:30 (NRSV), where Jesus claims to be one with the Father: "The Father and I are one." The Jews are upset with this claim and seek to stone him as a blasphemer, for how could a mere man claim to be God? These stories are not found in the earlier Gospels, but they do support John's attempt to elevate the status of Jesus.

Do you see the progression of divinity from earlier Christian writings to later portrayals—how the perception of Jesus changed as time went on? Jesus is first a powerful man like no other, followed by an exaltation where he is designated to be the Son of God, followed by adoption as God's Son at his baptism, followed by being born divine with a miraculous conception and birth, followed by a declaration that Jesus was the Son of God before he was even born. The progression doesn't stop there. A few centuries later, the creeds were developed, and Jesus would be defined even further as an equal member of the Trinity.

This idea of progression isn't new, for it is a part of our daily lives, and we see it throughout history. We see it in the realm of science, medicine, history, and every discipline of study. In the religious realm, we see how Jesus moves from the historical, pre-Easter Jesus to a post-resurrection portrayal. We see it in the progression of the Gospel stories. Perceptions expand. Explanations grow. Portrayals become more elaborate.

We even see this progression in our personal spiritual lives as we move from experiencing the divine; to reflecting upon our experience; to capturing our experience with words, metaphors, and symbols; to establishing doctrine in an attempt to set the experience in concrete. Every time we progress, we remove ourselves even further from the original experience to the point where we focus on the explanation rather on than the experience itself. If progress is a part of life, is it wishful thinking to believe that an explanation of the divine was finally and completely captured by words and concepts of the first century?

Pre-literary View

If Jesus died around 30 CE and the earliest Christian writings of Paul came into existence around 50–60 CE, then a gap of twenty to thirty years existed before any Christian writing was produced. What was the perception of Jesus during this period of time? This is a good question that is not explicitly answered in Scripture. Many turn to Acts for answers, but Luke wrote Acts around 85 CE, much later than Paul's writings and after Matthew, Mark, and Luke had been written. Because it is a later work and written in hindsight decades after the period in question, scholars don't rely on Acts as an accurate historical rendition of church history. Instead, they look for pre-literary clues within Scripture itself.

Pre-literary traditions simply refer to brief passages quoted by biblical authors that were in existence at the time of the authors' writing. We are not referring to Old Testament quotes, for they are readily identified as Scriptural quotes. Let's say I wrote you a personal letter and included in it a well-known phrase, such as "the early bird gets the worm" or "early to bed, early to rise." You would easily recognize and understand the phrase. Why? Because it was in existence long before I included it in my letter to you. That is the concept behind pre-literary traditions—quotes or phrases that an author uses in his literary work that existed prior to inclusion in the work itself.

Scholars have identified something similar in Scripture. If the biblical author is quoting a saying or phrase in his writing, then the quote is older than the writing itself and provides clues to the thinking that existed before the creation of the literary work. In other words, these quotes and phrases are pre-literary— existing before the letter itself. The point is that scholars have identified a number of these pre-literary quotes whereby we glimpse the early understanding of Jesus before the New Testament was produced.

One such pre-literary tradition is found in Romans 1:3–4 (NRSV): "The gospel concerning his Son, who was descended from David according to the flesh and was declared to be Son of God with power according to the spirit of holiness by resurrection from the dead, Jesus Christ our Lord." Scholars believe that Paul is quoting a common saying with which he and the Roman Christians were familiar. This self-contained, poetic saying uses phrases not found elsewhere in Paul, such as "descended from David" and "Spirit of holiness." If this is indeed a pre-literary tradition, as many scholars suggest, it may represent an early understanding of Jesus as having been designated the Son of God at his resurrection. This point of view would have existed before Paul wrote his letter to the Romans. Thus, it might reflect the perspective between Jesus's death and the emergence of Christian writings.

Another pre-literary example is found in Acts 2:36 (NRSV): "Therefore let the entire house of Israel know with certainty that God has made him both Lord and Messiah, this Jesus whom you crucified." And in Acts 13:32–33 (NRSV): "And we bring you the good news that what God promised to our ancestors he has fulfilled for us, their children, by raising Jesus; as also it is written in the second psalm, 'You are my Son; today I have begotten you.'"

Acts contains numerous orations attributed to Peter, Paul, and others. These aren't verbatim records of actual speeches, for there were no tape recorders or streaming audio to transcribe. No, these addresses were written by the author of Acts long after the words were said to have been spoken. This was common practice in the day and was not unusual. Words were placed upon the lips of the speaker by someone with a particular agenda. Within these speeches, we find snippets of pre-literary tradition that offer up clues to the perception of Jesus prior to the creation of Acts. We discover that Jesus was thought to have been made divine at his resurrection. He was a human who was raised into the heavens after his death and made divine by God. As time goes on, the writers of Scripture would add even more to their portrayal of Jesus.

A Changing Inadequacy

Many uninformed Christians believe that the Bible fell from heaven as a finished book. They believe that Jesus was a Christian, that the theology they hold has always existed, and that churches just like the one they attend burst on the scene immediately after Jesus died. In similar fashion, many believe that Jesus pre-existed as God before the world was created, descended from his heavenly glory, climbed into human flesh, was born of a virgin, died for our sins, bodily rose from the dead, and ascended back up into heaven. He did all of this as God. That's the story that they have been taught to believe literally and share with others.

They don't realize that Christianity experienced a progression of changes in perception and understanding along the way. Like everything else, the church grew into its current state of doctrine. It didn't just spring up out of nowhere fully structured and fully developed. The Bible wasn't dropped from heaven fully intact but progressed into its final form. The same thing happened with our Christology. It developed over time into the story that the church now proclaims. There is a difference between the historical Jesus and the Christ of faith. This change in perception developed over time like everything else develops over time. It was bound to happen and is, in a sense, a natural progression as earlier views are deemed inadequate and new views are brought forth. A close examination of Scripture reveals how this progression developed.

This evolving view of Jesus has to do with the moment they believed that he became divine. Early followers believed that Jesus was made the divine Son of God at his resurrection and exaltation, but as time moved forward, the moment he became divine moved backward—from exaltation, to baptism, to birth, to pre-existence.

This developing view of Jesus continued even after the Gospels had been written. In the second and third centuries, for instance, a variety of views existed regarding Christ's divinity. Docetists believed that Jesus was so divine that he couldn't also be human. The Gnostics believed that Jesus the man was different from Jesus the divine Christ. Modalists believed that Jesus was another expression of God the Father, who was simply appearing in human flesh as Jesus. As the doctrine of the Trinity was being developed, the Arian controversy of the fourth century asked whether Jesus was one in substance with God or a lesser created being. The Council of Nicaea addressed this question regarding the relationship between Jesus and God, solidified the issue, and declared the outcome to be the orthodox view.

This progression of thought regarding how and when Jesus became divine was an evolution of inadequacy where earlier views deemed inadequate progressed toward more advanced perspectives. The advanced views were then declared inadequate as new explanations arose, and so forth. Our outlook evolved over time. It happens in our own spiritual journey, as we see things differently today than when we were six years old. Earlier views are judged inadequate as we progress to new explanations and understandings. We get that.

But somehow, we want Scripture to be the absolute, unchanging repository of truth. Yet the progression we see in Scripture challenges our old understanding of traditional church teaching.

The oldest view that emerged after his death was that Jesus became divine at his resurrection when he was exalted to heaven. As time progressed, this view became inadequate, so Mark declares that Jesus became divine at his baptism. In this way, his entire ministry could be seen as the work of God. As time progressed, this view becomes inadequate, so Matthew and Luke declare that Jesus became divine at his conception and birth. He wasn't divine just during his ministry; he was divine his entire life. He was born that way. In time, this view became inadequate, as John declares that Jesus was always divine, even before his conception.

Even these views were deemed inadequate as various viewpoints arose in the second and third centuries regarding Jesus's relationship to God the Father (Docetism, Gnosticism, Modalism, Arianism, etc.). In the fourth century, these explanations were declared inadequate when the Council of Nicaea tried to settle the matter once and for all. The doctrine of the Trinity was developed, and the council officially decreed that Jesus was of the same substance as God the Father. Over time, as science progressed and biblical scholarship emerged, previous understandings of Jesus became inadequate, so theologians and biblical scholars provided new perspectives on the divinity of Jesus.

Other Support?

Aside from the declarations of divinity made at his resurrection, baptism, birth, and pre-existence, other attempts have been made to prove the divinity of Jesus. Some point to the fact that Jesus was called Messiah, the anointed one from God. Supposedly, this proves that he was divine. The Jews, however, didn't believe that the Messiah would be divine but that he would be someone sent from God, who was anointed by God, to bring about the kingdom of God. Jesus's followers may have sensed that he was sent by God, but in reality, they were slow of learning, slow of seeing, and slow of doing. It was only after his resurrection that he was portrayed as the full-blown, without-question, promised Messiah. Again, was this part of the post-Easter portrayal of Jesus after looking back upon his life and ministry? Other messiahs had come and gone who were also believed to have been sent from God. Were they also God? Being called Messiah doesn't prove divinity.

Did the many miracles that Jesus allegedly performed demonstrate that he was God? Elijah performed miracles—was he God too? Was Elisha? Is anyone who performs a miracle also a god? Was Oral Roberts a god? Are the numerous televangelists who focus on divine healing gods? Of course not. We don't really know whether miracles were performed by anyone, but if they were, does it necessarily prove the person was a god?

Jesus was said to forgive sins, and this proves that he was God, for only God can forgive sins. We have no proof that a sin was truly forgiven, only that someone declared that sins were forgiven. We see similar declarations in our world as mainline denominational ministers pronounce forgiveness of sins for their parishioners. That doesn't mean they are God. The Jewish priests also pronounced declarations of forgiveness on behalf of the nation and individuals through the Old Testament sacrificial offerings. Mainline ministers and Old Testament priests are not God simply by pronouncing forgiveness. They are merely declaring what God has already decreed.

People worshiped Jesus, and that proves that he was God. Really? We bow before a lot of things both physically and metaphorically; does that mean they are gods? There were thousands of gods in ancient days that people worshiped. Were they actually gods? Servants bowed before their masters, and subjects bowed before their kings. Were they gods? Even if Jesus was viewed as Messiah, forgave sins, performed miracles, and was worshiped by others, that still doesn't prove that he was God.

Chapter Summary

Designed to reveal the progression of thought regarding the divinity of Jesus, this chapter notes how the very concept of humans becoming gods and gods becoming human was not unusual in ancient culture, for we see it in the Greco-Roman world and within the Jewish and Christian Scriptures. This is the fertile soil in which the expression of deity came to be associated with Jesus.

Many seek refuge in a Bible they believe to be the fixed, immutable, inerrant Word of God to humankind, and yet they are troubled to learn how the perception of Jesus developed over time. What was supposed to be unchanging now reveals a progression right before their eyes. The later the Christian writing, the earlier divinity is bestowed upon Jesus. We have no direct words of Jesus, for he left us no writings. We only have the Gospels—stories about Jesus as told by others and words of Jesus that others claim he said. Did Jesus actually claim to be

God, or were words placed upon his lips to advance a particular understanding of him long after his death? The latter seems to be the more reasonable conclusion.

The issue is one of timing—when Jesus was said to have become divine. This is where we see the progression of thought surrounding the issue. The earliest view of divinity arose after Jesus's death, as Paul claims that he was designated the Son of God upon his resurrection and exaltation to the right hand of God. The next progression is found in Mark, where Jesus is designated the Son of God at his baptism. This is followed by Matthew and Luke, who move the moment of divinity to his birth. The last Gospel to be written is John, which portrays Jesus as having been divine even before his birth. By the time the Council of Nicaea convened in the fourth century, Christ was declared to be one in substance with God the Father. Orthodoxy was born, and the doctrine of the Trinity was established.

So, where does this leave us? We have discussed the virgin birth, the atonement, the resurrection, and the progression of divinity. In light of this information, what are we to make of Jesus? If the traditional teaching is no longer credible, what are we to believe? Who is Jesus? That is the subject of our next chapter.

13

WHO IS JESUS?
· · · · · · · ·

W E WRAP THIS SECTION UP BY ASKING, "WHO IS JESUS?" In deconstructing such cherished doctrines as the virgin birth, atonement, resurrection, and ascension, we realize that their literal interpretation makes no sense. In fact, it is the dogged adherence to literalism that generates such erosion of credibility.

This, of course, is frightening to those who place their entire bet on a literal understanding of Scripture. The light of reason, common sense, and scientific data are unable to penetrate their wall of blind faith. They simply aren't at a point in their spiritual journey where this makes sense to them, and that is fine, for when the student is ready, the teacher appears. Progressing beyond the limits of literalism isn't forced on others but pleasantly discovered along the journey, sometimes accidentally and when it is least expected.

This stumbling-into-learning concept reminds me of a conversation I had with a family member who belittled me for being so inquisitive and asking so many difficult questions about God and Scripture. Like that of so many others with probing inquiries, my faith was ridiculed. The solution, according to this well-intentioned relative, was to exhibit simple faith. A few years later, when the tide had turned and this individual was going through a rough stretch, all kinds of questions about God were raised. Of course, there was no self-loathing for lack of simple faith, for their questioning was seen as honest spiritual pursuit. Perspectives change when you are the one asking the questions, and yet it is the journey itself that prepares the soil of new understanding. Some are prepared for it, while others are not. Both love God, but the soil is at different levels of readiness for receiving seed.

We live in a time when difficult questions must be raised. Christianity can no longer hide behind the drapery of literalism while modern knowledge exposes its many shortcomings. Throwing back the curtain is meant not to embarrass the one hiding behind it but to show that hiding is unnecessary, for Scripture must now be examined in the light of present-day understanding. Where do we go from here? We move toward seeing Jesus in a way that maintains his immense value but also aligns our faith with current knowledge.

Two Layers

A contrast was made in previous chapters between the historical, pre-Easter Jesus and the later portrayals of him in the Gospels—the post-Easter Jesus.[13] This distinction is first-time news to many, for the church doesn't teach this perspective, even though its clergy have known about it for years. In an act of reverent faith, many read the Gospels as literal and factual narratives without the benefit of deep study, analysis, and critical thinking, which, of course, requires hard work. Literalism is always the path of least resistance, for no analysis is needed—you just effortlessly read, accept, and believe. While that may be the easier approach, it is also the least accurate. Never mind the absurdities and inconsistencies it leads to!

When approaching the Gospels, one must keep in mind the two types of material contained within its pages—two layers of tradition. One layer of content reflects the historical, pre-Easter Jesus, while another layer contains the developing tradition of the Christian community after his death—the post-Easter Jesus. One reflects the voice of the historical Jesus, while the other reflects the voice of the emerging Christian community. This sure complicates things, doesn't it?

Biblical scholars attempt to painstakingly sort out these two voices. Though it is difficult work, it helps us better understand the historical Jesus apart from the portrayed Jesus. Scholars look primarily to Matthew, Mark, and Luke because they are similar in nature, whereas the Gospel of John contains so much post-Easter material that its content is not very helpful in discerning the authentic voice of the historical Jesus.

It would be much simpler if the biblical writers had straightforwardly divided things out for us by saying, "In these passages, I am referring to the historical Jesus, and in these verses, I am sharing my developing portrayal of Jesus seventy years after his death." Unfortunately, that isn't how people tend to write. Instead, the Gospel writers combined the two. Intertwined in their post-Easter portrayal are snippets of material that extend back to the historical Jesus. Confused? Now you know why biblical scholarship and critical thinking are so important to understanding the historical Jesus and why we appreciate those who study Scripture so deeply. So, what might we surmise about the historical Jesus?

Jesus the Jew

Volumes could be written about Jesus, and while there is no shortage of available literature on the subject, my intention is to present key elements about him that capture my own attention. That Jesus was a Jew seems self-evident, but I am surprised at how many Christians diminish this truth. Instead, they think of him as a Christian. As a Jew, Jesus lived within the social and religious structures of Judaism. He read the Jewish Scriptures, held a Jewish worldview, and taught from a Jewish religious perspective, and his mission and ministry occurred within a small geographical region of Roman occupied Palestine. Even his disciples were Jewish. To our detriment, we tend to view Jesus through Christian eyes—Gentile eyes that detach him from his Jewish surroundings and influence.

We know very little about the early life of Jesus. His miraculous birth stories are only found in Matthew and Luke, for Mark and John do not mention it, and neither does Paul, the earliest Christian writer. Most biblical scholars view the birth stories as symbolic narratives rather than literal, factually accurate, historical accounts. In reality, we have no reliable historical data about Jesus prior to the beginning of his public ministry at which time he would have been close to thirty years of age.

Jesus was probably born around 4 BCE because he was born before Herod died, and Herod died in 4 BCE. Jesus's parents were probably Jewish, he had brothers and sisters, and he grew up in Nazareth of Galilee, located about one hundred miles north of Jerusalem. He more than likely grew up in a typical Jewish household, attended synagogue, and may have been a maker of wood products, placing him in the lower peasant class. Jesus would have been very familiar with the Jewish religion, along with its festivals and liturgical calendar.

According to Mark, Jesus began his public ministry when John was arrested, which may have been the catalyst that prompted him to step into John's shoes and carry on what he saw as an important ministry. It is Jesus's adult ministry that scholars scrutinize in an attempt to separate post-Easter portrayals from the historical Jesus.

Jesus did not speak of himself in post-Easter ways. In fact, he would probably be shocked to learn that he was portrayed as divine when he balks at even being called "good" in Luke 18:19. There is reason to believe, however, that his followers saw him as someone in whom the Spirit of God was present—someone who was deeply in touch with God in ways that others were not.

Jesus the Mystic

From the earliest writings of Paul, we get a sense that Jesus was intimately connected to the spiritual realm. We might even say that Jesus was a Spirit-person, a mystic, a religious ecstatic, or a holy man. In other words, he was someone who could perceive, interact with, and relate to another dimension of life beyond the physical, visible reality of which we are most familiar. Jesus personally experienced this spiritual realm that is difficult to define but is nonetheless real. For most of us, we struggle to muster up the faith to believe in the unseen world, but for Jesus, it was real. He lived it. He walked in it. It enveloped him. I am referring to a divine power, energy, presence, or what others might call the sacred or numinous that was upon him, within him, and emanated from him. Christians call it God or Spirit.

People noticed this about Jesus, and he realized it about himself as well. Although he became exhausted, hungry, tired, and withdrawn, like all of us at times, he also sensed the reality of God flowing within. We get so wrapped up in what Jesus said and did that we forget about the kind of man he was. He wasn't God and didn't see himself as divine, but he appears to know that the life of God is flowing through his veins in a way that moves him to be all that he was and do all that he did.

Seeing Jesus as someone in touch with the spiritual dimension is key to understanding the pre-Easter Jesus. The early followers sensed this connection, and his sensitivity to God was readily apparent. It was one reason why so many were attracted to him. Every religion seems to have its holy men and women who are more open and sensitive than the rest of us to this spiritual, nonmaterial world. It was only after his death that he came to be thought of as divine in the minds of his followers and was portrayed as something more than he really was. This after-death portrayal is referred to as the post-Easter Jesus.

That Jesus was a man anointed by the Spirit is revealed in numerous ways throughout the Gospels. Mark, for instance, includes the Spirit in his baptismal narrative. As Jesus's ministry is initiated, the Spirit descends upon him like a dove. He is further led by the Spirit into the wilderness of temptation. Mark wants us to know that the life and ministry of Jesus was lived in the anointing of the Spirit. Though Mark's baptism story is a post-Easter portrayal, it may reflect a pre-Easter understanding that Jesus functioned in the realm of the Spirit.

An Inner Strength

The Gospels portray Jesus as someone in close communion with God who spent long hours in prayer. Mark says that he rose early while it was still dark and sought a secluded place to pray (Mark 1:35). We find him climbing a mountain to pray (Mark 6:46). On one occasion, he spends the entire night in prayer (Luke 6:12). Scripture contains numerous verses to this effect.

By prayer, I am not suggesting that Jesus spent hours upon hours verbally petitioning God. I am not sure any of us could do that. Instead, he engaged in silence, meditation, and contemplation. It is a form of prayer with which our modern world is unfamiliar, for we are far too busy trying to accomplish some goal, possess some material item, or enhance our power and prestige. The kind of prayer Jesus was involved with is a form of prayer in which mystics from every religion engage. Long periods of silence, listening, reflecting, meditating, and contemplating allowed Jesus to peer behind the curtain—to touch the spiritual realm and experience the power and presence of God like few of us do. It was a powerful spiritual discipline in his life that we would do well to emulate.

He is said to have called God "Abba," which means "daddy" or "papa." It was a term of deep, intimate relationship. Jews imbued the name of God with such respect that God's name was deemed too holy to say aloud, and yet we find Jesus calling God his daddy. The Gospel writers are portraying his intimate communion with the spiritual realm.

Jesus is also portrayed as a prophet, for Mark has him saying, "Prophets are not without honor, except in their hometown, and among their own kin, and in their own house" (Mark 6:4, NRSV). Prophets were individuals who knew God, experienced God, and heard from God. They were people in close communion with the power and presence of the holy. Jesus may have viewed himself in a similar vein.

The point is that Jesus was a mystic—someone who experienced the Spirit in ways that others didn't. His connection with the divine provided an inner strength to draw upon. His followers saw this, and it was attractive and winsome to others. It was one of the reasons large crowds gathered to hear him teach. His authority came not from degrees, titles, position, wealth, tradition, or status. Instead, the difference was that he spoke and lived as one in touch with the Spirit. He was a Spirit-person, a mystic, a holy man who lived on the edge of sacred reality. Various religions have their own name for this sacred presence, but the point is that Jesus knew and experienced it. It became his inner strength, the source and power of his ministry, and the core of what attracted others to him. It allowed him to serve as a functional conduit between two worlds, the material and the nonmaterial—the world of mortals and the world of spirit.

The sacred dimension that Jesus experienced wasn't something outside this world—out there beyond the here and now. It was a present reality that was all around him, within him, through him, on top of him, under him, and beside him. He was a part of it, lived in it, and was acutely aware of it. In fact, we all live in the power and presence of God. The difference is that some are aware of this sacredness, while others are oblivious to its presence. Jesus was not only keenly aware of it but deeply connected to it.

Believing or Experiencing?

Unfortunately, we have made Christianity to be about correct doctrinal belief. This is seen in our creeds, doctrinal statements, and the many denominations that exist, each with its own twist on what correct belief entails. We systematize and categorize our beliefs, write creedal statements about them, and argue over whose beliefs hold worthier title and who has wandered off the beaten path. This emphasis on correctly worded propositional statements allows us to separate our belief, which we consider to be orthodox, from all other beliefs, which we consider to be heretical. Although Jesus certainly believed in the existence and reality of God, his spiritual life was not defined by the limits of religion. Instead of writing systematic theology textbooks and correctly worded doctrinal statements, Jesus simply touches the sacred and allows it to flow into him and out from him so that others might also touch the divine.

It was his daily experience of this presence that allowed him to be the person he was—a mediator between two realities. It was his ability to know and experience the sacred that gave him the spiritual authority to speak in ways that inspired others and prompted them to look at life differently. God speaks to us through the life of Jesus. We get a taste of the sacred through his life, and that motivates us to be more attentive to the presence of God all around us. Christianity isn't about checking off all the right doctrines one is expected to believe; instead, it is about experiencing God.

The life of Jesus says something about God. Rather than being an abstract principle or impersonal construct, Jesus demonstrates that God is real and experienced in personal ways. God is not an article of faith to believe but a present reality to be known. Though we will never fully define God, we can know the sacred presence in our personal lives. We can experience the same Spirit that Jesus experienced—the same sacred reality that touched his life.

Paul and the Spirit

Once again, we find ourselves going back to the earliest Christian writings of Paul to better understand what it means to say that Jesus was a person of the Spirit. In 1 Thessalonians, Paul's earliest writing from around 50–51 CE, we discover a connection between Jesus and the Spirit. Paul notes that Jesus came in the power of the Holy Spirit (1:5), the same Spirit was also given to us (4:8), and we are warned not to quench the Spirit's work in our life (5:23). Today, we read Paul's letters with the full-fledged doctrine of the Holy Spirit in mind, the third member of the Trinity, but the doctrine hadn't been formulated in Paul's day. That kind of understanding developed over time and was not a part of Paul's thinking. Paul didn't even relate to the Spirit in the same way Luke does in Acts, which was written long after Paul's letters. Instead, Paul believes that the same Spirit that Jesus experienced also augments our own spiritual experience.

Although the Spirit was a real presence that brought about a genuine experience, it couldn't be contained or described adequately with words. Human language is limited in its ability to capture what is beyond words. We experience holy moments and glimpse the sacred even as we struggle to articulate it. The early followers of Jesus saw him as someone who experienced the Spirit of God in extraordinary ways.

In Galatians, the second letter written by Paul, around 52–54 CE, we discover a contrast between the Spirit and the Law. Though both have their value, only the Spirit brings life and wholeness. Since the Spirit was associated with Jesus, we see life and wholeness evidenced in him. Paul goes on to say that the hope of righteousness comes through the Spirit (Gal. 5:5). The fruit of the Spirit is listed in Galatians 5:22, and we are encouraged to walk by the Spirit in Galatians 5:16. When we get to 1 Corinthians, written around 54–56 CE, we are told that "the Spirit searches everything, even the depths of God" (1 Cor. 2:10, NRSV) and that "anyone united to the Lord becomes one spirit with him" (1 Cor. 6:17, NRSV).

These are lofty concepts! The Spirit that was upon Jesus is also within us and brings a unity between God and humans. In essence, life and wholeness come through the Spirit, as evidenced in the example of Jesus. The vitality and wholeness seen in him is also present in our own being: "Or do you not know that your body is a temple of the Holy Spirit within you, which you have from God" (1 Cor. 6:19, NRSV).

Let's get this straight because it is a significant point. Paul saw in Jesus the intersection between God and man in much the same way the temple was seen as the dwelling place of God on Earth. We are the human temple of God's dwelling presence. Though we often struggle to recognize the sacred, Jesus was aware of the Spirit's presence in his life. More than that, the same Spirit that Jesus experienced resides in us and brings us hope that we can also experience abundant life and wholeness. God, Jesus, humanity, life, and wholeness are interconnected, and that is what others noticed and desired of Jesus.

Wind and Breath

Paul was trying to convey what inadequate words cannot. As a learned man, he was aware of the nebulous Hebrew concept of spirit, and it wasn't the doctrine we advance today. Two Hebrew words are key to understanding spirit. The first word is *ruach*, which means "wind," and the second word is *nephesh*, which means "breath."

Spirit is like the wind, as John 3:8 (NRSV) notes: "The wind blows where it chooses, and you hear the sound of it, but you do not know where it comes from or where it goes. So it is with everyone who is born of the Spirit." Though they couldn't explain wind, contain wind, or understand wind, people knew wind when they experienced it. It was boundless, with no beginning or end. Wind became a symbol for the Spirit—something that was real and experienced but unseen, unexplained, unconstrained, and uncontrolled.

Another interesting Hebrew word related to Spirit is *nephesh*, which refers to breath. We read in the Genesis creation account that God breathed the breath of life into Adam's nostrils, and he became a living being (Gen. 2:7). Breath was associated with the giving of life, the very foundation of human existence. Sometimes, even *ruach* carries this same connotation. When *nephesh* left a human being, life left. Later, *nephesh* was translated as "soul" or "spirit," but in the beginning, it referred to the breath of God within us—the very source of life itself.

The Law is unable to impart life and wholeness, but the Spirit can. Wind, breath, and Spirit are all interconnected. Today, such emphasis is placed on creeds, orthodox doctrine, and correct theology that we believe the life of God comes through them when it doesn't. In contrast, a spiritual person is one who experiences life and wholeness emanating from the Spirit, not the Law. Giving life is the very task of the Spirit. We are reminded of this in Ezekiel's vision as the wind-breath of God blows over dead bones and they come to life (Ezek.

37:1–10). In like manner, on the day of Pentecost, the arrival of the Spirit came like a mighty rushing wind. *Ruach* and *nephesh* are associated with life and wholeness.

Other people saw Jesus this way, as a Spirit-connected person—someone who possessed the life of God and who inspired life in others. Those who came in contact with the Spirit that animated Jesus also sensed life and wholeness flowing to them. Life begets life. I find this to be both fascinating and freeing. The very source of life, the breath of God, was radically experienced in Jesus, who in turn inspired life and wholeness in others. That same breath is within us, and if we are mindful, we can experience it to great depth and spread life and wholeness to others.

Jesus the Boundary Breaker

When you realize the breath of God within you, life is lived with spiritual attentiveness. This influences the way you perceive the world and others. You begin to move, live, and be in the Spirit. The barriers that once held you back and kept you in your place are no longer obstacles of restraint. In a world of darkness, you become light. Others experience you as a bundle of vitality. The life and wholeness implanted within you ignite the possibility of life and wholeness in others' lives. It is a wonderfully contagious cycle of influence.

The Gospel of John attempts to convey this very thought by placing these words upon the lips of Jesus: "I came that they may have life, and have it abundantly" (John 10:10, NRSV). When you come into contact with the power of Christ, that is, when you enter into the Spirit like Jesus did, you enter into abundant life and wholeness—the inevitable outcome of experiencing the divine.

The Spirit is always moving to overcome the obstacles that separate us from life and wholeness. Unfortunately, we live in a world full of barriers. Our houses are nothing more than boxes with walls that keep others out. We erect fences that separate us from our neighbors. We live in separate neighborhoods. The poor live here, and the rich live over there. Certain races live on this side of the tracks, while other races live on the other side of the tracks. We separate ourselves by gender, income, ethnicity, sexual orientation, age, religious preference, and so forth. The last and final barrier to our human existence is death. I am not suggesting we live under the stars in the open range, do without protection and privacy, or refuse to acknowledge differences. My point is that life built by humans is about barriers and separation.

Jesus, on the other hand, was seen as a boundary breaker, someone who broke down barriers of inequity and discrimination. When you encounter the Spirit like Jesus did, boundaries no longer exist. Life is no longer lived in isolation or from an "us versus them" mentality. Instead, the life-force of God becomes the source of your moving, seeing, and existing. You no longer need boundaries to provide security, worth, and sustenance. Life is lived differently because you now see the world with new eyes.

When God becomes the sustaining force of your life, you now have the ability to love without limits and without exclusion. You can love those who are different from you—those who live on the other side of the tracks. There are no barriers to the love of God that freely flows in you and through you. Life is lived with a sense of vitality that emanates from the Spirit to the physical world around you. Barriers diminish as our sense of God increases. Even though we live in a fragmented world, there are no obstacles that can prevent our divine connection and no barriers to living in wholeness. The obstacles of hurt, pain, and sadness are restored by the life-sustaining connection to the Spirit within.

We see this life-force in Jesus. The barriers of his own age didn't prevent him from living in freedom and personal wholeness. His Spirit connection prompted him to move beyond them. When the barrier of unforgiveness presented itself as he was dying on the cross, he asked that God forgive those whose actions led to his death. Who does that? Where does one find the power to forgive his murderers? Jesus had the freedom to do just that because he possessed the power and vitality of the Spirit. He rose above the barriers of bitterness, regret, and unforgiveness and allowed wholeness to flow from him into others—even his enemies.

Though his existence upon this earth was short-lived, Jesus experienced a quality of life that most of us never achieve. The sustaining life-force of the Spirit allowed Jesus to utter, "It is finished" as his last words. It is the word *tetelestai* from the root *teleo* or *telos*, and it means that Jesus had accomplished his purpose—his telos. He didn't live a long life, but he enjoyed a purposeful life—one that had reached its proper end. He died a completed life. Even in his death, the Spirit flowed through him. His life had reached its proper purpose. That is a life of quality—a life that is connected to the sustaining power of the Spirit.

Again and again we see Jesus breaking barriers. He eats with sinners and tax collectors instead of isolating himself among the self-righteous. He stops to engage a woman at the well who is both a despised Samaritan and a lowly female. His disciples are amazed that he would do such a thing. Barriers no longer exist for Jesus. The Samaritan woman is a fellow human—someone who also has the breath of God within her, and the false boundary needs to be reclaimed. We find Jesus doing good on the Sabbath, which infuriates the punctilious keepers of the law. Yet Jesus crosses the boundary and will not be restrained even by religious rules that are taken out of context and elevated to grand-barrier status. Instead, he knows that the Sabbath was made for humans, not humans for the Sabbath (Matt. 12:1–8; Mark 2:23–28; Luke 6:1–5). Numerous examples of Jesus's boundary-breaking efforts could be cited.

It made no difference to Jesus who you were, where you were from, or what your status was in life. You were always a "somebody" in his eyes. You could be an adulterer, a rich ruler, a Gentile, a despised Samaritan, a lowly female, or even his executioner, and the infinite and boundless love of God was extended to you. His love knew no boundaries. Even Paul realizes this boundary-breaker element in Galatians 3:28 (NRSV): "There is no longer Jew or Greek, there is no longer slave or free, there is no longer male and female; for all of you are one in Christ Jesus." Paul isn't naïve enough to think that Jew and Greek, slave and free, male and female don't exist or that there are no differences in life. Rather, he simply believes they are not obstacles to unity and value. In Christ, differences are cherished, not barriers erected between us, for we are all one in Christ.

The Spirit brings life and wholeness, not separation and fragmentation. Through the power of the Spirit comes the capacity to love all as the breath of God, just as Jesus did. Barriers based on gender, age, sexual orientation, ethnicity, race, religion, you name it, are all destroyed. Instead of estrangement, we rejoice in the diversity of God's breath. Barriers promote separation, power, and control, but the Spirit brings life and wholeness that overcome all obstacles to the inclusive love of God. All are holders of God's precious breath.

The final barrier to human existence is death. It is seen as the end of all there is—the finality that befalls all of us. It is true, we will all experience death, but death may not be our final reality. The world of spirit and the breath of God are the ultimate reality. Jesus was raised from death into the world of spirit. This gives rise to hope that our own death is merely an entrance into the ultimate reality itself as our breath returns to its source.

Jesus the Image of God

Not only is Jesus a mystic and a breaker of barriers; he also discloses God to us, for he is the image of God. Followers of the historical Jesus sensed that he was different—that he marched to the beat of a different drum. He was a

Spirit-person whose reality included both the seen and the unseen. He was a breaker of boundaries who saw the breath of God in every person. He was also someone who revealed the character and passion of God. If you want to know what God is like, then look to the life of Jesus as the human disclosure of God's image: "He is the image of the invisible God" (Col. 1:15, NRSV) and "Christ, who is the image of God" (2 Cor. 4:4, NRSV). Jesus wasn't God and would never have thought of himself in those terms, but he did teach and live in ways that revealed the heartbeat of God to his followers. The Gospel writers try to capture this in their literary portraits of him.

In a sense, Jesus becomes a metaphor for God—a sacrament, a window or doorway through which we see God. After his death, writers portrayed him as divine, but Jesus never claimed that title for himself. In reality, he was someone who reflected back to us what God must be like. Though he was a real person, he was much more than that because of the Spirit's presence in his life. His disciples noticed it, crowds caught a glimpse of it, and his Spirit-filled life transformed many. It was this anointing that prompted the attachment of various titles after his death, such as light, bread, living water, Son of God, Word of God, etc. All of these images and metaphors are trying to capture the fact that he mirrored the image of God. If you want to know what God is like, then look to the life of Jesus.

For Jesus, the Spirit was a present reality, assuring us that God can be known and experienced. The presence and power of the Spirit were real and accessible, and it is the reality of Spirit that matters to me. We can argue until the cows come home about various superficial details regarding the life of Jesus, but it is the substance underlying his life that piques my interest. What was behind his life that caused others to see the life of God in him? I want to experience the depth of Spirit that moved Jesus to love others without limit. God was not a doctrine, a textbook definition to be memorized, or the recitation of some religious statement, as if affirming it made it true. Jesus's personal experience of the divine didn't come through a priest, the institutionalized church, or belief in correct doctrine. God was accessible to Jesus just as God is accessible to us—a direct, nonmediated experiential reality.

A Compassionate God

Jesus experienced a God of compassion. Instead of an angry deity pouncing upon those who struggle to walk in total obedience to the rules of the great lawgiver, Jesus reveals a heart of compassion through such stories as the Prodigal

Son and the Good Samaritan. In fact, we are told that Jesus himself felt compassion toward those who followed him.

According to Luke 6:36, Jesus asks us to be compassionate just like God is compassionate. Although many versions use "merciful" rather than "compassionate," I find the concept of compassion to be the more appropriate wording. It speaks of both the character of God and a key quality of a God-centered life. To be compassionate is to be caring, loving, open, embracing, and nurturing. That's how Jesus experienced God, and it is the kind of God he discloses to us.

Rather than being limited to one's personal life, compassion is also an important social value that affects the element of community. Compassion is a core ingredient to living in relationship with one another. While the religious elite of Jesus's day practiced a religion of holiness and separation, Jesus practiced a religion of inclusion and compassion. For many, religion creates clear lines of demarcation—pure versus impure, holy versus profane, righteous versus sinner, whole versus broken, spiritual haves versus the have-nots, and so forth. But as noted earlier, Jesus was a boundary breaker. He shattered lines of demarcation that divided people into "us versus them" categories. Instead, he functioned from a compassionate core that saw God in all people. He practiced hospitality to the disenfranchised, broke constrictive and often ridiculous religious rules, and was accused of being a drunkard for eating and drinking with those deemed unworthy of such affection and attention.

I have met plenty of people in the church who view God as a trigger-happy judge anxious to throw the book at those who stray off the narrow religious path. Who wants to serve a God like that—a critical Heavenly Father always in attack mode? I have found these people to be harsh, critical, and joyless. They suck the very life out of the church. They are deadly purveyors of all things wrong with the church and leave a path of destruction in their wake, all the while believing themselves to be God's deputized holy standard-bearers who help God uphold the straight and narrow.

In Jesus's day, the dominant understanding of God was that of holiness, and yet that doesn't seem to be the picture of God Jesus discloses to us. Jesus's experience of the Spirit always led to life and wholeness, not self-righteous rule-keeping and holier-than-thou attitudes. To experience the Spirit is to experience the love, acceptance, care, compassion, and nurture of God. While compassion is a quality of God and an individual virtue worth emulating, it is also an esteemed social value within the Christian community. We relate to one another as God relates to us—with compassion.

Relationship or Rule-Keeping?

We learn many things from the life and ministry of Jesus. We see a contrast between life and death, wholeness and fragmentation, unconventional wisdom and establishment rules, internal and external focus, and the difference between relationship and rule-keeping.

Two roads can be traveled in this life that diverge at the point of choice—our choice. One takes you to the left, and the other takes you to the right. The road most traveled only sees this world—a journey without the Spirit. The other road, the path Jesus encouraged his followers to pursue, is a countercultural way of viewing life—a nonconventional approach to living and being. One road is well traveled, firmly grounded in this culture, and follows the conventional ways of talking about God. The other road is less traveled, firmly grounded in the Spirit, and leads to seeing things from a new perspective. In a sense, Jesus was the grand eye-opener because he walked in step with the Spirit and saw another side of reality often eclipsed by the traditional way of doing business as usual.

For Jesus, focusing only on external actions simply didn't go far enough, for life in the Spirit causes us to examine the internal motivation behind our thoughts and actions. Jesus's experience of the Spirit imbued life and wholeness into him, something every human needs. Trying to fix our bumps and bruises with materialism, power, and prestige is a duct-tape approach to patching up our fragmented souls. It is a temporary fix with no lasting value. Following the conventional wisdom of this culture leads to death because it is devoid of the power and wisdom of God. Chained to establishment thinking, nothing is risked, and nothing is ventured, whereas walking in step with the Spirit leads to promptings, nudgings, impressions, and internal alignment with the divine. Our eyes are open to another reality—a different path than the one we are currently traversing.

As Jesus demonstrates, the path of the Spirit leads us away from religious rule-keeping and into relationship with the divine. Over and over again, we see that the heart of this path is a relationship with the Spirit. Religion is filled with forms, symbols, and rituals that are useless in themselves. Their value isn't in the form itself but in the substance to which they point. Getting to the substance—to the heart of the matter—is what mattered to Jesus, and if it mattered to Jesus, it matters to God, and if it matters to God, it matters to us. Jesus had an uncanny ability to get at the heart of issues, to bypass external fluff, and to lead others toward personally experiencing the Spirit.

Jesus and the Social Order

In a culture filled with numerous social taboos, we glimpse Jesus's approach to relationships through his reported actions. The social order of Jesus's day ranked people according to worth, holiness standards, false criteria, and all kinds of erroneous evaluations. In stark contrast, Jesus saw worth in every human and demonstrated that value through his actions and his words. He often ate meals with the disenfranchised and downtrodden—those deemed less valuable. He invited despised tax collectors and unclean sinners to his table, and by keeping their company, his own character and worth were diminished in the eyes of his detractors. That was okay with Jesus, for sharing a meal with others was a way of showing love, value, and acceptance. It revealed to others that God was open, inclusive, and accepting and that inherent worth could be found in every human, for each person carries within them the *imago dei*—the image of God.

Jesus touched lepers who were ceremonially unclean. He allowed a woman with a bleeding issue to touch the hem of his garment. She, too, was ceremonially unclean and seen as someone with reduced value; and yet Jesus stops to converse with her, heal her, and ultimately restore life and wholeness to her being. The social order viewed these folks as impure, "less-than" people, and yet we find Jesus turning his face toward them. He traveled to Samaria to speak with a despised and lowly woman about living water. On the scale of social value, she wasn't worth much. Jesus risked his reputation to demonstrate the love of God for all people despite the many social taboos created by a value scale that was itself valueless.

Who does that? Who dances to the Spirit's impulse in the presence of danger and personal peril? What kind of person is not constrained by culture's erroneous assignments of value? As the revealer of God, Jesus demonstrated what was important to God. All humans, regardless of their place in the social ranking system, were loved and valued by God. Jesus promoted an egalitarian human perspective—everyone was of equal worth. We would do well to remember and live by this uniting concept.

The Ethic of Love

In addition to a life that demonstrated the worth of every individual, Jesus taught an ethic of love as the key component to following God. Jesus lived in a culture of commandments, obedience, purity codes, and rituals. Matthew 22:35–40 (NRSV) relays how one of the Pharisees, a lawyer, asks Jesus a question in order to test him: "Teacher, which commandment in the law is the greatest?" Jesus responds, "'You shall love the Lord your God with all your heart, and with all your soul, and with all your mind.' This is the greatest and first commandment. And a second is like it: 'You shall love your neighbor as yourself.' On these two commandments hang all the law and the prophets" (Deut. 6:4–7; Mark 12:28–31; Matt. 22:35–40).

These words were to be the heartbeat of Israel, a core social value within the community of faith. Unfortunately, these core values became encased in the performance of rituals. Instead of actually loving God and loving one's neighbor as God desires, rituals grew to replace the very commandment they were to represent. The focus turned from love to law, from internal communion with the divine presence to strict adherence to external rules and regulations as the core identifier of God's people. Jesus recaptured love as the heartbeat of faith—the ethic of those who follow God. In fact, for Jesus, the entire Law and the Prophets are summed up in loving God and loving people. In his mind, that's pretty much it, and it's pretty simple.

What does God care about? God cares about love, as demonstrated by the life and teaching of Jesus. Love is central to being a God-follower. It demands that we treat each other well and see value in every person. Jesus said nothing about affirming creeds, repeating the sinner's prayer, or becoming a member of a church. Instead, following God entailed loving God with all that is within you and loving your neighbor as yourself.

While loving God and loving others is a simple message, it is easier said than done. It is far simpler to establish a social order that ranks one's value, allows for comparisons, and erects scaffolding around the concept of love than it is to actually love. The simple message of love was added to until it became complex and difficult to understand and achieve. Can it really be that simple—that a relationship with the divine presence centers upon love and compassion? We have a tendency to twist things around. We take the simple message of love and add layers of complexity to it. We then focus on the complexity in order to prove our spirituality. We make what is simple hard, and we make what is hard simple. We have it backward.

Following God involves loving God and loving others. Living that simple message reflects the nature of our heart. Loving with purity is one of the most difficult things we can do, and yet to progress in love is to become more like the God of love. We would rather turn a simple message into a complex one so the true motives of our own heart remain unmasked. It is far easier to engage in an external ritual than it is to turn our hearts toward love.

Our inclination is to attach "if, but, when" conditions to the love of God. God will lavishly love you *if* you do this, say this, believe this, act this way, etc. God will lavishly love you *when* you do this, say this, believe this, act this way, etc. God will lavishly love you, *but* you must do this, say this, believe this, etc. The conditions we place upon God's love are not grounded in Scripture and are used to justify the social scale of who is worthy and who isn't. God's love flows freely to all, regardless of who they are and what they have done. God's love is unconditional, expansive, and all-inclusive, and it radiates to us, in us, around us, and through us. It is given to all without condition, without status, and without merit because it emanates from God, who is love.

The epistle of 1 John expresses the essential quality of love. We are told that love is from God and that God is love. Those who do not love do not know God, and if we claim to love God and yet hate others, it reveals that we do not love God. To abide in love is to abide in God. Paul echoes these very same values in his famous love chapter, 1 Corinthians 13. According to Paul, you can have all kinds of gifts and abilities, but if you do not have love, it profits you nothing. Without love, our comings and goings are like the annoying sound of clanging symbols. The greatest item in our arsenal of faith is love, and Paul lists its many virtues in 1 Corinthians 13:4–8 (NRSV):

> *Love is patient; love is kind; love is not envious or boastful or arrogant or rude. It does not insist on its own way; it is not irritable or resentful; it does not rejoice in wrongdoing, but rejoices in the truth. It bears all things, believes all things, hopes all things, endures all things. Love never ends.*

If there was an ethic that Jesus followed, it was the value of love in its many expressions. God is associated with love, and when you come into contact with the source of all love, you cannot help but love, for the divine love of God flows in you and through you. Love is the result of peering behind the divine curtain as Jesus did, and it becomes the hallmark of those who seek God.

Peace and Justice

Another item of social order worth noting in the life of Jesus is that of peace and justice. At no time do we find Jesus advocating for, or using, violence as a means of advancing his message. During Passover, he rides into Jerusalem on a donkey, a symbol of peace, in contrast to the horses of war ridden by Roman soldiers tasked with guarding the peace. When Peter draws his sword in violence against the arresting officers who come to take Jesus into custody, Jesus responds, "Put your sword back into its place; for all who take the sword will perish by the sword" (Matt. 26:52, NRSV). Jesus wanted no part of violence. He taught a different set of values with a different way of living life, but he did so through storytelling and the example of his own life, not through the weapons of war or the power of oppression.

There were always those who yearned to be free from Roman oppression and turned to guerilla warfare. They were called zealots and recruited like-minded individuals to pursue war and violence in their fight against the dominant Roman system. They killed in the name of God and justified their actions in religious terms. In the end, it was nothing more than the power of violence all dressed up in religious garb.

There is no inkling of violence in the life of Jesus, even though some find such support by taking verses out of context, like Matthew 10:34–36 and Luke 22:35–36. In Matthew, Jesus says, "Do not think that I have come to bring peace to the earth; I have not come to bring peace, but a sword" (Matt. 10:34, NRSV). But Jesus isn't calling for violence; instead, he is being brutally honest with his disciples and warning that following him will often bring resistance and division within the family, between a man and his father, a daughter and her mother, and that "one's foes will be members of one's own household."

We find another strange passage referencing a sword in Luke 22:35–36 (NRSV), where Jesus says to his disciples, "'When I sent you out without a purse, bag, or sandals, did you lack anything?' They said, 'No, not a thing.' He said to them, 'But now, the one who has a purse must take it, and likewise a bag. And the one who has no sword must sell his cloak and buy one.'" The point isn't to become armed revolutionaries who incite violence; instead, it is a Middle Eastern way of noting that Jesus will soon be gone, that they will be left on their own, and that their very existence will be in danger.

Jesus turned the tables on the temple moneychangers in a dramatic act to make a point, but he had no army, recruited no soldiers, carried no weapon, and taught the way of love, not violence. He didn't engage in or promote looting, destroying property, or inciting mob violence. Those on the receiving end of violence and oppression, he uplifted and befriended—even forgiving his executioners. The way of Jesus was the way of wisdom, authenticity, and love. He was a nonviolent individual who shared his message through nonviolent means in order to achieve his end. His was the power of influence and truth. His was the power of love—the ultimate barrier breaker. He was a peaceful man who promoted peace with God and others in peaceful ways.

In addition to being a peaceful man, Jesus was also concerned with justice. The way of peace, some believe, is the way of sissies and weaklings, and a more assertive approach would yield greater results without the need for patience. Yet Jesus was powerful, not because he implemented weapons of war or violent tactics but because he stood for the deeper things that mattered through nonviolent means. He taught with his life, actions, and words. He became a living example of what he believed.

Many are disappointed that Jesus didn't gather an army about him and take a vigilant stand in calling for the overthrow of Rome. They want him to call out slavery, heal every person, bring about instant equity in all things, and use whatever means necessary to achieve justice—even violence. We don't find Jesus doing that. Slavery was left intact and even used in his teaching to make a greater point. He cares for the poor, feeds the hungry, and heals the afflicted, but he doesn't eradicate any of it. The dominant power structure was not destroyed. Instead, it was the oppressive system itself that wielded its power to arrest, try, convict, and execute an innocent and peaceful man.

Just because Jesus didn't eradicate injustice doesn't mean he endorsed it. Far from it! His point was to demonstrate how life should be lived in the midst of it. We see a different ethic in the life of Jesus: the ethic of love. Where love abounds, justice ensues. This concept of love and justice isn't new, for it was spoken of by the Old Testament prophets. The relationship between God and Israel is that of lover and beloved, and justice is seen as a form of love. When love is central to one's life, justice is an automatic by-product—a natural expression of love for God and one another. Jesus seems to understand this.

In God's kingdom, love and justice go hand in hand. Too often we conceive of God's justice as punitive, mean-spirited, and overshadowing God's sense of love. God is often portrayed as a rules-and-rewards kind of God who will zap you for not measuring up. Strict obedience to God's laws is expected; otherwise, the Heavenly Enforcer will get you. This mean-spirited deity is a God of works, not grace, and a God who killed Jesus so that God's own sense of justice could be appeased. But what if the justice of God isn't about retribution or punishment? What if it is about alleviating the oppression of others and treating them as equals? What if justice is an outflow of love, not the result of anger and hatred?

From an individual standpoint, Jesus elevates the equality of every human being as valued and loved by God. Tax collectors, sinners, lepers, lowly women, despised Samaritans, the poor, the ceremonially unclean, and all others were equal in his sight. He demonstrated this value in his own life by lifting them up, standing with them, and involving them in his life. From a collective standpoint, he stood up to the oppressive religious authority of his day that misconstrued the things that really mattered. He envisioned a transformed world where the compassion and justice of God triumphed.

The prevailing social systems of our day are flawed and often oppressive. The social scale of who is valued and who isn't still remains. When you find Christians standing strong for justice, they do so out of deep passion for God, believing that justice is the by-product of love in social form. Aligning themselves with the Old Testament prophets, their pursuit of social justice is nothing more than the worship of God being acted out in this life. It is an important way that Christians worship God. Dismantling discrimination and injustice is to follow the model of Jesus, who showed us what life could be like when the boundless love of God is extended to all.

Injustice can be seen in how individuals treat one another, but more than that, it can rear its ugly head through social systems that are built unjustly— called systemic injustice. When you are the benefactor of an unjust system, its discriminatory practices can fly under the radar. Many seek fair and balanced social systems as an expression of God's love. When the value of human life is seen in terms of God's very own image, the love of God cannot help but flow into the lives of others and influence the systems that affect the disenfranchised.

What does God require of us, the prophet Micah asks: "He has told you, O mortal, what is good; and what does the LORD require of you but to do justice, and to love kindness, and to walk humbly with your God?" (Mic. 6:8, NRSV). Jesus was familiar with Micah's mandate and sought to demonstrate it through his life and teaching. The Jewish Talmud sums this teaching up in a powerful way: "Do not be daunted by the enormity of the world's grief. Do justly, now. Love mercy, now. Walk humbly, now. You are not obligated to complete the work, but neither are you free to abandon it." Jesus was a promoter of love and justice through peace and nonviolence. In like manner, it was Martin Luther King Jr., a modern-day prophet of the 1960s, who caught this teaching of Jesus and exemplified it in his approach to the civil rights movement.

Jesus the Prophet

Many Christians view the prophets as tellers of the future whose role was to predict and forecast forthcoming events that moved the plan of God forward. Their predictions provided God with plausible deniability for the events and actions that would occur. For instance, one might say, "You are on your way to hell, and it is your own doing. God revealed truth to you through the various Old Testament prophecies. You should have known. Don't blame God." All you had to do, according to this view, was read the prophets and believe the prophecies about Jesus, the end times, what happens to people and countries that offend God, the second coming of Jesus, etc. God now has the right to say, "Don't blame me; I told you so. Had you listened, you wouldn't be in this jam of yours." It is an alibi of plausible deniability.

The Jewish authors of the New Testament utilized the Old Testament in shaping their understanding of Jesus. They looked backward to Old Testament writings, discovered passages they could cherry-pick and apply to Jesus, and did so. Even though the ancient story had nothing to do with their contemporary circumstances, New Testament writers saw a correlation or a prefiguring that could be applied to their own situation. The Old Testament writers had no intention of writing with New Testament circumstances in mind. They were writing to address their own situations, not predicting the future.

Rather than foretellers of the future, prophets were clarion voices serving as the social conscience of the nation. The prophets arise during times of crisis and great difficulty. They cluster around two significant events in the life of Israel—the fall of the Northern Kingdom in 721 BCE by the Assyrians as they captured Samaria and the fall of Jerusalem and the destruction of the sacred temple by the Babylonians who overtook the Southern Kingdom in 586 BCE. The prophets appear around these important events in the life of Israel, and their role was to address the nation during these difficult times.

Their messages were very similar. They indicted Israel by saying, "Look at what you have done and how you have lived." Exploitation of others by the powerful and wealthy was disconcerting, and their relationship of fidelity to God was broken. They lived and trusted in themselves, and if they continued down this path of social irresponsibility, it would result in conquest and ruin. Powerful nations would take advantage of this chink in Israel's armor and pursue military conquest. You didn't have to be a rocket scientist to figure that out. This is exactly what happened as the Assyrians plundered the Northern Kingdom, while the Babylonians pillaged Jerusalem in the south.

Realizing the eventual outcome of such social irresponsibility, the prophets called for repentance and change. The nation as a whole was beckoned to get back on track, and the prophets did all they could to garner the attention of their beloved nation through fiery orations, judgments, indictments, stories, and even acting out their message in strange ways. They weren't predicting a foreordained future decreed in the heavens eons ago but rather trying to prevent the natural outcome of an irresponsible society amid the gathering storm of outside nations. They were, in essence, trying to change the inevitable, and their words were couched in the deep religious heritage of the nation. If Israel would change its ways, the eventual outcome could be avoided.

Jesus can also be thought of as a contemporary prophet of his day. There is evidence that he saw himself in this light, for we find him engaged in prophetic actions and describing himself as a prophet without honor in his hometown. He sensed an urgency to his mission, especially after being baptized and learning of John's imprisonment and beheading at the behest of a wicked king. Jesus also perceived Israel's social irresponsibility in relationship to God and others. He indicted the religious culture of his day and exposed the corruption and exploitation of others. He told stories and parables to advance his message. He denounced those in positions of religious power, who should have known better. Had they forgotten about compassion, loving God with a pure heart, and caring for others? People had their values mixed up and were focusing on the wrong things.

His compassion for others created a visceral response within him. At one point, he even wept for Jerusalem. He told parables and shared stories in an attempt to catch people's attention. It was his way of calling for change—deep change that would alter the individual and the nation. Jesus warned that the beloved temple in Jerusalem would be destroyed and that the familiar Jewish culture they took for granted would be forever altered if the nation didn't change its ways. Fed up with rebel Jewish guerilla warfare, Jesus's warning came to fruition in 70 CE as the Romans destroyed the center of Jewish worship—the treasured temple.

Jesus invited people to a new way of seeing, living, and being. Two paths lay before them: the broad path of conventional wisdom and the narrow path of inner transformation. He called for living life in a new, alternative wisdom. He journeyed to Jerusalem to proclaim this challenge, and it got him killed. Just like the prophets of old, Jesus summoned his own generation to a better way. He saw the crisis brewing on the horizon, pointed out the inequities and religious pretense of his day, and challenged others to walk a new path.

The Post-Easter Portrayal

On multiple occasions, I have mentioned the difference between the historical, pre-Easter Jesus and the post-resurrection portrayal of Jesus and how scholars search for hints of the historical Jesus amid the post-Easter portrayals. My comments about Jesus in this chapter are trying to capture the historical man who walked this earth in the first century rather than recount portrayals of him long after his death.

In identifying these distinctions, one may get the impression that there is no value in post-Easter portrayals of Jesus. Maybe we should discard them altogether as insignificant and inaccurate—nothing more than obstacles in our path to discovering the historical Jesus. It is true that post-Easter portrayals are merely that—portrayals, and not historical, factual actualities—but that doesn't mean they are without value, for we benefit from them because they reveal the impact Jesus had on the lives of his followers.

The historical Jesus is the man who actually walked this earth more than two thousand years ago. The portrayed Jesus is how others expressed his meaning for their lives at the time of their writing. We tend to look at everything the Bible says about Jesus as absolutely, 100 percent, factually and literally true. In reality, people interpreted the life of Jesus in various ways, depending on the age in which they lived, the cultural circumstances of their time, and their own personal leaning toward one agenda over another. They expressed the meaning Jesus had for them, and this is the significant thing about post-Easter portrayals.

Post-Easter portrayals point to something beyond the portrait itself—to the man and his impact upon the writers. He became Lord to them, which points to their seeing him as someone worthy of loyalty and allegiance—someone worth following. Jesus lived with such significance that it caused others to say of him, "He is Lord." The historical Jesus also functioned as someone under the anointing of the Spirit—someone connected to the spiritual dimension in ways that others noticed. It led them to conclude that the life and power of God were flowing through him, so much so that after his death, he was portrayed as divine. The portrayals are reflections of the historical Jesus and the impact he had upon others, not of the historical Jesus himself. They are not historically and factually true but stories and portrayals that reflect what Jesus had come to mean to them, not what Jesus actually thought of himself. They reveal the transformative nature of the Christ power.

The stories of Jesus's conception, birth, death, resurrection, and ascension were never meant to be taken as literal, factual, historical truth, but as profound and powerful truth that symbolized something more. There are no virgin conceptions without male seed. People who have been dead for three days are not raised back to human life. Jesus didn't literally lift off this planet and head into outer space in an ascension. These aren't literal facts but stories that symbolize and point to a greater truth. They are myths, images, symbols, motifs, and portrayals that speak of the significance and impact of Jesus.

Jesus is portrayed as the light of the world, but he is not a literal light. This is a metaphor—a symbolic way of showing how the message of Jesus brings light to our darkness. The story of his miraculous conception symbolizes that his teaching and ministry were of God. A path to God is symbolized in the death and resurrection of Jesus. It is the path of being born anew—experiencing a divine paradigm shift where our old way of thinking, seeing, and living gives way to a new way of thinking, seeing, and living. Paul says it this way in Galatians 2:19–20 (NRSV): "I have been crucified with Christ; and it is no longer I who live, but it is Christ who lives in me." An experience of Jesus was one of God being present. He is seen as Immanuel.

The list could go on and on, but the point is that these stories point to the significance of Jesus and reflect God's involvement in his life. God was seen in Jesus. His story is the story of God intersecting with human life. These interpretive portraits are valuable because they point to the meaning and impact of Jesus upon his followers.

Although I make a distinction between the historical Jesus who actually walked this earth in the first century and the post-Easter Jesus who later writers made him out to be, both are important. For me, it is not an either-or choice but a both-and phenomenon. Both add value to our understanding of Jesus and his impact. The historical Jesus is someone in whom the Spirit of God could be seen. He entered the world of spirit in ways and depths that many of us have never experienced. Living in the reality of the Spirit made him who he was—attractive, winsome, powerful, insightful, and transformational. Others experienced the moving of God in his life. On the other hand, the post-Easter portrayal of Jesus reflects what he became to others after his death. In other words, the stories represent the impact and meaning he made in their life. Both the actual Jesus and the portrayed Jesus are important. One represents who he actually was, and the other represents what he became to the early church. We can look at both and point to an extraordinary man who was led by the Spirit of God.

The Significance of Jesus

If Jesus is not divine, then is there any significance to him at all? What is his value? Volumes could be written on this, but for me, the significance of Jesus boils down to his relationship to the world of spirit and how that relationship expressed itself in his life. Jesus was human like the rest of us, but he was much more than that. He had the ability to peer behind the veil of perceived reality and into another dimension. He lived in constant contact with the Spirit, and as such, he demonstrated for us what God is like. He provided an example of how to live life in the Spirit.

He is the image of God—the revelation of God in human form being lived out within the sphere of humanity. If Jesus reflects to us what God is like, then we have nothing to fear, and he becomes a doorway to experiencing the divine. In this way, he is a central element to all that Christianity is. The life of God that touched Jesus is also available to us.

A Spirit-Filled Reality

I see Jesus as someone who was filled with the Spirit—someone who lived life with constant awareness of, and in tune with, the Spirit dimension. You say, "Spirit-filled person" in our contemporary religious environment, and our mind immediately goes to someone with outstretched hands, speaking in tongues, and dancing about in a holy hop while attending a Pentecostal church service. For some reason, I don't see Jesus jumping up and down at a church service, yipping like a dog, laughing like a hyena, or convulsing to the beat of a contemporary religious song. I am not against such expressions of faith, but it is not the image of Jesus portrayed in Scripture.

When I speak of Jesus as a Spirit-filled individual, I mean to say that he experienced the spirit world in genuine ways that marked him and allowed him to straddle the fence between two realities. Our modern-day religious structure emphasizes proper belief, adherence to creeds, and the affirmation of propositional religious statements. Jesus seemed to care very little about such things. Instead, he lived life in the Spirit. He demonstrated to us that the Spirit is real. If we want to know God in the depths of our being, it won't come through adherence and promulgation of religious doctrinal statements. That is a waste of time and energy. Jesus reveals that life is fully lived when it is lived in the Spirit. He demonstrates that reality is more than the physical world; it involves attentiveness to the world of spirit.

A Living Example

Not only does the Spirit-filled life of Jesus alert us to the reality of the Spirit; it also influenced how he lived life. In essence, his Spirit-filled life becomes an example to us. For instance, we find in Jesus a sense of joy, courage, and compassion. He lived life free of fear, worry, and anxiety. He had no preoccupation with self-adulation and would rather serve than elevate himself. In essence, his Spirit-filled life expressed itself in the fruit of the Spirit. By walking in the Spirit, according to Galatians 5:22–23, the fruit of the Spirit is evidenced in our own life. Jesus exemplified this for us. Living in the Spirit as Jesus did influences the quality of the life we lead—a life that produces the fruit of the Spirit.

As the image of God, Jesus discloses to us what God is like. That disclosure becomes a model for us to follow. We trust what Jesus trusted. He put his trust in God, and we should do the same. Jesus lived in the reality of the Spirit, and we should do the same. We care what Jesus cared for. He cared about people—loving them, serving them, and seeing the image of God in them. We should do the same. He broke down the cultural barriers that divide humans by treating slaves, tax collectors, women, the downtrodden, and the disenfranchised as equals. We should do the same. He practiced an open table where love, trust, and acceptance prevailed, and we should do the same. We value what Jesus values.

Jesus lived this way because he was in constant contact with the Spirit, which became his life source and inspiration. It gave him the drive and power to pursue his values. That Spirit connection ensured the quality of life he lived—one that evidenced the fruit of the Spirit. That Spirit connection prompted his moving beyond cultural barriers to demonstrate the value of all humanity. He had total freedom to be himself and pursue God without self-serving ambition and without fear or anxiety. That Spirit connection allowed him to live and teach an alternative path that leads to abundant life—the narrow way of wisdom and the road to personal transformation. When we live in the Spirit, we experience Jesus as a living spiritual reality. It is one way that we taste the world of spirit as he did.

God was profoundly and intimately present in the historical Jesus from Nazareth. In essence, Jesus put a human face to God and helped us see God as the source of life and love—a presence that touches us so deeply that we live life in the expansive love of God that knows no boundaries. The life of Jesus invites us to move beyond our limited perspective and experience God's life-giving Spirit.

I am ordained by a denomination that allows for great diversity of thought surrounding the interpretation of Scripture. This ability to be true to one's own conscience is rarely encouraged in our day. Instead of affirming creeds and doctrinal statements to become a church member, my denomination merely requires that one affirm that Jesus is the Christ, the son of the living God. That's it. Pretty simple. I can readily agree to these titles because they reveal something about the historical Jesus I have already discussed.

These denominational congregations are composed of members holding various theological outlooks. Some are conservatives, while others are liberals. Some are literalists, while others are not. Many are in between or haven't made up their mind yet. In the midst of this kind of diversity—each member pursuing her or his own conscience—there exists a unity and love that I have not seen in other denominations. It is refreshing. Each Sunday, when these diverse members come together to celebrate God, differences are laid aside. Common among them is a bond of love and unity. Congregants have the freedom to sing their own song and dance to the rhythm of their own view. Yet they all come together of their own volition to celebrate the unity and love found in Christ. The denomination isn't perfect, but I am proud to be a part of this extraordinary effort toward wholeness.

Chapter Summary

How can a discussion of Jesus be limited to a few pages in a book, especially when it involves alternative perspectives? It can't. These pages can, however, awaken our appetite for further learning, thinking more deeply, and pursuing the life-giving Spirit behind the historical Jesus. If this section on Jesus hasn't stirred your mind and heart, I don't know what will. Its contents cry out for an answer from you.

I challenged traditional understandings of the virgin birth, ascension, atonement, resurrection, and the divinity of Jesus. Because I am willing to point out the elephants in the room, some feel I have crossed the line of acceptable Christian behavior. Yet my observations are seen as a breath of fresh air to those seeking to make sense of their faith. This particular chapter rounds out the section by asking, "Who is Jesus?"

We saw that Jesus was a Jew, and to understand him, we must see him through Jewish eyes, not Christian or Gentile eyes. Jesus was a mystic—someone who held deep connection to the world of spirit. He straddled the fence between two realities, this world and the unseen world. Jesus was a boundary breaker who saw in others the image of God and treated them as worthy equals. He was a prophet who became the conscience of the nation, and he was the revealer of God. In him, we see the intersection of God in human life. He lived with the reality of God coursing through his veins and became a living example to us of what life can be like when it is lived in the Spirit.

Our next section takes us into even deeper waters as we delve into the traditional concept of God. Really? Am I going to go there? I absolutely must! Nothing is off limits to the inquiring mind and the fervent seeker. Don't worry, God is not threatened by our thrashing about in deep waters. It may be just what is needed to pry ourselves away from the false security and comfort we find in a dying past. You can abandon dying ideas without abandoning God. Let's talk about God.

LEAVING RELIGION

14

THE GOD PROBLEM

· · · · · · · ·

G OD HAS A PROBLEM THESE DAYS THAT'S BEEN brewing ever since the Enlightenment. Through no fault of God's own, the troubling issue has to do with the advancement of humanity. As human knowledge progresses, traditional notions of God retreat. The rise of one accelerates the decline of the other. We have gotten to the point where one wonders whether God has left the building and no one has the courage to turn the lights off.

In ages past, God was the answer to almost everything that couldn't be explained. Why were there sickness, storms, earthquakes, and volcanoes? The answer was obvious. God was offended and was unleashing divine wrath upon humanity. That's exactly how the bubonic plague was explained. God must be angry at something. The God answer sufficed for centuries until the explosion of new knowledge, and the human mind was released to initiate serious inquiry. When this happened, humans unearthed different explanations for things that had once been attributed to God.

For instance, we discovered bacteria, viruses, germs, and the causes of disease. We uncovered plate tectonics and the movement of Earth's crust as it relates to earthquakes. We learned that molten rock deep inside the planet was released up and out with great force through Earth's natural pressure valves. These were not the antics of an angry deity but the result of natural and explainable forces. Increased knowledge meant that what once perplexed us could no longer be attributed to God. In a sense, God is out of a job, and many think that God will forever be unemployable. If earthquakes, disease, volcanoes, tornadoes, roaring seas, and the like can no longer be attributed to the work of an angry deity, then what is left for God to do?

When I speak of the God problem, I am not implying that God is somehow deficient or defective in any way. God is God, whether our knowledge is advanced, developing, or in its infancy. The problem I speak of has to do with our concept of God. In other words, what makes God unemployable in our day is a deficiency not in the reality of God but in our understanding and explanation of God. If God is no longer the answer to the questions that once perplexed us, then it is time to rethink our notion of God and ask new questions! God isn't dead, as some have suggested, but it is time to bury archaic notions that no longer find relevancy in our day. We can abandon obsolete understandings of God without abandoning the reality of God. The inevitable result of new knowledge is the reordering of our worldview. This is a good thing and reveals that we are progressing in our understanding of the world.

Two Notions of God

Trying to articulate God concepts is a difficult thing to do, and who am I to tread on such holy ground? But if we can conceive of God, then surely we can talk about God, even though our discussions lack the certitude we desire. I enjoy God conversations, so I will share my thoughts on the subject with the high hope that it stimulates your own courageous reflection.

Two key notions of God can be seen throughout Scripture and the history of Christianity.[14] One is not a recent, modern view, while the other is an older concept, for both notions can be found in Scripture, and both have ancient roots. Only one, however, links well with our advanced knowledge of the world. Unfortunately, the notion of God we are most familiar with is faltering, and for good reason. When people speak of the death of God, it is the concept of supernatural theism they have in mind. The second notion we will consider is called panentheism. Don't be alarmed by these upscale terms; their meaning and importance will become clearer as we go along.

Supernatural Theism

Having grown up an evangelical, I was introduced to God as a supreme being—the highest being there was. God must be male, for he was always referred to as "he" and "father." This deity was a personlike being—a great big one of us, except bigger, better, grander, and more powerful. This all-powerful and all-knowing God sat on a throne in heaven, doling out justice or mercy—whichever was deemed best for the situation. God's subjects bowed their heads in worship and their wills to God's divine plan. Everything that happened in life was the result of God's sovereign will—a kind of Christian fatalism. This divine being could be moved to act on our behalf if we prayed hard enough, long enough, and with sincerity and right motives. This divine being was a transactional *quid pro quo* kind of God. If I was a good boy, I received mercy, grace, answered prayer, and God's favor. If I was a bad boy, I received justice, punishment, unanswered prayers, and the disfavor of God. If I do this for God, then God will do this for me—a *quid pro quo* arrangement.

The being I was taught to love was the creator of the universe who lived somewhere "out there," separate and distinct from the creation, and who intervened in this life to answer prayers and enforce divine sovereignty. My role as a human was to worship this deity, obey the divine decrees, and in return for my devotion, I would receive reward instead of punishment and eventually spend eternity with God in heaven. Does that kind of God sound familiar to you? It should, because it is the traditional notion of supernatural theism that has been promulgated throughout the centuries. It is, however, a dying concept. This problematic view makes little sense to the postmodern mind, and theologians have struggled mightily with it. Let's examine this traditional notion in greater detail.

The word for God in the Greek language of the New Testament is *theos*, and *theism* (theos-ism) simply refers to a belief in God. There are many forms of theism, such as pantheism, monotheism, polytheism, panentheism, deism, and so forth. All believe in God, but all represent different understandings of this deity. Atheism, on the other hand, is the disbelief in God. By putting the word "supernatural" in front of God, we are referring to a specific kind of deity—one that is beyond the natural world and the laws of physics. This brand of theism believes in (1) a divine, personlike being who (2) resides outside this world, and (3) intervenes in the affairs of humans. This is what is meant by supernatural theism—the brand of theism Christians in the Western Hemisphere are taught to believe.

A Personlike Being

Many envision God as a great big one of us—as if God were another human being, except bigger, brighter, and stronger. We have, in essence, made God in our own image, except God is the opposite of our human weaknesses and limitations. We are finite, while God is infinite. We are created beings, while God is the Creator. We are limited in knowledge, while God knows all things. We are limited in power, while God is all powerful. Human justice is skewed, while God's justice is perfect. We explain God as a personlike being just like us, without all the intrinsic flaws and limitations associated with being human.

We speak of God in human terms. For instance, it was the finger of God that wrote the Ten Commandments. It was the righteous right arm and hand of God that rescued Israel. God speaks, thinks, feels, acts, and even has a change of mind. God possesses physical properties, such as eyes, ears, feet, and a face, as well as human emotions, such as sorrow, jealousy, anger, and grief. We imagine God as a judge, father, shepherd, and lover. The impressive theological term for attributing human characteristics to God is "anthropomorphism." In other words, we have personified God to be a great big one of us.

I understand our impulse to personify God, for it seems to be a natural response to our personal experiences. How else are we to describe something that is indescribable without using human words and images? The real problem is interpreting these images as literal descriptions of God when they are simply human projections onto the divine—human-speak for our personal God encounters. They are not literal.

One Wednesday evening during a church Bible study, I read some scriptural passages that personified God. I asked those in attendance, elders included, whether they believed that God literally possessed a right arm. Each of them affirmed exactly what the Bible said. God possessed a right arm because the Bible said God possessed one. I asked them whether God literally had a right hand, feet, ears, and eyes, to which they nodded their affirmation. If Scripture said it, they believed it. After all, who were they to challenge the literal words of God? This is exactly the problem; they took literally what was never intended to be taken literally.

I followed my questions with a reading of John 4:24 (NRSV), where Jesus tells the Samaritan woman at the well, "God is spirit, and those who worship him must worship in spirit and truth." I then asked whether they believed that God is spirit. Of course, they all nodded their heads in firm affirmation; after all, that is what the Bible said. After pointing out that a spirit by definition was incorporeal—had no body—I asked how God could be both spirit and also possess literal body parts. They had no answer, had never considered the issue, and didn't seem the least bit concerned with resolving the dilemma. Who were they to question the Word of God? In their eyes, it was easier and far more spiritual to simply believe these illogical conundrums than to ask questions and critically think through the issues. Their response was not unusual, for many who hold the Bible in high esteem are unwilling to consider anything other than a literal approach to its contents, no matter how ridiculous the outcome.

I have found that people interact personally with life, and it is the same way with God. We experience God personally rather than as some inanimate object like a piece of plywood or sheet metal. Our experience of the divine moves us and affects our whole being—emotions, intellect, and behavior. This mysterious interaction is the zest of life and a motivating force behind our passion. We experience God personally, not impersonally.

Combine these profound encounters with the limits of human language, and about all we can do is speak of God in humanlike terms. If we don't find some way to express our divine encounters within our limited vocabulary and understanding, we are in danger of making God out to be an inanimate deity—like relating to a piece of plywood or sheet metal. That certainly isn't very satisfying, and I, for one, have never been deeply moved by a piece of plywood.

Speaking of God in humanlike terms reveals the personal nature of our experiences. It is one way we show devotion, love, and relationship with the divine. I take no issue with personifying God as an expression of worship, but when these personifications are literalized, we move into supernatural theism and get ourselves into trouble.

For instance, God is most often referred to in Scripture as "he"—a father. But God is not literally male, and God is not a literal father, for God is beyond gender and not subject to these limitations. Personifying God as a male and a father reflects the hierarchical society in which the biblical writers lived, not how God really is. God was imagined as a male father figure who provided comfort, protection, care, discipline, etc. This image fit their worldview, culture, and experience at the time. It is a mistake, however, to literalize these depictions, for they are far too limiting for a grand, indescribable God. We experience God in personal ways and personify those experiences in humanlike terms, but literalizing them is problematic. The reality is that God is certainly more than the humanlike expressions of our experiences.

Outside This World

Supernatural theism views God as residing outside Earth—somewhere beyond the blue sky. God is conceived not as an all-pervasive spiritual presence but as a being who is separate from creation. Creation is one item, and God is another item—separate and distinct from one another. Although God is the powerful grand designer whose artistic beauty is reflected in nature, this supreme deity is not to be confused with the universe but exists outside it and in addition to it.

As creator and ruler of the universe, God has absolute authority to set the rules of the game—what is right and what is wrong. The standard by which all else is judged, and by which our lives are measured for reward or punishment, is the holiness of this deity in the sky. Not only are these divine standards revealed to us in the Bible; they also become the basis of God's judgment upon us. To align our lives with the rules of God is healthy and beneficial. Otherwise, we face stern judgment, and who wants to stand before this powerful being to face divine wrath?

Intervenes in the World

If God is a separate and distinct being who dwells outside this world, the only way God can relate to this planet is by acting upon it—intervening in its affairs and operation. The writers of Scripture attribute all kinds of spectacular events to the mighty hand of God. Healings, resurrections, earthquakes, parted waters, and miracles of all sorts are ascribed to this supernatural being. According to Joshua 10, for instance, God miraculously stops the sun from its rotation around Earth for the sole purpose of extending the daylight hours so Joshua has more time to slaughter his enemies. That astounding event is attributed to a being in the sky who intervened in the rising and setting of the sun. Never mind that the statement is factually false, for the sun doesn't even rotate around Earth.

Today, we discover devout followers praying, pleading, sacrificing, and bargaining with God to intervene in their lives to cure cancer, guide the doctor's hand during surgery, obtain a college scholarship, win a sports championship, and so forth. In a sense, God is nothing more than a heavenly slot machine. Insert enough prayer coins, and out pops the answer to our fervent petitions. And when the answer isn't to our liking, we simply pray longer and harder in an effort to manipulate this being toward our preferred outcome.

Some unscrupulous ministers even promote a "name it, claim it" clanlike theology. It reveals their understanding of God as a being who can be coerced into acting on our behalf. When our prayers go unanswered, we even say it is the will of God. There is no way God can lose. I recently heard a local preacher say that God's answer to prayer is either yes, no, maybe, wait, or what were you thinking? That pretty much covers it. No matter the outcome, it is hard for God to lose when the odds are always in God's favor. If prayer is answered, God is benevolent—rewarding us for righteous living. If prayer is unanswered, it is simply God's will for our lives, and God knows best in teaching us valuable life lessons.

Most Christians I know hold this understanding of God. Supernatural theism is everywhere and has become the majority viewpoint. We hear it on the radio, on television, in our pulpits, and on the lips of devout followers throughout the world. It is part of our religious psyche, ingrained in us from an early age. God is a divine being who lives in heaven, rules over the universe, and intervenes in human affairs in response to our prayers and in accordance with God's sovereign will. This view is fraught with problems!

A Deficient View

What's wrong with supernatural theism? Just about everything! Portraying God as a supernatural being seems more like the mythical gods of Greece and Rome than a God who can withstand the scrutiny of the twenty-first century. If you grew up in evangelical land like me, this is the only God you knew. We were taught this literalistic dogma, and all of our God experiences were filtered through this framework. We knew of no other alternative viewpoint, and if someone had pointed one out to us, we would have flatly rejected it anyway. God was a supernatural being who doled out rewards and punishments. We prayed that this God in the sky would move the mountains in our lives. Sometimes it seemed to work, and sometimes it didn't, and when it didn't, we simply said it was the will of God. Will that kind of God stand in the twenty-first century and beyond?

Literalism

We have never met a literal being called God, nor have we been able to capture, analyze, see, or identify this divine entity. We are, in a sense, pushing the limits of human words in our attempt to describe the indescribable. How do we do that? We use reason, knowledge, and language to interpret and articulate our experience of something we refer to as God. Though our God encounters are genuine, palpable, and meaningful to us, we are constrained by the very limits of our humanity in articulating something we are incapable of understanding. Our experience of God is real, but our explanations are always found wanting.

Many preachers, armed with a literalistic view of Scripture, have God all figured out as they speak in absolute terms. Their theological perspective becomes *the* absolute view of God. Little do they know how thin the ice is upon which they tread, for we have never met God absolutely—in all of God's fullness. The only way we can speak of that which is indescribable is through metaphor. We can never say with certainty that God is this or God is that, for that is impossible. We can only say that God is *like* this or God is *like* that. We rely upon metaphors to do the heavy lifting of addressing things that are beyond our ability to grasp or articulate.

The Bible says that God is a rock, but God is not a literal rock; instead God is *like* a rock—firm and secure. The Bible portrays God as a shepherd, but God is not a literal shepherd herding sheep or people; instead, God is *like* a shepherd who protects and provides for the flock. These are images and metaphors. It is the language of devotion and intimacy, and it is not intended to be a literal depiction of God, for that simply cannot be done. They are merely images attempting to capture our experiences through time-bound words and worldviews.

God was likened to a shepherd because shepherds were well known to people in ancient times and helped serve up an image of God. In twenty-first-century America, we might liken God to a computer programmer or a great scientist—something of which the ancients wouldn't have a clue. In their world, God's home was just beyond the sky, but we know from space travel that there is no powerful being living just beyond the clouds. The description made sense in an age where restricted worldviews, limited knowledge, and a flat-earth perspective prevailed, but it makes little sense these days.

My point is that many devout God-followers in the current age interpret these images literally. Though they are well-intentioned, their God concept simply cannot be. Their experience of God may be real, but their explanation is no longer viable. We live in a different time with expanded knowledge. Many believe that these descriptions are divinely revealed by God through Scripture and that to question such depictions is to lack faith in God's Word—something they could never do.

Unfortunately, in trying to uphold the value of Scripture, their view actually limits the limitless being they purport to worship. For instance, it is limiting to say that God is male, for God is beyond gender. It is limiting to say that God is a rock, a shepherd, a king, or anything else, for the moment you say that God is one thing, you automatically imply that God is not something else, and that is limiting, especially when referring to a limitless, indescribable God. Do you see the dilemma we are in? These are images and metaphors, not literal descriptions. Speaking of God as a being up in the sky is yet another metaphor, not a literal description of God, and it, too, is limiting.

The Demise of God

It is understandable how God could be viewed as a personlike being in less enlightened times. After all, they couldn't travel in space and didn't have access to the kind of information about our universe we possess today. We live in the twenty-first century, a world of which they couldn't even conceive. How do we understand God in light of this explosion of new knowledge? We have been beyond the clouds, and the divine personlike being is nowhere to be found. Is it enough to simply move God's physical dwelling place to some distant planet, like Mars, instead of just beyond the clouds? Does that solve the problem for us?

We have taken pictures of Mars, and a space probe sits on the planet's surface, and still there is no divine humanlike being called God. We could simply keep moving the physical distance of God's dwelling farther and farther out into space—to places we haven't yet explored. After all, the universe is vast, and maybe God is hiding out in some nook-and-cranny. We keep telling ourselves that this powerful being must be out there somewhere. Isn't it time for a new image of God—a new metaphor for the twenty-first century?

The God of the past was a tribal God, called upon to win wars and defeat enemies. The God of the past was responsible for earthquakes, storms, lightning, tsunamis, and volcanoes. This past God was responsible for sickness and disease, plentiful harvests, and successful hunting trips. The God of the past punished sinners and rewarded saints while allowing some to die and sparing others. This God of the past is dying a painful death at the hands of increased knowledge.

We now know the reason behind earthquakes, storms, lightening, tsunamis, and volcanoes. We now know the reason for sickness and disease and what makes for a good harvest. Why some live and some die has a great deal to do with all sorts of things other than the will of God or divine retribution. Placing a divine and arbitrary being behind all the things we have yet to understand is to perpetuate the myth of this dying God. Images of the past have lost their meaning and power for the twenty-first century, and when taken literally, Christianity is reduced to a religion of clichés with little effect in the real world.

Let me be crystal clear: God isn't dead. What is dying is the notion of God as a supernatural being who works to meet our human needs. We think that this notion of supernatural theism is the same as God, when one is the reality and the other is merely a concept relative to the age in which we live. They are not the same. God is distinct from our *notion* of God. In other words, no human words, definition, or concept can cover all that God is. It cannot be done, for we cannot reason beyond our own limits. All that we know, perceive, and believe about God is limited by our own humanity. Some notions of God may fit better within specific cultures, but even our images and notions of God change over time as culture and knowledge evolve. To lock God into antiquated concepts of the past is to confine God to time and space—to a specific culture, language, circumstance, and worldview. Certainly God is beyond the limits of a relative point in time and space.

The God of the past looks a great deal like us—a deity with humanlike features. It is this literal, personlike notion that atheists reject. Some Christians strive to move away from this literal rendition and conceive of God as a bodiless spirit with humanlike properties, but this notion simply takes away God's physical features while still possessing humanlike attributes. Does a bodiless, humanlike being solve the problem? I hardly think so.

Is God Real?

We know that the universe exists, for we can see it and touch it. We are part of it. When people quarrel about the existence of God, they are most often arguing about whether or not a supreme, personlike being exists outside the universe. I believe in the reality of God, and this book assumes such a position. In simple terms, I ask myself, "Why is there something rather than nothing?" This leads me to the reality of God, even though I remain unconvinced that supernatural theism is the best way to articulate this reality. Contemporary atheistic authors who deny God are rejecting this supernatural theistic notion. They, like many others, are unaware that there is another concept of God worthy of consideration that correlates well with twenty-first-century knowledge.

What Alternatives?

If supernatural theism is lying on its deathbed, what other theistic options are available to us? There are plenty of them, but only one has merit for twenty-first-century Christianity, and, much to our surprise, it is even found in the Bible itself. But first, let me examine other theistic concepts so we can distinguish them from the notion of God that works best.

Because supernatural theism is no longer functional, some turn to atheism. In its early days, atheism meant a-theism, or non-theistic. It was possible to be a non-theistic Christian—that is, someone who believed in the reality of God but not in the supernatural theistic definition of God. Unfortunately, as supernatural theism achieved its current status as the literal go-to concept of God, this important distinction has largely fallen by the wayside. Today, atheism refers to a denial or rejection of God, and as such, it is not a viable option for Christians who believe in a divine reality.

Polytheism is a belief in many gods, whereas Christians believe in one God who exists in Trinitarian form (Father, Son, Holy Spirit). This made no sense to Jews, for in their mind, a Trinitarian doctrine was just another way of saying three gods, not one. Christians, of course, vehemently disagree, even though they are unable to adequately explain this triune doctrine.

Three great religions cluster around monotheism (belief in one God): Judaism, Islam, and Christianity. Each defines God differently, but they all agree on the theistic notion of one God. Most other religions exemplify some form of polytheism—the worship of many gods. Sometimes in polytheistic cultures, one god is elevated above others, which is called henotheism. This can be seen in the early life of Israel, where Yahweh was elevated above all other gods. Over time, however, their henotheism turned into monotheism. Polytheism isn't a good option for Christians because Christianity is centered upon a belief in one God, not many.

As scientific inquiry began its ascent, the notion of God as a miracle-working interventionist gave way to deism. How could one still believe in God and accept contrary scientific evidence? The answer was found in deism, the notion that God created the universe and set into motion the principles of self-regulation. Deists saw God as distant and uninvolved in human affairs. In other words, God created the world to operate on its own principles and physical laws without intervention by an outside deity. This once-popular view has declined in theological circles to be virtually nonexistent in today's world, for it is one step away from atheism. What is the difference between a distant God we are unable to experience and one that doesn't exist at all? This isn't a satisfying alternative for those who believe God is immanent, not absent.

Pantheism, on the other hand, believes that everything is God. In other words, all finite things in existence are merely parts or modes of one divine being. Trees, plants, snakes, cows, dung beetles, and humans are all part of an ultimate being. There is no transcendent element within the divine, for everything is God. This view has never been a part of the Christian concept of God.

Panentheism

The final theistic view under consideration is panentheism, a word I had to read several times over to ensure that I was reading it correctly—panentheism? Initially, I made two wrong assumptions that most Christians make. First, I read it as pantheism—that everything (pan) is God (theism), which isn't a teaching found in Scripture. Pan-en-theism is entirely different and means that everything (pan) is in (en) God (theism), a concept clearly found in the holy writings.

The second mistake I made was to think that panentheism was some weird, out-of-bounds, New Age philosophy. Because I wasn't familiar with the word, I dismissed it. It didn't fit into the evangelical jargon I grew up with, so I reacted strongly to it. Although panentheism is a recent term, it is a modern way of expressing an overlooked concept of God that has been around for a very long time.

Transcendence and immanence are more familiar terms to evangelicals and fundamentalists. Theological textbooks speak of God as being totally beyond us, wholly different—an otherness that is indescribable. This is known as transcendence. In ages past, God followers articulated transcendence in terms of a supernatural being who lived just beyond the sky. Pantheism, on the other hand, downplays transcendence and emphasizes the immanence of God by saying that God is everything in the here and now. Christians often note that God is everywhere present (omnipresence), but that is quite different from saying that God is everything. Supernatural theism emphasizes transcendence, while pantheism emphasizes immanence.

In panentheism, however, God is both beyond us and present with us—a balanced perspective without the extremes of pantheism or supernatural theism. By saying that everything is in God, we mean to say that God's presence penetrates every aspect of the universe and that the universe finds its existence within God. Mindboggling, isn't it? Panentheism says even more—the universe isn't God, but it exists within God, and God is greater than the sum of the universe. The following illustration shows how God was thought to be within the world, then outside of the universe, and now the universe is within God.

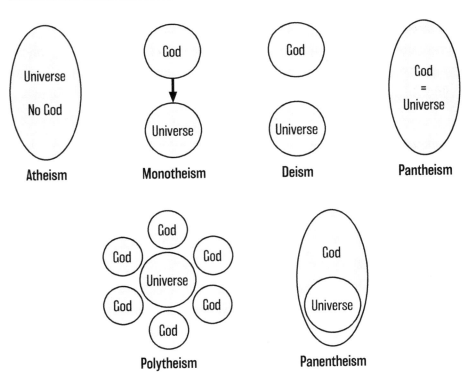

Panentheism sees God as an encompassing, pervasive, all-present Spirit, not as a supernatural being up in the sky. It is one way that theologians and philosophers advance a concept of God that connects with Scripture and the present age. If the word "panentheism" is not to your liking, find another word that suits your fancy. The point is to understand the concept, not become attached to a label. For me, panentheism makes tremendous sense. It doesn't limit God in any way to the universe or equate the universe with God. Instead, it maintains both the transcendence and immanence of God by noting that even as everything exists in God, God is more than everything. Panentheism is simply a new way of expressing an age-old notion of God.

Scripture

Several biblical passages speak of this panentheistic understanding. In Paul's sermon to the Athenians on Mars Hill, he notes that God is not far away but near, for "in him we live and move and have our being" (Acts 17:28, NRSV). Our relationship to God is that we live in God, we move in God, and we exist in God. Our very being is in God. It is difficult to exist in God if God is a separate being who resides beyond the clouds. But if the universe exists in God and God is more than the universe, then we get a sense that our very existence is somehow connected to the sacred presence that is in us and beyond us—both immanent and transcendent.

After declaring that Jesus is the image of the invisible God and that all things are created through him and for him, the author of Colossians states, "He is the image of the invisible God, the firstborn of all creation; for in him all things in heaven and on earth were created, things visible and invisible, whether thrones or dominions or rulers or powers—all things have been created through him and for him. He himself is before all things, and in him all things hold together" (Col. 1:15–17, NRSV). Paul echoes a similar thought: "For from him and through him and to him are all things" (Rom. 11:36, NRSV). There is this notion within Scripture that the existence of all things is held together in and through an ultimate reality that is both transcendent and immanent. This is the heart of panentheism. Other Scripture of interest includes 2 Chron. 2:6; Job 38; Ps. 19:1–2; Jer. 23:24; John 1:2–5; and Eph. 4:6.

The Old Testament speaks of the glory of God, often portrayed as a fog or cloud enveloping the tabernacle, and later the temple. Traveling through the Sinai desert on their way to the Promised Land, the Israelites were led by the presence of God, depicted as a pillar of fire by night and a pillar of cloud by day. This divine glory was thought to be a living presence that filled Earth. In a dazzling vision, Isaiah beholds magnificent creatures surrounding a throne and declaring to one another, "Holy, holy, holy is the LORD of hosts; the whole earth is full of his glory" (Isa. 6:3, NRSV). Ezekiel experiences a similar vision of God's glory filling the temple. The living presence comes from the east, and Earth shines with God's glory (Ezek. 43:1–2). The presence of God was thought to fill Earth, and, according to Psalm 19, even the night sky declares God's glory.

The immanence of God is found everywhere. As the psalmist declares in Psalm 139:7–10 (NRSV), there is no place outside the all-present, all-pervasive Spirit of God:

> *Where can I go from your spirit? Or where can I flee from your presence? If I ascend to heaven, you are there; if I make my bed in Sheol, you are there. If I take the wings of the morning and settle at the farthest limits of the sea, even there your hand shall lead me, and your right hand shall hold me fast.*

God's presence is even seen in a storm that sweeps across the land (Ps. 29:3–9, NRSV):

> *The voice of the LORD is over the waters; the God of glory thunders, the LORD, over mighty waters. The voice of the LORD is powerful; the voice of the LORD is full of majesty. The voice of the LORD breaks the cedars; the LORD breaks the cedars of Lebanon. He makes Lebanon skip like a calf, and Sirion like a young wild ox. The voice of the LORD flashes forth flames of fire. The voice of the LORD shakes the wilderness; the LORD shakes the wilderness of Kadesh. The voice of the LORD causes the oaks to whirl, and strips the forest bare; and in his temple all say, "Glory!"*

God's presence is in the heavens and upon Earth. It is everywhere and cannot be escaped. Scripture notes that Moses was so filled with the glory of God that his face glowed with a special countenance. Jesus is also said to be filled with the glory of God as a cloud surrounds him and his clothes become bright white on the Mount of Transfiguration. The point is that God's presence is everywhere. It is not just "up there and out there" but "here and now," in the everyday world in which we live.

In the birth of Jesus was seen "Immanuel"— that is, "God with us." God tells the Israelites not to be afraid for, "I am with you." The very name of God "I Am" is significant, for it speaks of the very presence of God. What great comfort this brings us, to know that the divine presence is always with us. As Saint Augustine laments his late coming to the grandeur of God, he realizes the wasted time spent searching for God elsewhere, when all along God was always within him—even though he wasn't always with God. The Catholic monk Thomas Merton realized the same thing. It is impossible to be anywhere without God, for our very being exists within God. There is no "me" outside the divine presence.

In the Old Testament, the Spirit of God was likened to wind (*ruach*), which couldn't be seen or captured; yet it could be powerfully experienced. With no boundary or destination, the Spirit moved at its own impulse. It was this wind—this Spirit of God—that was said to hover over creation in Genesis. The wind of God was experienced in this world, not outside it. The Spirit was also thought to be breath (*nephesh*), and it was this breath of life that was breathed into the nostrils of Adam, the first human. In other words, our very life is derived from the wind-breath of God. With each breath, God is within us, around us, over us, under us, beside us, and through us.

I was taught to envision God as a powerful creature who lived in heaven as the CEO of the universe. Through prayer and righteous living, we could manipulate this divine executive to intervene on our behalf. God was a God of rewards and punishments, and if I accepted Jesus as my Savior, I would, in return, be granted forgiveness and gain an entrance ticket to heaven.

Though we have laid these images upon God, they are not literal descriptions of deity. In my younger days, I took the Bible as the literal, once-for-all, authoritative and inerrant words of God to humankind, but now I see how outlandish that view really was. Like many others, I didn't see these depictions as human attempts to describe the indescribable within the limits of human words. It is impossible to speak of God in concrete, absolute terms, for we are referring to that which is beyond our ability to understand or describe (transcendence). Though we cannot speak in concrete, absolute terms, we do sense God's presence in personal ways (immanence). It is this immanence that we are attempting to convey within the limits of human words. There is a difference between our experience of God and our explanation of that experience.

All descriptions of God are mere metaphors. Jews were prevented from making physical representations of God, for God is beyond all images, physical or otherwise. God was a sacred presence. Though metaphors and images are woefully inadequate, they are the only instruments in our toolbox for articulating notions of God. When we attribute humanlike characteristics to God, we are saying that God has been experienced like a loving father, a nurturing mother, a strong and mighty tower, the stability of a rock, and so forth. God isn't literally these things any more than God can actually be a humanlike being. They are merely metaphors—nonliteral explanations of our experiences.

Even as I speak of God as Spirit or presence, I am still using the language of metaphor. Metaphors change as culture changes, and the image of God as a humanlike being no longer fits with our knowledge of the world. It is time to discard images that no longer work. We must remember that abandoning a metaphor for God is not the same as abandoning God. Panentheism is a modern term that helps us grasp that everything is in God—our existence, our being, our very life—and yet God is more than what we know. God is more than what is. Panentheism is an amazing concept that frees us from the literalized notions of the past as we balance both the transcendence and immanence of God.

God as Being Itself

Instead of viewing God as a supernatural being who lives up in the sky, theologian Paul Tillich articulates a notion of God that challenges us to think of God as something more. From Tillich's perspective, God can no longer be conceived as a being; instead, God is being itself. Tillich is trying to align our notion of the divine with our advanced knowledge.

During my training days at a solidly evangelical seminary, I viewed Tillich as a modern-day oddity. He was, in my naïve perspective, nothing but an overeducated fool, the kind of person whose advanced learning got in the way of simple faith. In those days, I wasn't open to anything other than what I already thought I knew. Now that I am in the second half of life and have clothed myself with greater humility, I journey with less ignorance and judgment than my sanctimonious seminary days. I didn't understand Tillich, so I did what many do: I mocked and belittled views that didn't align with my own. How foolish of me!

For evangelicals and fundamentalists, any talk of God outside the lines of literal interpretation is difficult to accept. From their vantage point, declaring that God is being itself is nothing but religious mumbo-jumbo. The concept extends far beyond their comfort zone, but it is Tillich's way of lifting our gaze beyond the boundary of words. The goal is not to create a new God or simply replace metaphors and images, although they will surely have to be replaced; the idea is to convey an understanding of God that is both relevant and pushes the limits of human conception.

By saying that God is a being, we imply that God is limited to time and space, when God is not subject to such limitations. We readily grasp how beings exist in time and space, for that is how we exist—at a specific place within a specific time. Referring to God as being itself, however, forces us to new levels of consciousness about the divine. Instead of God existing within time and space as a being, maybe time and space exist within God! This challenges us to think beyond the human images we project upon the divine.

We sense a bit of this understanding with the Jewish name for God—YHWH. The name was so sacred that no vowels were associated with it, and out of respect, Jews substituted other words, such as Lord (Adonai). When God directs Moses to be God's representative, Moses wants to know what to tell the Israelites, should they ask who sent him. The answer comes, "God said to Moses, 'I AM WHO I AM.'" He then says, "Thus you shall say to the Israelites, 'I AM has sent me to you'" (Exod. 3:13–14, NRSV).

Who has a name like "I Am"? Is this the proper name of a being, or is this a Jewish symbol for being itself—the ultimate reality from which all else exists? It makes our head spin, but it also compels us to think about God differently. Instead of existing as a being inside time and space or even outside time and space, maybe time and space exist within God. After all, according to Acts 17:28 (NRSV), "we live and move and have our being" in God.

Saying that God is being itself is a difficult concept to grasp, especially for those entrenched in supernatural theism. We are saying that God is the ground of being—the ultimate reality upon which all existing things depend for their own being. God is not a noun, the name of a supernatural being, but a verb, that which keeps all beings in existence. God is the mystical presence, the source, the all-encompassing presence that is in us and around us. God is not a distinct and separate being apart from the universe but a reality that includes the universe, and yet God is also beyond the universe. Many Christian mystics and modern theologians, such as Paul Tillich and Karl Rahner, imagined God in this way. While this concept may be unfamiliar to supernatural theists, it is not unfamiliar to many influential Christians throughout the centuries. God is the reality in which everything exists.

Chapter Summary

This chapter identified a God problem—a problem with the explanation and perception of God called supernatural theism. This view believes God to be a superhuman being who lives just beyond the clouds, sits on a throne in heaven, and intervenes in the affairs of humankind. Although this perspective has been the explanation of choice for centuries, it may not survive into the future.

It makes God out to be a personlike being—a great big one of us, except bigger, better, and stronger. Because this being is outside the planet, the only way God can interact with the world is to act upon it from the outside—either through coercive prayers or God's sovereign will. This view was unquestioned for centuries until the explosion of new knowledge arrived on the scene. God was once the answer to all the things we didn't understand, but many of our age-old assumptions have been upended. Viewing God as an angry deity stirring up floods, earthquakes, volcanoes, and sickness in order to punish humanity is no longer believable.

With supernatural theism unable to adequately address the religious needs of the twenty-first century, another notion of God is needed—a view called panentheism. Instead of a personlike being overseeing the affairs of the universe, God is conceived as an all-pervasive presence that is everywhere. God is not outside the universe; instead, the universe exists within God, even as God is more than the sum of the universe. Some modern theologians conceive of God as the very ground of being or being itself. In other words, God is the ultimate reality through which all things have their own being. This view addresses both the transcendence of God (beyondness) and the immanence of God (nearness).

The problem is that we have taken metaphors and images of God and interpreted them as literal descriptions. Locked into the limitations of being a finite human, we are incapable of speaking of God in concrete, absolute terms and must resort to metaphors and images as the language of God-talk. As time, culture, knowledge, and circumstances change, so must our images and metaphors if they are to have meaning, power, and relevance for our day. This means that our understanding and explanation of God will morph over time. In fact, they already have. God has a history in human thought. In our next chapter, we explore the evolution of God—how the concept of God has changed over time with the advent of increased knowledge.

15

THE EVOLUTION OF GOD

· · · · · · · ·

T HE MERE TITLE OF THIS CHAPTER AWAKENS THE slumbering fury of fundamentalists who find such sentiment to be preposterous and anti-biblical.
They declare their displeasure although everything around them changes, and
yet they are unwilling to admit that even the concept of God has evolved over
time. There is a difference between saying that God changes, which I am *not*
saying, and noting how our understanding and explanation of God have evolved
over time, which *I am* saying. No matter what era or culture we live in, God
remains God. In other words, God is the constant within Christianity. Yet it can
be demonstrated that, over time, our understanding and explanation of God has
evolved.

Such evolution of thought alters how God is perceived. The problem is that
we have cemented our understanding of God into first-century images, worldviews, knowledge, and prejudices when we live in the twenty-first century. Our
explanation and understanding of God have evolved from then until now, and I
suspect it will continue to morph long after the twenty-first century has ended.

In an earlier chapter, I revealed how the portrayal of Jesus evolved over
time—from being a mere human to being declared the Son of God. For Paul, the
earliest of the biblical writers, this declaration of divinity occurred at Jesus's
resurrection, while Mark felt it occurred at his baptism. Matthew and Luke
declare that Jesus was divine at his birth, while John, the last Gospel writer,
proclaims that Jesus's divinity existed long before his birth. Many Christians
refuse to accept this evolution of thought because it doesn't fit with the traditional narrative they were taught.

A similar evolution of thought regarding God also occurs over time. Why this
surprises anyone is beyond me, when everything about life changes as time and

knowledge progress. Perspectives change, shift, expand, shrink, emerge, and disappear. For example, there was a time in America when women were not allowed to vote simply because of their gender. How silly is that? We look back and say, "How could they have thought such a thing?" With the passing of time arose new perspectives, and with the Nineteenth Amendment to our Constitution, the right to vote was extended to women in 1920. Historians can document the evolution of thought surrounding this civil rights issue and identify key people and events that shaped this great change.

The same evolutionary process occurs within denominations that have had to reinvent themselves due to the changing nature of our world. Churches had to adopt to the impact of world wars, the Great Depression, racism, civil rights issues, unemployment, the role of women, and a host of other social matters. With increases in scientific knowledge, technology, globalism, aids, COVID-19, and the like, it is easy to see how denominations have shifted their focus, their resources, their mission, their outreach, and their methods in order to survive. Many started out one way and ended up another way in order to maintain some semblance of being relative during changing times. The church in America is aging and becoming less relevant by the day. Unless it adapts to changing conditions, it will soon lose what little foothold it currently holds.

People change. Organizations change. Perspectives change. Values change. Methods change. Everything changes, including the advancement of knowledge. Why in the world would we expect our understanding of God to remain shackled to the ancient world of the Old Testament or the first century?

Many to One

The evolution of God can be seen in Israel's move from polytheism to monotheism. This is difficult for some to accept because they feel that their current perspective of God has been around since the beginning of time. Moses and the prophets, for instance, are thought to have understood God exactly as we do today. The doctrine of a triune God, for example, was not formulated until the fourth century of the Common Era. Did Moses, Ezekiel, Jeremiah, Isaiah, and the minor prophets believe in and articulate a doctrine of the Trinity? Did they realize that the portrayal of Jesus would morph over time until he was considered to be divine after his death? More than likely, they would have asked, "Jesus who?" It is a shock for many to learn that the God of Israel evolved over time as culture advanced and knowledge increased. The way we think of God today wasn't always the way people thought of God, and though we want our understanding to be the perspective that everyone else possessed throughout the ages, it just isn't so.

Judaism, Christianity, and Islam are considered monotheistic religions, but they weren't always that way. Monotheism is the belief that there is only one God. Not two gods, three gods, or any other number of gods—just one, for no other gods exist. Was this the view of Israel since the beginning? The answer is no, for the understanding of God shifted over time, as it did in all three of the monotheistic religions.

We find scriptural references to other gods besides the God of Israel. The prophets didn't deny the existence of other deities, for they often chastised Israel for worshiping them. The temptation to stray was an ever-present reality. Verses such as "You shall have no other gods before me" (Exod. 20:3, NRSV) and "Who is like you, O LORD, among the gods?" (Exod. 15:11, NRSV) are abundant. There seems to be no denying the existence of other gods—only that Israel was not to worship them.

Israel didn't start off with a full-blown monotheistic view of God but came to that understanding over time. Plenty of scholars have written on this topic, but for our needs, let it suffice to say that the journey of God's evolution began with the worship of powers seen within the world of nature, which some would call animism.[15]

The next step is a move from animism to polytheism—the belief in many gods. The prevalence of polytheism can be seen in the history of Israel, as numerous gods existed in the ancient world. From polytheism, the evolution of God moved to the worship of national, tribal gods. This is called "henotheism," where one god is elevated above all others as god of the tribe. The Egyptians had their gods, as did the Persians, Babylonians, Amorites, Amalekites, and so forth.

Israel's national god was Yahweh, while surrounding tribes elevated other gods. It was Israel's tribal god who defeated Baal, the Phoenician god of Jezebel in I Kings 18. Each tribe called upon its god for victory in war, fruitful harvests, fertility, and so forth. The deity they elevated over all others became a key identifier of the tribe. God evolved from a god of nature to merely being one of many gods. Now this deity was acting within history on behalf of a specific tribe or nation. For the Israelites, it was Yahweh who called them to be a nation, rescued them from Egyptian slavery, led them through the Sinai desert, created a covenant with them, and led them in conquering the Promised Land.

The final step was the move from a tribal deity to the single God of monotheism. God progresses from nature to a multiplicity of gods, to a chosen, elevated tribal god from among many divine options, to the existence of only one God. Yahweh became the true God, the one and only God. All others were merely idols. The development of God's evolutionary journey is from animism to polytheism, to henotheism, to monotheism.

Jewish Boundaries to Greek Influence

Another way to view the history of God is through the influences upon it from a geographical standpoint. The God of Christianity evolved from Judaism when Abraham was called to leave Ur of the Chaldeans to become the father of a new nation. Of all the gods of the Chaldeans, Abraham sensed a call from a deity that would become the tribal God of Israel. Abraham knew nothing of North America, South America, Antarctica, or the North Pole. His knowledge, experience, culture, and God were limited to the small geographical footprint of the region in which he lived. These boundaries became the womb of God's birth in Judaism.

As time passed, knowledge increased, and powerful kingdoms enlarged their territories: the God of Judaism expanded from its initial, limited boundaries to the influences of a greater world. Judaism and Christianity were exposed to, and influenced by, the wider Gentile world of the Mediterranean and its Greek and Roman ways of thinking. Gentiles living outside the Jewish mindset knew nothing of Abraham, Joseph, Moses, Joshua, and other cherished heroes of the faith. Instead, their understanding of God was shaped by Gentile philosophers like Plato. As Christianity spread beyond its birthing boundaries, God was cast in the spirit of Plato. In fact, Christianity struggled to survive in the Gentile world until St. Augustine's influential writings of the fourth century came along and helped facilitate the development of Western philosophy and Western Christianity. The God of Christianity had to be reframed in order to survive the platonic thought forms of the Gentile world and expand beyond the influences of its limited boundaries.

My point is that the understanding of God within Judaism and Christianity evolved from its narrow geographical region to the influence of the Gentile Mediterranean world and its Greek philosophies. To survive in this new world, the understanding of God was cast afresh in order to make sense in a changing world.

Copernicus to Freud

The shaping of God by St. Augustine lasted for a thousand years, until the Renaissance, the Reformation, and the Enlightenment. The Renaissance ignited a cultural rebirth, and the Modern Age began. The invention of movable type allowed for greater distribution of new ideas. Though the effects of the Renaissance were not evenly experienced throughout Europe, it was a time of cultural change that laid the foundation for further evolution in our understanding of God.

The Renaissance was followed by the Reformation of the 1500s, when dissatisfaction with Catholicism gave rise to the Protestant church. Martin Luther, John Calvin, and others led this reform. Every Protestant church today can trace its roots back to the Reformation. This momentous event forever altered a Christianity that would no longer be defined solely by a Catholic understanding of God. With this schism emerged a new vision of God and Christianity.

If the rumblings of change were felt within the Renaissance, and a break with Catholicism's stronghold on religious interpretation was the result of the Reformation, it was the Enlightenment that set ablaze the fires of new understanding. During this time, often referred to as the Age of Reason, cracks in the foundation of traditional assumptions were exposed to the light of increased knowledge. The scientific method was born, and everything changed.

Questions lead to probing, which leads to new knowledge, which leads to new perspectives, which lead to more questions, which lead to more probing, which leads to additional knowledge, which leads to new perspectives. The cycle continues, and it was the Renaissance, the Reformation, and the Enlightenment that opened the door to the modern world and fueled our courage to question and probe like never before.

Copernicus, Kepler, Galileo, Newton

Nicolaus Copernicus was a Polish monk who lived in the sixteenth century. He was also a mathematician and astronomer whose inquisitive demeanor and brilliant mind led him to study the movement of celestial bodies with a newly invented instrument called the telescope. His studies instigated a new model of the universe in which Earth was no longer seen as the center of the universe. This, of course, was a shock to many, upset the conventional wisdom of the day, and had enormous implications for religion.

For centuries, Earth was viewed as the center of a three-tiered universe, and to think otherwise was to set yourself in direct opposition to the divine revelation of Scripture. If Copernicus was right, then the church was wrong.

In the seventeenth century, Johannes Kepler, a German mathematician and astronomer, discovered the laws of planetary motion. He added to the work of

Copernicus by noting that Earth's orbit around the sun was elliptical, not circular; thus, our understanding of the universe changed even further.

After Galileo Galilei, an Italian astronomer and physicist of the seventeenth century, pointed his telescope to the sky, he published his findings, which created quite a stir within Christendom. How could the church let this go, for Galileo was directly challenging its authority and its understanding of God? Because the Bible declared that the sun revolved around Earth (Josh. 10), and because the Bible was thought to be the inerrant, divinely revealed Word of God, Galileo had to be wrong. They couldn't both be right, for they were in direct opposition to one another. As a result, Galileo was charged with heresy and ordered to stand trial. How dare he undermine church teaching!

The church has always been slow to accept new knowledge, even more so when it contradicts the traditional concepts of God. Galileo's insight was unable to withstand the strength of the institutional church of the seventeenth century, but like all new knowledge, it could not be suppressed or hidden for long. Over time, as more and more people began to see the light of day, the understanding and explanation of God had to change. New knowledge, no matter how inconvenient it might be to our religious prejudices, will always have an impact upon our understanding of God. Instead of embracing new truth, we often do what the seventeenth-century Catholic Church did—we brand new knowledge as heresy and justify all means of protecting traditional belief systems. In reality, we are no longer seekers of truth but protectors of the past.

While Copernicus, Kepler, and Galileo opened the doorway to new insight about our universe, it was Isaac Newton, an English mathematician, physicist, and astronomer, who observed that the universe operated according to fixed laws, such as the law of gravity and laws of motion. The world was being explained in new ways, which meant that God would also have to be seen in a different light.

Was there really a God sitting upon a throne just above the clouds, running the universe on a day-to-day basis? Newton discovered that the universe functioned upon unchanging laws, not through the manipulation of a supernatural theistic being. The church taught that it was God who caused the rains to fall, the mountains to quake, and the sun to rise, but new knowledge proved otherwise. Realizing that the universe functioned upon immutable laws meant that our understanding of God as a controlling supernatural deity had to change.

Copernicus, Kepler, Galileo, and Newton led the way for an important evolutionary change in our understanding of God. Others would rise and continue the work of gaining new knowledge about our world. Brave souls would publish new insights, despite being excoriated and marginalized by the church. The church's understanding of God continues to be challenged by revolutionary insights into our world, which translates into revolutionary ideas of God.

Darwin

In the 1800s, Englishman Charles Robert Darwin initiated the science of evolution. From Darwin's study arose the theory that all species of life evolved over time from a common ancestor. While this approach to the origin of species is now the accepted explanation among scientists, Christians still struggle to accept such a view. Darwin's understanding of how the various species arose is different from what the Bible portrays. They both can't be right.

People sensed a conflict between the biblical story of human creation and the scientific knowledge we came to possess. The church promoted a literal, inerrant understanding of the Bible which led to a supernatural theistic understanding of God. Darwin's views not only undermined a literal approach to the Bible; they also undercut a foundational teaching of the church—the doctrine of original sin and the need for atonement.

The biblical account of creation proclaims that humankind was created perfect and without sin by the hand of God. The reason there is so much evil in the world today is because both Adam and Eve fell from perfection by disobeying God. This allowed sin and evil into the world as a punishment for their sin. The purpose of God is now to rescue humanity by providing a way out of this mess. Jesus's death is said to be the perfect sacrificial human offering that not only appeased the justice of a holy God but also provided a path for humans to be forgiven and restored to a right relationship with their Creator. All we have to do is believe, and we are good to go.

Darwin's studies offer another explanation of human origin, with tremendous implications for the Christian faith: if evolution is true, then there is no such thing as an original perfect creation that fell into sin and is now in the process of being restored through faith in Jesus's sacrificial death. Evolution says the exact opposite. Instead of being created as a completely finished and perfect product, incomplete and imperfect creatures evolve over time, according to this theory. They move from a less evolved state toward a more evolved state and are, in fact, in a continual state of evolving, adapting and becoming. They are never perfect, finished products and never have been.

The implication of such information is staggering and causes us to rethink our understanding of God. How can there be a fall from perfection when there is no perfection to fall from? How can humans be restored to a status that never existed in the first place? If there is no fall from perfection caused by original sin, then there is no need for atonement, forgiveness, and a substitutional human sacrifice to appease God.

Darwin's work has created a ripple in theological time that can be felt in every corner of the church. The very foundation of our understanding of God is under review. If saving us from sin is no longer the work of a heavenly deity, then what is the work of God? If the diagnosis of the human condition is wrong, then the remedy is also incorrect. Could the story of God's relationship with humanity be more about moving toward wholeness and completeness rather than forgiving sin and restoring us to a perfection we never enjoyed to begin with? The very concept of God is evolving as new knowledge arises. Many deny modern realities and refuse to let go of traditional understandings that bring comfort and security, but burying our heads in the sand and covering our ears isn't a credible approach that will last into the future.

Freud

Copernicus challenged our assumption that God lived just beyond the clouds. Newton challenged our assumption that the hand of a supernatural theistic being caused all the happenings in the universe. Darwin's theory of evolution challenged our assumptions about human origins and the doctrine of atonement. The Austrian Sigmund Freud presented another challenge to our concept of God that also had far-reaching effects.

Freud analyzed the unconscious element of human beings—something that had never been studied before. He concluded that religion was the result of humanity's need to calm the anxiety brought on by self-consciousness—where you know that you know that you know. In other words, when humans realized that they were self-conscious beings unlike other creatures, it produced anxiety. How do you deal with the realization that of all species, you are the self-conscious ones? Religion, according to Freud, was nothing more than the projection of human needs upon a supernatural being who was in control and watching over us. God wasn't self-existent but a human projection to mitigate against the angst of uncertainty and meaninglessness.

Freud's work challenged the very existence of God as a supernatural being whose job was to protect us and meet our every need. That kind of God was merely a figment of the human imagination, fueled by our need for comfort and meaning amid the realization of our own existence. That is why humans created a God who was just like them, except without all the inherent flaws and weaknesses of being human. Freud's theories certainly challenge our understanding of God.

Divine Revelation to Scientific Inquiry

The impact of Copernicus, Kepler, Galileo, Newton, and others upon Christianity was astounding. In a sense, they gave us permission to seek, inquire, explore, learn, and challenge. They opened the door to new understandings of our universe, and as a result, our perception of God was forever altered.

For centuries, Scripture was thought to be the divine revelation of God, and as such, everything was filtered through this paradigm of understanding. The human perspective saw everything through the spectacles of divine revelation. The Renaissance, the Reformation, and the Enlightenment allowed brave individuals to peer at the sky through telescopes and walk boldly through the doorway of new insight. It is difficult to question or critically study something thought to be so sacred, especially when a charge of heresy awaits you. Must God be protected from such inquiry? Must God be protected from truth that challenges old paradigms? Must God be protected at all? These new discoveries were much like a tube of toothpaste; once you squeeze out the paste, there is no getting it back into the tube.

Divine revelation as the basis of truth was being assaulted by truth itself. Our explanations of the universe, our basis for religious belief, and our understanding of God was losing its foundational support. Science brought with it the scientific method. If humans were going to inquire, observe, and form conclusions, consistent methods of doing so would need to be in place for testing truth. Testing truth? Do you see the change from assuming truth based solely on writings thought to be the divine revelation of God to observing and testing what is true?

This opened doorway led to new fields of study, such as geology, biology, sociology, psychology, and so forth. Geology allowed us to study geological time through the fossil record. Biology allowed us to study human origins. Sociology allowed us to study groups of people, while psychology allowed us to study the inner workings of the individual. I ask Christians flat-out whether they believe in evolution, and most of them refuse to answer. They hee-haw around like children caught with their hands in the candy jar, still wanting to cling to divine revelation while sensing the tension of scientific data.

Traditional Christianity holds that ultimate truth is found in a static, unchanging set of beliefs that stands upon the authority of divine revelation. What happens when the knowledge brought to us by science contradicts the Bible? What happens when another set of lenses becomes available for viewing the universe and God? What happens when the divine revelation of God is flat-out wrong?

The scientific method also made its mark on biblical interpretation. Instead of blind acceptance of the Bible as the divinely revealed, inerrant, authoritative, once-for-all words of God to humankind like the church proclaimed, the scrutiny associated with the scientific method would now be extended to the study of Scripture. Biblical scholarship came of age in the 1800s, and the study of Scripture has never been the same. We discovered that the Bible didn't just drop out of heaven fully completed but was carefully constructed and edited by human authors who wrote with a specific agenda, in a specific culture, in a specific way, with specific biases, for a specific audience. As vigorous methods of critical analysis arose, theologians brought forth new ways of understanding God.

Paul Tillich, for instance, a modern theologian of the 1900s, proposes that God is not a supernatural being at all; instead, God is the very ground of being itself. Anglican John A. T. Robinson popularizes this perspective in his 1963 book, *Honest to God*. The supernatural theistic definition of God was being scrutinized. Science and biblical scholarship keeps us honest in our approach to God. It allows us to speak with candor, and because of this, our traditional understanding of God is at a crossroads.

Tribal God to Universal Reality

If we look carefully, we see how the perception of God changes within the pages of Scripture itself. Early in Israel's history, God is viewed from a tribal perspective. Yahweh is one of many gods existing in the region and becomes the deity elevated to god-of-the-tribe status. As noted earlier, elevating one god over all others is called henotheism. Over time, however, Israel's henotheism evolved into monotheism where the elevated tribal god is thought of as the only god. All other gods are merely idols.

Once a tribal god was identified and proclaimed, Israel exemplified typical tribal mentalities. In many ways, gods were utilitarian—a god who led them in war, led them to victories over their enemies, and led them to conquered lands. Israel's god was stronger than the gods of other tribes. God overcame Egypt and killed the chasing Egyptian army. God stopped the sun in the sky to provide more daylight so Joshua could slaughter more Amorite enemies. Israel's tribal god ordered the killing of every man, woman, child, and animal of the

Amalekites. God hated everything the tribe hated. We see this throughout the Old Testament. It is called tribalism.

This limited perspective began to change with the prophets, as Yahweh fails to prevent the Northern Kingdom from being trampled by the Assyrians in 721 BCE and the Southern Kingdom from being conquered by the Babylonians in 586 BCE. Apparently, the tribal gods of Assyria and Babylon were stronger than Yahweh. Instead of being God's fault, however, these monumental downfalls were interpreted as Yahweh's punishment upon a sinning people. Israel got what it deserved. Yahweh would teach this stiff-necked people a powerful lesson.

In light of such destruction and humiliation, many of the prophets began to see God in a new light. With changed circumstances comes new perspectives, and the understanding of God seemed to expand. Instead of being confined to the limits of the tribe, Yahweh began to be seen in more universal ways. The fourth-century prophet Malachi, for instance, enlarged the concept of God: "For from the rising of the sun to its setting my name is great among the nations, and in every place incense is offered to my name, and a pure offering; for my name is great among the nations, says the LORD of hosts" (Mal. 1:11, NRSV). God was no longer limited to the tribe of Israel but would become a God to the nations consisting of Gentiles, the unclean enemies of the Jews. Do you see the shift? The boundaries of tribalism were expanding.

The New Testament echoes this sentiment in the Great Commission of Matthew 28:18 (NRSV): "Go therefore and make disciples of all nations." In other words, take the message of God's great love to every person, every nation, every language, every race, and every religion. Baptists evangelize and convert individuals to become Baptists. Other denominations do the same thing with their brand identity. But that isn't the message we are to proclaim. Our commission is not to convert others to some Westernized doctrinal statements of belief. No, we are to share God's untarnished, unbranded love for all people.

Unfortunately, the good news of God's love has become entrapped in a high-functioning, well-oiled conversion machine designed to produce more Christian widgets on the evangelism assembly line. Why can't we just share the good news that God loves all human beings fully, completely, and just as they are without trying to convert them to some denominational label?

In the eighth century, along came a prophet named Hosea. His life became a living symbol of God's great love for all people, no matter who they are or where they are on life's journey. Hosea's wife, Gomer, left him to become a prostitute. As time went by, and the novelty of her status as the choice play-toy among her many lovers wore off, she became all used up, emaciated, and good for nothing. When she was put up for auction as a slave to the highest bidder, Hosea offered fifteen pieces of silver for her, an exorbitant price for someone in her condition. What use was she? Who would want someone *like that*? Fifteen pieces of silver would have secured a healthy, strong male servant.

Hosea welcomed her back and crowns her his wife—just as if she had never left. This story symbolizes God's great love for the people of this world. No longer would God be limited by tribal boundaries, for God's love extends to the people of all nations. The New Testament echoes this very thought through Peter's vision in Acts 10. A sheet is lowered three times from heaven, containing all kinds of unclean animals that Jews are not allowed to eat. A voice commands Peter to kill and eat the animals. Realizing that this food is forbidden by Jewish law, Peter responds that he has never eaten unclean food. Peter's vision reveals that God's love has no boundaries.

After the vision, Peter is called to the house of Cornelius, and it is this encounter with a Gentile believer that expands his view of God. In Acts 10:34–35 (NRSV), Peter declares, "I truly understand that God shows no partiality, but in every nation anyone who fears him and does what is right is acceptable to him." This is a very different understanding of God from the protective, conquering, killing tribal God of the past.

Throughout the life of Israel, proper worship of the tribal God was essential. Ways, means, and rituals were established and enforced throughout the tribe as a way of honoring and appeasing their deity. As one might suspect, the elements of proper worship became corrupt with power, pride, and self-interest. It is Amos, another eighth-century prophet, who rejected such exploitation and enlarged the meaning of worship, for the Lord says in Amos 5:21–24 (NRSV):

> *I hate, I despise your festivals, and I take no delight in your solemn assemblies. Even though you offer me your burnt offerings and grain offerings, I will not accept them; and the offerings of well-being of your fatted animals I will not look upon. Take away from me the noise of your songs; I will not listen to the melody of your harps. But let justice roll down like waters, and righteousness like an ever-flowing stream.*

For Amos, the corrupt worship of his day was meaningless and offered little value. Instead, he called for human justice as a means of expressing worship. The two could not be separated. Followers of God must express their devotion in some way, and confining worship to corrupt rituals, festivals, and assemblies that have little to do with caring and loving other human beings is absolutely worthless. Amos presented an enlarged understanding of what it means to worship God.

The seventh-century prophet Micah noted a similar theme. The conventional understanding of Micah's day was that God primarily sought proper sacrifices, proper liturgy, and proper worship practices. God was concerned about rituals being performed just right. Micah saw through this and presented a different understanding of God, declaring, "He has told you, O mortal, what is good; and what does the LORD require of you but to do justice, and to love kindness, and to walk humbly with your God?" (Mic. 6:8, NRSV).

The understanding of God, the requirements of God, and the message of God morph over time from a tribal God to a universal God for all the nations. Is God to be understood as a tribal deity who chooses people, hates what the chosen people hate, kills enemies, and conquers land from others, or is God concerned with human justice and kindness—a God for all the nations? As time rolls on, so does our understanding of God.

A Changing Reality

How we view and practice religion is never static; rather, it's always in process of reacting and adjusting to present realities. In 70 CE, Jerusalem was sacked by the Romans. They had their fill of zealous Jews engaging in guerilla warfare. The Roman army taught the Jews a difficult lesson by destroying their cherished temple, the epicenter of Jewish religious life. Since that time, the temple has never been rebuilt.

Can you imagine the effect this had upon the worship of Yahweh? This event forever altered the very nature of Jewish worship and religious practice. No longer would Jews offer sacrifices at the temple, for it now lay in ruins. Where would they go? What would they do? How would they conduct worship without a temple and without sacrifices? They were forced to change. Prayer would now take the place of sacrifices, and the synagogue would now replace the temple. The very understanding of God would have to change since the center of their worship practices was forever altered.

Change is everywhere. We cannot escape it no matter how hard we try—even in our understanding of God. The ministry of Jesus worked to initiate an expanded, deeper understanding of God. In his interpretation of Old Testament Scripture, Jesus says, "You have heard that it was said to those of ancient times . . . but I say to you . . ." With these words, he altered the common understanding of God in his day. In Matthew 15, Jesus challenges the teaching of the Pharisees when he says, "Listen and understand: it is not what goes into the mouth that defiles a person, but it is what comes out of the mouth that defiles" (Matt. 15:10–11, NRSV). This upset the Pharisees, for Jesus was not only calling into question their teaching and practice but questioning the very dietary laws set forth in Leviticus. An expanded, deeper understanding of God was being initiated.

The cycle of change seems to begin with resistance. Fresh viewpoints, new methods, and novel concepts are initially resisted. They are then labeled and identified as harmful and dangerous. Over time, they become tolerated as an inevitable nuisance of life. Finally, they become accepted into the mainstream of current thought. I suspect this process occurs even with our understanding of God.

Most Christians whom I know have never considered how our understanding of God evolved over the centuries. This is a novel concept for them and is perceived as threatening and dangerous, for it means they must rethink their own understanding of God. Psychiatrist Carl Jung once said something to the effect that most people judge because thinking is difficult. Labeling something as dangerous or dismissing it altogether is much easier than trying to figure out the truth of the situation. It is far more comfortable to believe that our current understanding of God is exactly how God has been perceived in ages past and how God will continue to be perceived in ages to come. Unfortunately, that is nothing more than wishful thinking.

Is it a good thing that our understanding of God changes over time? My answer is a resounding yes, for how could it not change? Everything else in life changes as new information comes to light; why wouldn't our understanding of God? I am not suggesting that God changes, only that our understanding and articulation of God evolve over time. We live in the contemporary world with twenty-first-century realities. We see the world through twenty-first-century glasses, not the spectacles of ancient Israel or the lens of first-century Christianity. Life has changed. Our realities are much different. Knowledge has vastly increased, and the assumptions of the past are no longer relevant and meaningful for our day. If God is not relevant to the age in which we live, then what relevancy does God have at all? If Christianity cannot relate to the realities of each generation, then how can it survive in the generations to come? Our understanding of God must evolve as life evolves, or God has little chance of surviving into the future.

If God is bound by the culture, thought forms, and worldviews of ancient times, then God becomes less and less relevant as each day passes. Faith systems of the past will die off if they do not evolve. The Christianity that I value is one that is ever evolving, ever adapting to its surroundings, and ever in dialogue with its current milieu as a means of relating our God experiences to the real world in which we find ourselves. Our God experiences are not limited to or contained within first-century articulations. God must be understood and vocalized in a way that makes sense to those listening. The experience of God is for every person in every generation.

This is a mind-blowing concept for Christians who elevate Scripture to an unchanging status as the inerrant, literal, once-for-all time words of God to humankind. In essence, they imprison God in the explanations, worldviews, assumptions, and prejudices of ancient Israel and the first century. A God who is shackled to the past loses relevancy for today, for life moves not backward, but forward.

As I look back over my life, I am amazed at how naïve I was and how easily I accepted certain concepts without the requisite due diligence. Although I never question my passion, my love of God, or how deeply I experienced God's presence, I do shake my head in disbelief at my own prejudices and closed-mindedness, all the while calling it "truth." We live and learn, don't we? As I have aged and matured, I find the second half of my life more thrilling than the first. I see God everywhere, and I experience the divine presence in deep and moving ways while never being able to understand or articulate that presence to my satisfaction. I am okay with not being able to fully define God. I am okay with our ever-evolving explanations of God, for it is the divine presence that I seek to experience, even as I struggle to name it. Our understanding and explanation of God have morphed over time and will continue to do so, but the divine presence is real and constant, and for that I am eternally grateful.

Chapter Summary

This chapter examines how our understanding of God has transitioned over time. While I refer to this transition as the evolution of God, I mean that our understanding and explanation of God have progressed with the passing of time and the advancement of knowledge. I am not suggesting that God has changed.

I view these transitions from various angles in an effort to help us grasp the evolutionary history of God. I begin by showing that the perception of God moved from animism to polytheism, to henotheism, to monotheism. From the angle of geography, God was initially contained within the limited boundaries of the Middle East. As these boundaries began to expand under Greek and Roman influence, the concept of God had to adapt to the larger Gentile Mediterranean world.

Our understanding of the universe changed when people like Copernicus, Galileo, and others peered into the night sky with their telescopes, which greatly altered our understanding of God. Darwin's theory of evolution challenged our perception of human origins, while Freud challenged the very notion of God's existence. New insights into our world have translated into new understandings of God. Former perceptions based upon the divine revelation of Scripture are now subject to observation and testing. This new way of discovering truth was applied to Scripture when biblical scholarship came to fruition in the 1800s. Even within the pages of Scripture, we see God's transition from a tribal deity to a universal God for all people.

I conclude that our understanding and explanation of God have changed over time as knowledge has progressed. Is this a good thing? Of course it is! When we handcuff God to the worldviews, thought forms, culture, values, and prejudices of the ancient past, relevancy is lost for current and future generations. Although God doesn't change, our understanding and articulation of God must evolve in order to remain relevant to our contemporary world. We must, in a sense, move beyond the God of the past, and that is the topic of our next chapter.

16

MOVING BEYOND GOD

· · · · · · · ·

O UR UNDERSTANDING OF GOD, WE HAVE DISCOVERED, is a bit more precarious than we first imagined. We grew up thinking of God as a supernatural
theistic being who directs the affairs of the universe and miraculously intervenes to answer our prayers while sitting upon a heavenly throne. Why did we
embrace this image? Because that's what the church taught us. We didn't know
any better, and we didn't realize that these images were carried over from an
ancient culture with limited knowledge. We didn't question the church or
Scripture, for we were taught to simply accept ecclesiastical teaching in faith.
That's what good Christians do. Questioning only reveals a lack of faith. Little
did we know that God is not threatened by questions, the exploration of new
knowledge, or the advancement of civilization.

As we grew up, and as knowledge and civilization progressed, we noticed
disparities between our knowledge and the teachings of the church. We asked
questions, dug deeper, and discovered an ever-expanding gap between the
church's proclamation of absolute truth and new discoveries about our world.
What was once thought to be crystal clear wasn't so clear after all. In fact, since
the Renaissance, the Reformation, and the Enlightenment, humans have been
raising questions in rapid-fire succession. Our worldview has drastically changed
since ancient days, and our reservoir of knowledge far exceeds what was previously known. This has influenced our understanding of God.

What Is God?

It seems strange to ask, "What is God?" when we are so used to asking, "Who is
God?" I purposely phrased the question this way to expand our theological horizons. The word "God" is a referent. In other words, it isn't the proper name of

a supernatural being in heaven. We have no idea what God's proper name is—that is, if God even has one—and that assumes that God is a humanlike personal being who requires a name. I wonder what God's last name is?

Ancient Israel referred to God as "I Am," or Yahweh, and a host of other names, including Adonai, Elohim, El Shaddai, Elyon, and so forth. God sure has a lot of names. Which one is the correct actual name, or could it be that none of these are proper names of God but aliases, images, and mere referents that seek to name that which is personally experienced and yet indescribable and undefined?

We find ourselves in quite a predicament. On the one hand, we experience this sacred presence we call God, and on the other hand, we are unable to explain, contain, or define this reality. God is a mystery far beyond our ability to grasp or explain. So, how do we talk about something we can't see, feel, smell, taste, hear, or experience in the same way that we experience other human beings? We have to call this divine presence something, and so we call it God. "God" is the label we use to refer to the divine—the object or essence of our ultimate concern.

Because ancient worlds lacked the knowledge we now possess, they asked, "Who caused the earthquake? Who caused the sickness? Who caused the storm?" Their answer was God. Today, we don't ask *who* caused these things; we ask *what* caused them. Our answer to what causes earthquakes isn't God but the forceful pressure of plate tectonics. Our answer to what causes sickness isn't the divine will of an angry deity in the sky. The answer to what causes storms isn't God. The go-to answer in days of old was God. It was a reasonable answer, given the limited knowledge they possessed at the time. In fact, the answer to almost everything had to do with a supernatural theistic being interjecting his divine will upon Earth. Unfortunately, that doesn't fly in today's world.

Is God a who or a what? A who implies a personal, humanlike supernatural being residing somewhere in the heavens. The biblical writers often personalize God as someone who cares for us, protects us, disciplines us, feeds us, and watches over us. While this is a comforting image, one can't help but ask whether it is describing the essence of God or the experience and perception of people at the time of the writing. Things get a little murky when trying to articulate concepts of God. Even Paul seems to grasp this difficulty as he remarks, "For now we see in a mirror, dimly" (1 Cor. 13:12, NRSV).

Others assert that God is a what rather than a who. The author of 1 John declares that God is love. Love isn't a who but a what, even though the effects of love are experienced personally. Old Testament writers refer to God as wind or breath—a what, not a who. In God's self-disclosure to Moses during the burning-bush incident, God is called "I Am." That isn't a proper name but a recognition of the presence of God. It means "I will be what I will be," or "I am present," or what theologian Paul Tillich calls the "ground of being." God wasn't a *being* separate from all other living things; rather, God was *being itself*. In other words, God is to be experienced, lived, and breathed in rather than defined, analyzed, categorized, and systematized as a thing.

Let's admit it—we don't really know much about God at all, and the only data we have to go on are Scripture, the world in which we live, and our own personal experience. Looking to Scripture as God's once-for-all, divine revelation doesn't work, for we know the holy writings to be human expressions of God experiences written in the culture, language, worldview, values, and biases of the day. As such, it is a collection of human words *about* God, not the words *of* God. We are still exploring our universe, and so far, we haven't discovered a supernatural being called God; and our personal experiences are merely that, personal experiences, not the essence of deity. And yet making God out to be a "what" seems to depersonalize that which we experience in personal ways. But we dare not confuse the experience or the effect of God with the essence of God.

If God is so difficult to define and articulate, and if God cannot be equated with supernatural theism, is atheism the only alternative available to us? What a chilling thought that is! From my perspective, atheism throws the baby out with the bathwater by declaring an absolute negative. Just because there is no supernatural being sitting on a throne in heaven doesn't mean there isn't a God; it only means that a particular view of God is in question. Tillich's "ground of being" is trying to move us away from thinking of God as a separate superhuman entity, but it doesn't lead him to atheism. The word "God" is merely a symbolic term, and yet even in Tillich, we sense the struggle to articulate such deep mystery and speak of a limitless God within the limits of human words.

When we say that God is the reality upon which all existing things depend for their own existence, we find ourselves struggling to grasp a concept far beyond us. We must be careful when speaking of God, for we are entering a realm where our explanations always fall short. This is why we speak of God with metaphors and images.

We are limited human beings without the means to express God in terms other than human language. Even language changes and evolves over time so that words that meant one thing in the past may no longer hold the same meaning today, and new words are continually being added to address new realities. Despite our inadequacy to articulate the divine, we are able to conceive of God and experience the sacred presence, and once again, this brings up the distinction between our experience of God and our explanation of that experience.

Experience vs. Explanation

Confusing our explanation of God with the truth of God is an ever-present danger. The two are not the same, and this is a fundamental distinction that must be grasped. My constancy is God—not Scripture, theology, doctrines, creeds, or time-bound, cultural-bound explanations of God. Let me be clear: God doesn't change, for God is God. Always has been and always will be. How do you explain a constant, unchanging presence that is also a mystery? We do it the only way we know how: by using the language and knowledge available to us at the time in which we live. Our experiences of God are real and personal, and yet our descriptions of those experiences are always relative.

Because our sacred encounters are connected to divine reality, the experience lives on from culture to culture and age to age. That is, the divine presence is real, genuine, and accessible to every person of every age in every generation. Our explanations and descriptions of those experiences, however, change over time because they are culturally bound and always stated in terms of the world in which we live. Therefore, explanations die out because they are directly tied to the knowledge, worldviews, values, and biases of a specific era, whereas our divine experiences live on because they are connected to the constancy of God. This is exactly how God evolved from a tribal God to a universal God for all nations. It wasn't that God changed but the explanation and understanding morphed over time. Without this evolution of thought, we imprison God into an ancient worldview that cannot sustain itself in the days ahead.

Every experience in life, whether it is a God experience or some other kind of experience, is interpreted through the lens of culture. No experience is ever divorced from its cultural context. New Testament writers wrote from the reality of first-century worldviews. Old Testament writers wrote from the cultural realities of their own time. The Bible, then, is a collection of viewpoints from the first century and beyond. It is the reflection and perspective of the era in which the writers lived. The content of this book is no different, for I am writing about my experiences from a twenty-first-century perspective. I have no ability to define the essence of God; no one does. But I can articulate a view of God that grows out of my God experiences and out of the culture in which I live. My perspective is relative, and yours is, too, and as the ages pass, both of our perspectives will succumb to change.

This means that the explanations of God found in the Bible are time-bound and culture-bound human reflections, for we explain and interpret our experiences in light of the worldview, assumptions, and understanding of our day. Everyone has a frame of reference that cannot be escaped. If we say that the Bible is the inerrant, authoritative, once-for-all words of God to humankind, our God experiences are handcuffed to explanations of the past, complete with their own worldview, knowledge, assumptions, and prejudices.

How does one explain sickness apart from our modern understanding of disease? You label it a demonic spirit, the chastisement of God, or the result of sin. If you don't understand that Earth revolves around the sun within one of many galaxies, then you say that Earth is the center of the universe and that the sun revolves around Earth. If you are unaware that Earth is spinning on its axis and is spherical in shape, then you believe Earth is flat and God lives in heaven just beyond the clouds. Even the creeds of Christendom are nothing more than human attempts at explaining Jesus in fourth-century terminology.

Because our knowledge is ever increasing, our explanation of God is ever expanding. To literalize ancient explanations as "the" explanation of God is problematic, for it incarcerates all of our God experiences into a language and worldview that no longer exist. This is one of the reasons Christianity has lost credibility in the modern age. Surely God must transcend the language, images, worldviews, and explanations that have been frozen in Old Testament and first-century language! If the explanation of God, which is always relative to a specific time and culture, cannot be separated from the experience of God, then we are in a heap of trouble.

Definitions, articulations, and understandings of God are always about our personal experiences and never about the essence of God. Do you see the difference? This is clearly revealed to us in the evolution of God. This deity was initially intertwined with nature and then became one of many gods, then a tribal god, and finally the only God. Which view is correct? Jesus also evolved. He was a human teacher who dispensed godly wisdom, but after his death, he was declared to be the Son of God. Exactly when this declaration occurred changed with the progression of time. Was Jesus declared the Son of God at his resurrection, his baptism, his birth, or before his birth? Which one was it? That depends on which New Testament author you read. The experience of Jesus lived on, but the explanation changed.

Today, God is declared to be triune in nature—one God in three persons. Is the Trinity an actual, absolute truth about God? How *would* we know that? How *could* we know that? Can we ever have that kind of knowledge and certainty about the mystery of God? The doctrine of the Trinity arose during a specific age and speaks to the progression of our human experience of God. There is no doctrine of the Trinity in the Old Testament. Jews didn't understand God in this way. The early Christians didn't think of God in these terms. Paul wasn't a Trinitarian, for he says that Jesus was designated the Son of God at his resurrection, not equal with God.

Our God experiences live on; our God explanations do not. For me, it is the divine experience that is paramount. Knowing that God is a sacred mystery that cannot be adequately defined by the likes of us humans leaves me in a place of uncertainty and vulnerability. Hard as I try, I cannot get my arms around God. Instead, I must accept my inability to define this mystery and simply bask in my experience of God rather than arguing with others over things we don't know much about or advancing as certain that which is uncertain. I want to experience the breath of God within me, touch the divine, and allow that presence to transform me into becoming the very best me I can be.

Atheism is only one articulation of God that doesn't align with my experience or my view of reality. Supernatural theism is another articulation of God that held court for centuries. Yet that definition of God is gasping for air because it is unable to withstand the light of new knowledge. A distinction must be made between supernatural theism and God. We equate the two when we shouldn't. Supernatural theism is merely an explanation of God, not God. It seems to me that we will forever be looking for ways to explain our God experiences with images, language, and metaphors that make sense in the contemporary world. The experience of God lives on, but the explanation is always changing. We must be willing to let go of the images of the past that no longer ring true.

Freed from the Past

Our view of God is always influenced by culture. In other words, no thought about God can ever be divorced from its historical context, for it is time-bound, culture-bound, subjective, and relative. The thoughts about God in this book are no different.

We seek to embrace a certainty that just isn't there, for God is a mystery. Because the truth of God is never bound to a particular season of time, we are free to reframe our God images so they better relate to our contemporary world. Our understanding and articulation of a mysterious God will always be in a state of flux, for God transcends cultural and time-bound definitions.

Our twenty-first-century understanding of God is much different than the perspective of previous centuries, for we live in a different world, a different culture, with a greater reservoir of knowledge. Make no mistake about it—even today's explanation of God is subject to change in the future. We cannot shackle a transcendent God to the culture and time-bound definitions of any age. This should not come as a surprise to us, for it is actually a good thing. Time-bound definitions become outdated and disconnected, whereas our evolving understanding of God is always fresh and relevant.

Christianity is not a static, once-for-all, fully defined religion. Instead, Christianity is itself evolving, always seeking to relate the constancy and reality of God in ways that make sense with the ever-changing realities of life. Christianity is influenced by the past, but it is never chained to the past so that it becomes an island unto itself. Christianity is always fresh and meaningful to the times, for God is a constant reality that is assessable in every era. New understandings arise. New explanations overtake old ones. New symbols and rituals emerge that keep the reality of God meaningful to the present age.

Living with Ambiguity

If God is beyond our ability to adequately grasp, then about all we can do is relax and enjoy the divine journey without arguing over which conception of God is the correct one. We dare not speak too authoritatively on the subject, as though we have the corner on truth while others don't. This idea of uncertainty, ambiguity, and mystery seems so anti-biblical to those who prop up Scripture as God's inerrant, authoritative, once-for-all words to humankind. But making an assertion, or believing an assertion, doesn't make the assertion true. The assertion does, however, provide the cover they need for making all kinds of definitive, boastful, and judgmental declarations about God. It gives them something to rally around and instills a false sense of security that allows them to proudly proclaim, "Thus saith the Lord!" In reality, we know very little about the things of which they boast, for God simply cannot be codified in writing.

For instance, does God possess a gender? That was the subject of a blog post I once wrote. A longtime friend of mine was sorely disappointed in what she read and felt that I had abandoned the authority of God's Word. After all, the Bible refers to God as "he," and so should we. Maybe I had forgotten about the Lord's Prayer—the very words of Jesus in Matthew 6:9 (NRSV), who explicitly states,

"Our Father in heaven." For her, retreating from the masculine terminology found in the Bible was anti-biblical and undermined the certainty of Scripture.

I didn't have time to go into the many problems with such a viewpoint, like her understanding of Scripture, her understanding of God as having human body parts and the physical attributes of a specific gender, or the Lord's Prayer as the work of the Gospel writer, not Jesus. She wasn't open to other viewpoints, so why bang my head against a closed door? I don't argue with people over such things; I simply sow seed among the cultivated soil of receptive hearts and soft spirits.

These days, we find ourselves living in a politically correct world where the thought police are always on the lookout for those who use specific phrases or words that have been deemed unfit for human consumption. Would it be more politically correct to refer to God as a she? Is that the solution? All that does is substitute one gender for another in reference to a God that transcends gender. The use of masculine references reveals the hierarchical culture of ancient days, not the essence of God. It is merely an image—a term that made sense from their cultural perspective. We dare not confuse the time-bound, culture-bound images of God with the very essence of God. The two are not the same.

I am not a thought-police type of person. If you want to call God by male pronouns, then go for it. If you want to call God by feminine pronouns, that is fine too. If you want to avoid gender altogether and call God by some other name or image, please do so. Culture may prefer one term over others, but more than anything, I want you to experience the reality of God in your life and discover a personal and meaningful connection to the sacred presence. Call this experience whatever you like, but understand that you are connecting with a divine mystery that defies explanation, gender, and certainty.

A denomination is merely a collection of people who agree to articulate their God experiences in a similar manner. God is not defined by denominational boundaries any more than God is defined by images of the ancient past. God transcends all boundaries we attempt to place upon the mystery. I was introduced to God through one denomination and articulated my God experiences through the rituals and lingo of this religious franchise. One day it dawned on me that God was confined within the boundaries of thousands of denominations, each one claiming to possess the truth. It wasn't long before I began to see that God transcends all expressions of faith. Denominations can be useful tools in our quest for God, but that is all they are—avenues for articulating our God experiences. They are not to be confused with God, are not God's official representatives, and are unable to contain God within their doctrinal boundaries, for all they do is gather like-minded people together who find comfort in sharing similar viewpoints.

If God is a spirit and beyond our ability to comprehend or articulate, then we just need to sit back and enjoy the ride. The certainty we long for is nowhere to be found, and that may just be what was intended for us all along. Quit trying to figure out what can never be figured out. As the currents of uncertainty sweep us away, we instinctively reach out for something to grab onto that will dispel our fears. Instead of frantically thrashing about for false security, we are better off enjoying the thrill of the ride. In our attempt to latch onto certainty and security, we cling to insignificant minutia, elevate it to granddaddy status, declare it to be from God, feel superior to others, and place our trust in the sand-castle at low tide. This is why religions attribute divine origin to their Scriptures, but it is all for naught, for no words can ever capture God.

In my experience, religious folks have little tolerance for ambiguity. One Sunday morning, I offered two different interpretations of a particular passage, which irritated some outspoken critics, who loudly voiced their displeasure. Instead of taking a firm, authoritative, and declaratory approach to a difficult verse, I was perceived as wavering with regard to the certainty of God's Word. They left little room for any explanation other than the one they held dear.

The greater faith, from my perspective, is demonstrated in the midst of ambiguity and uncertainty—not by having all the answers. It takes great faith to say, "I live in an uncertain world without the security I desire, but I move forward with courage because I experience the mystery of God's presence in my life." There is no pompous attitude with that outlook. It doesn't dictate to others or stand upon false platforms of security; instead, it embraces both the transcendence and immanence of the divine presence. That is faith!

Without a sense of mystery, God has little room to influence our life. It takes courage to embrace this path, especially when so many denominations claim to have all the answers. As our knowledge of the universe increases, our certainty about God decreases. This, however, is a good thing, because acknowledging our uncertainty is an important step toward spiritual maturity.

Moving Beyond God

Is it time for us to move beyond supernatural theism—to think of God in other ways than as a separate, living, thinking, emotional, controlling, humanlike entity? Moving beyond God doesn't mean embracing atheism; rather, it is the discovery of new expressions, metaphors, and images that more closely align with the contemporary world. We are moving not beyond the reality of God but beyond concepts and articulations that are no longer worthy of consideration. Relinquishing treasured explanations that have outlived their usefulness doesn't equate to abandoning God.

There is no such thing as an officially approved God language for expressing our God experiences. There is only human language, which is always deficient and never definitive, for God cannot be bottled up in a string of words. Moving beyond old and familiar religious concepts is extremely difficult, for we are required to let go of something that has been dear to us for a long time. We desperately cling to this comforting illusion, while letting go of false security systems seems to be the path toward spiritual maturity. Moving from old paradigms to new realities is called transformation, being born again, or seeing with new eyes. It is by letting go that we experience a freedom of faith we never thought possible. We move beyond the boundaries that have tripped us up to discover a God that transcends all boundaries. Our souls begin to experience the abundant life of Christ, and we see the richness of life all around us, even as we traverse uncertain and insecure terrain. And yet unspeakable joy wells up within us. God is everywhere present!

Many have never experienced the thrill and freedom of this kind of journey—this kind of maturity. To speak of God as a presence, energy, spirit, wind, breath, or love is far too nebulous for them. They want definitive doctrinal statements, declaratory "thus saith the Lord" assertions, and absolute certainty and security in a connect-the-dots kind of faith. Spiritual maturity, on the other hand, realizes that the effects of God are not the same as the essence of God. The essence of God is a mystery, while the effects of God are experienced personally. This kind of maturity requires that we journey beyond the ancient, culturally bound images of the past and confront the uncertainty and insecurity of this life. We do this by loving with all that we are, living life to the fullest, and becoming the best version of ourselves. This is how we honor the God of love, the giver of life, and that in which our very being exists. We live, move, and exist in God.

By letting go of archaic images of the past, we are letting go of idolatry. When we imprison God in a supernatural theistic definition, or any definition, for that matter, we are tempted to worship an image of God instead of God. Try that concept on for size! When images of God are elevated to a God-like status, we wind up serving the image, not the essence. That is idolatry, and even if the image is good, helpful, and all dressed up in religious adornment, it is nothing more than an image—never the reality. It is a shadow—never the Shadow-maker.

Images and metaphors are merely tools that assist us in experiencing God; they are not God.

We do the same thing with our ceremonies and rituals. The tools we use to express our devotion can become idols unto themselves. Images and metaphors must evolve as life evolves, for our explanations of God are not God; they are mere tools that help us express our spiritual endeavors. Are you grasping the difficulty of trying to define the mystery of God? Spiritual maturity allows us to walk in loving devotion to that which we can only experience but never understand.

How do we move beyond our own hollow descriptions of the infinite? If you were asked to describe your experience of God in terms other than the super- natural theistic language of the past, could you do it? How would you do it? For Rudolf Bultmann, the famous German theologian, moving beyond God means de-mythologizing Scripture. In other words, we have to get beyond the articula- tions themselves to discover a God beyond God. For Dietrich Bonhoeffer, the imprisoned Lutheran minister murdered by the Nazis during WWII, moving beyond God means discovering a Christianity apart from religion—a God that is beyond all forms of religious expression. For the influential and controversial theologian Paul Tillich, moving beyond God means moving beyond the notion of a supernatural theistic being to God as the very ground of being itself.

Like a child who matures from a simplistic, naïve understanding of the world to a more complex, nuanced view, we must also let go of God concepts that no longer align with modern sensibilities. Even with our advanced knowledge, we are far from having all the answers we would like, and so we journey through this life of uncertainty and insecurity by embracing the mystery of God, cherish- ing our God experiences, and moving forward with courage. The thing we do *not* do is maintain a view of God that embraces nonsensical concepts. That isn't courage but foolishness.

The worldviews of an ancient era are no longer tenable in the present age. If Christianity is to survive into the future, it must abandon concepts from a bygone era and consider afresh the reality of God. There is no male supernatural theistic deity sitting on a throne in heaven whose sole job is to ensure our happi- ness and meet our every desire. God is more than that!

Scripture is not the inerrant, literal, once-for-all words of God to humankind that lock us into ancient worldviews, values, and prejudices. As human words *about* God, not the words *of* God, Scripture is merely a tool—a doorway that helps us experience the divine. There is no such thing as an infallible pope or one true religion, and the essence of God cannot be contained in propositional doctrinal statements. There is no God who causes earthquakes, diseases, and actively kills our enemies. We must let go of these ancient concepts that are no longer viable. God is more than this, bigger than this, beyond this—and that is the God we must rediscover. We must move beyond these antiquated, nonsensical concepts if the reality of God and the Christian religion is to capture the hearts and minds of future generations living in the age of space travel.

Moving forward will not be without its challenges. The church has never been open to new ideas unless it is forced to do so. When Copernicus, Kepler, Galileo, and Newton advanced new insights about our world, the church recoiled and, instead of embracing new truth, worked hard to condemn it, label it as heresy, and persecute those who dared to challenge ecclesiastical power. Reformers of the church are rarely encouraged or embraced until long after they are dead—after the church has been forced to accept new truth even while dragging its feet and mumbling the whole way. Reformers may well be excoriated and misunderstood in their day, but they help us see Christianity with new eyes. They are essential poets of the faith who help us see beyond our own noses.

Naming an Experience

Is God merely a human construct without real substance? Language itself is a human invention—a system of symbols that allows us to communicate thoughts and ideas. Although the word "God" is a culturally conditioned term, it is merely a symbol that points to something beyond itself. What does the word point to? That depends upon the age and culture in which one lives.

In one age, God may have referred to nature or spirits within nature. At another time in history, God may have symbolized mythology and folklore. The gods of Greece and Rome were one thing, while the God of first-century Israel was another. God became known as a superhuman being—like a great king. What lies behind these God symbols? Is God simply a human thought housed solely within ourselves, or does God actually point to a reality that exists outside our own mind?

The term is indeed a symbol pointing to a divine reality that we experience in the human dimension of life. In other words, "God" seeks to name a human experience that leads us to deeper dimensions of consciousness where awe, wonder, and worship result. It is a personal experience that connects us to something bigger than ourselves—the reality of a sacred presence. It doesn't happen outside our humanity, but it's something we experience deeply within our humanity—something that calls us to look at life differently and moves us beyond the boundaries of our own self to a universal love.

For me, God is more than a mere subjective experience with no reality outside ourselves. I believe that the term is trying to name that which is nameless, a reality that exists and is real, and one that we experience personally, even though we cannot fully explain it. We are in many ways like every other living thing, except that we are self-conscious. We are cognizant that we are aware and alive. We don't just exist; we *know* that we exist, and we ponder the value and meaning of our existence. We have the ability to move into a dimension of life and awareness that other species don't possess. They are stuck within their biological limits, but humans have the ability to experience the reality of God in unique ways. We are able to transcend our biological selves, grow in the awareness of life within us, and connect with the source of our own existence.

By becoming aware of the life of God flowing in us and through us, we see God in all things, for God is the source of all life—the ground of being in which everything else finds its existence. How does one articulate this kind of experience that is both within us and outside us, both immanent and transcendent? We create a symbol for the experience and call it God, and at the same time, we grasp and grasp, never fully reaching what it is we are trying to grab hold of. That is both the reality of God and the mystery of God.

It is difficult to name the nameless. Whatever we name this divine presence is only a symbol—a pointer. Yet it is enough for me to experience the life of God flowing in me and through me without wasting precious time trying to define, contain, analyze, or systematize God. Once we do that, we have distorted the very experience we are trying to describe. But that is what humans do. We try to put the experience of God into a form, a creed, a doctrinal statement—something tangible that we can worship, and, much like Aaron's golden calf created during a time of uncertainty, we wind up worshiping the image and not the reality. In our minds, it is far too dangerous to allow God experiences to exist on their own without commentary and definition, for that is messy and undefined and leaves us out of the equation for control.

I Believe in God

What does it mean to say, "I believe in God"? I suppose that depends on whom you are asking, what part of the world they live in, and what religious preferences they hold dear. We are saying, it seems to me, that on the subject of God, we see things a particular way. Believing is a way of seeing—our perspective about the matter. Next, we must determine what the word "God" refers to. Is God a spiritual presence, a supernatural theistic being, the ground of all being, a set of propositional statements, or something else? Because belief entails our way of understanding God, images and metaphors play an important role in expressing our religious perspective.

Images and metaphors are a reflection of our culture and our experience and, ultimately, how we perceive God. In other words, we view reality through the spectacles that we wear, and the spectacles that we wear are influenced by a culture that is never static. These glasses become the lens by which we arrive at our worldview—our picture of reality. How we understand God becomes our map for living life, determining our values, and assessing what is real and worthwhile. As images become outdated and irrelevant, new metaphors emerge that help us keep pace with a changing world. The images and metaphors of one generation may not work for another. It isn't that God has changed; rather, our understanding and articulation of God is reacting to an ever-evolving reality around us.

Because we experience the sacred in personal ways, we often describe God in humanlike terms with personal characteristics. This is called the personification of God, which we previously discussed. Because God is a mystery far beyond our ability to comprehend, we utilize images and metaphors to convey our experiences. They are a reflection of our own experiences rather than absolute definitions of God.

I can't tell you exactly what God is. How would I know? How can anyone know? I can't speak of God with certainty, for God is a mystery, and I haven't solved the mystery. I feel comfortable referring to God as a presence, a spirit, the holy one, the sacred, the divine, and other similar terms. It keeps me away from the impersonal side of things while also recognizing that God isn't a humanlike being. I look to the life of Jesus as a metaphor for what God is like, as Colossians notes: "He is the image of the invisible God" (Col. 1:15, NRSV).

My God experiences have transformed me, changed me from the inside out, and brought me to an entirely new level in my humanity. It matters very little to me what you call God, for that label is a mere referent, not the actual name of the divine. What matters to me is that the very life of God, whatever that mystery is, flows in you, through you, and out to others. It is in this divine reality that "we live and move and have our being" (Acts 17:28, NRSV). If God is the source of love, life, and my very existence, then I best honor God by loving with all my might, living life to the fullest each and every moment, and becoming the very best "me" I can be within my own existence. Because I lack certainty regarding the divine mystery, I simply maintain a soft heart and an open mind and focus on my experiences of God that change me for the better—experiences that create in me a new heart and allow me to more fully embrace my humanity. I am most attentive to God when I am in tune with myself.

Though I struggle to name my God experiences, I know that the image of a supernatural theistic being in the sky no longer holds value for me. Though life is filled with uncertainty, I choose to walk in the mystery of God and focus on the personal nature of my spiritual encounters. I allow those experiences to change me at the core of my being so that I can love more fully and, in so doing, become more fully human. I believe that God is real even though I cannot prove it, define it, or contain it. I believe that God is the source of love, life, and my very being. I believe that all things in existence have their very being grounded in the reality of God. I believe that we can experience God in this life. I believe that we are creatures who reflect the divine image and that all of life is a reflection of God.

This may not be concrete enough for some, but it is enough for me. Puffing out our little chests and declaring all there is to God while drafting propositional statements that must be affirmed in order to become an official God-follower is a whole lot to do about nothing. We must peer beyond the horizon to discover a God beyond these images we have conjured up. When we connect with *that* God, we will experience a bit of what Jesus himself experienced, and our lives will be forever transformed for the better.

Chapter Summary

This chapter encouraged us to move beyond outdated concepts of God that no longer bear weight in the present age. Rather than dogged adherence to the God language of the first century and beyond, Christianity is challenged to embrace new ways of conceiving and expressing the reality of God for a new age.

We asked if God was a who or a what and noted that the idea of God as a separate, living, thinking, emotional, controlling, humanlike deity was no longer a viable option. With the limited knowledge of the past, the ancients asked *who* caused disease, earthquakes, and storms. Today, we ask *what* caused these things. God was once the go-to answer for just about everything, and now that our knowledge has progressed, these go-to answers must be updated.

The differences between our experience of God and our explanation of God were highlighted. Genuine God experiences last forever because they are connected to divine reality, but explanations of those experiences die out as culture changes, for no explanation can be divorced from its cultural context. This means that our explanations of God are constantly in a state of flux.

We live in the twenty-first century, and yet our God explanations are still tied to ancient expressions of the past. New knowledge has made them irrelevant. Moving beyond these outdated images is imperative if Christianity is to survive into the future. God is the name we attach to our experiences of divine reality—to that which we experience personally but struggle to name or define. Instead of wasting precious time fiercely protecting antiquated explanations that have run their course, we are far better off enjoying the divine journey.

If God is not a supernatural theistic being and our advanced knowledge has undermined much of our God-talk, where does this leave us, and where do we go from here? What are the next steps, and how can we ensure that the message of Christianity remains relevant in the ages to come? That is the topic of our next section.

LEAVING RELIGION

☑ **The Problem of Behavior**

The Problem of Belief

☑ The Credibility of Scripture

☑ The Credibility of Jesus

☑ The Credibility of God

FINDING GOD
A New Beginning

AND FINALLY →

17

THE CHURCH OF TOMORROW
• • • • • • • •

AFTER DECONSTRUCTING CHERISHED BELIEFS OF THE past, one wonders what is left of Christianity. Where in the world do we go from here? How do you recover from something like that? Is there nothing left to stand upon, and can we even consider ourselves Christian anymore? One thing is certain: the age of believing in fairy tales is over, especially when the knowledge we now possess informs us that they can't possibly be true. This chapter sets the sails and points the boat in a new direction of reconstruction. It is time to finally begin putting the engine back together again. Do we start afresh, utilizing those pieces of Christianity that still work, or simply jettison the whole thing and call it a day?

The fact that you made it this far in the book reveals your interest in where this boat is headed. It is difficult to predict the future, and no one can definitively say what the church of tomorrow will look like, for we are still in the sea of transition. Though we are too far out to cry, "Land ahoy," and we realize it will take decades, maybe centuries, for the church to embrace new ideas, at least the boat is on the water, the sails have been set, and we are moving with the winds of change. The grand adventure has begun.

Many realize that remaining where they are is not an option. It is difficult to steer a parked car, so they put it in drive and begin moving. The days when you could have one foot in the boat and the other on the dock are forever behind us. The ship has left port and is under sail, for "the times, they are a changin'," according to the crooner Bob Dylan. Thanks for sticking around to this point and giving serious consideration to sailing the high seas of transition with me. I hope this chapter encourages you to think of God in new ways, add integrity to your faith, and come in from the cold to join countless others who have left religion behind only to rediscover a faith worth believing and a God worth following. You no longer have to be a sideline Christian hiding in the witness protection program. Instead, you can be a fully engaged, intellectually honest, full-fledged member of the God-follower club!

Crossroads of Faith

In 1971, rock star David Bowie released a song on his *Hunky Dory* album titled "Changes." It contains a catchy chorus line, "Ch-Ch-Ch-Ch-Changes," and I have been singing that famous lyric for a while now as I consider the significant evolution of thought the church has undergone since the 1500s. Like a snowball rolling downhill and gaining size and speed, the amount, type, and pace of change has caught the church off guard. Some would even say its effect has been devastating—that it has excised the heart of all that we believe. While it has certainly undermined many of our traditional notions of deity, it has not destroyed God. God lives on, even as our articulation of that reality changes over time.

Whether we recognize it or not, Christianity is at a crossroads where the gale-force winds of change drive us to rethink things. Now that we know what we know, we can never go back to old ways of thinking. Can Christianity survive without supernatural theism? Will liberation from dying concepts free us to move in new directions? I sure hope so, for new knowledge often makes past thinking obsolete. Like pulling the pin on a hand grenade, it is just a matter of time before the whole thing explodes. It might be easier to think of this crossroads in terms of maturity. When I was a kid, the world consisted of baseball, bubblegum, and Band-Aids. But was that an accurate depiction of reality? I wish! The world is far more complex than that. As I grew and matured, I saw the world differently. The point is that once our eyes are open, we can never go back to embracing baseball, bubblegum, and Band-Aid perspectives, no matter how much they are cherished. We have outgrown them.

The same holds true for our faith. By failing to recognize the colossal challenges staring us in the face, we swim in a pond that is drying up until there isn't even enough water for tadpoles to thrive. It is difficult to adjust our thinking if we don't acknowledge that a problem exists—that the very survival of the church is at stake. Ancient explanations built upon the limits of ancient knowledge leave traditional Christianity between a rock and a hard place, a dilemma for which traditional doctrines have no answer. Ch-Ch-Ch-Ch-Changes!

Responses to Change

What do we do with our sophisticated knowledge and its refusal to bow before archaic religious belief systems? Our response to the tsunami headed our way is not inconsequential, for these monumental changes will affect the future of the church whether we like it or not. Will our boat sail toward tomorrow's sunrise or sink to the ocean floor, courtesy of the oncoming tsunami? The choice is up to us, and we might as well take the time to consider our options.

The first option is denial and ignorance—the refusal to acknowledge the coming changes and their impact upon the church. See no evil, hear no evil, and speak no evil. If we don't acknowledge it, it doesn't exist. Maybe it will simply go away on its own. To their own detriment, these citizens of Pompeii ignore the rumblings of Mt. Vesuvius and proclaim, "Oh, it's nothing!" Good luck with that approach! Making no decision at all becomes the worst decision one can make.

A great number of people fall into this category, from the declining mainline denominations trying to figure out why young people no longer attend their church services to the robust evangelical congregations still promoting the past as the way forward. One knows something is up but doesn't realize how deep the change must be to survive, while the other doesn't recognize the threat for what it is and merely regurgitates stock answers from the past. Meanwhile, Mt. Vesuvius is erupting. The church is facing a monumental threat that is destructive and life-threatening. Cavalier business-as-usual approaches simply won't do, for the lava is already flowing. We're not talking about losing a church here and there for sundry reasons; we're talking about the demise of Christianity as a viable and survivable religion. Can we not read the tea leaves in our cup and realize the gravity of the situation?

The second option sounds the alarm to take up battle stations as defensive positions surround the fortress of the past. Hoping to preserve and protect it from the destructive forces of godless change, minds are made up, and there is a willingness to go down fighting. These folks see themselves as the only true remnant of the faith who, in martyr-like fashion, dedicate themselves to protecting and preserving their version of the truth. As they double-down on yesterday's message, they attempt to resuscitate a lifeless body, but nothing can save a terminally ill message. They are merely embalming the past for a museum of the future. In essence, they are fundamentalists who will never allow the taint of change to enter the hallowed halls of faith on their watch. Sadly, it is too late for such misguided heroism, for the state of decay is too far gone and the pace of new knowledge is accelerating, not slowing down.

The third option is to simply give up and walk away from Christianity altogether. The cost/benefit analysis no longer adds up. What is there to gain in propping up a belief system that doesn't square with reality? These folks find themselves in a thorny position. To believe the traditional doctrines of the church requires them to cast aside intellectual integrity. Forced to make a difficult choice, they sadly walk away. More and more individuals find themselves in this very situation. They long for a place to call home—where intellectual honesty is linked to vibrant faith. Unfortunately, those places are hard to find. But why must Christians be forced into this situation at all? I hope to present a path forward where faith and intellectual integrity can peacefully coexist.

Instead of denying, ignoring, protecting, or running away from the swift currents of change, our final option embraces the challenge and turns to face the wind. This approach takes faith seriously enough to rethink our position, ask hard questions, and seek new understanding in light of increased knowledge. Intellectual integrity is invited to the dance, and the truth of new discoveries merely increases our wonder and awe of God.

The church of tomorrow will not be the same as the church of yesterday. We simply cannot ignore the rising tides, for sooner or later, we will be under water if something isn't done to stay afloat. It is far more comfortable to maintain the status quo, but we are too far down the road to turn back, and we couldn't even if we tried. Change is easier to face when we recognize what is happening and why.

This is not an easy path to follow, for we become the minority in a majority world. It is risky to walk uphill against the flow of downward traffic. While we may not be the popular kids in school, we will walk with integrity in our task of being salt and light to others. We will be instruments of change in transforming our world and advancing a faith worth believing and a God worth following.

What's It All About?

What's at stake with all of this? The short answer has to do with the future survival of Christianity as a viable religious option, and that is dependent upon what the message of Christianity is, which is dependent upon one's view of Scripture. It's the domino effect. Literalists proclaim one message based on reading specific texts literally, while nonliteralists advance another message based on metaphorical understandings. This creates division within the ranks of Christendom, and onlookers are both dismayed and confused. It's almost as if two different religions exist, each calling themselves Christian.

People want to know what Christianity is all about. What are its claims and beliefs? Which story will win out? Will it be the story of the literalists, with their heaven-and-hell message of guilt and shame? Will it be the story of Jesus as the sacrificial offering who paid the ultimate price for our sins so the justice of a vindictive God could be appeased, and striving to live up to the plethora of biblical standards so we can go to heaven when we die? Is that what Christianity is all about? Is that the message that will stand the test of time and the scrutiny of increased knowledge?

The new insights of our age undermine the very message literalists promote, and when a message doesn't square with reality, it is discarded as an irrelevant relic of the past that soon fades into the forgotten pages of history. Christians read the same Scripture, use the same language, and arrive at different conclusions. It is the "two-trains" dilemma mentioned earlier in the book. It matters which train you board, for they arrive at different destinations, and I am convinced that only one train will take us into the future.

In reconstructing a church for tomorrow, I have no intention of replacing one list of doctrinal statements with another, for the Christian message transcends such dogma, and we would never agree on it anyway. Besides, it would just bring us right back to the current problem. It is always easier to analyze the past, for it has already occurred, but the future hasn't yet arrived. Even though we aren't yet at the "Land ahoy!" point, we can paint broad brush strokes of important concepts that assist us in sailing the sea of transition. They are, in essence, key items in my own vision of what the future church might look like, and as such, they become good discussion starters.

Symbol to Substance

Over the years, the church has established a glut of symbols, rituals, creeds, and religious practices that serve to express our faith and identify us as Christian. Even nondenominational churches that boast of no such entrapment find themselves engaged in similar routines, though they wouldn't dare label them as such. One church I pastored experienced tremendous stress over the fact that a huge cross was absent from the sanctuary wall behind the pulpit. How could a legitimate church call itself Christian without a prominent cross staring you in the face each Sunday? One day I counted all of the crosses I could find in the sanctuary, from the communion table, to the hanging lights, to the engravings on the pews, to wall banners, and so forth. I discovered that there were more than one hundred crosses staring us in the face each Sunday. Yet it wasn't enough. We had to have the big one, front and center. It dawned on me that the congregation yearned for a symbol, not the substance behind it.

There is nothing wrong with symbols and rituals, for they help us celebrate the things that are important to us—birthdays, marriages, births, deaths, etc.

Symbols stand for something and help us attach significance to things that matter. The church is no different. Religions will always utilize symbols and rituals as a way of expressing what is important, and I suspect they will change as the frontiers of new knowledge increasingly influence our understanding of life, God, and humanity. Since we are unable to speak of the mystery of God with absolutes, symbols become one way of remaining relevant against the backdrop of increased knowledge.

In the church of tomorrow, symbols and rituals will be reimagined and expressed in new ways—ways that are culturally relevant and align with present reality. When ancient expressions of faith no longer make sense, tomorrow's church will find ways to symbolize its faith in more enlightened ways. Symbols of the past are not bad, but they are subject to decay and irrelevance, since they are based on the limited knowledge and worldview of a world that no longer exists.

The evolution of our symbols isn't about change for the sake of change; it's about meaning—a renewed focus upon the substance behind them. They are mere tools for expressing the meaning, message, and experience of God. When our understanding changes in light of new knowledge, past tools of expression become outdated.

What new practices, symbols, and rituals will be necessary to reflect a more informed faith? Will the Christmas story be symbolized by a virgin birth even though such emphasis runs counter to everything we know about human reproduction? Will our Easter celebrations continue to emphasize a physical, bodily resuscitation back to life when we know that is scientifically impossible? Will communion be about a bloody human sacrifice offered to appease a bloodthirsty God whose warped sense of justice demands the death of an innocent man?

Increased scientific knowledge forces us to reconsider past symbols built upon archaic worldviews. The church of tomorrow will focus upon meaning, not maintaining old symbols. As Christianity is impacted by new discoveries, our perception of faith will morph right along with it. This means that more appropriate symbols, rituals, creeds, and religious practices will be developed that better align with our growing understanding of the world.

Doctrine to Experience

Christianity, we have been told, is about correct doctrine. One must believe rightly in order to be considered a Christian. But is that true? Is Christianity about believing the right things? Funny, I don't recall Jesus ever mentioning this. The church has spared no expense to defend its creeds, interpretations of Scripture, and doctrinal statements of faith, even killing or imprisoning those who challenge its authority or refuse to bow the knee to its orthodoxy. Its bloody history is yet another way of saying, "We are right and you are wrong," and sets up an "us versus them" mentality, for the only ones who know God, follow God, and experience God are those who believe the right things in the right way. And yet there are more than thirty thousand denominations in the world today, each with the same mentality. There seems to be little consensus about which doctrine is the correct one to believe.

It reminds me of the dieting dilemma facing so many Americans. What foods can and should you eat? Which diet is the right diet? Everyone claims their approach is the best, while expert doctors and dietitians disagree with one another. One day we are told a certain food is bad for us, and the next day the very opposite is encouraged. What in the world are we to believe? Religion is a lot like dieting—numerous choices amid conflicting information.

The early followers of The Way struggled to articulate their experience of Jesus. Though their understanding was fluid and ill-defined, they saw the reflection of God in Jesus. These diverse lovers of God articulated their experiences and understanding differently. This diversity of expression wasn't allowed to survive as competition for followers heated up. It would be centuries after the death of Jesus before many of the doctrines we call orthodox today were established. It took a while, but the church finally managed to weed out the less powerful viewpoints and create a single way of telling the Christ story, which was then declared correct doctrine—orthodoxy. All other views were deemed heretical.

Even if there is broad-brush consensus on the gist of the Christian story as told from an unenlightened past, which there is, is this what being a Christian is all about—intellectually affirming specific doctrinal statements or a denominationally approved storyline? Do you see the inherent contradiction? If God is a mystery far beyond our ability to comprehend or describe, how can we advance such absolute propositional statements as the litmus test of faith?

What is the correct test of faith? Is there one? What is the basis of our fellowship? Right practice? Right rituals? Right doctrine? Right symbols? Right lingo? There is no such thing as a right religious practice or a correct doctrine. Our practices and beliefs are merely culturally conditioned expressions of our God experience, not absolute descriptions of God that must be affirmed, or else! My point is that the core of our fellowship is based on our experience of God, not correct doctrine. This lack of control over the narrative of others is concerning to the institutionalized church. Though we gather with those who choose to articulate God in ways that appeal to us, it is entirely possible to embrace "correct" doctrine and live like hell. That isn't what I call a Christian, for, as Scripture notes, even the demons believe.

There has to be something different, something deeper than intellectual assent that unites our hearts and prompts us to live in communion with the life-giving Spirit of God. Since we are unable to adequately define God or speak of God in the language of absolutes, all we can do is experience the sacred presence in our lives and express that reality in terms that are meaningful to us instead of dictating to others what to believe and how to express that belief. Christianity is a shared lifestyle based on love, nonviolence, simplicity, and service. It is about transformation, change, and becoming. If we think for one moment that Christianity consists of merely believing "correct" propositional truths about God without engaging in the element of internal transformation, then our notion of Christianity is perverted.

Today's church emphasizes doctrine and culturally approved expressions of faith when it should focus upon our genuine God experiences. The church of tomorrow will be able to separate the two. People will seek unity around a common experience of the Christ power rather than strict adherence to approved articulations of our God experiences. This allows our expressions of faith to remain personal to us and at the same time relevant to the knowledge and culture of our age. We are free from outdated expressions of the past. It is time for a firmware update.

It's like using "thee" and "thou" in our speech. That was fine for the 1611 King James Version of the Bible, but no one talks like that anymore. We are free from an outdated litmus test of orthodoxy. Instead of demanding that Christians be card-carrying members of a specific doctrinal affirming denomination, fellowship is based upon a common confession of personal God experiences that transform us to be more like Christ. The church of tomorrow will distance itself from correct doctrine as the criterion for calling oneself Christian and will focus upon our genuine experiences of God that unite us in fellowship. Abundant diversity of thought will be welcomed and appreciated, for it is the love of God flowing within that embraces diversity in the midst of unity.

Biblical Revelation to Self-Communication

In Protestant denominations, the Bible plays a central role in the life of the church. In cultlike fashion, it is often elevated to God-like status and idolized—affirmed to be the authoritative, once-for-all, inerrant, literal words of God to humankind. This was the perspective that captured my attention for so many years, and as such, I spent a great deal of time memorizing it, studying it, safeguarding it, and living according to its precepts. After all, if it was the very words of God, it was worthy of the high esteem I ascribed to it.

Though my perspective has changed, my respect for Scripture is greater now than ever before. Elevating it to God-like status or viewing it as the authoritative, once-for-all, literal words of God to humankind is problematic for all the reasons previously noted in this book. For one thing, it borders on bibliolatry, when nothing is to compete with or replace our allegiance to God, not even good religious things like the Bible.

It is this literalistic understanding of the biblical text that will crash and burn in the future, for such a perspective simply cannot stand up to reason and reality. As a result, the emerging church will distance itself from literal understandings and view Scripture as a sacramental and metaphorical tool for opening windows into the divine. It will be seen not as the very words from God but rather words about God arising from the experiences and understanding of our forefathers who lived in a different age—an era fraught with limited knowledge, troublesome cultural biases, and an entirely different understanding of the world.

Scripture has fallen from its pedestal, knocked off by the advent of science and the discovery of new knowledge. No, the sun does not revolve around Earth, as noted in Joshua. No, humans aren't born without male seed. No, a person cannot lift off from Earth and ascend to heaven in a cloud. No, a person dead for three days cannot be physically resuscitated back to life. No, a crowd of five thousand people cannot be fed with five loaves of bread and two fish with twelve baskets leftover. No, a man cannot live in the belly of a fish for three days only to be spewed forth at an exact, predetermined location. These exaggerated stories are designed to communicate profound truth, not literal truth. The church of tomorrow will respect the nature of sacred storytelling and seek the deeper, more profound meaning behind the literal words on the surface.

It leads us to consider how God speaks to us. If the Bible is God's once-for-all communication to humanity, then all we have to do is consult the good book, for God has spoken—once and for all. What need is there for God to speak today? This is a past-tense God who has spoken long ago, is done speaking, and is now silent. Even if God were allowed to speak today, nothing could contradict what has already been written. For all intents and purposes, God has been muzzled, and what is considered the contemporary voice of God is merely the regurgitation of ancient writings. Is a past-tense God worth following? Is God unwilling or unable to speak in the present age? Mix in the various controversies and opinions as to exactly what God said in the past, and we are pretty well hung out to dry.

This warped perspective crumbles under the slightest push back, and yet it is the view that prevents so many from joining tomorrow's church. Fortunately, the emerging church will proclaim a God who is still speaking, not a bridled, past-tense God. While still retaining its value and esteem, Scripture will be placed in its proper sacramental role rather than on the pedestal of a once-for-all, inerrant, literal communication from God.

Theologians note that the revelation of God is seen in Jesus, in nature, and in the Bible. Divine reflection can certainly be seen in each of these, but none of them are God. There is a difference between the reflection and the original, between the shadow and the Shadow-maker. Jesus was pronounced divine after his death as a way of highlighting his life-transforming effect upon others. A man who lived the way Jesus did was surely filled with the presence of God and allows us to exclaim, "That must be what God is like!" Colossians 1:15 (NRSV) attests to this, for Jesus "is the image of the invisible God."

With wonder and amazement, we also look to nature, with all of its beauty, diversity, splendor, complexity, and intrigue, and reflect, "Why is there something rather than nothing?" It points us toward the divine. The creativity and diversity of God's sacred presence take our breath away. In a similar vein, Scripture also opens our hearts to the revelation of God. Though we don't take its contents literally, we see God's reflection in how our forefathers experienced the sacred presence and how they dealt with the vagaries of life.

But why would the revelation of God be limited to these three avenues of expression when the reflection of God's sacred presence is everywhere, even in you and me? If God is a presence from which one cannot escape (Ps. 139), and if we live, move, and exist in God (Acts 17:28), then God is everywhere present. What a profound truth. God is not a being who sits on a throne in heaven but a sacred presence in which we live, move, and exist. God is in us, through us, beside us, over us, under us, and around us. We see the revelation of God in our pets, in flowers, in thunderous storms, in joys and sorrow, in the transitions of life and death, and, most importantly, we see the image of God in each other. In fact, the next time you look in the mirror, it is the revelation of God that is reflecting back at you. God is in you, and you are in God. What a wondrous thought. If this doesn't excite your soul, then I don't know what will.

My point is that the future church will see the revelation of God everywhere and will understand the proper role of Scripture as a sacramental tool. The image of God is not something to be obtained but something to be lived and experienced—something that already is and something that we already are. God's revelation to us is a deeply personal self-communication that will be cherished by the church to come.

The revelation of God extends far beyond an ancient controversial book; instead, God is continually revealing Godself to us personally through inward self-communication. It's what Quakers call the light of Christ within each person. This is frightening to yesterday's church, for it takes away their declaratory "thus saith the Lord" control mechanisms and frees the sacred presence to minister to us personally, individually, and subjectively. When I say there is no one correct belief, correct practice, correct doctrine, correct symbol, or single revelation of God, I mean to say that God reveals Godself to us through self-communication from within, for the divine is inside of us. We are the revelation of God.

Certainty to Mystery

It was bound to happen, and it did. I clashed with a parishioner over the interpretation of a particular biblical passage during a Wednesday-evening Bible study. He vehemently set himself in opposition because the notes in his Bible differed significantly from the perspective I set forth. When I asked which version of the Bible he was reading, it happened to be The Ryrie Study Bible. Ahh, that explains it.

Charles C. Ryrie was a professor and dean at Dallas Theological Seminary, a school known for its dispensational theology—a fundamentalist perspective. I explained that the notes he was reading weren't part of the biblical text but the perspective of a specific theologian with a specific interpretation of Scripture. There are many interpretations that exist regarding the meaning of various biblical passages. The parishioner was resolute, for his Bible said one thing, while his pastor was teaching another. I lost credibility in his eyes because I didn't agree with Charles C. Ryrie or, in his eyes, the Word of God.

On another occasion, my words differed from the text of another man's Bible. This time, the issue wasn't one of interpretation but the specific words of Scripture. I discovered that he was reading The Living Bible by Kenneth Taylor, a paraphrased version of Scripture instead of the more accurate word-for-word translation I was utilizing. It provided an opportunity for me to explain why there are so many different versions of the Bible, something many parishioners don't understand. How can there be one Bible and so many different versions?

Since the original, first set of God-inspired writings are nowhere to be found, we possess only copies and fragments of various manuscripts that have been discovered over the years, and even they don't always agree. We translate manuscripts into English and print them in different versions, such as the King James Version, the New International Version, the New American Standard Version, and so forth. Rather than present word-for-word translations, some versions paraphrase the gist of the old manuscripts in an effort to make the Bible easier for our culture to read and understand. Each English version is based on specific principles and guidelines of translation that direct the process. Some are word-for-word, others thought-for-thought, others paraphrases, etc. Well-known Bible teachers from various theological persuasions add in their two cents' worth, slap their well-recognized names on the cover, and voilà, we have The Ryrie Study Bible by Charles C. Ryrie, The MacArthur Study Bible by John MacArthur, The Dake Annotated Reference Bible by Finis Jennings Dake, The Expositor's Study Bible by evangelist Jimmy Swaggart, The Thompson Chain-Reference Bible by Frank Charles Thompson, and a host of others.

These differences remind me of the church in Corinth whose members quarreled over their dedication to specific people and perspectives. Paul pleads for unity among the various factions. One group follows Paul, another Apollos, another Peter, and still another group swears allegiance to Jesus. My pastoral ministry often ran up against those with allegiance to Charles C. Ryrie, John MacArthur, Finis Jennings Dake, Jimmy Swaggart, Joel Osteen, T. D. Jakes, Joyce Meyer, and other famous individuals. How could anyone disagree with these prized authority figures?

This steadfast allegiance reveals our need for authority figures who interpret the Bible correctly and offer up certainty. The goods being sold are "thus saith the Lord" pronouncements. Just choose the charismatic figure most attractive to you, buy into the wares they are peddling, and you have all the certainty and security you need. I apologize for being so crass about it, but it is what it is. I was talking to a high school acquaintance who said to me, "I have studied the Bible, know what I have been taught, and no one can tell me otherwise." She had no formal seminary training, and yet she was claiming expertise. She knew it all. End of story. She was not open to discussing her faith but in promoting the certainty she had acquired.

How do you have an open and honest dialogue with people like that? You can't. There was nothing I could have said or done at the time to bring up other perspectives, so I simply extended love anyway! Your beliefs about the Bible, the end times, the rapture, heaven, speaking in tongues, the filling of the Holy Spirit, the resurrection, and a host of other theological distinctives are dependent upon what denomination you attend and where your theological allegiance lies. Please don't follow me. I don't want any groupies or allegiances; I simply want people to move beyond the certainty they can never possess and rest in the deep waters of divine mystery.

The craving for authority and certainty makes living with ambiguity more difficult. I get that. We want to declare definitive, absolute truth about God and confidently proclaim the right description, the right interpretation, and the right perspective that helps us feel secure. Out of all people, we are the ones who are right! When I was growing up, preachers declared with certainty that Mikhail Gorbachev, the former leader of the Soviet Union, was the antichrist because he had a birthmark on his forehead. When supermarkets implemented checkout scanners that read the bar codes on food items, spiritual authorities told us it was the dreaded mark of the beast described in Revelation—the beginning of the end. How wrong they were. Some sects within Christianity have even declared with certainty the exact date when Jesus would return to Earth, only to be embarrassed when it didn't happen. Certainty isn't so certain after all!

The doctrine of the Trinity, for instance, is a mainstay of Christianity and taught with conviction and authority. Ask someone to explain it, however, and watch them stumble in their words. Instead, they search for Scriptures that bolster their case and explain the Trinity with various images, like a triangle with three sides, or water that can have three forms (solid, liquid, steam) and still be of the same essence. These illustrations are supposed to strengthen our confidence in things we deem certain, even though they aren't.

The Old Testament contains no Trinitarian doctrine, and it isn't found in the first century, either. Paul, the earliest of the Christian writers, claimed no Trinitarian doctrine. Developed over time as a way to elevate Jesus to divine status, the doctrine of the Trinity wouldn't emerge until the fourth century of the Common Era, and yet we proclaim it as sure as the morning sunrise. Rather than being an absolute truth about God, the doctrine is an articulation of how Christ and God were perceived in the fourth century.

Christians often voice certainty on uncertain matters. If God is beyond our ability to describe or comprehend, how can we speak with such assurance about things we are unable to comprehend? We can't, and that is why we resort to the use of metaphors. Though our knowledge has advanced significantly since ancient days, we don't know everything, and we never will. There ought to be a sense of humility about us when we discuss God. The church of tomorrow will move away from false certainty and authority claims of the past in order to open wide the door to mystery.

As we strive to live, love, and be in an uncertain and insecure world, we will move into the mystery of God with courage and vigor. It will be our experience of the divine that will unite us rather than allegiance to various schools of theological certitude. Experiencing the love of God without having all the answers or feeling like our way is the right way will be acceptable. This frees God to move in diverse ways instead of a single church-approved path to experiencing the sacred presence of God. The future church will place little value on authoritative declarations of certitude and will embrace divine mystery as something to be experienced rather than explained, controlled, defined, classified, or restricted.

Faith is living with courage amid the ambiguities of life where tribal mentalities abound. This is what faith is all about, sojourning in an insecure and uncertain land armed only with our personal encounters of God. No false pretenses. No false security systems. Nothing but you and God. If you really want to experience the presence of God, strip yourself of all the absolutes that have spewed from your lips over the years and expose your naked self to uncertainty and insecurity. When there is nothing left to grab onto, there you will find God—that unexplained mysterious presence that flows within. That is what the emerging church will focus upon—embracing and experiencing divine mystery itself.

Literal to Metaphorical

The very book Christians espouse as the gold standard by which their lives are ordered has been the cause of rancorous division and provoked unspeakable acts of hatred toward those outside of the faith—even justifying the killing of others in the name of God. I say this not to denigrate the Bible but to expose how bad interpretation can lead to bad behavior. All religions deal with fringe elements who tarnish the faith. The way we interpret Scripture has significant implications, one of which is whether or not Christianity will survive into the future.

Previous chapters have outlined the many pitfalls of literalism, and there is no need to rehash it all over again. In light of the new knowledge science has brought us, a literalistic approach to Scripture has been exposed as inadequate and oftentimes comical. It just doesn't square with reality. Scholar John Dominic Crossan states, "We used to think that the ancients believed dumb stuff, told silly stories, and that, at the Enlightenment, we got smart and ceased to believe them. I think it is more accurate to say that the ancients told powerful parables and that, at the Enlightenment, we were dumb enough to take them literally."[16]

Instead of literalism, the church of tomorrow will relentlessly pursue the transforming truth behind the biblical stories. No one can walk on water, no one is resuscitated from the dead after three days, no one is whisked into the heavens in a chariot of fire, no one lives within a fish belly for three days, no one can instantly convert 180 gallons of water into premium wine, and no one can feed five thousand people with five loaves of bread and two fish with twelve baskets of leftovers. These exaggerated stories are to be interpreted metaphorically, not literally. Each of them is trying to convey a deeper, more profound truth, not a literal truth. Exaggerated stories like these have been the method of ancient Middle Eastern storytelling for centuries—a means of conveying something far more profound than the story itself. Tomorrow's church will recognize this and move from a literal interpretation of Scripture to profound metaphorical understandings.

Dying Christ to Cosmic Christ

Atonement theology may be the toughest weed to control in the garden, for its roots go deep and its level of resistance is fierce. Like a tick stubbornly buried in its host, this pervasive doctrine of atonement will be upended in the church of tomorrow and replaced with a larger, more inclusive vision of the Christ.

As noted earlier in this book, atonement theology is fraught with problems. For one thing, it makes God out to be an abusive father who orchestrates the death of his innocent son to appease a twisted sense of justice. Before God can forgive anyone, a sacrifice of human blood must be poured forth. What kind of father does that to his son? What kind of justice is that? Our human understanding of justice is more just than that, for we forgive our enemies without requiring the blood of an innocent human. This story from the past makes God out to be a vindictive, punishing, child-abusing God.

Atonement theology also makes Jesus out to be a victim—someone who was intended to suffer at the hands of an angry God, power-protecting Romans, and jealous Jewish leaders. Furthermore, it makes humanity out to be sinful, dirty, contaminated, and in need of redemption. In essence, we are worthless. Is that the story we are to proclaim to the world, that God is an abusive parent who needs a bloody victim in Jesus to satisfy his holy justice for a humanity that is absolutely worthless?

The implications of atonement theology are numerous, and the bottom line is that it presents a distorted view of God, Jesus, and humanity. Is the core of our problem that we are worthless sinners in need of a sacrificial offering of human blood to redeem us? What this implies about God, Jesus, and humanity is incredulous. This is the tale of mythical gods in need of appeasing sacrifices. It may have occupied the minds of people who lived in less enlightened times, but it certainly isn't a twenty-first-century understanding of God.

The work of Charles Darwin and his theory of evolution inflicted a mortal wound upon this distorted view of God. In direct opposition to the Genesis creation story, Darwin implies that humanity wasn't created perfect at all, nor did humans fall into sin through disobedience. The storyline of atonement is one of restoration back to a previous state of being. If evolution is correct, and there is a good amount of evidence to say that it is, then human origins are quite different than what the Bible portrays.

Evolution is about changes over time—moving from imperfection to something more advanced, whereas the Bible declares that we move from perfection to imperfection. The two perspectives are completely opposite of one another. How can we fall when there is nothing to fall from, and how can we be restored to a status of perfection that never existed in the first place? This will not fly in the church of tomorrow, with its penchant for intellectual integrity. If the human condition is misdiagnosed, then the prescribed remedy is also wrong. The problem with humanity isn't that we are fallen people in need of forgiveness but that we are evolving people in need of wholeness, and that is what the Christ power can do for us—lead us toward wholeness. We do not need to be restored to perfection after succumbing to sin; we need to become, change, and transform into a better self and become whole people.

A distinction is made in this book between Jesus and Christ. The historical Jesus was the flesh and blood man who literally walked Earth, taught his disciples, and was crucified. Christ, the anointed one, is a recognition that the Spirit was within him, upon him, and flowed through him. It is that power, that Spirit, that connection to the divine that the church of tomorrow will pursue. It is this Christ element that will capture the attention of the future church.

This thing we call the Christ, this empowering presence of the sacred, existed long before the man Jesus was born. It has been around for eternity, for it is the sacred presence of God. This is the powerful anointing followers recognized in

Jesus. This isn't some weird New Age philosophy but a biblical concept. Jesus was the Christ, the anointed one in whom the Spirit was powerfully present. Our eyes have been trained to see only what we have been taught to look for, and we have been taught atonement theology and the worship of Jesus when it is the anointing, the Christ element, that made Jesus so winsome and attractive to others.

The universe is billions of years old, and when the Big Bang occurred, or however the universe happened, it was a moment when God revealed Godself. Some have called it the first incarnation of God. In essence, the revelation of God was first revealed in the creation of the universe. Jesus was the second incarnation of God. In other words, God specifically and powerfully manifested Godself in Jesus. He was the individual in whom the sacred Christ was powerfully manifested, and he captured our attention. When this Christ power flows to us, within us, and out from us, it is what Paul calls the Christ mystery. Paul never knew Jesus in the flesh like the other apostles. He experienced Jesus the same way we experience Jesus, through the Christ mystery. This divine mystery revealed itself in the person of Jesus in extraordinary ways, and it is this cosmic Christ presence that Paul himself experienced. It was a mystery to him, as it is a mystery to us, and yet it was also very real. Jesus personified the power and presence of divine mystery, and it is that Christ mystery the emerging church will promote and pursue.

Instead of living in the Christ mystery and focusing on the sacred presence behind Jesus, we focus on Jesus the human individual. We worship him and see his death as an atoning sacrifice for sin. The way to God, we have been taught, is through accepting Jesus as one's Savior. Jesus arrived in the early first century and lived on this Earth about thirty years, and his public ministry lasted anywhere from one to three years. What happened to all of the people who came before Jesus and all of those who have never had the opportunity to hear the salvation message? I guess they are just plain out of luck and become throwaway people to God. Too bad, so sad for them. God only saves those lucky enough to live in a time after the death of Jesus with a potential chance of hearing the message and accepting Jesus into their hearts. This is absolutely ludicrous.

If the Christ power is eternal, then individuals from all geographic locations, all ages of history, and all religions have the ability to experience that which flows to us, within us, and out from all of us. All people, everywhere, can experience the cosmic Christ that is everywhere present. When we speak of the cosmic Christ, we are referring to the Spirit or anointing that was upon Jesus, that sacred presence which he lived in and experienced so deeply. There is a distinction between Jesus the man and the anointed Christ upon him.

Atonement theology will fall by the wayside in the church of tomorrow, and humanity will be seen as in the process of becoming—evolving into better, whole people who pursue love. When we can love like Jesus loved, care about the things Jesus cared about, serve others, and live in the presence and power of the cosmic Christ, then we are well on our way to becoming the best version of ourselves we can be. It is this Christ mystery, the experiential nature of knowing the sacred presence within us, that is transformative. It is this mysterious reality—this Christ anointing available to all that the church of tomorrow will pursue.

Tribal Deity to Universal God

Tribal gods are a thing of the past, arising from ancient "my god is bigger than your god" mentalities. We have previously examined the changing nature of our understanding of God, something I referred to as the evolution of God. Tribal gods are punishing, vindictive, killing machines that protect and promote the cause of the tribe.

In Israel's case, their tribal god chose them to be a special, distinct people set above all other nations. Their tribal god led them out from under Egyptian bondage with devastating plagues and the death of Egyptian firstborn sons while protecting the Hebrews from such calamity. When the Egyptian army chased after the fleeing Hebrews, the tribal god killed them all by closing in the waters of the Red Sea upon them. When Israel finally arrived at the door of the Promised Land, they charged into battle, slaughtered their enemies, and conquered new territories in the name of their tribal deity. The tribal god hated all of the things the Israelites hated.

Tribal gods weren't limited to Israel, for every nation had them, and each was competing for the right to be the most powerful. In 1 Kings 18, for instance, we read where the prophet Isaiah confronts the prophets of Baal. Each would call upon their tribal god, and the deity that answered was the true god. Yahweh wins the challenge, of course, and as a result, Isaiah captures all 450 prophets of Baal, leads them to the brook Kishon, and slaughters every one of them in the name of Yahweh, with the tribal mentality of "my god is bigger than your god" on full display.

Offering sacrifices to tribal gods wasn't unusual, and Israel implemented a sacrificial system where animals were slaughtered, blood was spilled, fat was burned, and carcasses were consumed. It was one way to appease their deity with pleasing aromas rising to his nostrils. With the destruction of the Jewish temple in Jerusalem in 70 CE, that practice was done away with and replaced with prayer in the synagogue.

Jesus grew up with this sacrificial system and the lingering effects of tribal mentalities. After his crucifixion, stunned followers looked for ways to explain this unfortunate event. They did the only thing they knew how: interpret his death through the sacrificial paradigm so integral to their religion. They searched the Scriptures, found verses and concepts they could apply to Jesus, and did so. It gave them peace to know that Jesus's death was not in vain.

This tribal understanding of God began to change when the prophets emerged. As Israel experienced decline, decay, and eventually destruction, it was the prophets who began articulating a renewed vision of God. The fall of the Northern Kingdom to the Assyrians in 721 BCE and the fall of the Southern Kingdom to the Babylonians in 586 BCE precipitated this softening of God. The god of the tribe would now be thought of in more universal terms—a God for all people, not just Israel.

Malachi, a fourth-century prophet, has God declaring, "For from the rising of the sun to its setting my name is great among the nations, and in every place incense is offered to my name, and a pure offering; for my name is great among the nations, says the LORD of hosts" (Mal. 1:11, NRSV). The eighth-century prophet Hosea becomes a living example of God's great love for all people as he takes back his prostitute wife. Amos, another eighth-century prophet, notes that the worship of God is meaningless without human justice. Micah, a seventh-century prophet, declares, "He has told you, O mortal, what is good; and what does the LORD require of you but to do justice, and to love kindness, and to walk humbly with your God?" (Mic. 6:8, NRSV). The old tribal mentality is deteriorating, and the image of God is changing and expanding.

This shifting view of God is further expanded in the New Testament. God's great love is to be shared with all the nations (Matt. 28:18). Peter's vision in Acts 10 shows that "God shows no partiality, but in every nation anyone who fears him and does what is right is acceptable to him" (Acts 10:34–35, NRSV).

The emerging church will move beyond a tribal, vindictive, killing God whose purpose is to serve the tribe. Instead, tomorrow's church will pursue God as a universal sacred presence that resides in every human being regardless of tribe, race, creed, religion, gender, sexual orientation, or any other barrier we erect between ourselves. This is freeing and allows us to embrace what Christianity is all about—loving God, loving others, and loving ourselves. Tribal mentalities seek to erect fences between us, whereas the universal God calls everyone in love.

Static to Evolving

The story of Christianity was told through an ancient lens and has been crystallized in a form that is no longer meaningful to the contemporary world. It's like trying to sell telegraph machines in an age of wireless cell phones. Can you imagine how hard it would be to earn your living convincing others of the many benefits of this antiquated technology? You certainly wouldn't sell many telegraph machines, as you would be laughed off the doorsteps of prospective buyers. It is absolutely incoherent to the informed mind. In today's world, it is hard to sell a religious telegraph machine that has been encased in outdated language, symbols, and literal understandings.

The story set in the language of first-century Palestine and beyond struggles to advance its cause. As each generation passes, the grip of Christianity loosens even further. The question is whether or not Christianity will remain locked into the language, symbols, and literal interpretations of the past, or is it meant to evolve as life progresses? Is Christianity a static message chained to past expressions of faith, or does the Christian message transcend the medium used to convey its truth?

The future church will understand that our practice of religion and our understanding of God is always reacting and adjusting to present realities. If God is shackled to the culture, thought forms, worldviews, and knowledge of ancient times, then God becomes a static God of the past. Fortunately, the message and meaning of Christ extends beyond these boundaries and adapts and shapes itself to new realities. That's the kind of faith that will survive into the future—not as something that once was but as something that is now—living, dynamic, and adapting to new knowledge.

The Christ power is alive and well and transcends the boundary of space and time. As our knowledge increases, so must our understanding of God. As a result, God is always relevant to the current age. The emerging church will not promote a static God of the past encased in the pages of an ancient text but will embrace a God of the present that keeps pace with the shifting nature of reality. Though God doesn't change, tomorrow's church recognizes that our understanding and expression of God will morph as humanity grows and evolves. This will not be seen as threatening to the faith, but exciting, expected, necessary, and affirmed.

Though our sacred experiences will be understood and articulated in differing ways, depending on the knowledge we possess at the time, it is the reality of that experience that is a constant thread throughout the ages. The church is a living heartbeat, not an embalmed corpse. Tomorrow's church will allow for changing explanations while embracing the constant reality of God.

Heaven to Earth

Heaven as opposed to Earth, then instead of now, is the focus of today's church. When we accept Jesus as our Savior, we become one of the privileged few who enter heaven when we die. How many times have you heard the mantra? I guess God's love and power aren't grand enough to save everyone! And what kind of God is it who sets up such a system of reward and punishment anyway? This view focuses our attention on heaven, not on Earth—on what will happen then, not now. This is a waste of resources, time, and energy.

I often ask people where heaven is located, and, of course, they cannot tell me. They have no idea where it is and what it is like, but they are absolutely certain they are going there when they die. It is a place of peace, love, and joy, where sorrow no longer exists. It is a place where we spend eternity eating food at a grand banquet, worshiping God, and engaging in a great deal of singing. God must surely look forward to an eternity of bowed subjects offering eternal adoration. It appears that we also receive our own heavenly mansion and walk on streets of gold. It doesn't matter that we have never discovered such a place and we have no idea what exists in the afterlife, if there even is one. It is merely another self-assured certainty that plays upon our fear of dying, provides the hope we long for, and helps us cope in an uncertain world.

I actually believe in an afterlife, even though I don't believe in literal mansions or streets of gold. In reality, we know very little about the afterlife and think that our current concept of heaven is the way it has always been. That simply isn't the case. Once again, we see a progression of thought throughout Scripture on the subject. Some biblical writers saw death as the end of things. Other writers emphasize the nation of Israel in referring to life after death. In other words, after being destroyed, it is the nation of Israel that will again rise to prominence. It led some to reason that if this could happen to a nation, it could certainly happen to individuals at the end of time. If God's judgment came at the end of time, some wondered why it couldn't come at the point of death. The idea of punishment and reward arising after death was a concept that developed over time.[17]

Where do we go after we die? Who really knows! How could we know? That probably isn't what you wanted to hear, but it's true. For me, I find comfort in the cycle of life, the great transformation from one form to another. According to Acts 17:28 (NRSV), "In him we live and move and have our being." Our very existence is intricately linked to the divine presence within us. According to the Genesis creation story, our very breath comes from God, as God breathed life into the nostrils of Adam (Gen. 2:7). I come from God, I exist in God, and when I die, I return to God. After all, we are "participants of the divine nature," (2 Pet. 1:4, NRSV). The breath that was placed inside of me returns to its origin, for I live, move, and exist in God and God is in me. The eternal Christ within me cannot be destroyed.

The afterlife reveals the limits of human knowledge and is another arena of uncertainty for us, even though we all have our opinions on the matter. The danger of focusing on the afterlife is that we are far too heavenly minded to be any earthly good. The focus of today's church is upon heaven, how to get there, what must be believed to enter, and all the glorious things we have to look forward to.

A focus on the rewards awaiting us in the afterlife removes us from this present life, the only life we know and currently possess. Should we focus upon an afterlife of which we know very little, or should the emphasis be upon experiencing God in this present life and engaging in constructive efforts to make it better? I am for the latter and believe the future church will not waste precious time, energy, and resources trying to save others from hell and converting them to a heavenly outcome. Instead, tomorrow's church will expend effort and passion in pursuing the love and justice of God in this life. There is much work to be done. Since the very breath of God is in all people, and that breath belongs to God, it seems reasonable that it will return to the sacred presence from where it came. If this is true, then there is nothing to fear, and the wisest thing we can do is focus on Earth, not heaven—the here and now, not the then and there.

Foe to Friend of Science

Science is the enemy of Christianity, or at least that is what many believe. It is seen as undermining the faith and must be condemned and quarantined. I suspect, however, that those with such an outlook are selective in what science they accept and what they condemn. Anything that contradicts their literalistic view of Scripture is evil, whereas science that leads to new diabetes drugs and cures for cancer is acceptable. Why is one acceptable and the other isn't? Both originate from science.

With the advent of science and the scientific method, new ways of explaining our world arose that didn't involve God. This is threatening to literalists who seek to preserve the God answer for all things. On the other hand, many scientists are brazenly anti-God and make a point of demeaning religion. The bias is that all knowledge must be scientifically provable, a statement that itself cannot be scientifically proven. It is a philosophical claim that merely exposes a bias. I thought science was supposed to be open, not closed.

As I was struggling to come to grips with my changing understanding of God, I wrestled with the dilemma of science. Was I to trust in science and believe everything the scientists tell us? How could I trust science when it is constantly changing? A scientific truth today could easily be disproven and replaced with another scientific truth as new data emerge. I didn't think science was bad, but I didn't want to dive all in with something that was in a constant state of flux.

For me, science is one tool for gaining knowledge about our world. When science and Christianity clash, I think through the data and their implications. I change my mind if the evidence is there. Some of the data I take into consideration are my own observations, my own experiences, my own intuition, historical data, scientific data, and so forth. I believe that all truth is God's truth and should not be feared. I am willing to go where the data take me. I am not threatened by science, and no matter what is discovered, it will not shake the foundational bedrock of my faith. In fact, it enhances my faith, for I see God with greater awe and wonder.

The theory of evolution was a difficult concept for me to accept. That wasn't what I was taught, and deep down, I didn't want it to be so. I wanted a Father God in the heavens who created me from dust just like the Bible said. At the same time, I couldn't ignore the data regarding the age of Earth, the expanding universe, the Big Bang, the fossil record, DNA, and so forth. Though I realize that new discoveries may even change the theories we now take for granted, I want to be open to new knowledge. I don't want to worship matter; I want to celebrate the God of matter.

I am not a scientist and have little background in this regard, but I marvel at the discoveries we have made, our advances in medicine, and the exploration of distant planets. More power to the scientists and their discoveries that serve to increase our awe and wonder of God. Christianity is an active participant in the changing world in which we live. Relentlessly clinging to an image of God created thousands of years ago when science didn't exist is foolish. Our understanding of God adjusts and adapts to increased knowledge. This doesn't mean there is no God or that God changes, only that our understanding and articulation of God are always adjusting and reacting to the world around us. In this sense, science and Christianity work together. They are not enemies but friends that can peaceably coexist.

The church of tomorrow is not threatened by scientific discoveries, and neither does it worship science. Science is one way of obtaining valuable information about our universe, which helps to maintain God's relevance to the world around us. In the future, science will turn from a threatening foe to a cherished friend that reveals the magnificence of God.

Chapter Summary

No one has a crystal ball to predict exactly what the church will look like in the future, but when you see the clouds darken, the temperature drop, and the winds pick up, you know a storm is approaching. In light of increased knowledge, this chapter presented several important items the church of tomorrow will embrace.

Tomorrow's church will take a very different approach to Scripture, Jesus, and God. The advent of science has hastened the demise of literal approaches to Scripture. Instead, the future church will embrace a metaphorical, nonliteral interpretation and pursue the profound meaning behind the stories themselves. Jesus will no longer be viewed as an innocent, holy sacrifice who takes away our sins. Instead, he will be seen as an example of one who lived according to the Spirit and shows us what God cares about. The eternal Christ power he experienced is within each of us. God will no longer be thought of as a supernatural being who rewards and punishes, sends people to hell, and is manipulated by our prayers. Instead, God will be seen as a sacred presence that flows within us. God is not outside of the universe, but the universe is within God. We will not live in addition to God, but God is in us, and we are in God.

The church of tomorrow will focus on the meaning behind our religious symbols rather than on the symbols themselves, which will be updated and reimagined as our knowledge of God, our world, and ourselves change. No longer will affirming "correct" doctrinal statements be the litmus test of faith and the basis of our fellowship. Instead, we will unite around love and our personal experiences of God. The future church will embrace a God who is still speaking today. Scripture is a sacramental tool that helps us experience God, but God is revealed to us personally, individually, and subjectively through self-communication.

The future church won't claim to have all the answers but will encourage inquiry and intellectual honesty. Science will be embraced as a useful tool for learning more about our universe, and yet we will be satisfied to live in the divine mystery. Certitude cannot be found, but courage and wonder will become commonplace. In light of increased knowledge, Christianity will be viewed as living, evolving, and reacting to the world around us instead of being housed within a static book encased in the language and symbols of the first century and beyond. God is relevant to our present life.

The perspective and passion of the future church will move from heaven to Earth, from getting people saved for heaven in the future to engaging in the passion of God in this life by helping others, sharing love, seeking justice, and making this world a better place.

Is this a church you could embrace? More and more people are waking up to this vision, and I see the excitement in their eyes. "I could go to a church like that," you say. I could, too—a church where Christianity and intellectual integrity thrive together is a wonderful place to be. How does this new vision of Christianity affect us personally? How should we live in light of this new perspective? That is the subject of our next chapter.

18

HOW SHOULD WE LIVE?

· · · · · · · ·

T IS ONE THING TO DECONSTRUCT ANTIQUATED BELIEF systems and envision
a church of tomorrow, but how should we live today? If we seek to move beyond
senseless doctrines that no longer ring true, and the future church has not fully
arrived on the scene, how should we live in this in-between time? This rubber-
meets-the-road question personalizes our deep thinking and brings it down to
the real world of everyday living. What I present in this chapter isn't revolutionary;
it is quite simple, merely the extension of all that we have talked about so far.

My personal thoughts on how we should approach life are not exhaustive by
any means, but they may help to crystalize important guiding principles. This
section allows us to finally arrive at "so what?" implications for living in the present age. Jesus summarized the entire "so what?" of the Old Testament Law and
the Prophets with "Love the Lord your God with all your heart, and with all
your soul, and with all your mind" and "You shall love your neighbor as yourself"
(Matt. 22:35–40, NRSV). Mine won't be so short, but I will do my best to provide a few helpful signposts.

After reading a book like this, some may not want to move forward. I understand that kind of thinking, but I cannot agree with it. Are you giving up or
staying put because God doesn't fit into the predefined God-box you constructed? Just because past beliefs, past narratives, and past expressions of faith
that worked in a previous age no longer align with current realities doesn't imply
that God is not real. It only means that your God-box is too small, for our understanding and explanation are always trying to catch up with the reality of God.
For you, the question may not be "How should we live?" but rather, "How can I
go on?" This chapter may put some meat on the bones of practical living and
encourage you to pursue the sacred presence in fresh and authentic ways.

Living in God

When God is viewed as a supernatural being in need of constant appeasement, we endeavor to do the right things, say the right words, and pursue compliant obedience so the will of God in heaven can occur in our lives on Earth. Our gaze is focused upon doing, accomplishing, and appeasing. We work hard to earn the divine stamp of approval through blind obedience and doing the right things in the right way.

I don't know how many times I have heard well-meaning Christians declare that God's favor rests upon those who obey the rules, while God's disfavor is conferred upon the noncompliant. This is nothing more than a works-oriented religion that allows us to compare ourselves to others who are in the same boat. Our religious value fluctuates, depending on how well we adhere to the rules. The more we obey, the more God is pleased with us. Our value skyrockets as we rack up more blessings. Though we dress this perspective in religious adornment, it is nothing more than working hard to do more than others, do it better than others, and do it the right way, while others struggle to keep up. It becomes a religious game of one-upsmanship.

What a tiresome approach to life this is. It was the mindset of the Pharisees, who turned the joy of the Lord into a heavy burden that weighed people down. This perspective drained the life and joy right out of me and left me spiritually exhausted. Did I do enough? Did I do it right and more often than others? Was God pleased, or was there still more I could and should do? To top it off, I wondered exactly what the right way was, because I sure received a great deal of criticism for even trying to do it right. This didn't seem like the abundant life Jesus speaks of in John 10:10. Something was amiss. The initial joy I experienced in the faith was turning into another sweltering system of oppression. I was becoming trapped in a religious institution that stunted my ability to experience God's sacred presence. I needed to leave this kind of religion and find God. It wasn't easy.

I quit trying to appease a mythical being in the sky who rewards and punishes based on blind obedience, sends people to eternal hell for temporal sins, and requires the death of an innocent man before forgiveness can be extended. No longer do I expend energy, time, and resources trying to ensure that I won't become a crispy critter in the eternal fires of hell. Those days are gone forever. Far too many Christians live their lives trying to please this angry deity in the sky, praying they have done enough to make it into heaven when they die.

Instead of living *for* God, I am learning to live *in* God. What a vast difference this has made in my life. God is no longer the celestial cop hiding behind the religious billboard, waiting for me to come speeding by in my broken down-vehicle of disobedience. I have given up on being religious and now bask in the love of God within me. I haven't been issued a spiritual speeding ticket for years! What a tremendous sense of relief this has been. I no longer worry about doing religious things in the right way, doing enough religious acts, or comparing myself with others.

You see, my entire perspective has changed. God isn't someone out there in the deep blue sky—someone to be appeased; instead, God is in me, and I am in God. Even the universe in which I live exists within God, even though God is more than the universe. This concept blew my mind. I don't exist *for* God or *outside* of God, but I exist *in* God. I realized that the cosmic Christ, the sacred presence of God, dwells within me, and I dwell within God. How could I live *for* something that was already a part of who I am? How could I seek to obtain a status that I already possess?

If God is the source of all life, even my own life, then my very existence is tied to the existence of God. I am an extension of God's presence. This gave my life meaning, for now I was free to live with zest and gusto, without the cloud of a punishing God hanging over me. The best way for me to honor God as the source of all life is to live my own life fully and in the best way I know how. I stopped worrying about doing the right things in the right way, pleasing people, and appeasing an angry deity who was always keeping score. Instead, I was free to be me, to pursue the desires of my heart, release my giftedness, and make decisions that felt good to me. This wasn't selfish living but godly living that celebrated the divine life within. When I live life fully, I become a living testimony to the reality of God—the source of life itself. That's a pretty simple principle. Just embrace life and live it fully as best you can. Quit striving. Start living.

Living in Love

Love is the transformative power of the universe. When the enchanted journey of God's life-giving love weaves its way into our hearts, we are changed from the inside out. Love is meant to be given away. As a universal language that people recognize, it has the power to break down the mighty walls of division, and it may just be the very language of God. Throughout history, people have associated love with God, as Jesus did when he summed up the Law and the Prophets in Matthew 22:37–40 (NRSV): "'You shall love the Lord your God with all your heart, and with all your soul, and with all your mind.' This is the greatest and first commandment. And a second is like it: 'You shall love your neighbor as yourself.' On these two commandments hang all the law and the prophets."

The author of 1 John reveals that God is love and that God's followers are loving (1 John 4). Paul, the author of 1 Corinthians 13, notes that love is the supreme outcome of knowing God, for without it, we become noisy gongs and clanging symbols—annoying. Love is associated with divinity, because God is the source of love. When we love and are loving, we connect with the key identifier of God. We honor God as the source of love when we allow that love to flow out from us to others. We are fully capable of living this way, as Paul acknowledges in Romans 5:5 (NRSV): "God's love has been poured into our hearts through the Holy Spirit that has been given to us." The issue is not one of obtaining love but of actually loving.

Part of living life fully is loving extravagantly. Our survival-of-the-fittest mentality is to protect ourselves, seek our own good, and love only those we deem worthy of such affection. Can an object be loved simply because of what it is or who it is—for the intrinsic worth that resides within rather than for what it can do for us? I seek to be loving to all instead of scanning the horizon for deserving subjects. God is love, and when I love others for who they are, I am honoring God as the source of love. It's pretty down-to-earth. I see the God of love within others. I live life fully, and I love extravagantly. Simple concepts. Hard to do, but worth the effort, for it honors God as the source of life and love.

Living in Your Best Self

In addition to living life fully and loving extravagantly, we also pursue our best self. This approach to living stems from the fact that God is the ground of all being and that we are continually evolving. Instead of seeing God as a supernatural granddaddy sitting on a throne in heaven, I view God as a sacred presence that is everywhere present—the ground of being itself. By that, I mean that God is the ultimate reality on which all existing things depend for their own being. I am who I am, because I exist in God. I wouldn't be alive without a connection to the ground of all being. Because of this, I live, move, and exist in God, and I honor God by being my best self—by being all that I can be.

Being my best self also stems from the fact that I am in a constant state of evolution—that is, I am always becoming, progressing, and changing—never arriving. Christians often refer to this as transformation. I am not trying to attain a status of being right with God, for I already exist in God, and God exists in me. You can't get any "righter" than that. I am not seeking God's approval by accepting Jesus as my Savior or by believing a set of religious propositional statements, for how can we not be welcomed by God when God is already within us and shares divine life and love in our heart?

If God is the source of life and that life has been breathed into us, there is no other status we can obtain than to already possess the breath of God within us. If God is the source of love and that love has already been poured into our hearts, then we already possess the power, ability, and freedom to love extravagantly. We may not always act lovingly, but we are learning to become more loving as we grow, mature, and evolve. If our being is connected to, and dependent upon, God as the ground of all being, then we already possess an approved-by-God status, for we already exist in God. The life, love, and presence of God are already within us. In essence, there is no status we must attain that we do not already possess. In this life, we evolve, change, grow, and mature in our journey to become our very best selves. We never arrive, but we are always in the process of moving toward wholeness—becoming more fully human after the manner of Jesus. It is called transformation—allowing the life of God within us to change us and flow out from us.

How should we live our life? In its simplest form we live, we love, and we become.[18] Notice that I didn't say anything about joining a church, believing propositional statements of faith, adhering to legalistic mandates, or aligning ourselves with a political party or some socially charged issue. Those are all time-bound, culture-bound items that place people into categories of acceptance or rejection in the name of religion. Instead, we simply live life fully, love extravagantly, and become our very best selves.

How freeing is that? Could loving and following God be that simple? There is no status to obtain, for we already hold the status of being in God and God being in us. There is no litmus test of doctrine to adhere to, for Christianity isn't about agreeing to propositional statements of faith but about experiencing the divine. There is no long list of rules and regulations that meticulously control our life, for Christianity is about allowing the life of God within us to flow out from us. Just live life fully, love extravagantly, and be your best self. Could that really be the essence of what it means to be a God-follower? Quit trying to make it more complex than it is. Relax and enjoy. Live. Love. Be. In this way, you honor God as the source of life, love, and your very being.

Living in the Example of Jesus

Expressions of love come in many forms, as does living life fully, and the example of Jesus alerts us to what we should care deeply about in this life. What values and principles will guide our journey upon this planet? In looking to Jesus, we discover that he was a boundary breaker. In an effort to extend the life and love of God to others, he lived beyond the cultural and social constraints of tribal boundaries.

Jesus valued people. He cared about them, and they often moved him to compassion. He spent time with them. Taught them. Fed them. Ate with them. Traveled to meet them. Healed them. Answered their questions. Accepted help from them. Lived his life among them. People were important, and being in their midst helped him live fully and love extravagantly.

People matter, so we try to be kind, listen to them, serve them, and be among them. We may not be Mother Teresa, and we shouldn't try to be, for we are our own individuals and possess unique personalities, skillsets, and interests. We don't have to be like anyone else as long as our own lives are lived in ways that value and care about others. This allows us to honor the life of God within us and be our best selves in a manner that aligns with who we are as individual expressions of God. So, just be you and live out the life of God within you in a way that cares for and values others.

While Jesus extended an invitation for all to follow him, we frequently find him among downtrodden, disenfranchised, and despised people who were receptive to his ministry. Sadly, we have not arrived at a point in our world where every person is equally valued. If you are old and decrepit, you are viewed as taking up resources that could go to others deemed more valuable. If you are disabled, you are seen as a burden to society and are less prized than others. If you are in the womb of your mother or on death row, you are perceived as less than human and become subject to the killing instruments of the abortionist and the executioner. If you are LGBTQ+, female, foreign, Jewish, a minority, or a member of another despised category, you are considered to be a less valuable human, unworthy of the care, rights, and dignity attributed to others. This doesn't bode well for humanity or Christianity. We have a long way to go in our evolutionary journey and the alignment of our religious values with the way we live life.

Jesus faced similar first-century boundaries in his own Middle Eastern culture. If you weren't a Roman, you were a "less-than" individual. Jews looked down upon Gentiles and Samaritans. Pharisees looked down upon Sadducees.

The Essenes looked down upon all other Jews as less devoted. The Zealots looked down upon those who didn't support their cause. Males looked down upon females. Tax collectors were loathed for supporting the despised Roman invaders. If you were infirmed or a leper you became a social outcast. The poor were marginalized. The list could go on and on.

It wasn't that Jesus simply cared about people, which he did, but that he gave time and attention to those least valued by society—the poor, the tax collector, the sinner, the Gentile, the female, the Samaritan, the infirmed, etc. Those who look down on others feel no need to love certain categories of people. It is beneath them, for love isn't freely extended to all but dispersed only to worthy individuals. No wonder the message and ministry of Jesus were so unappealing to them. It required of them that which they were unwilling to give. Those who were looked down upon knew full well what it felt like to be cast aside onto the trash heap of humanity, and they opened their hearts to the loving, accepting ministry of Jesus.

What does this tell us about living life? It tells us that we are to love all people equally while noting that the downtrodden, disenfranchised, and despised are often more accepting of our love because they know what it is like to be at the bottom of the pile. Jesus identified with those on the bottom and sought to lift them up. In doing so, he provided a wonderful example for us.

He took time to speak with a despised Samaritan women in spite of cultural taboos that discouraged such interactions. He shared meals with tax collectors and sinners as a way of demonstrating value, respect, and acceptance—for they were equals. He is seen healing the infirmed, feeding a crowd of five thousand people, and providing wine at a celebratory wedding event. These stories reveal the joy, compassion, and love Jesus felt and displayed toward others.

Our contemporary world isn't much different when it comes to cultural boundaries of who matters and who doesn't. Clear lines of demarcation are drawn regarding who is to be ignored, ill-treated, and forgotten. We are still throwing people onto the trash heap of humanity. If you happen to be one of the despised, disenfranchised, or downtrodden, the care, concern, and love of Christ go forth to you. Jesus was a breaker of boundaries and extended the love of God to all people. What part of "all" don't we understand? We are always looking for something to align our life toward, so why not break down the boundaries that separate people into categories of value? Love all people. It will be one of the hardest things you have ever done, for it will cause you to look deep within your own heart, and yet it will be one of the most rewarding displays of God's presence in your life.

As Jesus engaged in love, he did so in nonviolent, peaceful ways. He wasn't a revolutionary who took up arms against injustice, and he didn't use force to get his way. Instead, he broke down boundaries by actually loving, actually valuing people, and becoming a living example to others. When we use violence and coercion, we have abandoned the principle of love, and who can withstand the force of love? Becoming a living example of what it means to care for, value, and love all people forces us to confront our own prejudices and internal boundaries, and yet it frees us to live more authentically in following The Way.

Living in Justice

When our focus shifts from heaven in the future to Earth in the present, we align our passion, energy, and resources with the things that matter to God. Looking to the life of Jesus and the Old Testament prophets can help us discern what matters in this life. What Jesus was passionate about is what God is passionate about. We know that Jesus cared for and valued people, especially the disenfranchised among us, but his actions also extended into equality and dignity.

Jesus pursued justice through his life, words, and actions. When love and justice are woven together, the ability to uplift life and move us toward seeing and treating every human with dignity is possible. For Jesus, tax collectors, lepers, women, sinners, Samaritans, the poor, the ceremonially unclean, and all others were of equal value.

The social scaling of human worth influences our laws, our financial systems, our housing systems, our politics, our religion, our view of others, and just about everything in life. Injustice can taint the very systems we develop and depend upon for navigating our world. Devaluing humans is an abstract term for many who have never been on the receiving end of inequity based on race, age, gender, religion, sexual orientation, and the like. When human life in seen as the very image of God, however, we move toward love and justice—not away from it. The eighth-century prophet Micah had his fill of the false piety around him and wrote what is now referred to as the Micah Mandate: "He has told you, O mortal, what is good; and what does the LORD require of you but to do justice, and to love kindness, and to walk humbly with your God?" (Mic. 6:8, NRSV).

How should we live? We should pursue the passion of God as seen in the passion of Jesus. When we treat others with love, dignity, and value, we break down the boundaries that divide us and begin treating all humans as equals. How inspiring is that? By living out God's passion, we become agents of change in creating a more just world.

Living in the Present

People live with different orientations toward life. Some have a tendency to preserve and protect the past. Others live in the present moment, with little thought given to the past or the future, while some are always looking to the future. My personality seeks to peer beyond the future, and I often find myself so far ahead that I sometimes travel alone. These elements of our personality are gifts that come with an upside and a downside. Part of being our best self is understanding and embracing our personality preferences, strengths, and weaknesses. We become a tremendous blessing to others by just being ourselves—the way God made us.

When it comes to experiencing God, our attention is upon a present spiritual awareness. Since God cannot be defined or adequately comprehended, our focus is upon the experience. In other words, God is a verb, not a noun. This prompts me to become more aware of God's presence in my life. Even if I remember past spiritual encounters, that act of remembering occurs in the present. Even if I expectantly look to future divine encounters, my expectancy is a present experience. Everything happens in the present, for it is the only moment that we have in our lives to be sensitive to God.

The issue isn't one of getting more of God, for God already exists within you and you within God. Why are we trying to obtain what we already possess? It is a futile and meaningless effort. The issue is one of greater awareness and sensitivity to the divine life within. People experience God in diverse ways. Since I am a thinker, I can read a book, consider a concept, or learn a new truth and deeply experience God's presence. Sometimes I am so moved that I break down crying, for the moment is holy. God speaks to me through my unique personality, and yet God is more than my personality. I live, move, and exist in God, so there is no place I can go or nothing I can do where God's presence isn't with me, in me, and moving forth from me.

Jesus was acutely aware of this divine presence in his own life. It allowed him to minister in powerful ways that were attractive and winsome to others. Jesus said that he only does and says what the Father instructs him to do and say. The Spirit seems to guide his instincts as to where to travel, whom to meet, and how to address the crowds. His life movement was orchestrated by the sacred presence within.

Compartmentalizing Life

We have a tendency to compartmentalize life and keep things separated from one another. One compartment is for religion, another for friends, another for family, another for work, another for relaxation, another for sports, another for exercise, etc. We separate them in our mind, whereas Jesus didn't function from this framework. The sacred presence upon him wasn't separated out into a few small containers; it influenced every aspect of his life.

Years ago I interviewed for a senior position within a non-profit organization that asked me to articulate a Christian worldview of my academic discipline of study. I stumbled through it in a very unimpressive manner as I wove the values of my faith into my academic discipline, but I could tell by their reaction that I wasn't scratching where they were itching. Through our discussion, I realized that they sought a Christian worldview for every element of life.

I knew this wasn't the job for me, and they felt the same way, so I asked whether one must, for instance, have a Christian worldview for riding a bicycle. They responded affirmatively, probably wondering how I could ask such an uninformed question. Of course one should have a Christian worldview of bicycle riding! I found that to be ridiculous, for I would have to formally articulate a Christian worldview for every element of life. What is the Christian way to evacuate your bowels, the Christian way to eat cereal, change a sparkplug, or blow your nose? This made no sense and reminded me of the legalism of the Pharisees. It majored on the minors and is the kind of petty-mindedness that makes for judgmental Christians.

I explained that I didn't compartmentalize my life in that way; instead, I illustrated God as the hub of a wheel that touches every spoke and holds everything together. In other words, the presence of God was central to every aspect of my life; there was nothing that wasn't influenced and touched by the presence of God. There is no such thing as a Christian worldview of riding a bicycle, but whenever I decided to ride my bike, the presence of God was with me and within me. Needless to say, I didn't get the job. This example is one way we divide our life into distinct and separate compartments rather than seeing life as a whole, where every aspect of our being is influenced and touched by the presence of God, the wheel hub.

Listening

My point is that God is with us in the present moment—in every moment. If we seek to experience the divine within, we must become more aware of the sacred presence in our life. That means less talking and more listening, less noise and more contemplation, and seeing beyond mere sight. Life is filled with noise and distraction—the tyranny of the urgent that competes for our attention. That which we hear is the thing shouting in our ear the loudest. The still small voice of God, however, doesn't shout over the crowd; instead, God speaks loudly through silence and contemplation, for it is a whisper arising from within.

How did Jesus know what to say, how to say it, when to say it, where to say it, and to whom? Did he possess a divine instruction manual that fell into his lap from heaven? Of course not. Jesus's life moved at the impulse of the Spirit. He was keenly aware of the sacred presence upon him, within him, and flowing out through him, so much so that it influenced every aspect of his life. He sensed opportunities to speak up. He sensed when others were down and in need of encouragement or instruction. He was emboldened to speak truth without fear. He courageously endured crucifixion at the hands of a dominant power system that saw his presence as a threat. He even forgave his executioners. How does one do that other than through a close communion and awareness of the divine presence within?

Jesus spent time alone in prayer, often on a mountain or in the wilderness. He was listening, not speaking—being still on the inside. He was reducing the internal noise level for the sole purpose of hearing the whisper of God. This is what we call contemplation. It was moments like these that kept him sharp, sensitive, and aware of the divine spark within. It was times like these that allowed every moment of his life to become sacred. It allowed him to see the image of God in others—valued in their own right. It allowed him to see beyond the cultural boundaries that prevented others from experiencing God. It allowed him to see beyond human sight.

How do we experience God? The sacred voice comes to us in diverse ways, for the wind blows where it may. Yet we rarely notice it apart from internal awareness. The danger of the contemporary world is that we get caught up in hamster-wheel living, chasing after all of the goods this world convinces us that we can't live without. Life is busy, hectic, and often confusing. How can we hear the voice of God when so much noise is competing for our attention?

It is difficult to quiet the heart, still the soul, and be present with the sacred voice. The interruptions of life and the busyness of my own mind make for a constant struggle, for I am a doer, not a sitter, and yet the moments when I experience God in my life are the moments when I am most aware of the sacred presence within me. I maintain my unique song and dance, but I am learning to quiet my soul and listen attentively. Experiencing God is being aware of the Spirit within me and finding ways to quiet myself and listen internally for the sacred whisper.

Radical Amazement

Another way I attempt to increase my present awareness is to live in radical amazement. Each moment is a gift, and I don't want to take anything for granted. I seek to live with awe and wonder at my surroundings. Everything is stunning. Every person I meet is the reflected image of God. My every encounter tells me that I am alive and God is in me. As life progresses, we can become jaded, sarcastic, and bitter, but I never want to stop living with spiritual amazement at the life that is given to me, around me, and within me. The joy and amazement I seek are found right where I am. With every step I travel in this uncertain and insecure land, the very heartbeat of God is with me.

I don't want to sound too mystical, but the point I am making is an important one. How should we live? We should live with present awareness of the sacred within us and see the world around us with radical amazement. God is everywhere if we will just open our eyes and see. This requires reducing the noisy clutter in our lives and treasuring the present moment.

Living in Integrity

Integrity is most often linked to morality. Don't steal from your employer. Don't murder. Don't cheat, and the like. While living a moral life is a good thing to do, I want to enlarge the concept of integrity beyond being a good member of society. I want to apply integrity to our faith, to ourselves, to justice, to the elephants in the room, to our theology, and to our body, soul, and mind. In other words, I want to apply integrity to all of life, not just moral behavior.

For instance, do we apply integrity to our understanding of God? This book seeks to do just that. When it comes to intellectual honesty and religious beliefs, the church struggles to connect the two, and its credibility is severely damaged. Millions exercise sincere faith in a set of beliefs that no longer rings true. It makes the church look silly, prejudiced, and irrelevant. It isn't intellectually honest.

This book has debunked many of those beliefs in an attempt to advance integrity of faith. Without it, the Christian message is diluted and misunderstood. No longer can we believe the unbelievable and label it as faith. That just won't do in an age of space exploration, scientific discovery, and new data regarding our universe. This book promotes a new direction in our understanding of Scripture,

Jesus, God, and the Christian message. It provides a path for embracing Christianity that is both intellectually defensible and true to Scripture. We are wise to hold our theology loosely and embrace our experiences of God firmly.

Personal Integrity

In addition to integrity of faith, we must also live with integrity regarding ourselves. In other words, it is important to embrace who we are without reserve. This integrity allows us to view ourselves as the blessed image of God. We live in a world that demeans the human body and assaults the human psyche in ways that encourage devaluation. But that is opposite of our actual situation. I rejoice in you and who you are—your God image. I rejoice in me and who I am—my God image. Living in this kind of integrity allows us to love and accept ourselves and others. We are fearfully and wonderfully made. We are partakers of the divine nature, possess the very life of God within us, and reflect God as the source of life, love, and being.

When we grasp our human identity, we are free to be loving to ourselves and others. Striving for perfection no longer drives us, and comparing ourselves to others is a worthless activity, for we are already loved and accepted, and we all carry the same status as image bearers. Too often, we put ourselves down as unworthy, flawed individuals. We don't like our nose, our ankles aren't skinny enough, we don't like the way we have aged, you name it—we want to be different than what we are, and we demand that others be different, too. That isn't living with integrity; that is embracing a false standard promoted by the media—that we are "less-than" people, always lacking something.

Instead, accept yourself. Accept your abilities, your giftedness, your body, and see it as it is, the image of God. There is nothing you must do to earn God's love, to be in God's presence, or to attain a status that you don't already possess. You have it all. Embrace it. Can you imagine what this kind of integrity would do for our lives? It would allow us to be true to ourselves. Those with same-sex orientations could live with internal consistency and be true to themselves. That takes courage and honesty. Those who are looked down upon in society will embrace the intrinsic value that is rightfully theirs and realize they are not defined by what they do, how they look, what they possess, or by any other false standard utilized to separate people into categories. Love yourself. See yourself with radical amazement. Be true to yourself. Be kind to yourself. Live with personal integrity in all aspects of your life. Don't let others define your world, for when they do, they will always make it too small.

It didn't take me long in ministry before I ran into trouble with who I was and what others wanted me to be. I enjoyed my serving role, but there was always a group within the church that I could never please. I didn't do enough here, I overdid it there, and I could do nothing right. I was nitpicked until I was bloodied and bowed. Life was becoming miserable. I had the wrong gifts, the wrong personality, the wrong sermon, and I could never measure up to the unrealistic expectations of those who wanted to control my life and define who I was. It was affecting my health, and I didn't want my children to grow up seeing the nasty side of church life, for it would destroy their own faith and damage the credibility of God.

So I made a decision. I decided to live with personal integrity with regard to myself. I wasn't any good at trying to be someone else, and I was tired of trying to measure up to someone else's impossible standard—a standard they would never apply to themselves. No, I was done trying to please people. I was done living on the hamster wheel of someone else's expectation. Instead, I chose to honor the life of God within me by being true to myself, wherever that led me in ministry or in life. I embraced me, and decided to let the chips fall where they may. This was the result not of a rebellious attitude but of a humble recognition that I was to simply be the way I was made to be.

I can't tell you how freeing this was. I wasn't perfect by any stretch of the imagination and had a great deal to learn about myself, life, and a whole lot of other things, but I would at least be true to myself as a way to honor God as the source of my being. This decision cost me my pastorate, because I couldn't please the right people all of the time. So be it. As difficult as it was, it was the best thing that ever happened to me. Sometimes being true to yourself is costly, but it is always essential, for it honors the life and image of God within you. These days, embracing me is not nearly so difficult. I have had years of practice, and it all goes back to the day I made a decision to live with personal integrity regarding my own image of God.

Elephant Integrity

My life is not perfect, and I have made my share of bonehead blunders, but my heart seeks to live with honesty when it comes to elephants in the room. I call it elephant integrity—the ability and willingness to point out the issues everyone recognizes but no one is willing to address. While having lunch with a pastor friend of mine, he noted the thousands of dollars his church had spent on things that didn't make sense, all because no one was willing to address the elephant in the room. As is often the case, churches are heavily influenced by those with the loudest voice, with the most money, with longevity and heritage, or with antagonistic tendencies. They hold the church hostage, yet no one holds them accountable for their behavior. They are elephants that suppress integrity, and no one calls them out on it.

I refuse to play the game. Never have and never will. Instead, I am willing to identify the elephants in the room. Everyone knows they are there, and no one buys into the outcome, because elephant decisions are not based in integrity. Living with integrity entails a willingness to surface that which prevents honesty so that issues can be dealt with squarely and openly.

My point in all of this is to encourage us to live with personal integrity. Integrity isn't limited to morality but relates to every aspect of our life. Integrity touches our head, our heart, and our soul. We live with integrity in our relationship with others, in our theology, in our work, and with ourselves. We are not perfect, and we often become blind to the elephants in our own lives, while quickly pointing out the faults in others. The greater our personal integrity, the freer we are to embrace our own God image. By living with personal honesty, we move toward wholeness. How should we live? Live in integrity.

Living in Courage

Many times throughout this book, I have stated that life is uncertain and insecure. Who wants to hear that nugget of truth? As self-consciousness dawned upon humanity, we began asking all of the who, what, when, where, and why questions of life. Living in a vast universe without answers and without control exacerbates fear and anxiety. At the heart of self-consciousness is insecurity. That's why we imagined a great big God in the sky who takes care of us and provides the certainty we long for. We desire control, but in reality, we have no control over life, our health, our longevity, or much of anything. We are but a speck of dust in a vast universe that we don't comprehend. Life is insecure and uncertain, and that's just the way it is.

It takes courage to live in the midst of such uncertainty, but that is what faith is all about. Living for God isn't about believing the right things or doing religious things in the right way. Rather, it is about moving forward, becoming, changing, and growing in the midst of insecurity and uncertainty. The only thing we can hold on to is our own personal God experiences. We can't explain God, capture God, or control God, but we can experience the divine within us during our short journey upon this planet. It is this connection to the unseen world of spirit that makes us realize we are a part of something more—something bigger and grander than ourselves.

I have accepted the ambiguities of life and my inability to arrive at certainty. I have accepted my lack of control and my inability to provide the answers that I seek. There is nothing I can do about that. How do I live in light of such uncertainty? I move forward with courage and trust in the self-communication of God to me personally. It is my personal God encounters that allow me to sense the source of life, love, and being within me. That must be what my life is about—not getting somewhere, not amassing a hoard of materialistic wealth, not trying to measure up to others, or earning salvation, but living out the life of God within me and connecting with the sacred presence within.

Though I am unable to speak of God in absolutes, I have experienced moments where the unmistakable presence of God flows through me—now, in this world, in the present moment. It is these experiences that alert my soul to the world of spirit and the divine presence housed within. I stopped trying to figure it all out; instead, I float upon the waters of courage, aware of the sacred presence flowing in and out of me.

Chapter Summary

This chapter encouraged us to live *in* God instead of living *for* God. We honor God as the source of life when we live life fully. Loving extravagantly is another way of honoring God, the source of love. We also honor God as the very source of our existence when we seek to be our best selves. Simply put, I encouraged us to live fully, love extravagantly, and be our best selves. It isn't some highfalutin theological talk, and it certainly doesn't sound very spiritual, and yet it is the best way I know to allow the life and presence of God to flow in me, through me, and out to others. Acknowledging the sacred presence within us is a simple way to live life.

I also encouraged us to live in the example of Jesus and care about the things he cared about. That includes valuing others and going beyond the boundaries that divide us. Living in justice is another principle worthy of our attention as we uplift every human as equal in value and worth. It means that we treat others with dignity and pursue this value in all that we do. I also encouraged us to live in the present moment and become aware of the life of God within us.

Living life with integrity is another guiding principle that allows us to pursue intellectual honesty in our faith, in ourselves, and in others. Without integrity, life becomes nothing more than self-serving strategic navigation. Instead, we seek to be true to ourselves, which bestows upon us the freedom to live with integrity.

Finally, I invited us to live with courage in an insecure and uncertain world—to focus on the self-communication of God within ourselves. It is in those personal God encounters that we feel alive, real, and connected to something greater than ourselves. Go and live, love, and be.

Since explanations of the past have been firmly ingrained into our religious psyche, how do we get from where we are to where we want to be? How can we overcome the obstacles that hold us back from boarding a new train? The next chapter provides insight into making this faith transition.

19

GETTING FROM HERE TO THERE

• • • • • • • •

W E HAVE NOW COME TO THE POINT WHERE DECISIONS must be made. What will you do with this information? Which train will you board? Some, I imagine, will cast this book aside as heresy and double-down on defending the faith from the likes of my kind. Others will chew on it for a while and think things over. There is much to consider, and this book will have upended their religious equilibrium and brought discomfort to the certainty they once possessed. Others will gladly jump on board, shouting, "It's about time! I have been seeking a way to connect my faith with the integrity it requires."

I can't do much about the first group, for no amount of information or reasoning will budge them from their entrenchment. They are encased in concrete, and a power greater than my words will have to open their eyes. I understand the second group, for I was once in their camp. I chewed on things, processed new information, and gave myself some space to think. These folks won't board a new train until it makes sense to them. Think away my friends. I encourage it. The third group is ready to jump on the bandwagon and feel like liberated prisoners who see the light of freedom for the first time. They sense hope for the church and can finally approach faith with integrity. Welcome home, sisters and brothers!

There is another category of individuals who understand the contents of this book, have been processing things throughout their reading, agree with much of it, but struggle to make the leap from one train to another. They want to jump and know they should, but they don't know how to get from here to there. These are my fundamentalist and evangelical sisters and brothers who love the Lord deeply and experience great tension between what they have been taught and the information now before them. Guilt, fear, disappointment, and betrayal overwhelm them.

Switching trains at this juncture in life is scary and takes a lot of backbone. I hope this chapter brings you the courage and comfort needed to see with fresh eyes. Once the new train is boarded, you will sense a great deal of freedom and relief, and God will become more real to you than ever before. It is like learning to ride a bicycle. Fear is present in the early stages as the training wheels come off, and you may even fall down and scrape your knee on occasion, but the joy of riding all over town is thrilling. It is time for you to experience the adventure of riding a new spiritual bike.

Head, Heart, and Spirit

In my own journey toward integrity, I had to deal with issues surrounding the head, heart, and soul. In other words, I had intellectual, spiritual, and emotional baggage to sift through. I suspect you may be in a similar situation, and these issues must be addressed if you are ever going to make a move. Why jump trains in the first place? After all, if you are content with your situation after reading a book like this, then you aren't ready to consider new alternatives. I couldn't do that; I couldn't sit back and accept a past faith riddled with inconsistencies and intellectual pitfalls that no thinking person could rightly accept. I couldn't sit back and accept explanations that directly opposed the knowledge we now possess about our world. I couldn't sit back and accept a story simply for the emotional comfort it provided when I knew deep inside that it couldn't be true. I had decisions to make that involved my emotions, my spirit, and my mind. Of the three, the emotional element was the most difficult.

From an intellectual standpoint, was I going to follow evidence, scientific data, reason, and common sense, or would I stubbornly ignore or refuse such data in order to maintain my comfortable worldview? What would I do with the overwhelming evidence presented to me? Would I continue believing the unbelievable, or would I alter my perspective in light of the evidence? I had a decision to make, and I wanted to come to my conclusion with intellectual honesty.

From a spiritual standpoint, I knew that my God encounters were genuine and that I could never let go of the sacred presence in my life, but was I willing to let go of the explanations and interpretations of those experiences that I had been taught throughout the years? I didn't know there was another way of telling the Christ story. It dawned on me that I was not being asked to give up God, only outdated explanations that had lost credibility in light of the many discoveries of new knowledge. What was I interested in preserving, God or my explanation of God? These are two very different things. Could I preserve my God experiences while at the same time arriving at new expressions of faith? I had a decision to make, and I wanted to come to my conclusion with spiritual integrity.

From an emotional standpoint, the journey was a bit rocky, especially after being so heavily trained in the evangelical way of sharing the Christian message. I had mastered the old story, become familiar with its symbols, practices, and interpretations, and invested my life in such a view. After devoting so much time, energy, and resources into one way of thinking, jumping trains meant giving up my comfortable security blanket and packing up the certainty I had acquired. It meant that I would be hiking in unfamiliar territory. Was I willing to overcome my fear and emotional discomfort to journey into new regions of faith and see God in new ways? Would this be a betrayal of God or a journey into God? I had a decision to make, and I wanted to come to my conclusion with emotional integrity. If I wasn't honest about my faith from an intellectual, spiritual, and emotional perspective, then I couldn't be honest about much of anything in life. I was determined to approach my faith with the integrity it deserved. Are you?

Change is all about transition.[19] Implementing change is the easy part; making the transition is much more difficult. If your employer decides to switch from PCs to Macs, the company only has to purchase and replace the computers. Presto, the change has been made. But that isn't the real issue, is it? The problem with change isn't so much the change itself but the transition in one's mind. Familiarity with PCs and the routines associated with them was comforting and well-known. Changing to Mac computers meant that all of that would be upended, and the familiarity and comfort employees once relied upon would now be up for grabs. They would be thrust into the wilderness of discomfort and uncertainty. The transition from PCs to Macs would not be complete until employees feel just as comfortable with their new system as the previous one. Change is all about the transition.

If you move from New York to California, all you have to do is pack up your things, shove them in a truck, make the drive to your new residence, and voilà, you are there. The change has been made. End of story, right? Hardly! It will take time before you actually make the transition. Until you find new friends, a family doctor, a new church that feels comfortable and become familiar with your new city, the change won't feel like home. The transition is successfully made when California feels like home, just like New York felt like home. Until that time, we walk in the wilderness of adjustment, struggling to get back to the comfort of the familiar. This chapter is designed to help you make both the change and the transition. Let's begin with the emotional aspect of the transition, move on to spiritual considerations, and finish up with the intellectual element.

Dealing With the Heart

Christianity is an emotion-filled religion, and I say that respectfully. It is a good thing, for our beliefs and experiences powerfully move us and shape us toward action and transformation. We feel deeply about the role of God in our lives. I can describe numerous occasions where my heart was moved by a sacred stirring from within. Those times are memorable and become one way I relate to the divine presence in my life. I don't ever want to lose that kind of personal and meaningful communion. The danger is to think of Christianity as some cold, philosophical exercise in abstract thinking that doesn't connect with our hearts. The last thing I want to do is remove God from personal experience, for I cannot deny the deep stirrings in my life.

Would thinking of God in new ways undermine my deep heart connection to God's sacred presence? As I began to seriously explore new ways of seeing, I realized that I was not being asked to give up my personal experiences; instead, I was being asked to embrace them as the authentic moving of God in my life, something I was already doing. The issue wasn't doing away with my personal God experiences but rather choosing to articulate those experiences in a more authentic, relevant way.

Betrayal and Judgment

The biggest conflict train jumpers encounter is the feeling of betrayal—disappointing God and others. Jumping trains isn't as simple as deciding whether or not you want hot or cold cereal for breakfast; this decision feels weighty and comes with perceived consequences, one of which is feeling as if you just betrayed God, walked away from your faith, and are now the one lost sheep the Lord is calling back home. Who wants to wander away from the shepherd? But is that really what we are doing, or is that an emotional guilt trip laid upon us by our religious upbringing?

Our traditional understandings have been so deeply ingrained in us over the years that even thinking about other ways of articulating God puts the fear of judgment in our bones. God will be angry with us and we will face severe punishment. We had better walk the straight and narrow plank, or we may jeopardize our entrance into heaven. Who wants to risk that kind of outcome? But this is merely riding the coattails of a failed theology, a religious way of keeping us from questioning, thinking, and moving away from nonsensical beliefs. Christianity becomes a religion based on the controlling power of fear. Have you ever thought about what this says about the God you believe in?

Think of it—for years we were raised in the traditional doctrines of the church. We participated in church Christmas plays, celebrated numerous Easter services, attended a host of Bible studies, and learned what our parents had learned—the blessed once-for-all faith delivered to the saints. How we thought of God became one way we identified ourselves as believers. How can we walk away from that without feeling like we have abandoned the faith, betrayed God, and will face stern judgment for our rebellious actions? It goes to show just how deep the inroads of past explanations run in our lives.

I understand this sense of guilt, for I experienced it myself, and yet I didn't allow it to overtake my internal obligation to discern and pursue truth. I would not give in to fear, religious or otherwise. A vindictive, punishing, judgmental, fear-mongering God who resorted to threats of severe punishment for questioning, thinking, and pondering the sacred presence in my life was not a God worth following. What did this say about the church, that it promoted a doctrine of divine punishment for considering the reality of God in new ways? I wasn't denying God but merely questioning why I was locked into believing past doctrines built upon limited knowledge and an antiquated understanding of the world. How is God threatened by that?

Emotions are wonderfully powerful motivators in life, but they are not always dependable. They must always be checked against our ability to think and our ability to experience God. Our emotions are subject to internal processing—the checks and balances of our intellect and spirit. While emotions are real and experienced deeply, they are not the best adjudicator of truth. They are merely one source of information to be checked against other sources of information. That may sound far too mechanical for some, but how many times have our feelings prompted emotional outbursts or withdrawals that we later regretted? I felt it would be much more appropriate to validate my feelings while at the same time assessing them for their accuracy. We must do the same thing with our feelings of betrayal and our fear of judgment. These are true emotions, but are they legitimate when balanced by our intellect and our spirit?

Where does our fear of disappointing God or being punished by God come from? Is God the originator of those emotions? Is God the one making us feel bad about ourselves, dumping a heavy load of shame and guilt upon our shoulders, and instilling in us the fear of divine punishment that risks our salvation? If you believe in a God who acts like that, I respectfully ask you to consider whether that kind of a God is worth serving, believing, trusting, and following. That is the very God we are trying to get away from: a punishing, vindictive, trigger-happy God who keeps score and is ready and willing to hurl lightning bolts from heaven to zap those who disappoint, disobey, question, think, or challenge traditional church teaching. How dare you engage your mind, listen to your spirit, and view God in some non-approved way! Heaven forbid we continue holding on to that understanding of God. It is no wonder most evangelicals and fundamentalists struggle to embrace new concepts. I should know; I was one of them.

And you are feeling guilty for walking away from that? Seriously! Check your fear, guilt, and shame at the door. It doesn't come from God, who imparts joy, life, and love. Those feelings arise from the guilt-driven, self-serving interest of the church that has set itself up as the self-proclaimed controller of all things God.

Have you ever thought about who benefits from such a view? The church does, for it has profited from a vindictive, punishing God for centuries. The church declared itself to be the only place where the Bible could properly be deciphered, forgiveness could be dispensed, and rules and regulations governing proper living could be decreed. The institutionalized church was the bastion of religious edicts that were nothing more than power grabs in the quest to control others. This pursuit of power is so far removed from the example of Jesus as to be laughable, and yet, over and over again, we succumb to its abusive power over us. We have bought into a God who is vindictive and punishing to the point where we feel guilty for the slightest use of our God-given senses.

A new understanding of God—a more biblical way of articulating the divine— isn't a recipe for free-for-all living but a reclamation of a view of God that even Jesus embraced. I take to heart the words placed upon his lips in Matthew 11:28– 30 (NRSV): "Come to me, all you that are weary and are carrying heavy burdens, and I will give you rest. Take my yoke upon you, and learn from me; for I am gentle and humble in heart, and you will find rest for your souls. For my yoke is easy, and my burden is light." Combined with John 10:10 (NRSV), "I came that they may have life, and have it abundantly," we see a very different picture of the God whom Jesus followed.

Emotional Hijacking

Would I allow emotional baggage to hijack my ability to deal with reality? Would I allow emotional baggage to cast aside the weight of scientific evidence and good old-fashioned common sense? Would I allow the false fear of a vindictive, punishing deity to keep me from moving forward in my faith? Would I allow the emotional turmoil within me to dictate my life without the checks and balances of my intellect and spirit? My emotional attachment to the past kept me from living in the present. It became my religious pacifier that I was unwilling to surrender. It was my grungy church blanket that I dragged around as a source of comfort. Would I constrain God to the pacifier and the blanket, or was it time for me to move beyond these emotional constraints? I do not say these words lightly, for I wrestled with my emotional connection to the past just as you are. I know what it feels like to let go of treasured ways of thinking that bring comfort and meaning to your faith.

I personally understand the courage it takes to move beyond such emotions and embrace a view of God that actually fits with reality. I can tell you with sincerity that once you make the transition, you will experience a freedom of faith you never dreamed possible. Like a new set of eyeglasses that bring sharpness of vision, you will never desire a return to the old ways of thinking. How could you, now that you know what you know? Now is the time to assess your emotions, fears, guilt, and shame and put them in their place. Acknowledge the emotions you are feeling, but do not allow them to control the decision you must make.

What good comes from adhering to an understanding of God that is in direct opposition to current knowledge and is no longer relevant and believable? How does that provide comfort to us? It is rather odd that we feel shame for relinquishing antiquated beliefs of the past, but we feel no shame in actually believing them even though we know they are not true. The emotional struggle we go through is not uncommon or unexpected. The question is whether or not we will deal with them head on, assess them in light of other information, and check and balance them against our intellect and our spirit. If not, we will be held hostage to the comfort of our religious pacifier, even though we have outgrown it. We will continue to live life in fear of the divine deity we serve. The fact that you are reading this book tells me that you may now be ready to give up your emotional baggage. Are you courageous enough to live with integrity and let go of the controlling influence of misplaced feelings?

Believe me, I wrestled with the very same thing. As much as I loved past explanations that held precious memories, I exposed my emotions to the light of other information, such as my intellect, my spirit, my observations, and my intuition. What would win out? In good conscience, I couldn't allow my emotions to rule the day. I acknowledged them, understood why they were rebelling, and then told them to quiet down, for my faith journey was taking me in a new direction. My emotions would be the caboose, not the engine at the front of the train.

Since that decision was made, I have not looked back. Not one regret! I have embraced a truer, more biblical understanding of God that has led me to greater joy, freedom, and an articulation of faith that is reasonable and relevant in light of the knowledge we now possess. I still drink from the river of my God experiences, but now I appreciate them more, stay a little longer, hold them closer to my chest, and see God's presence everywhere, even within me. I originally thought that by letting go I was losing something, until I realized that letting go was God's way of moving me into deeper waters. I gave up what I had outgrown only to gain new breathtaking views of God that I could never have imagined. By letting go, I experienced internal transformation, and that is what Christianity is all about. My God is no longer a vindictive, punishing deity in the sky but the same sacred presence Jesus himself experienced. The same Spirit that pulsated through Jesus was now flowing through me, and I was becoming more and more aware of it each day.

Disavowing the Past?

Sometimes train jumpers want to run from their past like a dog seeks shelter from an abusive master, but living in a sterile bubble to prevent contamination isn't the answer, let alone feasible. In fact, the church has not reached the point where new symbols, rituals, hymns, liturgy, and instruction have been firmly established. In other words, we live in a period of transition, beyond where the church currently resides but not yet where it will be. I am not asking us to decontaminate ourselves but to see God in a new way. This means we must unlearn certain things, but there is no reason to hide from past expressions of faith. Instead, we now understand them for what they were—articulations based on the limited knowledge and worldviews of a different age that are no longer credible.

Does jumping trains mean we disavow all elements of the past? Of course not. The problem is that there are not many churches that allow for these broader theological outlooks, and the ones that do are often so knee-deep in identity politics and social agendas as to be distasteful. I suspect, however, that over time, your spirit will ache for a form of worship where you won't have to constantly make mental adjustments with the language, doctrine, and expression of faith found in most traditional churches.

I understand this dilemma and have experienced this tension myself. If I am in a church with traditional articulations of faith, I participate in the symbols, rituals, songs, and various elements of the service, but I understand the meaning behind them in a different light. I still recite the creeds, but I do so with new insight that no longer considers them to be literal renditions of truth. Instead, I see them as the expressions of faith that our forefathers articulated in a different age with limited knowledge. I participate in their attempt to articulate their genuine God experiences without accepting a literal understanding of the expression.

The same could be said of the great hymns of old. I don't cast them aside as radioactive contaminates. I was raised on the hymns and love their familiar tunes. In fact, they touch my soul deeply and stir my emotions. I don't agree with all of the lyrics, the doctrines set forth, or the portrayal of God, but I understand that people were trying to express their devotion within the knowledge they possessed at the time. I can respect their genuine God experience without agreeing with the elements of their expression.

I am not asking you to live in a basement behind closed doors in fear of contamination. There is no need to look down upon those who express God in ways that do not align with the present age. I don't believe their expression of faith will survive into the future, but I don't cast aspersions upon those who hold such views. Their God experiences are real, just as mine are, but they articulate their experience in ways that no longer ring true.

I prefer to expose my faith to intellectual honesty and choose to ride a different train. It gets old having to worship in churches that are stuck in the past. If you find a church that allows and promotes new perspectives of God, be grateful, for you have found a jewel. Don't cling to your emotional struggle so tightly that you can't move beyond it when you know deep down it is the right thing to do. Appreciate past expressions of faith for what they were, articulations of God from a different age to which you were emotionally connected, but don't let this stop you from making the necessary transition to new understandings. Don't allow the past to dictate your transformation of today.

Need for Certainty

From an emotional perspective, I felt good about the certainty I had obtained regarding my faith. I knew the doctrines, had my story down, and could explain it clearly to others in need of such clarity. I was proud to have mastered the old articulations of God. Little did I know that my certainty was nothing more than a time-bound, culture-bound explanation of God that offered little more than emotional comfort. I didn't realize there was a difference between my genuine God experiences and the framework in which I described those experiences. Our God experiences are genuine, while our explanations change with the passing of time and the increase of knowledge.

I entered into faith through the doorway of evangelicalism and learned to articulate God in its terms. Had I spoken of God as a divine mystery, a sacred presence, or the ground of being, I would have been speaking a foreign language, and more than likely would have been corrected or excoriated, for God was a supernatural being sitting on a throne in heaven. The proper way to address this deity was as a male father. Each denomination teaches its own expression of God in terms that are dear to it. The lingo I had come to know was now comfortably embedded in my psyche and provided a level of certainty that I had down pat. I had learned to function well in the religious world of institutionalized evangelical land. Was I now to give that up?

While my emotions were connected to familiar words, phrases, and ways of expressing my love for God, I began to see that I had placed my certainty in a familiar religious system with a familiar God language. Had I grown up in another system, another denomination, my emotional certainty would have been attached to that particular God language. I had to assess my loyalties. Was the comfort of my certainty based upon the evangelical expression of faith, or did my comfort lay in the God behind the system? These are two different things.

The emotional certainty gathered about me was connected to the lingo, phrases, terms, systems, processes, practices, rituals, and doctrines that I had grown up with, was familiar with, and had mastered. My emotional certainty was misplaced, for I had elevated the expression of one particular system that was comforting to me. I had to make a distinction between exactly what I was certain about, and once I understood the distinction between the authenticity of my God experiences and how I chose to express those experiences, the answer was obvious. I decided to place my comfort in the reality *behind* the system rather than in the system itself.

Do you see the subtle distinction? When I realized what it was that I was emotionally clinging to, it helped me to move forward. I don't think negatively of my old comfort system, for it was useful at the time. It simply doesn't have enough staying power to see me through the rest of my journey. All expressions of faith are merely time-bound, culture-bound articulations arising within a specific worldview, knowledge base, and theological understanding. The traditional articulation of the past will not survive into the future because it cannot be grounded to the reservoir of knowledge housed by the modern world.

Combine this distinction between God and the explanation of God with the realization that the essence of God cannot be captured by human words, and you begin to understand that *all* systems of expression are merely attempts to articulate what cannot be captured by human words. Emotionally, we are holding on to human attempts at defining the undefinable. Our emotions are wrapped around a system of expression and not the substance behind it. I was emotionally invested in the wrong thing. My certainty hung upon the peg of human attempts at describing God. This was totally different than the essence of God. I realized my emotions were locked on to a false sense of security, and this helped me to move beyond the lure of misplaced emotions.

If all expressions of God are merely human attempts to describe the indescribable, am I simply encouraging you to exchange one human system for another? Great catch! In a sense, that is exactly what we are doing—exchanging one time-bound, culture-bound expression of God for another. I am asking you to jump trains so your understanding and expression of God makes sense for the age in which we find ourselves. The expression of the past is no longer credible, because it requires belief in doctrines that have been debunked by current knowledge. It is time to trade in the old paradigm for a new one. Why become attached to an outdated, irrelevant, intellectually indefensible understanding of God? That's like holding on to ancient medical practices when science has given us so much more knowledge to work with.

So where should our security come from? If we live in an insecure and uncertain world, and if God is a mystery beyond our ability to describe and adequately comprehend, then we must see our religious system of choice as nothing more than human attempts to capture our experiences of God. The certainty we long for evades us, for it is nowhere to be found. We have looked in all the usual places and now discover that even our religious system doesn't provide the certitude we seek. This is why I can release my grip on the certainty I thought I once knew. Instead, I live in the joy and authenticity of my experiences of God. That is what I find to be real and genuine. The assurance I cling to is not found in a religious system but in the fact that God is real to me, is in me, and that I am in God. That's it. What more could we ask for? The sacred presence of God is within us. We live, move, and exist in God. That's what I trust in.

Letting Go

It is difficult to let go of that which has comforted us for so long. But when we consider exactly what it was that comforted us in the first place, we realize that it wasn't God but the system surrounding God. On a recent trip to Minnesota, I stayed at a hotel near my old stomping grounds where I attended seminary, worked at a furniture store to help pay my way through graduate school, and later served in academic leadership at a local university. It was a wonderful trip down memory lane, but I wouldn't want to live there anymore and do it all over again. I value the role it played in my life, but I have moved on and let go of the past.

There is nothing wrong with remembering the past and what it meant to us, but as we begin to see things with new eyes, we could never return to live in the old neighborhood. It has changed, and we have changed. Although we value the role it played in our life at the time, we have progressed, let go, and moved on. It must be emphasized that by letting go, we are not letting go of God; rather, we are letting go of God explanations that no longer hold weight in the present age. Our emotions were misplaced, for we were confusing the reality of God with the ancient explanation of that reality. What would we rather cherish, the explanation or the reality? I kept the reality and let go of the explanation.

Isn't transformation what Christianity is all about—moving from one way of seeing to a more enlightened way of seeing? Jesus illustrated this principle with a grain of wheat that is placed in the ground and changes into a productive plant. By letting go of past explanations that no longer make sense, we release the emotional baggage that holds us back. Rather than focusing on a denominationally approved explanation, we discover and experience afresh the reality of God and focus on the experience itself—the self-communication of God to us.

Are you willing to let go of the fear that prevents you from experiencing newfound freedom? Will you hang on to guilt or release it so you can experience the abundant life of Christ? Will your emotions fuel shame, or will they rejoice in the sacred presence within? Will you let go of a vindictive, punishing God who holds you captive to fear, guilt, and shame, or will you embrace a welcoming, approachable, and loving God? I wrestled with all of these things, and in the end, I waved goodbye to an outdated explanation and said hello to a new perspective—one that articulated the reality of God for a modern world. It took courage, but it has been life-changing. I assessed my emotions, checked them against other sources of information, and realized how misplaced they were. I refused fear and allowed common sense to prevail. I now experience the sacred presence of God in ways that I never dreamed possible.

Dealing with the Spirit

In addition to assessing my jumbled emotions, I examined the deep part of my humanity that related to the spiritual side of the equation. With my feelings in check, I could now consider the reality of God in my life and how I experienced that reality. People are profoundly touched and marked to the core by the moving of the Spirit. On numerous occasions, I have sensed God's sacred presence upon me, within me, and going forth from me. These experiences mean something to me, for they are treasured moments when I peer behind the curtain separating this world from the world of spirit.

Throughout this book, I have encouraged us to experience God rather than waste time on arguing about God. Our lives are made up of head, heart, and spirit—intellect, emotion, and soul—and all three are engaged in our God experiences. Some have labeled our God experiences as emotionalism and chasing one mountain-top experience after another, like a spiritual junkie in need of another fix. That is not at all what I am referring to.

When we experience God, our whole self is in play. New insight can stimulate the mind to greater heights of awe and wonder. When compassion pours forth, our emotions are stirred like the churning of the ocean. In moments when our God experiences touch our whole being, we sense the life of God flowing in us and through us. These cherished moments are genuine encounters where our spirit connects with the world of spirit.

Writing this book has been a spiritual experience for me that involved my entire being. My intellect was moved as I pondered profound truth and sifted through new insights. My emotions were deeply touched as I wept with joy and at other times danced across the room at the truths discovered and the freedom they brought to me. Let me assure you, that was not a pretty scene, but it was the spontaneous expression of a happy heart. Had I known such things earlier in my life, I could have bypassed many of the potholes and road construction in my life. In all of it, my spirit was quickened with a divine comradery. It has been an experience of the mind, the heart, and the spirit, but it has been more than that; it has been an experience of God where the curtain to the world of spirit was pulled back.

Experiencing God isn't a matter of prospecting for the Spirit like some wide-eyed miner during the gold rush. Because the life, love, and presence of God are already within us, the issue is one of recognition, awareness, and sensitivity—not possession. Like a dog that can't focus for all the squirrels, rabbits, birds, and rustling leaves before it, our attention is easily captured by the noise of the physical world rather than the unseen and soft-spoken world of spirit. It is when we become internally quiet that God becomes loud. It is when we open up an attentive spirit that we hear the divine voice within. Our God experiences are moments of spiritual awareness.

Focusing on our God experiences is a move toward greater awareness, greater sensitivity, and recognition of the divine within us. Who could disagree with that? How we explain our experiences is of little consequence, for they are merely time-bound, culture-bound words, whereas our experience of the divine is a timeless connection to the eternal sacred presence of God. This communion with God is the core of our Christian faith. Everything else is merely attempts at explanation. How do we move from where we are to where we want to go? We focus on becoming more aware of the sacred presence within. That is a step I have enjoyed taking, for now I see the presence of God everywhere. I still have a long way to go, but my internal gaze has refocused on the life, love, and being of God within me. You will be surprised at how this changes your perspective.

Transformation

Growth plus change equals transformation. We are most open to transformation when our sensitivity to and awareness of the Spirit is heightened. In other words, our God experiences have the power to change us from the inside out. When we live with spiritual awareness and sensitivity, the Spirit is allowed to shine forth, and we see the world with new eyes. Imagine, the same Spirit that Jesus was plugged into is the same Spirit that flows through us. They aren't two different Spirits. Jesus was just more in tune with the divine than we are. The same Spirit that stirred him to compassion, led him to value others as being in the image of God, and moved him to serve with love and humility is the same Spirit that is within us. His spiritual sensitivity was the defining mark of his life that caused others to declare his divinity. They recognized the sacred presence upon him, within him, and flowing out from him. It was life-transforming.

We all face battles when trying to increase our sensitivity to the Spirit. I struggle to quiet my mind, others wrestle to calm their emotions, and still others search for any sign of the spiritual. It's similar to living in a congested inner city with its share of noise pollution, traffic, fast pace, police sirens, and hordes of people and then spending the night at a bed and breakfast in the middle of Iowa farmland. The silence is deafening. The only sounds are one's own thoughts amid the chirping of the summer cicadas.

But even that kind of quiet isn't what I am referring to, for our ability to listen to the voice within can occur anywhere—in a noisy inner city or the serene farmland of Iowa or, in Jesus's case, from the quiet wilderness to the strenuous Garden of Gethsemane to the agonizing crucifixion. The point is to quiet the soul and listen to the voice within, wherever you are. The mystics call this contemplation. Paul calls it praying without ceasing and walking in step with the Spirit. The train I am asking you to board doesn't argue over which denominational dogma is correct; instead, this train seeks greater awareness and sensitivity to the life, love, and being of God within you. These divine experiences become the common language that connects us—that allows us to rise above dogma and see with new eyes. The result is transformation—the process of becoming, growing, learning, and changing.

Moving Beyond Systems

I have encouraged you to move beyond denominational dogma and debates over who is right and who is wrong in their doctrine, statements of belief, and religious practices. In fact, I have portrayed all of that as off the mark and encouraged you to focus on experiencing the life, love, and being of God within you. In that way, you connect with the eternal sacred presence rather than adhering to some doctrinal statement that must be confessed in order to be declared accepted by God. In my opinion, these things are inconsequential to the reality of God. They are merely human concoctions, not the essence of the divine.

As strange as it sounds, these systems can actually prevent us from experiencing the very God they attempt to promote. It happened in Jesus's day, as the religious system became oppressive and heavy-burdened. The Old Testament sacrificial system often upended God. Corruption and greed became so rampant that it caused the prophets to speak up in condemnation.

We grew up in a particular faith system, whether that be Catholic, Episcopalian, Methodist, Baptist, or some other religious expression. We learned to articulate our understanding of God through the language, rituals, practices, and doctrines of the system that enveloped us. The dangerous temptation is to elevate the system over the reality behind it. Since our preferred system of expression has become a significant part of our religious experience, we struggle to let it go and view other traditions as equally valuable. It essence, it becomes another form of tribal identity and another form of idolatry.

I happened to grow up in the Christian and Missionary Alliance system, a solidly evangelical denomination. I attended evangelical schools of higher education, pastored in evangelical churches, and taught in evangelical universities. It was a tradition close to my heart. When I began to see God in new ways, I realized that my new understanding would not be accepted, so I let go and searched for a system where my authentic spiritual self would be welcomed. No denomination is perfect, and I am not sure we even need them, but it is what it is. I have high regard for the Christian and Missionary Alliance and the role it played in my life, but it was time to thank its members, leave with grace, and move on to the next leg of my spiritual journey. God was real to me in that denomination, for God can be found in various systems, but I realized that God was not contained within that denomination. God is bigger and grander than any religious system.

God in a Box

As an all-pervasive sacred presence that permeates the universe, God cannot be put into the box of any one system or denomination. God is not a jack-in-the-box, stuffed inside with the lid tightly closed; instead God is inside the box, outside the box, through the box, beside the box, on top of the box, under the box, and around the box. God transcends all boxes we create as avenues of religious expression. Systems can be helpful, but they do not contain God any more than the Jewish temple could house God. These systems merely serve as a vehicle for articulating God. Unfortunately, our focus is misplaced when we mistake the system for the reality.

Let me illustrate it this way. If I walk down the Magnificent Mile of Michigan Avenue in downtown Chicago, I see the city one way. If I stand atop the observation deck of the John Hancock Center one thousand feet above the ground, I see the city differently. If I fly in a small airplane five thousand feet above Chicago, my view is completely different. If I fly over the city on a commercial airliner at thirty thousand feet, my perspective changes even further. Now imagine the view from the International Space Station, from Mars, from another galaxy, from outside of the universe.

The point is that when we put God in a box, the only perspective we see is our God-in-the-box view. We must move beyond this limited perspective and recognize how confining it really is. We come to faith in a manner that is personally meaningful to us. But it is a street-level view. Over time, we expand our horizon and find ourselves atop the observation deck and notice a host of other evangelical boxes. As long as their box is similar to ours, we are fine—we just didn't know there were so many. We then experience the thrill of flying over our faith at five thousand feet, where we discover a plethora of different God-boxes. We see liberal God-boxes, mainline God-boxes, progressive God-boxes, and fundamentalist God-boxes and realize there are vast differences in how God is articulated. It is frightening and causes us to recoil in defense of our own box as being the right box out of all other Christian boxes. We have experienced our own God-box so deeply that we can't imagine any other box producing such powerful and personal experiences of God.

Later in life, we make our way onto a commercial airliner of faith and view the religious landscape at thirty thousand feet, and we are surprised to see a host of other religious God-boxes across the globe that are dissimilar to our own. We see a Jewish box, a Muslim box, a Hindu box, a Buddhist box, and so forth. We don't know what to make of this, since they look so different from the God-box familiar to us, so we reinforce the protection surrounding our God-box while declaring all others to be evil.

I am encouraging you to see your God-box from a new perspective. God is not limited to our street view, our John Hancock Center view, or any other view. God is inside our God-box and outside of our God-box. In fact, God transcends all boxes. Rather than being limited to one view, God is found at every view and at every level. God isn't contained within the box, but is in the box, through the box, and beyond the box. Seeing God as located within one tradition is far too limiting for a sacred presence that is everywhere. While many want to argue over which box is the best box, we are better off moving beyond boxes and focusing on the sacred presence that permeates all boxes.

Christianity is the box I feel most comfortable with and the one that best articulates for me my experiences of God. Though I sense God within my own view, I realize that God is beyond my box and beyond all boxes. Religion is merely a system that helps us articulate the sacred presence of God. It is scaffolding, not the building itself. When I let go of the Christian and Missionary Alliance denomination, I let go of a narrow perspective, for I was now flying high above it and seeing things from a different altitude. I was progressing and enlarging my faith. I was transforming and becoming more fully human. We progress not by holding on but by letting go—by dying to one way of seeing and embracing a new way of seeing. A narrow one-box perspective is to see the world through a straw. The church of tomorrow won't be looking through a straw; it will see the entire universe and all God-boxes as the playground of the divine.

Value the God-box you were raised in, for it was part of the journey that shaped you. My goal is not to move you from one denomination to another; I am trying to move you beyond denominations—to let go of your God-box as the sole container of God and realize that as an all-pervasive Spirit, God's presence transcends all boxes. People from various faith traditions can experience God just as you do, even though they articulate that experience in different ways, with different language, symbols, rituals, practices, and doctrines. We must ask ourselves what is important, the system or the reality, a specific God-box or the God beyond all boxes?

Don't confuse a religious system with the reality of God. I suspect that when we peel the onion back, we will discover that much of our reticence to let go is due to system loyalty and not the reality of God itself. It is time to jump trains and focus on the experience of God as a transcendent sacred presence that is above all boxes and yet within all boxes. In dealing with spirit issues, I decided to jump trains because my loyalty was to the reality of God in my life, not to a system or denominationally approved God-box. I wanted to experience this reality without the constraints of street-view thinking.

Dealing with the Head

In dealing with emotional obstacles to moving forward, I realized that my emotions were wrongfully placed. The feelings I experienced were real, but the basis for them was not, and I had to be honest about that. In dealing with obstacles of the spirit, I realized that my experiences of God were genuine, but I was substituting my evangelical explanation for the experience itself. I had to be honest about things and separate my experience from my explanation, which was merely a preferred religious God-box—a view that was personally meaningful to me but was not the sole container of God. It was simply a system for expressing my God experiences, and if I didn't separate the system from the reality behind it, I could easily become trapped in the system itself. It was merely the explanation that had become dear to me over the years, but it wasn't the essence of God. It was now time for me to deal with the intellectual obstacles to jumping trains. After all, God gave me a brain; I might as well use it.

Scripture

For me, everything hinged on my view of Scripture, for it was the linchpin that held everything else in place. The Bible, I was taught, was the literal words of God to humankind. As such, they were to be revered, obeyed, and believed without question. If the Bible really is the literal, inerrant, once-for-all words of God to humankind, then that is pretty much the end of the story. It became imperative for me to determine where I stood on this issue, for how I answered the Bible question would have enormous implications on how I perceived God.

I began to inquire, ask questions, read books, learn from others, put two and two together, and get to the bottom of this foundational doctrine. If the Bible wasn't the very words of God, then what exactly was it? Believe me, I wanted to hang on to my old belief, but common sense, reason, and the embarrassment of new data would simply not allow it. I had to take a hard look at the facts and follow the evidence wherever it led me.

It wasn't long before I realized that the rationale for believing Scripture to be the inerrant, literal, once-for-all words of God to humankind was so flimsy as to be propped up by religious declaration and a couple of verses taken out of context. Simply declaring something to be true doesn't make it true, no matter how loudly we shout it, and the biblical support for such a view is virtually nonexistent. As disconcerting as that was, there is more.

The implications of such a view are incredulous. It means that God hates and kills certain people, such as the Egyptians, Amalekites, Amorites, and others. God even kills chosen Jews who disobey. It means that God hates homosexuals and requires their death, not to mention the death of children who disobey their parents. God promotes slavery, demeans women, and requires the death of an innocent man in order to forgive humans. God created hell as the place where sinners receive eternal punishment for temporal sins. It means that all of the biases found in the first century and beyond have been ordained by God. It means that God's message to humans is wrapped up in time-bound and culture-bound words. Since God has already communicated in a once-for-all manner, there is no longer a need for God to speak in the present age, and if God were allowed to speak today, God could say nothing new. Once-for-all means exactly that—once for all time.

It means that the original set of God's written communication is nowhere to be found. For being the very words of God to humankind, there sure is enormous disagreement as to what God is actually trying to communicate. It means that Scripture was written from a Jewish mindset, was birthed in Judaism, but was later overtaken by a Gentile world that knew nothing of Jewish sacred storytelling. The Scriptures began to be literalized when they were never meant to be. For these reasons, and a host of others listed in this book, I had to face the facts. Declaring Scripture to be the inerrant, literal, once-for-all words of God to humankind just couldn't be. Would I be intellectually honest with the data before me, or would I regurgitate the mantra taught to me by the church? Would

I arrive at a reasoned conclusion or feel guilty for even questioning the holy writings? No longer would I be brainwashed by such religious methods of control.

Being intellectually honest with my view of Scripture allowed me to function with integrity regarding other doctrines that relied upon this view of the Bible. For instance, I could no longer interpret the Gospel stories literally. Instead, I saw them in the light of Jewish sacred storytelling, where profound truth was being conveyed, not literal truth. I began to see that the Bible wasn't words *from* God but human words *about* God through the lens of writers utilizing the language, knowledge, and methods of their time.

Scripture was a sacramental doorway that helped me to experience God, not unquestioned literal words that required me to leave my brain at the front door of the church in order to enter the halls of faith. I began to understand that I could still value and respect Scripture even though my view progressed from what I had originally been taught. This took courage and intellectual honesty. If we don't apply intellectual integrity to our faith, then we can believe just about anything. All we have to do is declare it to be the Word of God that must be obeyed without question. I could no longer travel down this path. I would value Scripture for what it was: human words about God written from the experience of my religious forefathers who expressed their understanding in light of the worldview, knowledge, and culture of their day.

Jesus

Once I had my view of Scripture squared away, it was time to consider Jesus, the central figure of our faith. Was he actually God? Was he the once-for-all perfect sacrifice whose blood washed away our sins? What was I to do about Jesus? Again, I examined the data, applied common sense, and obliged myself to embrace intellectual honesty. I discovered a distinction between the historical Jesus who actually walked this planet and the post-Easter Jesus portrayed after his death. Designed to portray him in a favorable light that would advance their cause, the stories about him were written long after his crucifixion. The Gospels weren't penned by eyewitnesses, and we have no writings of Jesus, only what others said he said decades after his death—hearsay.

The stories, I noticed, were seeking to elevate Jesus in the mind of the reader. People sensed something different about Jesus—that the Spirit of God was upon him and flowed through him. Writers sought to explain this spiritual dimension by connecting it to their Jewish Scriptures, something that was familiar to them. The unexpected death of Jesus caught them off guard. How can one possess and demonstrate the sacred presence of God only to be killed by the Romans? This didn't make sense to them, so they looked back into the Jewish Scriptures and cherry-picked specific verses they could apply to Jesus that would lend meaning to his death. They did this with images of a sheep being led to slaughter and making his death to be about sacrifice, an integral component of Jewish worship.

They went further and declared that Jesus was divine, for how could someone live like Jesus did without divinity? Paul insists that divinity was bestowed upon Jesus at his resurrection, when he was spiritually exalted to be with God. Mark, however, confers divinity upon him at his baptism, whereas Matthew and Luke portray him as having been born divine. The last Gospel to be written, John, indicates that Jesus was divine even before his birth. The portrayal of Jesus morphed over time until 325 CE, when he was finally declared to be co-equal in substance with God as the doctrine of the Trinity took shape.

The early followers of Jesus held diverse views of who he was and the meaning of his life. All, however, seemed to be in agreement that the Spirit was upon him and flowed through him and that people were changed by his teaching and ministry. I realized that Isaiah 7:14, the basis for the doctrine of the virgin birth of Jesus, actually says nothing about a virgin birth. Besides, humans are not born without male seed. I realized that the resurrection stories of Jesus were inconsistent and changed over time. Paul saw it as a spiritual exaltation, not a literal, physical resurrection. Jesus's resurrection appearances occur only to those who had faith to see him. In other words, the stories were about having one's eyes opened to the meaning and value of Jesus. He lived on, not physically but spiritually in their lives.

It was the doctrine of the atonement that was most difficult to rescind. The crucifixion of Jesus was all about dying for my sins and saving me from hell so that I could be forgiven and restored to a right relationship with God. This is a central theme of faith, and it was deeply ingrained in me. It was the story that I was told, that I embraced, and that led me to became a Christian in the first place. But was it true? Did it make sense?

Darwin's theory of evolution upended this cherished belief. If human life originated from a common ancestor that evolved over millions of years, then we weren't created in original perfection, which meant that there could be no original fall or original sin, which meant that there was no need for atonement, which meant that we cannot be restored to a status we never possessed in the first place. We are in the process of moving from a less evolved state to a more evolved state, not perfection to imperfection.

The implications of atonement are stunning. It makes God out to be the ulti-mate child-abusing deity who seeks an innocent victim in Jesus to save a wretched and deplorable group of humans. God is vindictive and punishing and requires a bloody sacrifice in order to forgive. What kind of God is that? Jesus isn't a glorious Savior but the victim of an angry God who can't appease a holy sense of justice without killing someone. And what does it say about us humans? We are dirty, wretched, sinful people—so unworthy that we need to accept Jesus as our Savior in order to be right with God. Christians call that the love of God. I call it a warped view of God, Jesus, and humanity.

As you might suspect, my mind was no longer willing to embrace a view that made little sense in light of new information. I now see Jesus as a profound example of what the fullness of humanity can be. He reflects back to us what God is like—the image of God. In the life of Jesus, we see someone who lived in the world of spirit. What matters to Jesus is what matters to God. He could not be both God and man melded into one person at the same time, for to be one precludes the other. His example would be a farce, for that would be cheating and setting an example we could never attain, for we are mere mortals. Instead, Jesus shows us how full humanity can become when the life, love, and being of God is allowed to flow through us.

God didn't see to it that Jesus was executed according to some divine plan. Jesus died because of his message, the risk taken for speaking in terms that offended the power system of his day. Yet even in his death, we see the influence of the Spirit, for who faces death with such grace and inner strength? Instead of believing unbelievable doctrines about Jesus, I wanted to live like Jesus, who saw value in others, broke down barriers that divided us, displayed compassion, pursued the ethic of love, sought peace and justice, and lived life with a Spirit-filled reality. That is the example he provides and the image of God he reflects. I want to be like that! I jumped trains and saw Jesus with new eyes.

God

Like all good evangelicals worth their salt, I saw God as a supernatural being who sat upon a heavenly throne, directing the affairs of the universe. In fact, he was also in charge of my life as well. After all, he knew the number of hairs on my head. For some reason, that must be important to know. That might have been a worthy feat in my younger days, but now I think even I could count them on one hand! God looked a lot like humans, males to be exact, except he was stronger and wiser, knew all things, and was all-powerful. I prayed to this God, beseeching him to heal illnesses, direct every step of my life, and provide items that I needed and wanted, all the while believing that my fervent prayers could move him to act on my behalf. If I obeyed the words of God, I would inherit eternal life and live with God in heaven when I died.

I never thought much about my view of God until I reached the second half of my life, when I had plenty of road miles under my belt. Life will do that to you, make you rethink things, and things were no longer adding up for me. It prompted me to be honest and reexamine my understanding of God.

It dawned on me that God as a supernatural deity in the sky was collapsing under the weight of increased knowledge and the critical analysis of Scripture. God wasn't a male or a father. In fact, God wasn't female either. God transcends gender. God wasn't a being in heaven, for God was an all-encompassing spirit that was everywhere present. God wasn't a great big one of us, but something far beyond that.

If God was in control of everything, why did so much of life seem out of control? Why would God, who had the ability and the power to do good, allow evil in this world from earthquakes, mudslides, cancer, miscarriages, and all sorts of suffering? Why didn't God stop Hitler from exterminating six million Jews? Why does God need to be worshiped for all eternity in heaven? Isn't that overkill and narcissistic? We would never ask that of our own children. Why would God communicate a once-for-all message when God's original letters can't be found? If they were so important, you would think that God could actually preserve the original once-for-all documents. It would have made more sense to wait until the advent of technology when things could have been communicated worldwide and documented as evidence.

Why did God require the death of an innocent man to satisfy a holy sense of justice before mustering up the will to forgive us? How is that just? Did God really set it all up so that one bite of an apple would do all of us in? God established the game and the rules, all the while knowing we would fail. Does that seem right to you? How am I responsible for the actions of Adam and Eve? Why was God so hateful, killing the Egyptians, Amorites, Amalekites, and chosen Jews who disobeyed? Why would God command the killing of homosexuals, disobedient children, and adulterous women and engage in a host of other unthinkable acts?

This supernatural being was becoming nothing more than a slot-machine God. Put in enough coins of praise, push the right buttons, and out pops your answered prayer. If you were really obedient, God's favor would rest upon you, implying that others did not possess God's blessing. This God was a tribal God who led in wartime victories, demanded sacrifices, and hated everything the chosen people hated. He was a God of our own making. I can no longer believe in a God like that. Can you? It is intellectually indefensible.

Instead, I began to see God as a sacred presence that was everywhere present. In fact, God is the ground of all being—not a he, a she, or a supernatural being in the sky acting as the CEO of the universe. Instead, God is an indescribable sacred presence that I experience personally. As Acts 17:28 notes, I live, move, and have my being in this sacred presence. My very being exists because God exists. I am intimately connected to this sacred presence that is outside of me, is within me, and flows forth from me. No more slot-machine God for me. No longer did I have to cajole the grand being in the sky. Instead, I possessed the life, love, and being of God within me. This was eye-opening and changed my entire perspective.

Early in my life, I was captured by an articulation of God grounded in the evangelical persuasion, and it blinded me from seeing a much larger perspective. I had the system down and spoke confidently of this great deity in the sky. I began to see that if God is indescribable, then our attempts to speak of God are merely human attempts at capturing our experiences in human language—an imperfect vehicle of communication fraught with human limitations. The only language I could use to speak of God was the language of metaphor, not absolutes. This is why I speak of God as a sacred presence, and even that is a metaphor, but it helps to remind me that God is experienced, not explained. I had to face the facts and hold myself to intellectual honesty. In doing so, my view of God changed.

Science

As I wrapped my mind around new understandings of Scripture, Jesus, and God, I also had to think through my concerns with science. How much stock was I to put in scientific data, especially when so much of this information rubbed against the grain of traditional Christian teaching? I am not a scientist and in many ways am pretty naïve about all of it, but I do understand some of the implications upon the faith of old. I realize that human conception isn't possible without male seed. I understand that Jesus didn't escape the passing on of a sinful nature simply because a story substituted God as the father, and not a human. We learned that women contribute 50 percent of the DNA to the forming child. Out the window goes that doctrine. Evolution tells us that we are moving from less evolved creatures to more evolved creatures, not perfection to imperfection, as the Bible states. I realize Earth is not six thousand years old but billions of years old, and so forth.

Science has been good for humanity. It has brought about medical cures, understanding of the human body, new findings about our universe, and much more. We are benefactors, and I am thankful for the many contributions of science. It has also brought about a structured way to inquire, gather evidence, and determine whether a theory is correct. I am not threatened by science and its impact upon religion, for if God is unable to withstand such scrutiny, then God is in the wrong business. The discovery of new truth only adds to the richness and beauty of the sacred presence, and we are filled with greater awe and wonder.

My problem was that science itself was changing and evolving. A theory that is labeled scientific truth in one generation may be upended in the next. How could I put stock into something so fluid? But that is the way science is and the way life has to be. New information is always forthcoming, and if we aren't open to it, we become stuck in outdated explanations and old ways of thinking. Isn't that what I am asking you to do—consider new information and change your thinking based on new information?

I wasn't being asked to replace my faith in God with a newfound faith in science. I could never do that, but I could appreciate science for what it was, a tool for discovering new insights about the universe. Certainly, there is nothing wrong with that. We have many tools for discerning information—science, intuition, personal experiences, observation, etc. Science has debunked a supernatural being who lives just beyond the clouds. Does that mean God is a ruse? No, it means that explanations of God based on the worldviews and limited knowledge of the first century and beyond are no longer relevant to the current age. In one way, science keeps God honest and relevant to our time. God is a reality we experience, but outdated explanations lose their appeal, because we know they cannot be true.

Today's Christianity focuses on correct doctrine, but what happens when those traditional doctrines crumble under the weight of new knowledge? Do we hold on to outdated, nonsensical beliefs, or do we maintain our God experiences and change our explanations? I chose the latter. Science is merely a tool for learning more about our world. It is changing and evolving as new information comes to light, but it is not a threat to the sacred presence of God, only to explanations that no longer make sense.

Choices

With honesty, I examined my emotional resistance to new ways of seeing God and discovered that my feelings were wrapped up in the explanation itself and the system that encouraged them—not the reality of my God experience. My emotional loyalty was misplaced. Once I understood this, I was able to move from an explanation to the reality of God. It gave me permission to address my misplaced feelings and transition to a new train.

With honesty, I examined my spirit and discovered that my God experiences were real and that I was transformed from within because of these encounters. Was I clinging to the substance behind those experiences or the avenue by which they came? I saw the distinction between the two and made a conscious choice to pursue the reality behind my experiences rather than dogged insistence upon the form in which they traveled—time-bound and culture-bound explanations. When my spirit recognized the difference between a system of articulation and the essence of God, I was able to make the transition to a new train—one that focused on the reality of my God experiences.

With honesty, I examined the traditional doctrines of Scripture, Jesus, and God and found them wanting, for they didn't square with new information about our universe. How could this be, and what would I do about it? I had to be intellectually honest about things. When old explanations were no longer credible, I chose new explanations that aligned with both Scripture and new knowledge, and in so doing, preserved the reality of God without being strapped to archaic explanations. I wanted to experience the profound truth of God, not feel obligated to a human explanation of that experience. When I realized that old paradigms no longer aligned with reality, I realigned my explanation rather than getting rid of God. This allowed me to make the transition to a new train.

It took time for me to make the full transition to a new train, and I found myself doing it in stages rather than in one fell swoop. I had to process, adjust, think things through, and become comfortable with a new direction. We all have a choice to make. Will we remain on the train that takes us into the past, or will we transition to the train of the future with new understandings of God? I chose the latter and have not regretted it for one moment. I feel a tremendous sense of relief and freedom from the bondage of outdated views, and I am beginning to see the sacred presence of God everywhere and in everyone. I am beginning to live with renewed fervor and with greater love and compassion. I am beginning to experience what it feels like to live, love, and be in Christ.

Transitioning to a new train has helped me take the next step in my own transformative process.

Will you join me? Take my hand and let's ride the rails together. If you decide to remain on your current train, know that I love you and will never judge you for that decision, for I see God within you, whatever train you ride. I am hopeful, however, that we can journey together. To those of you who have left the faith or placed it on the backburner, I invite you to board the train and come home. You no longer have to leave your brain behind. I have reserved a seat for you. Welcome back from the land of exile.

Chapter Summary

This chapter encouraged us to approach issues of the head, heart, and spirit with integrity. The head represents our intellect, and as we consider such key doctrines as Scripture, Jesus, and God, we must do so with honesty and apply the same kind of scrutiny, common sense, reason, and integrity we would employ with any other subject.

Scripture, we discovered, cannot be the inerrant, once-for-all words of God to humankind. Instead of words *from* God, Scripture is human words *about* God, written in the language, culture, knowledge, and worldview of the ancient past. We discovered that Jesus was deeply in sync with the divine presence flowing in and through him, which allowed him to reflect the image of God to us. Jesus shows us what a Spirit-filled humanity could be.

We also discovered that God is not a supernatural heavenly being supervising the affairs of the universe and answering fervent prayers on our behalf. Instead, God is a sacred presence—the ground of all being in which we live, move, and exist. Furthermore, we noted that science is not the enemy of God but a useful tool for understanding the universe. As such, it can never undermine the reality of God, only human explanations that no longer align with contemporary knowledge. Transitioning to a new train is easier when we approach our faith with intellectual honesty.

The heart represents our emotions and is one of the more difficult obstacles to overcome because we are so heavily invested in explanations of the past. We experience intense feelings of fear, shame, and betrayal when considering new perspectives, and while these emotions are deeply felt, they are nothing more than misplaced devotion. By checking our feelings against our intellect and spirit, we realize that they are attached to the religious system we grew up in. In other words, we became emotionally committed to the lingo, rituals, practices, and beliefs of a specific way of explaining God instead of the substance behind the explanation. Instead of loving God, this misplaced devotion loves the avenue by which our God experiences travel. This is a subtle form of idolatry. Transitioning to a new train is easier when we approach our emotional resistance with honesty.

The spirit represents that deep part of our being that communes with the sacred presence of God. Our God experiences are transformative moments when the curtain is pulled back and spiritual insights are revealed. Since the Spirit is already within us, our task is to live with greater awareness and sensitivity to the whisper of God within. A distinction between our genuine God encounters and the various ways we try to explain these encounters must be rendered. Our God experiences are real because they are connected to the eternal Spirit, whereas explanations are time-bound, culture-bound articulations that change with the passing of time and the surge of new knowledge. Transitioning to a new train is easier when we approach our spirit with honesty and distinguish between the reality of our God encounters and the human explanations given to them.

A contemporary faith requires integrity of head, heart, and spirit; otherwise, Christianity becomes a relic of the past. We are not giving up on the essence of God; we are merely casting aside outdated human explanations that no longer align with the knowledge we now possess. I encouraged you to embrace the reality of God, become sensitive to the sacred presence within you, and articulate this reality in a way that makes sense in the present age. The pathway for transitioning to new perspectives involves intellectual, emotional, and spiritual honesty.

Many questions remain, and though this book is unable to address every nuanced implication, the next chapter speaks to many of these questions in an effort to tie up loose ends.

20

Q & A SESSION
· · · · · · · ·

THIS CHAPTER PRESENTS COMMON CONCERNS OFTEN voiced regarding the contents of this book. The list of questions is not exhaustive, and neither are my answers. I certainly don't possess all the answers, and this chapter doesn't come close to raising all of the questions. However, providing short replies is an apt way to conclude the book and tie up loose ends.

Can I claim to be a Christian if I embrace new perspectives of the faith?
Absolutely! I refuse to abdicate my claim to be called "Christian" because the contemporary church is unwilling to be real and honest. Falling back upon primitive positions so divorced from the modern world makes Christianity irrelevant and unrecognizable. In many ways, Christianity has been hijacked by a cultural orthodoxy where propositional statements must be confessed without question.

Our understanding of God morphs over time as new knowledge comes to light. God evolved from a spirit among the wind and the trees to a God outside of the universe, and from one of many gods to a tribal god, then to an elevated tribal god, and on to the one and only God. The understanding of Jesus also evolved over time, as described in this book. The early followers of Jesus held diverse views regarding the meaning and message of his life and death. Despite these diverse perspectives, they all sensed the reality of God, and it is this reality they were trying to capture in human words.

The heart of Christianity isn't assent to religious propositional statements. Instead, it is about connecting to the Christ power, the Spirit that flowed within Jesus—that reality the early followers of Jesus experienced so deeply. This is what Christianity is all about—experiencing the universal Christ that transforms us to become more like Jesus, who exemplifies what a Spirit-filled humanity could be. I am a Christian who desires to live after the manner of Jesus, and I wholeheartedly embrace new perspectives of faith.

Can I still be a Christian and remain a biblical literalist?

Yes, but why would you want to? Why interpret Scripture in a manner that makes little sense, is not sustainable into the future, isn't the original intent of the authors, and has far too many holes in its intellectual bucket to hold any water? There are Christians who interpret the Bible literally and Christians who do not. Both love God and are devoted to their particular understanding of the Christian message, but because of differing interpretive approaches, there is disagreement on what the Christian message is all about.

I have illustrated this dichotomy as two different trains traveling in two different directions to two different destinations. One is indefensible in light of modern knowledge and becomes a return trip into the past. It is a train that moves backward. Metaphorical approaches to Scripture, on the other hand, move us into the future with breathtaking views of God that reveal the original intent of the biblical writers. This book doesn't determine who is a Christian and who isn't, for that is outside of my pay grade. I don't have the requisite skill or knowledge to make such pronouncements, and there are good Christians on each train. Instead, I make a distinction between a message that has been mortally wounded by the sword of increased knowledge and articulation of a faith that aligns with Scripture and modern knowledge and is a faithful understanding of Scripture, Jesus, and God.

How should I interact with those who still embrace the traditional, literal doctrines of faith?

Quite simply, you should extend to them the love, patience, and dignity offered to all humans. Though they ride a different train, possess a very different outlook on life, and interpret Scripture literally, they are still followers of God and worthy of our love and respect, even though we disagree with their articulation of the faith. Arguing with them does no good; in fact, arguing rarely does anyone any good. You don't win others over through arguing, making belittling comments, or attacking individuals personally. That isn't the way of love. We share God's love for all people and to all people, including those with whom we disagree.

Our role isn't to convert others to our way of thinking but to extend love to all while always being ready and willing to provide a reasoned defense for why we see things the way we do. Like plowed ground primed for seed, people have to be ready for new perspectives, and quite often, it is the power of life circumstances that turns an obstinate heart into receptive, fertile soil for receiving the seed of new insight. Some people chew on things for a long time before making a move, while others seem to stumble into new perspectives. Either way, when the student is ready, the teacher appears. Until then, we love with patience, grace, and dignity.

How should we view science, since it often conflicts with Scripture?
Science does, at times, conflict with Scripture—that is, if you interpret the Bible literally. The age of Earth, the origin of humankind, the virgin birth, the divine origin of Scripture, the passing on of a sinful nature through male seed, and the sun revolving around Earth are a few biblical examples. Does this disprove the existence of God? No, it only tells us that literal interpretations of Scripture and human explanations of the past are inaccurate. Articulations of God are always relative to the culture, worldview, knowledge, and circumstances of the age in which they are uttered.

Science isn't the nail in God's coffin. Instead, science thrills the heart, as we stand in greater awe and wonder at the reality of God. Science is a useful tool for understanding our world, even as our articulation of God is always morphing with the increase in human knowledge. I think of science as a wonderful tool for enhancing life, understanding the universe in which we live, and increasing our awe and wonder of God.

Realizing that our understanding and articulation of God change with the passing of time and the increase of knowledge is a good thing, for it keeps God before us in relevant ways, and it keeps our expressions of God intellectually honest. We see the understanding of God and Jesus morphing throughout Scripture. God moves from one deity out of many deities, to becoming a god elevated over other gods, to becoming the only God, to becoming a God for all people. Jesus morphs from being a human to being a God-sent itinerant teacher. As time passes, later writers confer divinity upon him at his resurrection, then earlier at his baptism, and earlier still at his birth, until finally he is declared divine even before his birth. As the doctrine of the Trinity develops centuries after his death, Jesus is declared to be co-equal with God. The reality and essence of God never change, but our explanations are always being refined in response to increased knowledge. Science is often the catalyst that spurs us on to see things differently

What do we place our faith in if not in past articulations of Christianity?
To be honest, I don't place my faith in any doctrine, Christian or otherwise. Christianity is a system for articulating our experience of God. There are various systems of religious expression in the world, and most of them disagree with one another on key items of belief. That's all they are—systems, agreed-upon ways of expressing our experience and understanding of God. I do not, and I will not, place my faith in a man-made system or doctrine, even though I choose to associate and identify myself with one religious expression over another.

Had I placed my faith in the traditional doctrines of Christianity as seen through the eyes of a biblical literalist, my faith would have crumbled long ago under the crushing weight of new knowledge. The result of scientific inquiry has made many of those doctrines obsolete. We function within systems of religious expression, but we do not place our faith in them. They are human constructs, not the divine essence of God.

Instead, I place my faith in the reality of God, as indescribable as God is. I don't understand God, can't get my arms around God, and certainly can't control God, and yet I experience God personally. The sacred presence moves me, shapes me, and marks me on my journey to becoming more fully human—more loving and more like Jesus. Christianity becomes the framework from which I articulate my God experience, but my faith is in the reality of God, not in the explanation of that reality.

How do we participate in today's church when it is so full of traditional symbols, creeds, and literal understandings? Why would we continue to celebrate communion, baptism, Easter, and Christmas?
One option is to find a church that teaches and accepts a broader understanding of the faith. This is difficult when the majority of Christian churches are of the literal sort. Another option is to give up on institutionalized religion altogether and go it alone. This is unappealing for a variety of reasons, one of which is that Christianity encourages community, family, and loving and serving within a dedicated fellowship of faithful followers.

Another option is to attend a less enlightened church while constantly making mental adjustments as we translate metaphorically what others take literally. With this option, we become incognito nonliteralists—camouflaged and closeted. This may be the only option available to some. Others attend in-person traditional congregations that provide the relational network they seek while watching online sermons from more progressive-minded churches. In this way, they touch both worlds. Over time, however, this gets old, as we long for others of like mind.

Let's face it, we are minority Christians in a majority world of faith. Things are changing as more and more churches make the move to broader understandings, but I wouldn't give up my new way of seeing for a return to the majority world. I couldn't do that with integrity. Communion, baptism, Christmas, and Easter are traditional elements within the Christian system, and no one is asking you to give them up, and we shouldn't, but they do take on new meaning with a more enlightened view of Scripture.

Communion, for example, is deeply meaningful to me, but instead of being about the blood of Jesus that saves such an unworthy and wretched person as I from hell, it becomes a method of connecting with the message, meaning, and life of Jesus. Eating bread and drinking wine were commonplace in the Middle East and consumed within a shared meal, not while sitting in a pew with bowed heads. As a way to offer inclusivity, value, and dignity to all, Jesus shared meals with all kinds of people, especially the disenfranchised. Communion reminds me that Christ is the sustaining bread and drink of life, and I renew my commitment to live after the manner of Jesus. Through both life and death, the Spirit flowed through Jesus. The Lord's Supper is one way I commune with God. I sense a deep desire to experience God the way Jesus did so that I can enter life and death after the man who taught me how to live and die.

Similarly, baptism becomes a visible, symbolic act of transformation—dying to old ways of living and rising to new understandings. Christmas isn't about a virgin birth but about the presence of God demonstrated in human history through the life of Jesus, who showed us what living in the Spirit looks like. Easter isn't about a literal resuscitation of a dead body coming back to life but about dying to one way of understanding and rising to new ways of seeing— transformation. We experience many resurrections in this life as we die to old perspectives and grow into new ways of seeing. Easter gives me joy and hope that I can experience the same Spirit that Jesus experienced so deeply.

The church of tomorrow will create new symbols and expressions of faith as it develops in the centuries to come, but the current symbols still possess profound meaning when understood at a deeper level. The challenge isn't to do away with them but to see them differently—as metaphorical symbols of a more profound truth than outdated literal perspectives can provide.

Living with uncertainty is scary. Where do we find comfort?
Life certainly can be scary, but it need not be. In other words, it is how we approach uncertainty that makes all the difference in the world. For centuries, the church has sold security to the frightened masses. If you accept Jesus as your Savior, you are sure to go to heaven. If you believe the traditional teachings of the church, you possess undeniable truth, while others follow lies. If you are baptized, your sins are washed away, and you are counted among the household of God. We buy into the various methods of control the church has promoted in an effort to secure comfort amid the ambiguities of life.

Part of our evolutionary development entails the realization that we are self-conscious beings. Unlike all other creatures on Earth, we know that we know we know. We ask questions that no other creature considers. Realizing our own realization brings with it a certain amount of angst, and we look for ways to assuage the anxiety associated with self-consciousness.

We feel better when we can declare a sense of certainty. Of all people, we possess truth, we inherit heaven, we follow the right religion, and so forth. But is it true? Is it certainty we possess or the declaration and feeling of certainty? One is an actuality, and the other is an illusion. I am aware of my absence of control, my tiny position within a vast universe, my want of understanding, and my lack of certitude about all sorts of things. I can make all kinds of declarations, but they are merely what I *believe* to be certain, not what is *actually* certain. We can declare there is a heaven, but no one really knows for certain. I can declare to the world that I am Teddy Roosevelt, but my declaration doesn't make it true. The declaration is not a certainty; it is merely a hope, belief, or opinion. Setting up camp on one side of the fence and yelling assertions at those on the other side might make us feel better about the camp we are in, but it is not backed up by the substance of actuality.

Encouraging or not, that's the way life is, and we can't do much about it. Forced to deal with it, we certify specific beliefs to be absolute truth. It makes us feel like we are doing something to combat our feelings of insecurity and uncertainty, and this is what the traditional doctrines of the church are selling—security and certainty, and by the looks of it, it sells pretty well in evangelical land. But it is merely a colorful Band-Aid covering up what everyone knows to be true in their heart of hearts.

So where do we find comfort in a precarious world when the certainty we long for cannot be found? Would we rather find comfort in a *declaration* of certainty or in the *ultimate reality* of God's presence within us? To me, the answer is obvious. Though the symbols, rituals, and language of our chosen religious system bring about a level of familiarity, they don't quite scratch where we itch because they are merely human systems that help us express our love and devotion to God. They are tools of expression, not the source and substance behind the expression. All too often, we grab on to the medium by which truth travels rather than the truth itself.

I accept insecurity and uncertainty as the way life is, and instead of spouting off certainties that do not exist, I simply rely upon my personal God experiences as genuine encounters with the divine. I find comfort in the self-communication of God to me, and I focus on becoming more aware of the divine life-flow that touches my heart, transforms me, and moves me to becoming a better human. This provides me with both comfort and courage. In this vast, uncertain, and insecure universe, my spirit is joined to the eternal source of life. As long as the heartbeat of God's breath is within me, I am connected to the divine. That's all I have, and it is enough. This gives me the comfort and courage to keep moving forward.

If the Bible isn't to be taken literally, how do we know what is real and what isn't?

Biblical literalists see the Bible as the inerrant, literal, once-for-all words of God to humankind. They read it with literal eyes and search for literal truth. I view the Bible from a metaphorical perspective—stories our forefathers told in their attempt to convey profound truth, not literal truth. Is profound truth real? Of course it is, but it is not literal truth. The Bible uses stories, metaphors, symbols, and sacred storytelling as methods for helping us understand profound insights.

Our tendency is to read the Bible literally as we cherry-pick verses that meet a momentary felt need in our life. We often approach it devotionally, without the benefit of deep study and critical analysis. After all, we can't all be doctoral-level theologians trained in ancient languages. Additionally, the Bible was written from a Jewish perspective, something most of us know very little about. Fortunately, we live in an age where we can engage in as much study, reading, discussion, conferences, online videos, learning, and training as we have time and interest. Anyone can read the Bible literally from the perspective of contemporary culture, but reading the Bible from the world of its authors is quite another thing.

As scholars engage in the critical study of Scripture, new discoveries are frequently made regarding ancient Israel, archeology, culture, and religion. This influences our understanding of Scripture. It is fascinating, for sure, but it isn't a prerequisite for experiencing God. The Bible is a sacramental doorway into the divine. That means we can read it, whether devotionally or critically, and experience the sacred presence of God through its pages. It is a valuable tool for drawing us toward our own God experiences. The profound truth of the Bible is real, not the literal interpretation we force upon it.

If God is indescribable, does it really matter what we believe as long as we experience God?

This question recognizes both the transcendence of God and the immanence of God. God is both indescribable (beyondness) and personally experienced (nearness). If we are unable to comprehend or describe God—my "catfish trying to describe what it is to be human" analogy in this book—then it is true that all systems of faith are mere human attempts at capturing our God experiences in human language. The experience is real because it connects our spirit with the eternal Spirit, but the articulation of that experience always falls short and is relative to the time, circumstances, knowledge, and worldview of the age in which we live.

Which system of religious expression best relates to our God experiences? That may depend upon where you live on this planet. If you grew up in the Middle East, Islam or Judaism becomes the major system of religious expression. If you grew up in India, you might express your experiences another way. In Vietnam or China, yet another way. In the United States and Europe, Christianity has been the main thoroughfare for articulating God.

Is one system right and all others wrong? That is the way most people understand their faith. I don't believe any one religion has a corner on truth, not even Christianity. In fact, if God is beyond comprehension, we cannot speak of God in absolutes—only images and metaphors.

I understand that religions do not agree on a great many things and that their claims are often contradictory. In monotheistic religions, for instance, Judaism follows Yahweh as the only true God, Islam claims Allah as the one true God, and Christianity promotes one God in three persons. They are different from one another and can't all be right. They each express the reality of God in differing ways, and it is the reality of God—the God behind and beyond all systems of expression—that I pursue. The mystics from all of the great religions seem to have reached a similar point, where language simply falls by the wayside as one experiences the divine presence that is beyond all systems of expression.

Our religious system of choice becomes very personal to us as we discern which view most expresses our personal God experience and our understanding of the world. I was raised in the Christian system and feel most comfortable with that form of expression, but I don't believe for one minute that it is absolutely, 100 percent correct in all matters of faith, even though it is the expression that makes the most sense to me. Yet I honor all religions, not because I agree with their teachings but because they are attempting to express the reality of God. I don't argue with people of a different persuasion, but neither am I unwilling to share my own expression of faith. I honor all people and their personal God experiences.

Does it really matter what we believe? Sure it does, for beliefs have consequences that guide our behavior, our treatment of others, our ethics, our perception of reality, etc. One reason I value Christianity is its emphasis on unity amid diversity, loving God, self, and others, and the life of Jesus as a reflection of what God cares about, such as justice, human value, seeing God in everyone, breaking down barriers of division, etc.

Seeing one system of faith as the only, true, correct expression of God reflects the certainty so many long for in this life. God, however, is beyond all human expressions, which are merely attempts to distill divine mystery into the language, culture, knowledge, circumstances, and worldview of our day. Religious systems often denounce one another as false, but could they all be human attempts at explaining the divine? Without question, I prefer one system over others and notice that every system has extremists within the ranks, but how can I denounce the genuine God experiences of others that lie beneath the human attempts at expression? It is the genuine experience of God that interests me, not the denigration of various religious systems.

If experiencing God is paramount, how can we increase our awareness of the Spirit?

The sacred presence of God is within you, around you, beside you, under you, over you, through you, and beyond you. In essence, you live, move, and exist in God. You cannot escape it. The issue is one of awareness, not possession. Jesus seemed to understand this, and his life becomes an amazing example to us primarily because of his deep connection to the Spirit within him. He shows us what humanity can become when we increase our spiritual sensitivity and allow the Christ power to flow through us.

Sensitivity to the Spirit is paramount to the process of transformation. Jesus, for instance, spent time alone in the wilderness and on a mountain in an effort to quiet his internal being so he could align himself with the sacred presence within. He wasn't flooding God with a long list of verbal petitions. Instead, he spent extended periods of time quieting his soul and listening to the whisper of God. The mystics call this contemplation.

Contemplation is a misunderstood term. You can stand in front of a great work of art and contemplate its meaning and the artist's intent, but that kind of mental activity isn't what we mean by contemplation. It is not assessment, analysis, or intellectual processing. Instead, we are talking about opening ourselves up to the divine voice that touches every aspect of our being. We do this by quieting our internal selves so we can be fully present with the whisper of God. It often involves surrender, insight, a stirring within, and coming to the place where there is no difference between the sacred and the secular. In other words, we come to the point where contemplation becomes a way of life, a way of seeing, and a way of being. We see the mystery of God in all things, even the simple, mundane things of life.

Brother Lawrence, for example, was a seventeenth-century lay brother assigned to kitchen duty in a Carmelite monastery in Paris.[20] He is best known for his joyous ability to practice the presence of God in the common, ordinary affairs of life. He discovered the presence of God in the kitchen as he was washing pots and pans on behalf of his Carmelite brothers just as much as he sensed God while on his knees before the holy Eucharist. For Brother Lawrence, the presence of God had become a reality in all of life, even the mundane daily task of washing dishes in service to others.

People employ various methods for quieting their internal selves. Some engage in centering prayer, some go for walks, some go on personal spiritual retreats, some listen to music, some read Scripture, some meditate, and some utilize other creative means to become quiet enough to hear the still small voice of God. The noise level of our fast-paced world screams loudly in our ears, and it takes intentionality to be present with the divine. Our relationship with God is often seen as something we do for an hour on Sunday morning or while reading a two-minute devotional every day. Those are good things to do, but they are not contemplation. Contemplation is not *doing* something for God but *living* in

God and *listening* to God—being aware of the constant presence within so that we see all of life, every moment, and every person as sacred.

Contemplation is not so much something we do but something we are, something we become as we habitually live in the moment of God's presence. It takes a while to learn this posture of life, and it is not some trophy we place on the fireplace mantle as a prized accomplishment; rather, it is something we experience and live each and every day. The path of contemplation is an intentional way of being that sensitizes us to the divine presence within us.

How can the sacred presence of God be in someone who engages in acts of atrocity?

How can they *not* have God within them? If God is the very ground of being, the source of human existence, then simply by being human, they possess the breath of God within them. Every person on this planet derives their very being from God—the ground of all being. Irrespective of how one acts, God is in all people, because all people exist in God.

Not everyone is aware of the sacred presence within, nor do they all walk in step with the Spirit, for if they did, they would produce what Paul calls the fruit of the Spirit in Galatians 5:22–23, which is love, joy, peace, patience, kindness, goodness, faithfulness, gentleness, and self-control. These are all positive and productive qualities, the very qualities Jesus himself exemplified for us. If you are unaware of the divine within and do not walk in step with the Spirit, it is possible to engage in all sorts of actions that produce fruit of another tree. Evil actions are never condoned, and they are not the work of God. We possess the life of God within us, as our very existence is tied to the existence of God.

What does it mean to be born again?

This phrase has been held hostage by evangelicals and fundamentalists who interpret it to mean we must get right with God in order to inherit eternal life. We do this by accepting Jesus as our personal Savior and receiving the forgiveness of sins. We come into the faith through a process called being born again that goes something like this: acknowledge that we are sinners before a holy God, recognize Jesus's death as the perfect human sacrifice that satisfies God's justice, seek forgiveness from God for our sins, and believe that Jesus's death on the cross saves us from the penalty of sin and restores us to a right relationship with God. The born-again phrase is also identified with a particular brand of Christianity most often associated with evangelicalism, fundamentalism, and biblical literalism. I once worked for a boss who said to me, "I don't mind Christians; I just can't stand those born-again ones." He recognized the brand.

Rather than being a reference to salvation, forgiveness, or specific brand of Christianity, the term is actually a metaphor for the powerful transformation that occurs in our life when we allow the Christ power to flow through us. The term only occurs in John 3 with the story of Nicodemus and in 1 Peter 1, where the author recognizes the recipients of his letter as being born again.

Jesus informs Nicodemus that unless he is born again, he cannot see the kingdom of God. Some translations say born from above or born anew. Nicodemus, the quintessential literalist, asks how he can reenter his mother's womb. Seeing things literally was an obstacle for Nicodemus, for Jesus was speaking symbolically through the use of metaphor. This is what happens to biblical literalists; they often miss the profound point being made, and we wonder whether Nicodemus ever got it.

Speaking further, Jesus states, "What is born of the flesh is flesh, and what is born of the Spirit is spirit," and "Very truly, I tell you, no one can enter the kingdom of God without being born of water and Spirit" (John 3:5–6, NRSV).

The point Jesus is making has nothing to do with accepting him as the perfect, sinless sacrifice for our sins, for Jesus hasn't even died yet, and Nicodemus would have no clue as to that meaning. Jesus isn't speaking literally of a new birth, for Nicodemus is right: how can someone reenter their mother's womb? This is the difference between reading the Bible literally, which leads to nonsense, and understanding a deeper, more profound truth. Jesus is speaking metaphorically to emphasize a new way of seeing, having one's eyes opened, and a spiritual rebirth. It is one way he addresses internal transformation, where the old is replaced with the new. Being born again is an essential theme in Christianity, but it doesn't refer to accepting Jesus as the sacrifice that saves us. Rather, it speaks of transformation.

Paul describes this transformative process as dying to self and rising with Christ, being crucified with Christ, and becoming a new creation in Christ. These are metaphors that point to the power of transformation. The death and resurrection of Jesus are another powerful metaphor of dying and rising. We undergo our own death and resurrection in this life, metaphorically speaking. Being born again speaks to the radical transformation that occurs when following the way of Jesus. Nicodemus wasn't sure he wanted to do this. He was stuck in literalism when he needed to embrace a new way of seeing, thinking, and living.

What about John 3:16?

This is one of the most recognized passages in the New Testament and is the signature verse for biblical literalists and their heaven-and-hell perspective. It is the summation of what evangelicals and fundamentalist strive for in this life—saving people from hell by accepting Jesus as their Savior.

A couple of items are worth noting. God's giving of the Son is referring not to Jesus's death but to his life, for God loved the creation so much that God was personified in the life of Jesus. God did this so that everyone who believes in him, or, as I noted earlier in the book, those who belove him, finds new life. We are not asked to mentally ascribe to a set of propositional claims *about* Jesus but to *belove* Jesus. In other words, there is a difference between *believing* someone and *believing in* someone. One focuses on the doctrine, and the other focuses on the person. We experience eternal life by believing in (beloving) Jesus. We extend our loyalty and allegiance to the person and his way of living, being, and seeing.

For evangelicals and fundamentalist, this refers to the bliss of heaven once this life is over, but for John, the author of this verse, it also refers to something we experience in this present life. John says it a little differently in John 17:3 (NRSV): "And this is eternal life, that they may know you, the only true God, and Jesus Christ whom you have sent." This is written in the present tense, not a future tense. What is eternal life? According to John, it is knowing God and Jesus now. By allowing the divine presence to flow in us and through us, we experience the eternal life of God in the present moment.

Just the other day, I heard a local preacher on the radio declare that if we didn't accept Jesus as our Savior, we would spend eternity in the raging fires of hell. He knew this because, as he stated, his King James Version of the Bible, the only true version of the Word of God, said so. That's the kind of God he served—a vindictive, punishing God who damns people to the fires of eternal torment for their temporal sins. John 3:16 isn't requiring assent to theological claims about Jesus, who rescues us from eternal damnation. Instead, God loves the creation so much that God is revealed in the life of Jesus, who reflects to us the image of God. When we belove Jesus and give ourselves to following the way of Jesus, we participate in the eternal life of God on this Earth.

Is Jesus the only way to God?

That salvation is only found in Jesus has been a mainstay in the Christian church for centuries. John places these words upon the lips of Jesus: "I am the way, and the truth, and the life. No one comes to the Father except through me" (John 14:6, NRSV). The church sees this as an exclusionary claim that prompts our efforts to convert as many souls as possible before the end of time.

The great God in the sky was gracious enough to exit heaven, assume the form of a human, live a perfect life, and then die for our sins. Have you considered what this implies? Any God that can be killed isn't a God worth believing in. Furthermore, it implies that Christians hold the keys to heaven, and the only way anyone can get in is if we open the door of understanding for them. We are right, and all others are wrong.

If God is all-powerful, all-knowing, and all of that good stuff, God sure has a funny way of showing it. Jesus's ministry lasted between one and three years during the early part of the first century. Knowledge of his identity wasn't widespread outside of Israel. The people in China, Australia, America, and other places across the globe were simply out of luck. The generations before Jesus didn't have a chance to believe, and those in distant lands didn't either. People went to hell simply because they didn't hear and accept Jesus as the only way to God. This is so strange and unjust as to be jaw-dropping. Luckily for us, out of all people throughout all of time, our understanding of God is the correct one! This is ludicrous.

Scripture, we recall, contains human words about God that reflect the experiences and understanding of ancient people writing within the knowledge, culture, circumstances, and worldview of their day. When John declares that Jesus is the way, the truth, and the life, and Luke declares in Acts 4:12 (NRSV) that "there is salvation in no one else, for there is no other name under heaven given among mortals by which we must be saved," they are sharing their experience of Jesus within the limits of their world at the time.

Their experience of Jesus was liberating, for they sensed freedom and transformation. For them, Jesus was the doorway that opened their eyes to new sight. He was the bread of life, the light of the world, the way, the truth, and the life. It is the language of devotion, love, and deep appreciation.

In what way is Jesus the way, the truth, and the life? Is the doorway to God opened by believing propositional religious claims, or is it something deeper? If believing propositional claims about Jesus is how we gain salvation, then the eternal destiny of millions is dependent upon our sharing the message so all can ascribe to the approved statements. This is what the evangelical mission is all about—converting others. It means that every other religion is false and disconnected from God. Besides, if we really believed this, we would all quit our jobs and spend every minute of every day convincing others to believe, for our eternal destiny hinges on believing the right things.

There is another way of viewing Jesus as the way, truth, and life that is much more profound than merely getting people to hear his name and believe specific claims about him. This view focuses upon the way of Jesus, not the propositional claims about Jesus. In other words, it is what we see in the life of Jesus that leads us to God; it is *the way* of Jesus that leads us to experience the kingdom of God. He is the image of God personified in human form. Jesus loved people, was in tune with the Spirit, and broke down barriers of division as he modeled value, dignity, and justice to others. In essence, when we say that Jesus is the way, the truth, and the life, we are referring to the way he lived, not to propositional statements about him. When we live like Jesus lived, we experience the kingdom of God like Jesus experienced it, and that is salvation to us—liberating, freeing, healing, wholeness, and seeing with fresh eyes.

How is Christianity about living, loving, and being? That seems so simplistic.

It is pretty simple, isn't it? We have a tendency to make things much more complex than they really are when it comes to knowing God. The Old Testament law became complex and convoluted, and the religious elite in Jesus's day turned God into a punctilious rule keeper. They invented quite a few rules themselves and spent time arguing over them. That sucks the wind out of our sails, and even Jesus had to correct this misperception of God.

Quite simply, if God is the source of life, then we honor God by living our life fully and intentionally. In this way, life is lived as the outflow of the life given to us. Quite simply, if God is the source of love, we honor God by loving extravagantly. God is identified with love, and when we act in loving ways, we reveal God to others. Quite simply, if God is the source of our very being, then we honor God by being our best selves. Our life is intricately connected to God; we exist because God exists. We transform, evolve, and become all that we can be as a way to honor God, the ground of all being.

How should we understand the meaning of salvation?

This word is packed with significance for evangelical and fundamental Christians, who understand salvation to be about a Savior who died in our place, rescued us from sin, and secured our entrance into heaven. Salvation, saved, and Savior are all related terms. Are you saved? Have you heard the plan of salvation?

Do you know the Savior? One better hope so, for, according to these folks, this is how one gets to heaven, and it would be a shame if you weren't there.

Salvation, however, is rarely used in connection with the afterlife. In the Old Testament, for example, salvation speaks of deliverance from bondage when Israel was liberated from Egyptian slavery. Salvation speaks of a return from exile when Israel came home from Babylonian captivity. Furthermore, it speaks of being saved from danger, as seen in the book of Psalms where rescue from personal harm is attributed to the salvation of God.

The New Testament continues this theme of deliverance and transformation with various images. For instance, we were once blind but now see, we were sick but are now healed, we were dead but now have life, we were fearful but now trust, we were in bondage but are now free, we were in exile but have now returned, we were in danger but now find safety, and we have moved from injustice to justice. Even the resurrection story is about transformation, as are the symbols of baptism and communion. This theme of deliverance and rescue is seen throughout Scripture, but it is not referring to entering heaven. Instead, it has practical meaning in this life, as our communion with the Spirit transforms us. Metaphors become a way of speaking of the profound movement of God in our lives.

How should we understand the meaning of sin?

According to traditional Christian teaching, salvation is associated with sin, for that is what we have been saved from—the devastating effects of sinful humanity that result in eternal damnation. We are sinners by nature (passed on to all humans by Adam and Eve) and by personal choice. I never could figure out why we are held responsible for our sinful actions if they are the result of an evil propensity intrinsic to who we are as humans. Additionally, I could never figure out why I was held responsible for the sin of the first two human beings. This makes me responsible and guilty for something I didn't do back in the Garden of Eden and for something I can't help but do in light of my sinful nature. Be that as it may, this is supposedly why we need to be forgiven. The human condition is defined as sinful; we are wretched, filthy rags in the sight of God. But is this how we should understand sin and the human condition? If sin is a metaphor for what ails us, we had better find out what ails us.

In looking at some of the ways salvation is used in the Bible, we see that Israel was not enslaved to Egypt because they sinned. In fact, sin wasn't what ailed them, so receiving forgiveness was not an appropriate remedy. They needed deliverance from bondage and liberation from their oppressors. When Israel was carried off into exile by the Babylonians, they weren't in need of forgiveness. What ailed them was exile, and they needed a way to return to their homeland. The psalmists who speak of God saving them were in need not of forgiveness but of personal rescue from dire situations. The parable of the Prodigal Son in the New Testament isn't a story about sin and forgiveness. Instead, it is about returning home, where welcome and celebration exist, not forgiveness. Those who experienced healing in the Bible weren't in need of forgiveness; they needed a way to be made whole—to move from infirmity to healing and from blindness to sight. The bleeding woman who touched the hem of Jesus's garment was in need of healing and wholeness, not forgiveness. In this way, God saved them. The point is that sin is simply a metaphor to describe our need to move from incompleteness to wholeness.

I was taught that sin is missing the mark of God—disobeying the laws and regulations as revealed in Scripture. It is true—we do act in ways that are unbecoming, hurtful, and less than our best selves. No doubt about that. But if sin is a metaphor for what ails us, then what actually ails us? Is the real issue that humanity is by nature dirty, filthy, deplorable, and in need of forgiveness, or is this a metaphor for moving from incompleteness to wholeness?

If salvation is spoken of in terms of liberation from bondage, returning home from exile, and seeing things with new eyes, could sin be speaking of our need for transformation from what keeps us in bondage, what keeps us in exile, and what keeps us from seeing? The issue of humanity isn't sin that must be washed away by the cleansing power of Jesus's blood, for we don't possess an internal, invisible, infectious disease passed down to us from Adam and Eve. Instead of being fallen creatures in need of forgiveness, we are incomplete people in need of transformation and being made whole.

As evolving creatures, we yearn to be liberated from the bondage that holds us back from becoming all that we can be. We seek to experience the welcome and celebration of coming home—of discovering the joy of God in us. We desire to see with fresh eyes. We do not need to be restored to a perfection we never enjoyed in the first place; instead, we evolve, change, and transform so that we become whole people who live, love, and be.

Where do we go when we die? Is there a heaven?

I think we would all like to know the answer to this question, but I am afraid it cannot be answered with any degree of certainty. Since death is a threshold we pass over but do not come back from, our ability to know is beyond us. Do we simply stop existing? Do we live on in a different form? Do we go to a literal place called heaven, where we walk on streets of gold, live in a promised mansion, and spend eternity worshiping God? I have performed many funerals as a minister and brought comfort to others with the familiar New Testament texts that bring hope in difficult times of loss. We love and miss those who have passed on, which makes it more difficult to accept uncertainty regarding the afterlife.

We see throughout Scripture and other ancient texts that the concept of heaven and hell is an evolving one. Some passages speak of the grave as being the end. Others refer to the resurrection of Israel as a nation, and some passages speak of a place called heaven. The concept has morphed and advanced to the point where heaven is now the reward for accepting Jesus as our Savior. The truth of the matter is that no one really knows what occurs after death. Some Christians believe that when we die, we die. That's it. Others view the idea of heaven as experiencing God in this life, not an afterlife. Others believe in a literal heaven, where we are rewarded with a crown atop our head, live in a mansion, eat at banquets, and sing to God all day long.

For me, I focus on the life of God within me. God is said to have breathed life into the nostrils of Adam and if God is the ground of all being, then I exist because God exists. As Peter notes, we are partakers of the divine nature. I live in God, move in God, exist in God, and am a part of God, even though I am not God, for God is more than the sliver of life within me.

I happen to believe in an afterlife where a part of us lives on, for how can the life of God end? Although I don't believe in a literal wonderland with streets of gold, I do think it is entirely possible that even as our body decays, the life of God within us returns to its originating source. Paul indicated that Jesus was exalted to be with God after death. I wonder whether that will be our end as well. At our own death, will we be exalted into God as Jesus was? If God is the source of our life, then it is possible that the breath of life within us will return to God.

Since no one really knows what happens after we die, I focus on experiencing the life of God within me while I am here on Earth. My connection to the divine gives me purpose, direction, and peace of mind. Just as Jesus faced his own demise with courage and grace, I hope to approach my own death in a similar fashion—not holding on to physical life but experiencing divine life flowing through me even in death. When we are connected to the Spirit in that way, a calm envelops us as we accept our own mortality, even as the life of God within us returns to its source.

If God is not a supernatural being managing the affairs of the world, what does that say about prayer?

If prayer isn't asking God to heal a disease, secure a dream job, come up with a down payment on a house, find a spouse, and the like, then what are we asking God to do for us? Whom are we praying to, and for what? If the Big Guy isn't even upstairs in the control room, are our prayers fruitless endeavors that have little religious meaning?

I believe in prayer—I just don't believe prayer is the petitioning of a controlling deity in the sky that acts on our behalf. If we behave right, believe enough, obey God's commands, and are sincere in our fervent petitions, we can move God to receive the answer we desire. Like Pop-Tarts from a toaster, this is a slot-machine God who pops out answered prayers when enough coins of praise are inserted. Sometimes we even bargain with God in prayer as a last resort. I simply do not understand God in this way, and I don't understand prayer to be naming and claiming all the things we want from this supernatural Santa Claus.

If we cross the railroad tracks right before a train comes barreling down the rails to collide with the car behind us, we praise God for divine protection, but the car that got smashed wasn't so lucky, since God didn't protect it. We have all gone through the loss of a loved one who, had God acted on our behalf, could have been healed of cancer, heart disease, brain tumors, and the like. If God is an all-powerful, all-knowing, all-loving deity with the power and ability to help us and does nothing, is God not malevolent or culpable in some way? We don't think much about that, and in fact, God can never lose. If our prayers are answered, God is good, and we experience divine favor. If our prayers are unanswered, God's will is being served. Tell that to the hurting mother who just lost her teenage daughter in an automobile accident when a drunk driver crossed the center line.

Prayer has to be something different than this—something far deeper and more profound than a Pop-Tart God who can never lose. We view prayer as an activity to engage in rather than a way of life—a way of being. I have struggled with the activity part of it all my life. I fold my hands and make my way through the list of prayer concerns only to feel my mind wandering. I notice how rough my hands are and begin working on a hangnail. Prayer was an activity—something I was expected to do, and as an obedient believer, I gave it my best shot. I always fell short. It wasn't working for me, and I was floundering. Trying to muster up the fervency expected of a holy prayer warrior was a constant struggle. Was this what prayer was all about, pleading with God to do something I felt needed to be done? After all, God had the power and ability to answer prayer. If I could just be spiritual enough to earn the answer I longed for!

I hold people in loving thought as I consider their situations. There is nothing wrong with that—after all, that is what we do for individuals who are in need. The kind of prayer that makes sense to me, however, is one that entails a way of being—a habitual way of living. Prayer is how I experience the life, love, and being of God within me. Am I not in perpetual conversation with the Spirit within, and is that not a way of being? Is that not prayer—to be in constant communion with God?

Christianity is about experiencing the eternal presence within. I don't run around all day apart from God only to come home and rush through ten minutes of prayer and devotional reading. For me, prayer is about living, loving, and being in communion with the Spirit as a habitual way of being. That is why I seek to be much more contemplative these days, for it helps to keep me centered on God. Prayer is life. It is sharing the life, love, and being of God with others. In this way, I am praying without ceasing, as Paul encourages, and I spend time listening to the whisper of God within my own soul, as Jesus did. Prayer has taken on a deeper meaning for me and is something I am—something I live rather than something I do to check off my list of holy requirements that please the Big Guy in the sky.

What is the gist of what you are saying? Can you sum it all up?
The time has come for me to put this book to rest. It has been two years in the making and I could use a little down time before traipsing off to my next creative project. Thank you for reading this work, making it to the end, and allowing yourself to be spiritually challenged. Whatever the outcome of your thoughts regarding the content of this book, I am grateful to have been a part of your journey. I love you for who you are, what you are, where you are, just as you are, and I embrace all that you can become. The life of God dwells in you, and the image of God shines forth from you.

This book exposes the church's credibility problem stemming from its behavior and its beliefs. Its behavior, both historically and in the present era, undermines the very message it is trying to communicate. But it is the message itself that struggles to survive, because it is built upon the limited knowledge and worldview of ancient days. What the church believes and teaches no longer makes sense in light of the knowledge we now possess about our universe. That is a devastating predicament to be in, and yet it must be confronted, as I did with the doctrines surrounding Scripture, Jesus, and God.

For Christianity to survive into the future, its behavior and beliefs must become relevant to the current age. Beliefs of the past, based on inadequate understandings of our world, become outdated and irrelevant, not to mention just plain wrong. I describe a path forward that allows us to maintain vibrant faith while approaching Christianity with integrity—from both the head and the heart.

Scripture, I note, is not the inerrant, literal, once-for-all words *from* God to humankind but rather human words *about* God by writers expressing their experience and understanding of God in the language, concepts, paradigms, worldviews, and circumstances of their day. Scripture becomes a sacramental doorway for experiencing God as we learn from the experiences of our predecessors.

Jesus, I note, was the personification of God—someone who experienced the divine life within and lived life accordingly. His awareness and sensitivity to the sacred presence became winsome and attractive to others. In essence, Jesus mirrored for us the image of God. We look to the life of Jesus to see what God must be like and what God cares about. We model our own life after the manner of Jesus so we can be in tune with the Christ power—the divine presence flowing in and through us.

God, I note, is not a supernatural being sitting upon a throne in heaven, running the universe and responding to all of our wants and desires. Instead, God is a sacred presence, the ground of all being. Since God is beyond our ability to describe or comprehend, we simply experience the life-flow of God within us. It is our God experiences—the self-communication of God to each of us—that transform us from the inside out and enable our connection with the eternal.

This led me to some conclusions about how to live life. We should live life fully as a way to honor God as the source of life. We should love extravagantly as a way to honor God as the source of love. Finally, we should seek to be our best selves as a way to honor God as the source of our being. We would do well to follow after the manner of Jesus, our example of a Spirit-filled life.

May you live life fully, love extravagantly, and be your best self as you follow after the manner of Jesus. Good night and Godspeed!

ENDNOTES

· · · · · · · · ·

1. This chapter is based on (1) the many works of Dr. Lloyd Geering, a prolific author and deep thinker, who has challenged our understanding of God; (2) Dr. Robert Jones's summarization of Geering's work in *God, Galileo, and Geering*; and (3) Dr. Robert Funk's chapter titled "An Enlightened Faith for an Enlightened Age," found in *The Future of the Christian Tradition*. Dr. Funk was a biblical scholar and founder of the Jesus Seminar and Westar Institute. The concept of "axial age" goes back to the German-Swiss philosopher and psychiatrist Dr. Karl Jaspers in his work *The Origin and Goal of History*. Jaspers saw a time of pivotal change in the development of religion—a time when human understanding turned on its axis. His concepts have been popularized by Dr. Karen Armstrong in *The Great Transformation: The Beginning of Our Religious Traditions*.

2. This section arises from the work of Marcus Borg in his book *Speaking Christian*, pp. 55–63.

3. For a detailed look at how the biblical author ridicules literalism throughout this Gospel, see John Shelby Spong's book *The Fourth Gospel: Tales of a Jewish Mystic*, from which much of this section is drawn.

4. John Dominic Crossan and Richard G. Watts, *Who Is Jesus: Answers to Your Questions about the Historical Jesus*, p. 63.

5. The Moses connection described in this chapter, as well as the liturgical nature of the Gospels, is based upon the many works of John Shelby Spong, with particular attention to *Liberating the Gospels: Reading the Bible with Jewish Eyes* and *Biblical Literalism: A Gentile Heresy*.

6. Marcus Borg has written extensively on Jesus and this pre-Easter and post-Easter theme. Much of what I have written in this section is based upon his excellent writings, such as *Speaking Christian*; *The Heart of Christianity*; *Jesus: A New Vision*; *The God We Never Knew*; and *Meeting Jesus Again for the First Time*.

7. Walter Bauer's book *Orthodoxy and Heresy in Earliest Christianity* describes this concept in great detail.

8. This distinction comes from Marcus Borg in *Speaking Christian* and *The Heart of Christianity*. Borg's differentiation between believing and faith is derived from the works of Wilfrid Cantwell Smith, *Belief and History* and *Faith and Belief: The Difference between Them*.

9. This list comes from John Shelby Spong in *Born of a Woman: A Bishop Rethinks the Birth of Jesus*, p. 55, and Raymond E. Brown, *The Birth of the Messiah*, p. 522.

10. Many of the concepts found in this chapter arise from the works of John Shelby Spong and Marcus Borg. Examples of Spong's books include *Unbelievable; A New Christianity for a New World;* and *Why Christianity Must Change or Die*. Examples of Borg's books include *Speaking Christian; The Heart of Christianity*; and *Jesus: A New Vision*.

11. Many of the concepts in this chapter emanate from the works of John Shelby Spong and Marcus Borg. See the bibliography for their works consulted.

12. For the concepts presented in this chapter, I am grateful to the following: Lloyd Geering, *Christianity Without God*; Bart Ehrman, *How Jesus Became God*; John Shelby Spong, *Born of a Woman* and *Why Christianity Must Change or Die*; Raymond E. Brown, *An Introduction to the New Testament* and *The Virginal Conception and Bodily Resurrection of Jesus*.

13. The concepts in this chapter originate from the works of Marcus Borg and John Shelby Spong. Borg's books include *Meeting Jesus Again for the First Time; Jesus: A New Vision*; and *A God We Never Knew*. Spong's books include *The Easter Moment* and *Why Christianity Must Change or Die*.

14. The concepts in this chapter arise from the following authors: Marcus Borg, *The God We Never Knew*; John Shelby Spong, *Why Christianity Must Change or Die* and *Unbelievable*; Lloyd Geering, *Christianity without God*; John A. T. Robinson, *Honest to God*; and Paul Tillich, *Systematic Theology*.

15. Many of the concepts in this chapter stem from the works of Karen Armstrong, *A History of God*; John Shelby Spong, *Unbelievable* and *Why Christianity Must Change or Die*; and Lloyd Geering, *Christianity without God* and *Christian Faith at the Crossroads*.

16. The Jesus Seminar, *The Once and Future Jesus*, p. 113.

17. See Bart D. Ehrman, *Heaven and Hell: A History of the Afterlife*; and John Shelby Spong, *Eternal Life: A New Vision*.

18. The concept of living, loving, and being comes from the many writings of John Shelby Spong.

19. Transition in the change process originates from William Bridges, *Transitions: Making Sense of Life's Changes* and *Managing Transitions: Making the Most of Change*.

20. Brother Lawrence, *The Practice of the Presence of God*.

SELECTED BIBLIOGRAPHY

· · · · · · · ·

Armstrong, Karen. *The Great Transformation: The Beginning of Our Religious Traditions.* New York: Alfred A. Knopf, 2006.

———. *A History of God: The 4,000-Year Quest of Judaism, Christianity, and Islam.* New York: Ballantine Books, 1993.

Bass, Diana Butler. *A People's History of Christianity: The Other Side of the Story.* New York: HarperOne, 2009.

Bauer, Walter. *Orthodoxy and Heresy in Earliest Christianity.* Philadelphia: Fortress Press, 1971.

Beilby, James K., and Paul Rhodes Eddy, eds. *The Historical Jesus: Five Views.* Downers Grove: InterVarsity Press, 2009.

Bridges, William. *Managing Transitions: Making the Most of Change.* Reading: Addison-Wesley Publishing Company, 1991.

———. *Transitions: Making Sense of Life's Changes.* Reading: Addison-Wesley Publishing Company, 1980.

Borg, Marcus J. *Days of Awe and Wonder: How to Be a Christian in the 21st Century.* New York: HarperOne, 2017.

———. *The God We Never Knew: Beyond Dogmatic Religion to a More Authentic Contemporary Faith.* New York: HarperSanFrancisco, 1997.

———. *The Heart of Christianity: Rediscovering a Life of Faith.* New York: HarperSanFrancisco, 2003.

———. *Jesus: A New Vision: Spirit, Culture, and the Life of Discipleship.* New York: HarperSanFrancisco, 1987.

———. *Meeting Jesus Again for the First Time: The Historical Jesus and the Heart of Contemporary Faith.* New York: HarperSanFrancisco, 1994.

———. *Speaking Christian: Why Christian Words Have Lost Their Meaning and Power—And How They Can Be Restored.* New York: HarperOne, 2011.

Borg, Marcus J., and N. T. Wright. *The Meaning of Jesus: Two Visions.* New York: HarperOne, 1999.

Brother Lawrence. *The Practice of the Presence of God.* Old Tappan: Fleming H. Revell Company, 1982.

Brown, Raymond E. *The Birth of the Messiah: A Commentary on the Infancy Narratives in Matthew and Luke.* Garden City: Doubleday and Company, 1977.

———. *An Introduction to the New Testament.* New Haven: Yale University Press, 1997.

———. *The Virginal Conception and Bodily Resurrection of Jesus.* New York: Paulist Press, 1973.

Carroll, James. *Constantine's Sword: The Church and the Jews: A History.* New York: Houghton Mifflin Company, 2001.

Chilton, Bruce. *Rabbi Jesus: An Intimate Biography.* New York: Doubleday, 2000.

———. *The Way of Jesus to Repair and Renew the World.* Nashville: Abingdon Press, 2010.

Crosson, John Dominic. *The Historical Jesus: The Life of a Mediterranean Jewish Peasant.* New York: HarperSanFrancisco, 1991.

———. *Who Killed Jesus: Exposing the Roots of Anti-Semitism in the Gospel Story of the Death of Jesus.* New York: HarperSanFrancisco, 1995.

Crosson, John Dominic, and Richard G. Watts. *Who Is Jesus: Answers to Your Questions about the Historical Jesus.* Louisville: Westminster John Knox Press, 1996.

Edwards, David L. *Christianity: The First Two Thousand Years.* Maryknoll: Orbis Books, 1997.

Ehrman, Bart D. *Heaven and Hell: A History of the Afterlife.* New York: Simon and Schuster, 2020.

———. *How Jesus Became God: The Exaltation of a Jewish Preacher from Galilee.* New York: HarperOne, 2014.

———. *Jesus before the Gospels: How the Earliest Christians Remembered, Changed, and Invented Their Stories of the Savior.* New York: HarperOne, 2016.

Funk, Robert W. *Honest to Jesus.* New York: HarperSanFrancisco, 1996.

Geering, Lloyd. *Christian Faith at the Crossroads: A Map of Modern Religious History.* Santa Rosa: Polebridge Press, 2001.

———. *Christianity without God.* Santa Rosa: Polebridge Press, 2002.

———. *Resurrection: A Symbol of Hope.* London: Hodder and Stoughton, 1971.

———. *Tomorrow's God: How We Create our Worlds.* Santa Rosa: Polebridge Press, 2000.

———. *The Word to Come: From Christian Past to Global Future.* Santa Rosa: Polebridge Press, 1999.

———. *Wrestling with God: The Story of My Life.* Charlottesville: Imprint Academic, 2007.

Gould, Stephen Jay. *Rock of Ages: Science and Religion in the Fullness of Life.* New York: The Ballantine Publishing Group, 1999.

Gulley, Philip. *The Evolution of Faith: How God Is Creating a Better Christianity.* New York: HarperOne, 2011.

———. *If the Church Were Christian: Rediscovering the Values of Jesus.* New York: HarperOne, 2010.

———. *Unlearning God: How Unbelieving Helped Me Believe.* New York: Convergent, 2018.

Gulley, Philip, and James Mulholland. *If God Is Love: Rediscovering Grace in an Ungracious World.* New York: HarperSanFrancisco, 2004.

———. *If Grace Is True: Why God Will Save Every Person.* New York: HarperSanFrancisco, 2003.

Hedrick, Charles W., ed. *When Faith Meets Reason.* Santa Rosa: Polebridge Press, 2008.

Hitchens, Christopher. *God Is Not Great: How Religion Poisons Everything.* New York: Twelve, 2007.

Jaspers, Karl. *The Origin and Goal of History.* New York: Routledge, 2010.

The Jesus Seminar. *The Future of the Christian Tradition.* Santa Rosa: Polebridge Press, 2007.

———. *The Once and Future Faith.* Santa Rosa: Polebridge Press, 2001.

———. *The Once and Future Jesus.* Santa Rosa: Polebridge Press, 2000.

Jones, Robert. *God, Galileo and Geering: A Faith for the 21st Century.* Santa Rosa: Polebridge Press, 2005.

Kertzer, Morris N. *What Is a Jew?* New York: Touchstone, 1996.

Otto, Rudolf. *The Idea of the Holy.* Mansfield Centre: Martino Publishing, 2010.

Powell, Mark Allan. *Jesus as a Figure in History.* Louisville: Westminster John Knox Press, 1998.

Robinson, John A. T. *Honest to God.* Louisville: Westminster John Knox Press, 2018.

Rohr, Richard. *What Do We Do with the Bible?* Albuquerque: Center for Action and Contemplation, 2018.

Smith, Wilfrid Cantwell. *Belief and History.* Charlottesville: University Press of Virginia, 1977.

———. *Faith and Belief: The Difference between Them.* Oxford: Oneworld, 1998.

Spong, John Shelby. *Biblical Literalism: A Gentile Heresy.* New York: HarperOne, 2016.

———. *The Birth of Jesus.* Gig Harbor: ProgressiveChristianity.org, 2014

———. *Born of a Woman: A Bishop Rethinks the Birth of Jesus.* San Francisco: HarperSanFrancisco, 1992.

———. *Dialogue: In Search of Jewish-Christian Understanding.* Haworth: Christianity for the Third Millenium and St. Johan Press, 1999.

———. *The Easter Moment.* New York: The Seabury Press, 1980.

———. *Eternal Life: A New Vision*. New York: HarperOne, 2009.

———. *The Fourth Gospel: Tales of a Jewish Mystic*. New York: HarperOne, 2011.

———. *Honest Prayer*. Haworth: Christianity for the Third Millenium and St. Johan Press, 2000.

———. *Into the Whirlwind: The Future of the Church*. Minneapolis: The Seabury Press, 1983.

———. *Jesus for the Non-religious*. New York: HarperSanFrancisco, 2007.

———. *Liberating the Gospels: Reading the Bible with Jewish Eyes*. New York: HarperSanFrancisco, 1996.

———. *The Living Commandments*. Haworth: Christianity for the Third Millenium and St. Johan Press, 2000.

———. *Living in Sin? A Bishop Rethinks Human Sexuality*. San Francisco: Harper and Row, 1988.

———. *A New Christianity for a New World: Why Traditional Faith Is Dying and How a New Faith Is Being Born*. New York: HarperSanFrancisco, 2001.

———. *Re-claiming the Bible for a Non-religious World*. New York: HarperOne, 2011.

———. *Rescuing the Bible from Fundamentalism: A Bishop Rethinks the Meaning of Scripture*. New York: HarperSanFrancisco, 1991.

———. *Resurrection Myth or Reality: A Bishop's Search for the Origins of Christianity*. New York: HarperSanFrancisco, 1994.

———. *The Sins of Scripture: Exposing the Bible's Texts of Hate to Reveal the God of Love*. New York: HarperSanFrancisco, 2005.

———. *This Hebrew Lord: A Bishop's Search for the Authentic Jesus*. New York: HarperOne, 1993.

———. *Unbelievable: Why Neither Ancient Creeds nor the Reformation Can Produce a Living Faith Today*. New York: HarperOne, 2018.

———. *Why Christianity Must Change or Die: A Bishop Speaks to Believers in Exile*. New York: HarperSanFrancisco, 1998.

Spong, John Shelby, and Denise G. Haines. *Beyond Moralism: A Contemporary View of the Ten Commandments*. Haworth: Christianity for the Third Millenium and St. Johan Press, 2000.

Strauss, David Friedrich. *The Life of Jesus, Critically Examined*. New York: Cosimo, Inc., 2009.

Tillich, Paul. *A History of Christian Thought: From Its Judaic and Hellenistic Origins to Existentialism*. Edited by Carl E. Braaten. New York: Simon and Schuster, 1967, 1968.

———. *Systematic Theology*. Chicago: The University of Chicago Press, 1967.

.

CPSIA information can be obtained
at www.ICGtesting.com
Printed in the USA
LVHW082118170721
692992LV00008B/86